Jossey-Bass Teacher

Jossey-Bass Teacher provides educators with practical knowledge and tools to create a positive and lifelong impact on student learning. We offer classroom-tested and research-based teaching resources for a variety of grade levels and subject areas. Whether you are an aspiring, new, or veteran teacher, we want to help you make every teaching day your best.

From ready-to-use classroom activities to the latest teaching framework, our value-packed books provide insightful, practical, and comprehensive materials on the topics that matter most to K–12 teachers. We hope to become your trusted source for the best ideas from the most experienced and respected experts in the field.

For more information about our resources, authors, and events, please visit us at www .josseybasseducation.com.

You may also find us on Facebook, Twitter, and Pinterest:

 Jossey-Bass K–12 Education

 Jbeducation

 jbeducation

The First-Year Teacher's
Survival Guide

Ready-to-Use Strategies, Tools & Activities
for Meeting the Challenges of Each School Day

FOURTH EDITION

JULIA G. THOMPSON

JB JOSSEY-BASS™
A Wiley Brand

Library of Congress Cataloging-in-Publication Data
Names: Thompson, Julia G., author.
Title: The first-year teacher's survival guide : ready-to-use strategies,
   tools & activities for meeting the challenges of each school day / Julia
   G. Thompson.
Description: Fourth edition. | San Francisco, CA : Jossey-Bass, 2018. |
   Includes index.
Identifiers: LCCN 2017061587 (print) | LCCN 2017054190 (ebook) | ISBN
   9781119470366 (pbk.) | ISBN 9781119470410 (epub) | ISBN 9781119470304 (pdf)
Subjects: LCSH: First year teachers--Handbooks, manuals, etc. | Teacher
   orientation--Handbooks, manuals, etc. | Teaching--Handbooks, manuals, etc.
Classification: LCC LB2844.1.N4 T47 2018 (ebook) | LCC LB2844.1.N4 (print) |
   DDC 371.1--dc23
LC record available at https://lccn.loc.gov/2017061587

Cover image: © airdone/Getty Images
Cover design by Wiley

Printed in the United States of America

FOURTH EDITION

PB Printing   10 9 8 7 6 5 4 3 2 1

Contents at a Glance

V. Create a Well-Managed Discipline Climate

Contents

Section Two: Develop Professional Productivity Skills 31

Section Three: Collaborate with Colleagues in Your School Community

II. Establish a Productive Classroom Environment

III. Teach the Whole Child

IV. Use Effective Instructional Practices

Section Ten: Measure Student Progress with Summative Assessments

V. Create a Well-Managed Discipline Climate

Please visit www.wiley.com/go/fyt4e for free online access to templates, checklists, video clips, and other useful content.

About the Author

Julia G. Thompson received her BA in English from Virginia Polytechnic Institute and State University in Blacksburg, Virginia. She was a teacher in the public schools of Virginia, Arizona, and North Carolina for forty years. Thompson taught a variety of courses, including freshman composition at Virginia Tech, English in all secondary grades, mining, geography, reading, home economics, math, civics, Arizona history, physical education, special education, graduation equivalency preparation, and employment skills. Her students have been diverse in ethnicity as well as in age, ranging from seventh graders to adults.

Thompson recently retired as a classroom teacher but continues to be an active speaker, consultant, mentor, and advocate for first-year teachers. Author of *Discipline Survival Guide for the Secondary Teacher*, *First-Year Teacher's Checklist*, and *The First-Year Teacher's Survival Guide*, Thompson also provides advice on a variety of education topics through her website, www.juliagthompson.com; on her blog, juliagthompson.blogspot.com; and on Twitter, https://twitter.com/TeacherAdvice.

For Phil, with gratitude, love, and admiration

Acknowledgments

I am grateful to my editor, Kate Gagnon, for her encouragement and patience during the preparation of this book.

Thank you to the faculty, staff, and students of two excellent schools: Windsor High School in Isle of Wight County, Virginia, and Langley High School in McLean, Virginia. I was honored to have been a teacher in both of these schools. It was a privilege to work with so many knowledgeable, caring teachers who represent the highest standards of professionalism.

Special thanks to the following thoughtful educators who offered their wise counsel and who could remember what it's like to be a first-year teacher:

Michael A. Barrs

Jennifer Burns

Anna Aslin Cohen

Edward Gardner

Kevin Healy

Vivian Jewell

Betsy Jones

Mary Landis

Deborah McManaway

Laura Moore

Jay O'Rourke

Shelly Sambiase

Margaret R. Scheirer

Luann West ScottJared Sronce

Jessica Statz

Jeff Vande Sande

About This Survival Guide

This is the book that I needed as a first-year teacher. I knew a great deal about the content I was expected to teach, but I did not know very much at all about the students who would be occupying the desks in my new classroom. I did not know how to set up a grade book or administer a test or grade papers. I did not know what to do when a student talked back, told me a lie, or stopped paying attention to my carefully planned lesson. Worst of all, I did not even know where to begin to look for the answers that I needed then.

If you are like me, there is a great deal about our profession that intrigues you. You may feel uncertain at times about what to do, but you can also feel pretty confident when things go as planned. It's a great feeling to look around your classroom and to realize that everyone is learning. As a first-year teacher, you know what you and your students are supposed to achieve, but you are not always sure how to proceed.

Almost everyone begins a teaching career with the same emotions. Many veteran teachers also suffered through the tough days when they didn't know what to do and gloried in the days when they were able to engage every student in the magic of learning. Even though you may have a great deal to learn about your new profession, your teaching career can still be immensely satisfying. Every day is a new opportunity to make a difference in a child's life. Your first years as a teacher can be years of dynamic professional growth and personal fulfillment as you learn how to master your new responsibilities.

Helping you enjoy success in the first years of your career is the goal of *The First-Year Teacher's Survival Guide*. The suggestions and strategies in these pages can help you develop into a skillful classroom teacher who remains enthusiastic about the possibilities in every student. For instance, in this book you'll find

- Assistance in identifying your professional responsibilities and establishing priorities to accomplish them
- Resources that can help you collaborate with other educators at the school level and online

- Methods of reflecting on your current teaching skills and establishing goals for your professional life
- Advice for learning to work well with parents or guardians as a member of a collaborative team to support student learning
- Strategies for managing your school-related stress so that you can find a successful balance between your personal and professional lives
- Advice about how to fulfill your legal responsibilities and protect yourself from lawsuits
- Efficient ways to manage grading, professional paperwork, and other routine tasks so that you can focus on teaching
- Recommended digital tools to design and deliver innovative, engaging, and relevant lessons
- Inspiration, insight, and practical advice from successful veteran teachers
- A wide variety of innovative and time-tested classroom management activities, strategies, and techniques to help you create a positive learning environment
- Suggestions about how to get the new school term off to a great start
- Advice about how to find teacher freebies and to create a productive classroom environment on a budget
- Advice about how to plan instruction for the entire term, for units of study, and for each day
- Suggestions for using both formative and summative assessments to measure progress
- Advice about how to support students with a variety of special needs
- Suggestions for handling homework and other concerns from parents or guardians[1]

In response to the numerous requests for advice I receive from first-year teachers, in the fourth edition you will find a great deal of information and help on how to prevent, minimize, or handle classroom discipline issues, including a quick how-to guide to some of the most common problems all teachers must deal with. You will also find a wealth of advice about how to create those important relationships with your students to help them be successful in a supportive classroom community.

Other new material in the fourth edition includes information and resources about such timely topics as

- Taking charge of your own professional growth
- Creating a professional portfolio

---

[1]As a classroom teacher, you will find that some of your students will live with biological or adopted parents while others will live with guardians. Throughout this book, you will find the use of "parents or guardians" or "parents and guardians" to indicate this relationship.

- Increasing your workplace productivity
- Using digital resources to inform instruction
- Organizing your workday with a professional binder
- Becoming a capable and confident classroom leader
- Establishing your reputation as a competent professional
- Helping students develop a growth mindset
- Developing positive relationships with parents or guardians
- Building positive relationships with students
- Creating a supportive learning community with student-to-student connections
- Developing the leadership qualities of a teacher who is a warm demander
- Incorporating the concepts of the whole child and social emotional learning movements into your teaching practice
- Adapting instruction through differentiation to support all learners
- Using restorative justice concepts in your classroom
- Establishing a calm and confident classroom authority to successfully manage discipline issues

The First-Year Teacher's Survival Guide was written to help K–12 teachers meet the challenges that each school day brings. In these pages, you will find the answers to the most common how-to questions that many first-year teachers have:

- **Section One:** How can I handle my new responsibilities as a professional educator?
- **Section Two:** How can I develop efficient workplace productivity skills?
- **Section Three:** How can I develop successful collaborative relationships with my colleagues and establish my professional reputation?
- **Section Four:** How can I develop the leadership and classroom time management skills I need to become a capable classroom leader?
- **Section Five:** How can I organize my classroom and connect with students during the first days of a new school term?
- **Section Six:** How can I foster positive classroom relationships with and among my students as well as with their parents or guardians?
- **Section Seven:** How can I meet the special needs of all students in my classroom?
- **Section Eight:** How can I use differentiated instruction so that every student can be successful?
- **Section Nine:** How can I design and deliver lessons that will meet the needs of my students?
- **Section Ten:** How can I use summative assessments to measure student progress?
- **Section Eleven:** How can I establish a framework for classroom management by using effective classroom policies, procedures, and rules?

- **Section Twelve:** How can I prevent or minimize discipline problems from disrupting the positive learning environment that I want to establish?
- **Section Thirteen:** How can I successfully handle discipline problems once they occur?
- **Section Fourteen:** How can I quickly find advice for dealing with some of the most common discipline concerns many teachers experience?

The First-Year Teacher's Survival Guide is designed to be a helpful resource tool for busy teachers. Don't start at page one and try to slog through to the last page. Instead, think of this book as a reference or guidebook—a resource filled with classroom-tested knowledge for teachers who need answers and advice in a hurry. There are plenty of topics written with your needs in mind. Here's how to get started:

- Skim through the table of contents and the index to get an idea of what the book offers. Use sticky notes to mark the sections that will address information that you already know will be helpful to you and that you would like to come back to later. You'll notice that there's a title bar across the top of each right-hand page to indicate just where you are in the book and to make it easier to pick and choose information as the need arises. You'll also find that the book is divided into five categories of information:
  - Learn the Skills Necessary to Be a Professional Educator: Sections One, Two, and Three
  - Establish a Productive Classroom Environment: Sections Four, Five, and Six
  - Teach the Whole Child: Sections Seven and Eight
  - Use Effective Instructional Practices: Sections Nine and Ten
  - Create a Well-Managed Discipline Climate: Sections Eleven, Twelve, Thirteen, and Fourteen

After you have a good idea of the layout of the book, you can then find the specific information that you need to know. Here are some tips to help you with this:

Learn the Skills Necessary to Be a Professional Educator:
Sections One, Two, and Three

Turn to these pages to find information about

- Learning from professional observations and evaluations
- Starting your own professional development
- Establishing a work-life balance
- Becoming efficient at managing your time
- Developing your professional productivity skills

- Setting up your work area
- Collaborating with colleagues
- Establishing your professional reputation

Establish a Productive Classroom Environment: Sections Four, Five, and Six

Turn to these pages to find information about

- Creating your classroom persona
- Establishing yourself as a classroom leader
- Managing class time effectively
- Instilling a growth mindset
- Starting the school term positively
- Creating positive relationships with parents or guardians
- Creating positive relationships with students
- Creating positive student-to-student relationships
- Building a classroom community

Teach the Whole Child: Sections Seven and Eight

Turn to these pages to find information about

- Incorporating the whole child approach into your classroom practice
- Incorporating the social emotional learning movement into your classroom practice
- Creating a risk-free environment
- Creating a culturally responsive classroom
- Supporting students with various special needs
- Teaching basic school skills all students need to know
- Using differentiated instruction strategies
- Measuring mastery with formative assessments

Use Effective Instructional Practices: Sections Nine and Ten

Turn to these pages to find information about

- Planning instruction
- Creating engaging lessons and activities
- Planning with technology resources

- Using summative assessments
- Helping students succeed with standardized tests

Create a Well-Managed Discipline Climate:
Sections Eleven, Twelve, Thirteen, and Fourteen

Turn to these pages to find information about

- Creating a framework of policies, procedures, and rules for classroom management
- Using specific strategies to prevent or minimize discipline issues
- Using appropriate interventions for misbehavior
- Using proactive and not punitive approaches to classroom management
- Finding effective ways to redirect off-task students
- Coping with individual student misbehavior
- Handling classroom misbehaviors

However you choose to use this book, it was designed to be an interactive experience. Use a pencil to fill in the assessments, set your goals, and scribble notes as you read each section. Highlight. Underline. Annotate information about the links and resources. Dog-ear the pages. Place bookmarks in the sections that appeal to you.

The information in these pages is there to help you become the self-assured and knowledgeable educator that you dreamed of being when you chose your new career. From the first day of school to the last day, you can be one of the greatest assets that our world can have—an effective teacher.

With patience and practice, you can realize your professional dreams. Millions of others have done it; you can, too. Your first years as a teacher can set you on the path to achieving the satisfaction that only a career in education can bring.

Best wishes for a gratifying and enjoyable first year!

Julia G. Thompson

For more information on how you can have a successful first year, visit www.juliagthompson.com, juliagthompson.blogspot.com, or https://twitter.com/TeacherAdvice.

SECTION ONE

Begin Your
Professional Growth

When you decided to become an educator, you entered a very special universe—one where your unique insights, energy, skills, and knowledge can be used to change the world. Change the world? Yes, that is what educators do. Just think of what a career in education means to you and to the millions of classroom teachers who are your colleagues across the globe.

Our jobs are about far more important ideas than just the content we teach. Countless studies indicate that teachers are the most significant factor in any student's schooling. Although you may be tempted to think peer pressure or a student's home environment have more influence than you do, keep in mind that it is teachers who inspire students to become lifelong learners and to believe in their ability to achieve their dreams.

It is a classroom teacher who teaches a child to read, to do math, to cooperate with others, to write sentences, to think analytically, to do neat work, and to solve problems. It is a classroom teacher who protects a child from bullies and who is the first line of defense in the battle against racism, ignorance, and poverty. It is a classroom teacher who helps young people learn how to navigate life. To be kind. To be successful. To accomplish dreams. To be good citizens of the world.

What a weighty responsibility we face each school day. What a privilege it is to be an educator.

As a classroom teacher, you will never be rich, even if your district should come to its senses and pay you what you are worth. You will, however, be rewarded repeatedly because when you help your students achieve their dreams, you will achieve yours.

Few careers can claim to be as impactful as a career in education. Classroom teachers do change the world—one classroom at a time. Never doubt that, even on the toughest days, you are making a difference in the lives of your students. What you do *matters*.

Welcome to your new profession.

How to Handle Your New Responsibilities

If you are like most new teachers, you may already be concerned about how well you will handle the responsibilities that accompany managing a classroom filled with a diverse population of students—each one with individual needs and abilities. Just how do successful teachers keep those responsibilities from morphing into demoralizing anxiety?

Good teachers take it one day at a time. They work to maintain a balance between their personal and professional lives by paying careful attention to their own well-being. Good teachers manage their professional challenges by realizing that they are not alone in their struggles and that it's okay to not always know the best solution to a problem. They reach out to a colleague next door or down the hall or in an online professional community to seek help. And even when they are dealing with the pressing details of each school day, good teachers stay focused on the big picture—the success of their students.

All teachers experience professional challenges. First-year teachers, experienced teachers, and teachers at every grade level cope with complex problems, no matter how ideal their school situation. Anytime you feel overwhelmed, remember that all teachers have had to deal with what you are going through. In fact, here are some of the most common challenges that all teachers experience:

- Finding a work-life balance
- Stacks of tedious paperwork
- Difficulty in connecting with parents and guardians
- Integrating technology appropriately
- A culture or generation gap with students
- Not enough equipment, materials, or time
- Short student attention spans
- Students with overwhelming family problems
- Uncertainty about the right course of action to take

If some of these problems seem all too familiar, remember that the hallmark of a great teacher is not the absence of problems but the ability to generate and implement innovative and effective solutions to an array of classroom challenges. With a positive attitude, a professional approach, a bit of creativity, and plenty of practice, you will soon be able to manage your new professional responsibilities.

Develop the Mindset of a Professional Educator

Although many educators use the term *professionalism* when referring to excellent teaching practices, it's not always a term with a straightforward definition. Instead, we tend to recognize it when we see it in action, but we may not be able to articulate exactly what it means. For many educators, though, professionalism means being the very best teacher that you can be every day. When you choose to develop the mindset of a professional educator, you send the message that you are in control of your classroom, your professional responsibilities, and yourself.

It is not always easy to be an educator, especially when you are just starting out, but resolving to act in a professional manner is a sound decision with far-reaching effects. You will earn the respect of your students, their families, and your colleagues. You will be able to enjoy your school days instead of struggling with the unpleasant consequences brought about by poor decisions.

> I do everything I can to make my students feel successful, safe, and cared for. That means arriving before the expected time so that the classroom is organized and ready for students. It means having lessons thought through and implemented effectively. It means modeling for my students good behavior, thoughtfulness, and a positive outlook.
>
> *Betsy Jones, 12 years' experience*

What's Expected of Twenty-First-Century Teachers

As a twenty-first-century teacher, you will be expected not only to maintain a well-managed classroom but also to establish a classroom culture of high performance for your students. All teachers, no matter what subject matter they teach or the age and ability levels of their students, are expected to create this culture in their classes. Although this can seem difficult at first, this expectation can make your life as a teacher much more rewarding as you watch your students master the material they are expected to learn. How will you know when you have created the productive culture of high performance that you want for your students?

- The classroom is student centered, with students taking ownership of their learning and responsibility for their success.
- Students are fully engaged in meaningful, respectful, and appropriate learning tasks.
- The overall focus of the work is goal oriented and purposeful.
- The teacher has classroom management structures in place so that students are confident about expectations for mastery of material, social interactions, and self-regulated behaviors.
- The teacher uses current research findings and best practices to inform instructional decisions.
- The teacher makes instructional decisions based on a thoughtful analysis of available data.
- Students move forward in their learning, mastering the assigned material and then moving on to the next topic under study. Students learn what they are supposed to learn.

Creating a culture of high performance is not a task that can be done in a day or two but rather requires consistent and sustained effort. It begins with the expectations that you have for your students. Set high goals and expectations; make sure that these expectations and goals are ones that students perceive as achievable.

Knowledgeable teachers have found that it is impossible to create a culture of high performance without encouraging collaboration. Students who work together learn to support one another. Successful teachers also focus on helping students understand the importance of practice and effort in achieving success.

Finally, in classrooms where there is a culture of high performance, the students and their teachers take the time to acknowledge their triumphs and to celebrate their successes. The culture of this type of classroom is overwhelmingly positive and conducive to creating more success.

Even though the expectation that you will create a culture of high performance in your classroom is daunting at first, it is a worthy goal with far-reaching rewards. Start small. Plan carefully and with the needs of your students in mind. Others have achieved this. You can as well.

Professional Growth: Develop Your Skills and Add to Your Knowledge

As a classroom teacher, you will become a lifelong learner just by the very nature of the profession. It is simply impossible to be a good teacher and to not want to know more about the content you are teaching or about the best methods to instruct your students. One of the most intriguing recent educational movements is the proactive role that teachers now take in determining the kinds of professional development activities that work best for them.

No longer do teachers rely only on their districts' professional development programs; instead, proactive educators determine for themselves the professional development activities that serve them best. Becoming a teacher who is actively involved in a program of self-directed sustained professional development is one of the wisest decisions you can make as a novice educator.

Fortunately, there are many different professional development opportunities available for interested teachers. As you begin to take ownership of this important aspect of your new career, you may want to consider some of the options on the following pages. Learning to use the resources that are available to you is a productive step in your quest to develop into the kind of teacher you dreamed of becoming when you first considered a career in education.

Use Action Research to Inform Classroom Decisions

The term *action research* has been part of the glossary of education terms for many years; it is a very personal and very effective way to learn how to solve common classroom or school-based problems. Action research is simply the research that educators do as they go about testing new strategies and ideas, analyzing the resulting data, and then deciding how to implement their findings. It differs from scholarly or theoretical research in that it is solution-oriented and controlled by the members of a school community themselves.

In fact, at any given time in a school, there may be many different types of action research projects under way: individual teachers may be investigating ideas for their classroom, collaborative groups of teachers may be testing ideas that affect their grade levels or departments, and the entire school community may be involved in a large-scale exploration of a topic of interest to all. To begin the procedures in the action research process in your own classroom practice, follow these proven techniques for successful action research:

- **Step One:** Determine an issue or problem that you want to investigate. It can be as simple as asking why your students don't always complete their homework assignments or as elaborate as helping your students learn to use effective reading practices.

- **Step Two:** Formulate a potential solution and apply it to the problem. The solution that you apply should be something that you believe has the potential to resolve the issue or problem. Once you have determined a possible solution, systematically put it into practice.

- **Step Three:** Collect data. Depending on the problem or issue that you are investigating, the data can be examples of student work, standardized test scores, formative assessment results, or products of any other method that allow you to test the effectiveness of your possible solution.

- **Step Four:** Analyze the data you have collected. Your analysis will indicate if you should continue the implementation of your possible solution or if you should formulate another one based on what you have learned from your original data collection and analysis.

Action research will enable you to be methodical in the way you assess the effectiveness of new ideas; assume responsibility for your classroom decisions; contribute in a meaningful way to the culture of your school; and increase your own knowledge, skills, and confidence as an educator.

Attend Conferences

As a first-year teacher, you may not believe that attending a professional conference is a good use of your time when you have so much work to do that you struggle not to be overwhelmed. However, if your school district offers you an opportunity to attend a conference, accept it. You'll benefit from the opportunity to learn new strategies and network with other professionals.

Participate in an Edcamp

An important part of the proactive professional development movement, edcamps (often referred to as *unconferences*) are participant-driven gatherings where K–12 educators can collaborate informally to share ideas and concerns with other like-minded educators in an inclusive and friendly environment. You can learn more about edcamps that would benefit you most from the Edcamp Foundation (www.edcamp.org).

Join Professional Organizations

One of the best ways to acclimate yourself to your new profession is to join an organization for education professionals. Joining a professional association is an excellent way to stay abreast of the latest developments and trends in education. Through collaboration and networking, you learn from other teachers with shared interests and concerns. Here is a list of some of the national professional organizations for teachers:

- **American Federation of Teachers (AFT) (www.aft.org).** The AFT is a teachers' union allied with the AFL-CIO. With 1.3 million members, AFT has been a strong voice supporting the classroom teacher for decades.

- **Association for Middle Level Education (AMLE) (www.amle.org).** With more than thirty thousand members, AMLE is the largest national education association committed to the educational needs of young adolescents.

- **Association for Supervision and Curriculum Development (ASCD) (www.ascd.org).** This group is a nonpartisan, nonprofit national and international organization for educators at all grade levels.

- **Coalition of Essential Schools (CES) (www.essentialschools.org).** This organization provides professional development and networking opportunities, conducts research, and serves as a policy advocate for public education.

- **National Alliance for Public Charter Schools (NAPCS) (www.publiccharters.org).** This nonprofit organization works to shape federal and state policy and advocate for funding as well as to improve the public understanding of the charter school movement.

- **National Association for the Education of Young Children (NAEYC) (www.naeyc.org).** This organization is the nation's largest organization for early childhood educators. Its focus is to provide support and resources for the educators of young children.

- **National Education Association (NEA) (www.nea.org).** With more than three million members, the NEA is the largest organization for public school teachers in the United States. It provides strong national support for educators at all grade levels.

- **National High School Association (NHSA) (www.nhsa.net).** This nonprofit association is dedicated to improving the professional knowledge of high school educators.

Read Professional Journals

Just as attending conferences can help you develop professional expertise, so can reading professional journals. Through such reading, you can learn a great deal about the interests you share with others in your field. Subscribing to one of these journals will enrich your teaching experience in many ways:

- *Educational Leadership* (www.ascd.org). This journal is the voice of the Association for Supervision and Curriculum Development and a useful resource for teachers at all grade levels. Here you can find professional resources for your classroom as well as for schoolwide issues.
- *Education Week* (www.edweek.com). This journal is a weekly periodical devoted to up-to-the-minute news and commentary about education-related topics.
- *Instructor* (www.scholastic.com). This widely read magazine devoted to K–8 educational concerns offers practical support through a variety of timely articles.
- *Kappan* (www.pdkintl.org). This professional journal produced by the international organization for teachers, Phi Delta Kappa, addresses issues of policy and serves as a forum for debates on controversial subjects.
- *Learning* (www.learningmagazine.com). This is another supportive resource for teachers of younger students, offering practical advice on a wide range of topics.

Investigate the National Board for Professional Teaching Standards

As a first-year teacher, you may not be eligible to work toward national certification, but it is a positive choice for teachers to make as early in their careers as they can. As you work to improve your overall teaching skills, you will also learn how to effectively teach the material in your state and district standards. You can learn more at the website of the National Board for Professional Teaching Standards (www.nbpts.org).

Explore Educational Websites

From elaborate and carefully curated sites to more humble offerings, online resources are a valuable resource for twenty-first-century educators. Once you have spent some time exploring some of the more well-known websites, additional research can help you find online resources tailored to your needs. Here are just a few of the more popular and useful sites available to teachers across the globe:

- **A to Z Teacher Stuff** (www.atozteacherstuff.com). This teacher-created site is designed to help teachers find lesson plans, thematic units, teacher tips, discussion forums, and printable worksheets as well as many more online resources.

- **Discovery Education (www.discoveryeducation.com).** This site offers an enormous wealth of resources for teachers—digital media, hundreds of easily adaptable lesson plans, worksheets, clip art, and much more.

- **Education World (www.educationworld.com).** This is an excellent general site for K–8 teachers in particular. It offers plenty of valuable resources, including free weekly newsletters.

- **Edudemic (www.edudemic.com).** Offering hundreds of articles on wide-ranging topics, Edudemic provides information on teaching trends and techniques as well as educational news.

- **Edutopia (www.edutopia.org).** This is a wonderful site for K–12 teachers. It offers timely articles, sage advice, videos, and a wide range of materials.

- **HowtoLearn (www.howtolearn.com).** An extensive and popular site, teachers can participate in various learning communities, enroll in online courses, learn new teaching strategies, and research various educational topics.

- **MiddleWeb (www.middleweb.com).** At MiddleWeb's extensive site, middle school educators can find many resources, articles, and useful advice geared to help them reach and teach middle school students.

- **Share My Lesson (www.sharemylesson.com).** At Share My Lesson, educators can access greater than four hundred thousand lesson plans, activities, and other resources shared by the more than one million members of the American Federation of Teachers who maintain the site.

- **Teaching Channel (www.teachingchannel.org).** Funded by the Bill and Melinda Gates Foundation and the William and Flora Hewlett Foundation, Teaching Channel is a video showcase of innovative and effective teaching practices. Instead of traditional lesson plans, teachers can watch brief videos of effective teaching ideas that they may want to implement in their own classrooms.

Establish Your Own Plan

Many teachers use social media to create a PLN, or personal learning network. A PLN is simply a way for individuals to use social media to connect with other educators to collaborate, share ideas, and explore common professional interests. Many educators who want to establish a PLN start by following bloggers who post about topics they want to explore further and investigating social media sites such as Twitter, Facebook, Instagram, and Pinterest.

Educational Bloggers

- There are hundreds of insightful educational bloggers whose posts are not only interesting to read but also thought-provoking. Subscribing to several blogs with a variety of viewpoints can help you keep up with educational trends while learning about new resources and strategies. In the following list, you will find just a few sites to begin this aspect of your professional development:

- **BAM Radio Network (www.bamradionetwork.com/educators-channel).** This site offers a wide variety of blogs for educators to follow. Carefully curated, the posts offer sound educational advice and insights on an enormous number of topics.

- **Cool Cat Teacher Blog (www.coolcatteacher.com).** Vicki Davis writes on a variety of useful topics and has interesting guest posts. She often has extensive lists of online resources that appeal to teachers of all grade levels.

- **The Cornerstone for Teachers (https://thecornerstoneforteachers.com).** At Angela Watson's blog, readers can find useful advice about many of the challenges facing classroom teachers.

- **Cult of Pedagogy (www.cultofpedagogy.com).** Jennifer Gonzalez's blog offers interesting, easy-to-read, practical tips about various classroom matters for all K–12 teachers.

- **Larry Ferlazzo (http://larryferlazzo.com).** Larry Ferlazzo's extensive offerings cover topics of interest to K–12 teachers, including a curated daily list of online articles. A prolific contributor to national publications, Ferlazzo also writes a blog for *Education Week* called Classroom Q&A (blogs.edweek.org/teachers/classroom_qa_with_larry_ferlazzo).

- **My Island View: Educational, Disconnected Utterances (https://tomwhitby.com).** Tom Whitby's intriguing blog offers many ideas about educational technology, and its balanced and big-picture approach to major issues in education make it an unusually interesting and helpful resource for classroom teachers.

- **Smart Classroom Management (www.smartclassroommanagement.com).** On this site, readers can easily access the many useful, easy-to-implement tips and techniques related to a positive classroom environment found in Michael Linsin's frequent posts.

- **Teach Like a Champion (http://teachlikeachampion.com/blog).** Author of *Teach Like a Champion 2.0* and several other helpful books, Doug Lemov's blog offers well-written insights on many topics that can help you grow as an educator. In particular, his classroom management strategies are especially helpful for first-year teachers.

Social Media Sites

- **Facebook (www.facebook.com/FBforEducators).** With dozens of groups dedicated to educational topics, it's easy to connect with like-minded educators on Facebook. A good place to begin your investigation is the Facebook for Educators page.

- **Instagram (www.instagram.com).** Although it is possible to use Instagram as a classroom instructional resource, it is also an excellent site for anyone who wants to connect with other educators and bloggers to explore topics of common interest.

- **Pinterest (www.pinterest.com).** At Pinterest, users can create personalized boards to organize their search information as they gather classroom arrangement ideas or find information about a variety of topics from innovative activities to the latest educational trends and classroom management techniques.

- **Twitter (https://twitter.com).** Twitter is an easy and productive way to join the global community of educators, stay current with education policies and trends, and learn from experts. In addition to maintaining your own Twitter account, you can participate in one of the many Twitter chats to share ideas and to learn from other educators. A good site to learn more about the many Twitter chats related to education is Participate (www.participate.com/chats).

Take Learning Walks and Make Snapshot Observations

Although it is not always easy to find the time to observe other teachers as they deliver instruction, the benefits of this practice far outweigh the hassles involved in arranging such classroom visits. A *learning walk* usually takes place when you and a colleague visit another teacher's classroom to observe a few minutes of class and then share your observations. A *snapshot observation* usually involves the same procedure but without a partner. Both techniques are excellent ways to learn new strategies and techniques from colleagues.

When you arrange either a learning walk or a snapshot observation, first ask permission of the colleague you want to observe to arrange a day and time and to discuss where you should sit. Usually a brief ten-minute visit is sufficient to gather information about a specific aspect of the class that you are interested in. While you are in the room, be respectful of that teacher's work by sitting in an unobtrusive spot and taking notes without interacting with students. Enter and leave the classroom as quietly as possible.

Both learning walks and snapshots are especially good ways to learn more about how your colleagues manage the opening and ending of class, transitions, direct instruction, classroom routines, group work, and assessments. You can also learn how to improve your own classroom leadership by observing how other teachers interact with their students.

Set and Achieve Professional Goals

Setting professional goals not only will give you direction and purpose as you begin to focus on the larger issues involved in developing into an effective educator but also will provide valuable baseline data so that you can chart a clear path for career success year after year. Goals tend to energize and motivate those who set them because they allow us to focus on what's important and thus to prioritize our efforts.

Experienced teachers also know that it's important to set SMART goals (goals that are *specific, measurable, attainable, relevant,* and *timely*) because they are easier to achieve than vague ones. Many teachers find that writing down their professional goals makes it easier to assess their achievements throughout the school year and to track the professional skills they know they want to improve.

If you are uncertain about how to begin, Teacher Worksheet 1.1 offers a checklist of suggested competencies for first-year teachers to focus your goal setting and inspire your thinking. In addition, Teacher Worksheet 1.2 offers a template to track your professional goals, and Teacher Worksheet 1.3 will guide you as you take ownership of your professional growth as a teacher.

Suggested Competencies

Consider some of these competencies appropriate for first-year teachers as you assess your strengths and the areas of your professional practice you would like to improve.

First-year teachers should be able to

1. _____ Set up and organize a classroom for maximum student achievement
2. _____ Collaborate effectively with colleagues and parents or guardians
3. _____ Take ownership of their professional development
4. _____ Manage professional responsibilities and duties
5. _____ Maintain a consistent work-life balance
6. _____ Manage stress with appropriate strategies
7. _____ Work with students from diverse cultures
8. _____ Teach students with various types of special needs
9. _____ Use student prior knowledge and preferred learning styles to differentiate instruction
10. _____ Plan lessons that align to state standards and district curriculum
11. _____ Vary teaching strategies to appeal to all learners
12. _____ Use data from formative assessments to inform instruction
13. _____ Engage students in student-centered learning activities
14. _____ Provide meaningful feedback to students and parents
15. _____ Adopt a problem-solving approach to resolve problems
16. _____ Appropriately assess student mastery of mandated content
17. _____ Establish an orderly discipline environment
18. _____ Prevent almost all discipline problems from occurring
19. _____ Use appropriate strategies when discipline problems occur
20. _____ Integrate available technology into instruction when appropriate

From *The First-Year Teacher's Survival Guide, 4th Edition*, by Julia G. Thompson. Copyright © 2018 by John Wiley & Sons, Inc. Reproduced by permission.

Track Your Professional Goals

Using this template, teachers can record their goals and then record their progress for each semester of a school term.

Goal	Semester 1 Progress	Semester 2 Progress
Sample: Hold a quick recognition ceremony/celebration each Friday.		
1.		
2.		
3.		
4.		
5.		

TEACHER WORKSHEET 1.3

Be Proactive about Your Professional Growth

To guide you as you take ownership of your professional growth as a teacher, consider using this quick worksheet.

- If you have already used a method in the list, write *Complete* in the blank.
- If you plan to use one of the methods but have not yet done so, write *Yes* in the blank.
- If you do not want to use a method, write *No* in the blank.

1. _____   Use action research to inform classroom decisions
2. _____   Attend conferences
3. _____   Participate in an edcamp
4. _____   Join professional organizations
5. _____   Read professional journals
6. _____   Investigate the National Board for Professional Teaching Standards
7. _____   Explore educational websites
8. _____   Establish your own personal learning network
9. _____   Take learning walks and snapshot observations
10. _____   Set and achieve professional goals
11. _____   Create a professional portfolio

Other Strategies for a Successful First Year

In addition to the responsibility of taking ownership of your professional growth, there are several other strategies that can help you become a successful teacher in your first year: developing a reflective practice, learning from role models and mentors, seeking feedback on your performance, using the evaluation process to improve your performance, creating a professional portfolio, and maintaining work-life balance.

DEVELOP A REFLECTIVE PRACTICE

It does not take long to realize that no one is a natural teacher. As educators, we cannot just rush through the hurly-burly of a school day, paying cursory attention to what we are expected to accomplish and then hope to be successful. Reflecting on our teaching should be part of every aspect of our professional lives. Such reflection needs to be systematic, methodical, and purposeful.

There are different ways to reflect on your teaching practice. Reflection can be as simple as a sticky note on a lesson plan or an audio recording stored digitally on your phone. Examining the information that you gather in these ways will allow you to discern trends and patterns in your teaching as you seek to improve your skills.

One very common and useful method of maintaining a reflective teaching practice can also involve recording ideas and observations in a journal on a regular basis. Whether you choose to maintain a journal online, in a computer desktop folder, on paper, or even in an audio format, it is important to be diligent about recording regularly. The questions that follow can help you use the time you dedicate to reflecting on your teaching practice as efficiently as possible:

- Are my goals for lessons reasonable and appropriate?
- Are my students challenged to do their best?
- Do students learn what they are supposed to master? How can I ensure that they always do this?
- At what points in a lesson did I have to change strategies or activities? Why? How productive was this flexibility on my part?
- How can I offer remediation or enrichment activities to the students who need them?
- What data do I need to collect before moving on to the next unit of study? How can I gather this information?
- What can I do to improve my skills when it comes to collaborating with colleagues?
- What worked in today's lesson? What did not work?
- How do I want my students to interact with one another as part of a whole group?
- What can I do to help my students collaborate with one another in small groups?

To this day, every time I teach something, I write on sticky notes with ideas on how to improve the lesson for next year. I am currently in the second week of the school year, and half of my desk is covered with sticky notes. I still have some on my desk left over from the end of last year. I will keep those notes adhered to my desk until I get the chance to revise those end-of-year lessons.

Vivian Jewell, 25 years' experience

- How can I integrate technology into my lessons?
- What problems did I have to manage today? How well did I manage those problems?
- How well do I listen to my students? What can I do to make sure that I model good listening skills?
- Which students were off task? What caused them to be off task?
- When were my students on task? What can I do to make sure that continues?
- How did I show that I was enthusiastic about the subject matter?
- How effective were the motivational techniques I used? How can I modify them for future lessons?
- How can I foster an atmosphere of mutual respect and courtesy among my students?
- How well do I manage my classroom? What can I improve?
- How much progress am I making in improving my teaching knowledge or skills? What can I do to improve?
- How can I use my strengths as a teacher to full advantage in my classroom?
- What are my strengths as a classroom leader?

Teacher Worksheet 1.4 offers a template for professional self-reflection.

TEACHER WORKSHEET 1.4

A Template for Professional Self-Reflection

Using a template such as this one will make finding the time to reflect on your classroom practices a manageable daily routine task.

Date: _____

What lessons did I learn today?

_____

_____

_____

_____

_____

How can I improve the way that I handled my academic responsibilities?

_____

_____

_____

_____

_____

What problems did I find solutions for today, and what problems do I still need to solve?

_____

_____

_____

_____

_____

What successes did I have today, and how did I achieve them?

_____

_____

_____

_____

_____

LEARN FROM ROLE MODELS AND MENTORS

One of the most important ways to become an effective teacher is to find good role models and mentors. No matter how long you teach, you will be able to learn from colleagues who are generous with their time, energy, and knowledge.

New teachers often find themselves reluctant to ask for help for various reasons, such as embarrassment at not knowing information or feeling intimidated by the expertise of their colleagues. If you find yourself hesitating to ask for help, keep in mind that teachers in general tend to be friendly and supportive people who remember what it's like to be a new teacher. Most of them will be glad to help you become a successful member of the school community.

Reach out. You are not expected to know everything about teaching during your first year. It is far better to ask for help than to be stressed because you are not sure about what to do.

Tips for Finding Appropriate Role Models

Even though you will probably be assigned an official mentor, you can learn a great deal from other colleagues as well. If you look around your school, you'll find an organized teacher or two who can serve as role models when it comes to productivity. You will find someone who is masterful at dealing with upset parents or who can make even the most disruptive student remain focused and on task. Soon you will see that role models for just about every aspect of your school life are all around you if you take the time to look and learn.

Tips for Working Well with an Official Mentor

Most school districts will assign official mentors to help new teachers during their first year. It's not always easy to begin a dialogue with a near stranger about your concerns at the start of a school year, but it is important not to hesitate to ask for help. Your mentor was also a new teacher once and has some understanding of what it's like to be in your place.

What should you ask of a mentor? Although novice teachers will have a wide range of needs, there are some common concerns that all teachers share. These usually can be divided into two levels of questions that you will discuss with your mentor. The first is the practical level: the daily concerns that are difficult to manage at first. Here are just a few of the day-to-day concerns that you can discuss with your mentor:

- How to handle planning and curriculum concerns
- How to use school technology
- How to obtain materials, equipment, and supplies
- How to work with parents and guardians
- How to manage paperwork
- How to arrange schedules and other school routines

The second level of questions that you should ask a mentor focuses on issues that are more complex. After you have settled into the school term and mastered the general information you need, you will be able to expand your focus to the art of teaching. Some of the complex issues your mentor can discuss with you can include topics such as these:

- How to solve common classroom problems
- How to help students with special needs
- How to increase student motivation
- How to design differentiated instruction
- How to handle diverse groups of students
- How to evaluate students fairly
- How to incorporate a variety of teaching strategies

SEEK FEEDBACK ON YOUR PROFESSIONAL PERFORMANCE

One of the most useful ways to grow professionally is to proactively seek feedback from a variety of sources. You can do this informally in many ways, such as watching your students' body language, looking at test scores, or paying attention to how often students are off task. No matter how you choose to seek feedback about your professional performance, it is a wise idea to use a variety of instruments to gather as much data as possible about your skills. To make sure that you have an accurate view of your strengths and the areas in which you could improve, try these methods of obtaining feedback:

- Ask your students their opinions about classroom matters using the free surveys at SurveyMonkey (www.surveymonkey.com).
- Record or video yourself as you present a lesson.
- Ask a colleague to observe you for part of a lesson you teach.
- Use exit slips or reflection questions at the end of class to ask your students to comment on the day's lesson.
- Install a suggestion box so that students can offer advice and suggestions about classroom concerns.

Make the Most of Peer Observations

Just as it is helpful for you to observe other teachers as they work with their students, it is also beneficial for you to ask colleagues to observe you as you teach. One of the advantages of this type of informal observation is that the observer does not need to stay in your room long to observe the specific part of the lesson you would like examined. A quick snapshot observation of you at work is often enough time for a colleague to be able to discuss what happened in class.

It is also beneficial for a colleague to take a more detailed and systematic approach to the observation. One way to ensure an optimal benefit to this approach to peer observation is to use a worksheet like the one in Teacher Worksheet 1.5.

Make the Most of Peer Observations

Use this worksheet to make peer observations as beneficial as possible.

Date: _____   Observer: _____

Planned class activities:

_____

_____

Special observation requests:

_____

_____

Observed teacher's areas of concern noted in advance:

_____

_____

Observer's response to the areas of concern noted in advance:

_____

_____

Positive teacher actions observed:

_____

_____

Positive student actions observed:

_____

_____

Questions for the observed teacher:

_____

_____

Suggestions for the observed teacher:

_____

_____

From *The First-Year Teacher's Survival Guide, 4th Edition*, by Julia G. Thompson. Copyright © 2018 by John Wiley & Sons, Inc. Reproduced by permission.

USE THE EVALUATION PROCESS TO IMPROVE YOUR TEACHING SKILLS

Evaluations can be of enormous benefit to you, or they can turn you into a nervous wreck; the difference is in your attitude. If you want to grow as a teacher, then adopt the attitude that your evaluators will offer you advice in areas in which you need to improve. Remember this: no teacher is perfect. Every teacher has areas of performance that can be improved.

One way to identify those areas is through evaluations. You can suffer through the process, or you can benefit from it. The choice is yours. As a teacher, you can expect to be evaluated on a variety of criteria often during your career. The evaluation process has several components.

First, you can expect one of your supervisors to discuss your goals and effectiveness with you in a pre-observation conference. If you do not already have a copy of your district's evaluation form and the other district information related to it, you should obtain these items. This is a good time to mention any problems you are having and to solicit advice.

You can also expect to discuss specific goals for the school year with your administrator. You will be expected to collect data and other evidence throughout the rest of the year to track how well you have met your goals.

Sometime after your pre-observation conference, your evaluator will make a planned classroom observation. At this point, the evaluator will be looking for your strengths and weaknesses as an educator. After the observation, you will meet with your evaluator again. At this conference, the evaluator will talk with you about the lesson you taught as well as about your strengths and weaknesses as a teacher.

You can also expect other observations during the year. The number varies from school district to school district. Expect to have many informal visits from administrators over the course of your career but especially during your first few years, when you are not a tenured teacher.

Near the end of the school year, you will have a final evaluation conference. This conference will involve more than just a discussion of the formal classroom observations you have had throughout the year; it will address your overall effectiveness as an educator. There should be no surprises in your final evaluation. If your supervisors believe that you are not an effective teacher, you should certainly have received some indication of that before the final meeting.

How to Prepare for an Observation

In many ways, informal visits by evaluators are much easier to get through than the planned, formal observations. You do not have time to worry about an unannounced visit, whereas knowing that an administrator is going to observe you in a few days gives you time to feel anxious. In addition, taking the following steps can help you feel confident both before and during the observation:

- **Step One:** Be proactive. Make sure that you have a copy of the supervisor's observation form if there is not a copy in your faculty manual. In fact, you should do this as early in the term as you can. Study the form so that you know what the observer will be looking for as you teach.

- **Step Two:** Keep your lesson simple so that you can do it well. The observer will want to see you interacting with your students, so do not plan a test or a video. Elaborate activities, such as a class skit or student debates, may not highlight your instructional skills very well.

- **Step Three:** Tell your students what is going to happen. Inform them that there will be a visitor in the classroom and that you would appreciate their cooperation.

- **Step Four:** Write out your lesson plan and collect extra copies of all handouts, textbooks, or materials needed for the lesson for the observer. Select an unobtrusive place for your visitor, and put these materials there. Be ready to show your lesson plan book as well as your grade book.

- **Step Five:** Get control of your anxiety. This is the most important step in your preparation. If you are ready and have a well-planned lesson, you do not have to worry. Expect to be nervous, but also expect to do well because you have prepared thoroughly.

Turn Criticism into a Positive Experience

One of the most difficult aspects of being observed and evaluated is hearing negative things about your teaching performance. Veteran teachers will tell you that although it is not easy to have a supervisor discuss the problems with your performance, such criticism can be conducive to professional growth. With a professional, open-minded attitude, you will find that discussing your teaching performance during the evaluation conference can be a valuable way to improve your teaching skills. Here are some suggestions to make an evaluation conference a positive and productive experience:

- Go into your evaluation conference with paper, a pen, and an open mind. Be prepared to hear negative as well as positive comments about your performance.

- Listen objectively. Most of the criticism will probably cover issues you have already started to address yourself. If you find yourself becoming defensive, stop and try to remain objective and open-minded.

- Listen more than you speak. Ask for advice and suggestions for improvement, then listen carefully, write them down, and follow them.

- After the conference, when you have had an opportunity to correct some of your weaknesses, keep the administrator updated on your progress in following his or her suggestions.

The Impact of Value-Added Assessments on the Evaluation Process

The term *value-added assessment* refers to the way that evaluators assess the performance of a specific teacher by comparing current standardized test scores with past test scores for that teacher's students. The intended result of these comparisons is to determine the contributions to student achievement made by each teacher in a single year.

Although the intent of value-added assessment is to provide a reasonable and objective method of assessing teacher effectiveness, the practice is controversial. Some of the problems with the use of value-added assessments can include missing past test scores, past test scores that are not comparable to present ones, or even test scores that could be skewed by various factors.

As controversial as this method of assessment may be, many school districts today use value-added assessments as a part of a teacher's evaluation process. The implications of this are significant for all teachers. There are several actions that you can take to avoid being adversely affected by a value-added assessment:

- Look at your students both as individuals and as part of an entire group. Although you may design instruction for the group, keep in mind that it is individual students whose test scores will be compared.

- Assess your students' strengths and weaknesses in terms of their knowledge and skill level at the beginning of each unit of study. Use that early assessment as a guide when you differentiate instruction for the unit.

- Make sure to maintain accurate records of your students' mastery of the subject matter. This will allow you to correct gaps in knowledge or skills as necessary.

- Be aware of the populations in your class, such as the children of poverty, students who are reluctant to learn, and students who do not speak English as a first language, who are at the highest risk for poor performance on standardized tests. This knowledge will enable you to intervene early to help them succeed.

- Teach the academic vocabulary and test-taking skills that are appropriate for your students. Offer practice sessions so that your students will not be intimidated by unfamiliar test procedures.

- Don't hesitate to ask early in the school term for assistance for those students who may be struggling. Involve support personnel as well as adult and peer tutors to help those students.

What to Do if Your Evaluation Is Poor

Almost every thoughtful evaluator will offer recommendations on how you can correct weaknesses in your teaching performance, but there is a difference between those constructive recommendations and an evaluation that indicates that your classroom performance is not acceptable according to your school district's standards.

If you receive a poor evaluation, it is very likely that your first reactions will be anger, frustration, shock, and despair. Although such emotions are understandable, the best course of action for you to take is to master these feelings quickly so that you can respond in a professional manner. Next, you should strive to be as objective and proactive as possible in dealing with the situation. Ask yourself these questions:

- Am I clear about exactly what my noted areas of weakness are and what I am expected to do to remediate them?

- To whom can I turn for assistance?

- What immediate changes can I make to improve my teaching performance?
- How can I contact my local education association representative for guidance?
- How can I learn more about my district's evaluation and firing policies?
- What long-term plans should I make to ensure that I have remediated the areas of poor performance indicated?

You should also keep in mind that your poor performance evaluation is not a topic that should be the subject of gossip at school or, even worse, among your students or their families. Do not vent indiscriminately or discuss your evaluation with anyone other than trusted colleagues and friends. Keep in mind that you want to solve this problem, not spread the news. Even though your evaluation may be a poor one, employees are still expected to sign the evaluation. If you want to write a letter to rebut or explain any part of the evaluation, you should feel free to do so and to ask that it be added to your personnel file, along with the evaluation itself. Refusing to sign the evaluation can be regarded as an insubordinate act on your part.

Finally, you should learn about your legal rights as an employee of your school district. Contact your local education association representative as well as your district's human relations office to learn as much as you can about how to manage your situation most effectively.

CREATE A PROFESSIONAL PORTFOLIO

Creating a professional portfolio serves two purposes. As a tool to showcase you to prospective employers, a portfolio can reveal a great deal of useful information about you and your teaching experiences. However, as a new teacher, you will find that another valuable result of the creation and maintenance of a professional portfolio is the opportunity it gives you to reflect on your teaching experiences and philosophy. It does not take long to set up and maintain a professional portfolio if you take the time to plan what you want to include in it. Although many teachers keep a paper portfolio, it is also easy to maintain a digital one or even a combination of both.

Whichever method you choose to use, the key to managing the portfolio process is simple: plan what you want to include and file that work as you encounter it. A lesson plan here, a survey there, a copy of some of the snapshot observations you've done, and soon you will have a representative sampling of your work.

Most professional portfolios contain materials that can be grouped into two parts: evidence or artifacts from your career and your reflections on various aspects of your teaching experiences. Here are some of the items you can include:

Artifacts

- Formal observations and evaluations
- Peer observations

- Student responses to surveys about your class
- Representative lesson plans—usually a week's worth
- A description of your classroom management plan
- A video or audio recording of a lesson
- Photographs of your classroom setup and decor
- Photographs of students working
- Lists of committees you've served on
- Lists of extracurricular work and activities
- Annotated samples of student work
- Letters of recommendation
- Awards or honors
- Evidence from professional development workshops or courses
- An explanation of your teaching responsibilities

> Schedule a gym class, hobby, or something else that starts one to two hours after the school day ends, at least two days a week. It will help you prioritize what needs to get done. Staying at school too long can lead to poor time management because you feel like you have forever to accomplish things. It can also lead to burnout.
>
> *Margaret R. Scheirer, 12 years' experience*

Reflections

- Sample pages from a journal recording your reflections on your teaching practice
- Responses you've made when observing other teachers
- Annotated lesson plans

MAINTAIN A WORK-LIFE BALANCE FOR LONG-TERM SUCCESS

Education is often ranked as one of the most stressful of all career choices. The chief cause of this ranking frequently lies in the unfortunate combination of too many pressing responsibilities and the idealistic dedication that many teachers feel about their work. Emotionally, mentally, and physically challenging, teaching is a compelling profession where teachers find it all too easy to immerse themselves in their school duties to the detriment of their personal lives. The result is that many teachers report significance stress due to a harmful work-life imbalance.

Because being a teacher means that daily responsibilities begin early and seem never to end, it is not always easy to leave the demands of school at school. Because we are in the business of changing lives, we feel the weight of those responsibilities long after we have left the building. One of the occupational hazards all successful teachers face is that it is all too easy to take home not only our paperwork but also our worries about our school days.

Successful teachers who want a long-term career in education must learn how to juggle the demands of being in a classroom all day long and still maintain a satisfactory personal life. The key? Finding a balance between the challenges of a new career and such personal needs as maintaining friendships, meeting family responsibilities, and pursuing other endeavors that bring fulfillment and joy to life. To learn how to be one of those successful teachers who seem to have found the right balance between their personal and professional lives, consider putting some of these suggestions into practice:

- Make time for yourself. Eat well. Exercise. Count your blessings. Plan enjoyable activities. Your students will not thrive if their teacher is exhausted and stressed. Take good care of yourself if you want to be able to focus on caring for your students.

- Don't lose sight of the big picture. No one can teach every part of the curriculum or reach every student or make every school day a success. What you can do, however, is realize that each school year is not a sprint but a marathon. It takes patience, determination, and a clear idea of the desired outcome for runners to complete a marathon; the same is true for teachers.

- See the opportunities in your problems. When you have a problem at school, try to think of it as an opportunity to learn new professional skills.

- Work efficiently while you are at school. Prioritize the tasks that you must accomplish and work steadily at them. Use your planning time and any spare moment to their fullest advantage. The more you accomplish at school, the less you will have to do at home, leaving you with the time you need to enjoy life away from school.

- Focus on the tasks at hand. Too often teachers find it easy to second-guess their decisions or to replay troublesome scenarios from the day. Instead of endlessly rehashing what went wrong, focus on productive tasks, such as designing the plans you need to create or new activities to spark your students' interest.

- Set boundaries. No one expects you to be on call twenty-four hours a day. For example, it is not wise to give out your personal phone number. Although there will be many after-school demands on your time, learn to gently refuse those that will be too demanding or unproductive.

- Keep your career worries in perspective. When something goes wrong, ask yourself if you will still be affected by it in a year, in a few months, or even in a week. Try to focus on the big picture instead of allowing nagging small issues to rob you of your peace of mind.

- Always have something to look forward to. Make a point of planning a weekend excursion or an outing with family and friends or even setting aside time to work on a hobby. Looking forward to something pleasant in the future will help you maintain your equanimity in the present.

- Don't forget that your new profession is only one part of a rewarding and busy life. If you find that you are spending too much time at school or worrying about school after you have left for the day, then it's time to take steps to manage that school-induced stress.

- Stop trying to control everything. Choose your battles wisely by asking yourself if the issue that is troubling you is worth your time and energy.

- Allow yourself time to make effective transitions from one class to another. This is particularly difficult when you have many classes each day. One way to manage this is by having an opening routine that your students can do independently. This will free you to make the mental, emotional, and physical switch from one group of students or from one content area to another.

- Keep a flexible attitude. Get into the habit of looking for solutions instead of dwelling on your problems. If you are open to alternatives, you will be able to assess your options much more quickly.

- Delegate responsibilities. Decide who you want to do a task, clearly explain how you want it accomplished, and then step back and allow the people you selected to get busy.

- Stop rushing from one responsibility to the next. Slow down. Here are some ways to slow your school life down: take the time to eat lunch, allow yourself ten minutes to relax with colleagues at some point during your day, and use a journal for reflection.

- Learn to pace your instruction to allow for some less intense teaching periods. You should not be "on" day after day. Instead, allow your students time for independent work, small-group work, or even such activities as viewing films related to the subject under study.

- Add structure to your life. Routines will prevent many stress-inducing problems. Putting your keys in the same place every day, for example, will save you frustration later.

- Reflect on the positive things that happen at school. When it comes time for that important self-reflection, be sure to think about the positive things that happen each day. Focusing on your strengths and your successes is just as important as improving weaknesses and correcting mistakes.

- Think before you act. If you plan your responses to unpleasant situations, you will prevent many problems. Situations that you should think about before you act include dealing with incomplete homework assignments, angry parents, defiant students, cheating incidents, tardy students, and other frequent classroom disruptions.

> I try to leave the emotion of work at work. I take paperwork home, but I try not to take the emotional stuff home. My husband and I have a ten-minute rule. We can each vent about our jobs for ten minutes at dinner, then that is it. No more. Move on. Tomorrow is another day.
>
> *Mary Landis, 22 years' experience*

- Take advantage of the assistance your district may offer its employees. Many districts offer various types of mental health assistance to its employees. Often referred to as an EAP (Employee Assistance Program), this district-wide assistance can take many forms, such as counseling referrals, wellness activities, online stress reduction classes, support groups, financial coaching, help with substance abuse, and many others.

- Start to put together a network of supportive and positive people who can help you. Being connected to others is an important way to avoid the stress that can make every day miserable. Supportive colleagues can help you figure out the solutions you need.

Twenty-Five Strategies Specifically Geared for an Educator's Tough Times at School

Having a bad day at school? Try the following strategies to banish the stress that comes with a bad day at school:

1. Go to your school's media center and escape into a good book or read a newspaper for a few minutes.
2. Talk things over with a sympathetic colleague or mentor.
3. Take a brisk walk around the perimeter of your building.
4. Refuse to take it personally when students are rude or disruptive.
5. If you have too much to do, divide each task into manageable amounts and get busy.
6. There are several free apps for mindfulness or meditation. If you would like to try one, a good place to start is with Calm (www.calm.com).
7. Take a break. Change activities. Do something you enjoy instead of dealing with drudgery.
8. Close your classroom door. Set a timer for five minutes. Allow yourself to just rest and be quiet.
9. Grab a sheet of paper and a pencil. Brainstorm solutions to the cause of your stress.
10. Listen to relaxing (or energizing) music for a few minutes. The Internet radio station Pandora (www.pandora.com) makes it easy for listeners to create personal listening stations.
11. Eat a healthful snack. Junk food will cheer you up for only a few minutes.
12. Even though using mindfulness activities in class for students is now a widespread practice, there are plenty of benefits for teachers as well. A useful site for teachers is Mindful Teachers (www.mindfulteachers.org).
13. Acknowledge that you are genuinely upset. Denial doesn't solve problems.
14. Plan a fun activity that you can anticipate with pleasure.
15. Ask your students for their advice if the problem is one where they can help.

16. Clear up some clutter. Tidy your desk or your classroom.

17. Shift your activity. Move to another location, if possible.

18. Ask for help. Doing this can allow you to move closer to a positive resolution to a problem.

19. Post a funny cartoon, meme, or photo where you can see it when you need a laugh during the school day.

20. Tackle busywork: grade quiz papers, answer e-mail, anything to be productive instead of paralyzed in negative emotions.

21. Deal systematically with the problems that cause stress. Don't procrastinate. Cope.

22. When you find yourself dwelling on the negative things that can happen at school, make a conscious effort to reframe those thoughts in a positive manner. For example, instead of thinking, "My students are always out of control after lunch," try "My students need ways to channel their energy after lunch."

23. Remind yourself once again that today's problems likely won't be important a year—or maybe even a week—from now.

24. Choose your battles. Is what you are stressed about worth your time and energy?

25. Take a deep breath. Hold to the count of three. Exhale slowly. Repeat until you feel calmer.

Questions to Discuss with Colleagues

Sharing ideas with colleagues is a helpful way to devise solutions to some of the problems that you must manage successfully at school. Here you will find several topics to open discussions with colleagues about successful instructional practices:

1. You have had a stressful day at school in which nothing seemed to go as you had planned. What can you do to remain confident while learning from the events of this tough day?

2. You just received an e-mail from your principal telling you that she will visit your classroom later in the day. Your lesson is not a very exciting one, nor is it particularly well structured. What should you do? Who can offer advice?

3. You and your mentor do not have a common planning period. How can you find the time to work together?

4. Although you are sure that you want to create a supportive network of colleagues to share ideas with, you are not sure about how to begin. How can you and your colleagues near and far benefit from your own professional learning network?

5. What problems can you anticipate that you will have as a first-year teacher? Where can you find help for them?

Topics to Discuss with a Mentor

Although the topics that new teachers need to discuss with a mentor vary from teacher to teacher and from school to school, there are some that most first-year teachers should be comfortable discussing with a mentor or a trusted colleague. You should ask your mentor about these topics from this section:

- How to learn about professional development opportunities in your school district
- Tips for making sure your evaluation process goes well
- How to set appropriate goals for your first year
- Which teachers at your school would be interested in observing you and in being observed themselves
- How to manage school-induced stress and maintain a work-life balance

Reflection Questions to Guide Your Thinking

1. What are your personal strengths as a teacher at this point in your career? How can you use these strengths to overcome some of the problems that you will face this year?

2. If you are like other teachers, you are understandably nervous about the evaluation process. How can you make sure that you know what to expect and how to prepare for it?

3. How can you find the time to start a program of sustained professional growth and still take care of your classroom responsibilities?

4. What part of your school life has been stressful so far? How have you managed this stress? Are you comfortable with your work-life balance so far? If not, how can you improve it?

5. What can you do to maintain your fresh idealism as you go through the ups and downs of your first year as a teacher?

SECTION TWO

Develop Professional Productivity Skills

When you were planning to become an educator, many of your daydreams probably centered on images of yourself in front of a class delivering instruction. Although that pleasant image is certainly a crucial aspect of an education career, it just can't happen without a great deal of behind-the-scenes effort and plenty of education-specific workplace skills. Developing professional productivity skills is one of the hallmarks of confident and capable teachers who can maintain a work-life balance.

As you work through the information in this section, you'll learn about the practical skills that can help you become an efficient teacher. The most important skills you need to manage your classroom well are learning to arrange your work space so that you can be productive, becoming proficient at time management, devising methods to manage professional documents, and grading papers quickly and efficiently.

Arrange Your Work Space for Maximum Productivity

Your personal work area may determine whether you will be comfortable in your classroom or not. Because you will be spending so many of your daylight hours in your classroom, your personal workstation should be comfortable as well as businesslike. The area you designate as your workstation should include a lockable drawer, your desk and chair, a coat cabinet, file cabinets, and other spaces that are solely for your personal use.

Your Desk Area

Your desk area is probably the most important part of the work space in your classroom because it is your most personal space. Here are some suggestions for making sure that it functions well for you:

- Keep the top of your desk as free of distracting clutter as you can. Although the items on your desk can reflect your personality, you should keep them businesslike as an example for your students and to make it easier for you to get your work done. Here are some of the items you should have within easy reach:
  - Trays for folders and papers
  - A calendar (Even if you rely on an electronic calendar, a paper version is often helpful.)
  - Pens and pencils
  - A notepad for reminders and to capture good ideas
  - A stapler (Label it "Teacher Use.")
  - Paper clips
  - Trash can
  - A charger for your computer

- You will probably be issued a laptop or other type of computer. Be sure to leave room on your desk for it and to arrange the cords and chargers that accompany it so that they are unobtrusive.

- Because your desk is a space allotted for your personal use, you should discourage students from taking items from it. To make this easy for students to remember, set up a student work center at a spot away from your desk. In this area, place a stapler (labeled "Student Use"), a hole punch, a trash can, a recycled paper bin, and a tray for collecting student papers.

- Do not place your cell phone, scissors, liquid paper, tacks, markers, glue, tape, or any sharp object on the top of your desk. If an item would tempt a student to steal or could cause harm or be used as a weapon, it should be stored inside your desk.

- You will need a safe place to store and lock away your personal belongings, such as your cell phone. Experienced teachers seldom have credit cards or much cash at school.

- You should set aside an area inside your desk to place your keys so that you can quickly find them. If you use a paper grade book or professional binder, these should also be stored inside a desk drawer when you are not using them.

- If you place your desk in the back of the room, you can monitor your students' activity while you are seated, confer with students without having the entire class as an audience, and you will not block students' view of the board.

- If possible, your file cabinet and other personal storage areas should be set up near your desk for quick access.

- It is always a good idea to leave your desk clean at the end of each school day. If you

> If I had a chance to do my first year over, I would be more organized. I would not hide my fear of failure behind bravado but ask for help from fellow teachers instead.
>
> *Deborah McManaway, 23 years' experience*

do this and leave the next day's to-do list in a convenient place, you will be able to start each day productively.

Supplies You Will Need

You will need more than just red pens and a grade book to provide dynamic and engaging instruction. Unfortunately, many schools do not provide teachers with enough money to pay for the supplies they need. Teachers everywhere have learned to adjust to a tough economy by recycling, asking parents or businesses for help, and making good use of the supplies they have. Many teachers have been able to obtain supplies by asking for donations or creating wish lists on such sites as:

- **ClassWish (www.classwish.org/teachers)**
- **Craigslist (www.craigslist.org)**
- **Donors Choose (www.donorschoose.org)**
- **Freecycle (www.freecycle.org)**

Another way that many teachers can obtain school supplies is by searching for freebies online. Here is just a small sampling of the many sites you can search for items that could benefit you and your students:

- **Cool Freebie Links (www.coolfreebielinks.com/Teachers_Freebies).** At this site, there are hundreds of free resources for K–12 teachers.
- **Print-A-Poster.com (http://print-a-poster.com).** Here teachers can download and print free posters on a wide variety of topics.
- **SchoolExpress (www.schoolexpress.com).** This site offers thousands of free worksheets, games, and awards of various types.

The following are lists of some of the supplies you may find useful as you go through the school year. If your district can't supply these items for you, start with the basics and add items as you can. Many of these can be purchased at discount stores during back-to-school sales. You can also ask your mentor or colleagues for assistance in obtaining classroom supplies.

Basic Items You'll Need

- Pens—blue and black
- Colored pens for grading
- Pencils with good erasers
- File folders

- Labels
- A hole punch
- A calculator
- Transparent tape
- Glue
- A flash drive or other memory storage device
- An easy-to-find key ring
- Rubber bands
- A pencil sharpener
- Staplers (one for students and one for you)
- Paper clips of all sizes
- Scissors
- Three-ring binders
- Sticky notes
- Lined paper
- Printer paper
- Notepads
- Stackable trays
- Board erasers
- Board markers
- Desk cleaning wipes
- Hand sanitizer
- Tissues
- Paper towels
- Reward stickers
- Mints

Useful Items That May Come in Handy

- Colored pencils
- Markers for student use
- Colored printer paper
- Poster mounting putty
- Envelopes of various sizes
- A personal first-aid kit
- Safety pins
- Wrapping paper for classroom decor

IF YOU SPEND TWENTY-FIVE DOLLARS ON YOUR CLASSROOM SUPPLIES

Although there are many ways to find free, reusable, gently used, recycled, or inexpensive materials for your classroom, it is not always easy to know how to allocate the money you may have available to you. Although every classroom is different, if you are not sure where to begin and you have twenty-five dollars to spend, you would be wise to focus your spending on these items:

- Bulletin board materials
- Storage containers
- Organizers for your paperwork
- Organizers for student papers
- An extra stapler
- Pencils, markers, and pens
- Crayons
- Scissors

IF YOU SPEND FIFTY DOLLARS ON YOUR CLASSROOM SUPPLIES

If you have a bit more money to spend on your classroom, then you should purchase the items in the twenty-five-dollar budget and then choose which of these would be appropriate for your classroom:

- Extra lighting
- Poster board
- Colored paper for student use
- Colored pencils or markers
- A rug

The Dos and Don'ts of Your School Computer

One of the most exciting moments of any orientation program for new teachers is the issuance of school computers. No matter what type of computer you have, it is exciting to be connected to the other employees in your district and to have access to the same resources that are available to them. Being issued a school computer also means that new teachers need to adopt a professional approach to the way they use this ubiquitous tool.

After years of working on personally owned computers, many new teachers are not always sure which behaviors are acceptable and which are not, even though they may have signed a document outlining their district's acceptable use policies. To make sure that your use of your school computer is as professional as possible, be guided by these lists of dos and don'ts:

School Computer Dos

- Do remain aware that the computer is the property of your school district.
- Do be cautious, conservative, and professional when using your school computer.
- Do transport your computer in the case or bag that was issued with it if it is portable.
- Do periodically go through your files to keep them organized and updated.
- Do back up your work to an external drive.
- Do follow your school's protocol for saving to a school network.
- Do use bookmarks to keep your topics easy to find in a hurry.
- Do use your computer for school business only.
- Do create passwords for your various school accounts that are logical and easy to recall and that can be updated periodically.
- Do respect the intellectual property rights of others.
- Do make sure to lock a portable computer in a secure place if you don't take it home each day.
- Do make sure that you are aware of your district's acceptable use policies for both school employees and students.
- Do keep your virus protection and other updates current.
- Do report problems with your computer as quickly as you can.

School Computer Don'ts

- Don't download any software program without permission—preferably in writing.
- Don't have food or drink near your computer. Spills can be costly.
- Don't forget that district personnel may monitor your e-mail account and search history.
- Don't leave your computer unattended when you leave your classroom.
- Don't allow students to use your computer.
- Don't follow your students on their social media accounts.
- Don't visit sites with such content as pornography or extreme political views that could indicate that you are not a good school employee.
- Don't decorate your computer with stickers, images, or anything that has not been approved by your school district.

- Don't knowingly open attachments or visit sites that could infect your computer.
- Don't share your passwords with others.
- Don't conduct personal business on your school computer.

Tips for Managing E-mail

Most teachers will admit to having mixed feelings about school e-mail. On the plus side, it is an efficient and quick way to communicate with parents or guardians, students, and colleagues. On the minus side, angry e-mails from colleagues, students, and parents or guardians can ruin any teacher's day.

Responding to e-mails often consumes far too much of a busy teacher's time. Also, an e-mail cannot always convey your tone, and so it's easy to send confusing messages with the potential to create or exacerbate unpleasant situations. To avoid unpleasantness and to create a positive relationship with those with whom you correspond, try these tips for making sure that your e-mails reflect your professionalism:

- If you are considering sending an e-mail about a discipline incident, make a phone call instead. Not only is it more courteous, but you are far more likely to resolve the problem.
- Be very careful about forwarding any messages that may embarrass the original sender.
- When you write the subject line, take care to be as clear as possible so that the receiver can prioritize the e-mail.
- Protect the privacy of your students by not mentioning them by name in e-mails to colleagues about sensitive issues.
- Before you send an e-mail, take the time to proofread it carefully.
- Be careful before you decide to "reply all" to group e-mails, avoid being too casual with your greeting or jargon, and be aware that attempts at humor can often be misread.
- Make a time management plan detailing how you will check and respond to e-mail during the school day. Many teachers check e-mail only at established intervals to avoid being distracted from their teaching duties.
- Adopt a systematic approach to how you manage your e-mail folders. Create a system that allows you to retrieve an e-mail quickly when needed. Many teachers group e-mail that they need to archive into folders with reasonably limited categories, such as meeting notes, special projects, or specific students.
- When you create your e-mail signature, remember that it should reflect your status as a school employee. If you include a quotation or motto, it should reflect your pride in your school and your profession rather than make a statement about your personal philosophy about life.

Time Management for Teachers

Poor time management is one of the most debilitating bad habits of any profession and especially for educators. We have so much to do and so little free time to accomplish it that many of us often feel overwhelmed and stressed. With forethought and attention to detail, however, you can develop the time management strategies that will make it easier for you to manage your workload and to create a rewarding work-life balance. Effective time management begins with making deliberate choices about prioritizing your professional tasks.

HOW TO PRIORITIZE YOUR PROFESSIONAL TASKS

With the workplace pressure that most teachers experience, it is crucial to prioritize your tasks so that you can accomplish everything you need to do, move forward in meeting your goals, and reduce your stress level so that you can have the work-life balance that you need to succeed. Here is a simple five-step process to help you prioritize your work:

- **Step One:** It's only common sense to begin by brainstorming a list of the tasks that you need to do. Jotting them down in a list will make it easier for you to visualize the work that must be done.

- **Step Two:** After you have made a task list, go over it carefully to determine the urgency of each task. Highlight the tasks that should be completed before you leave school for the day. Some examples of an urgent school task could include:
    - Responding to an e-mail from a parent or guardian
    - Responding to an e-mail from a supervisor
    - Making a phone call to a parent or guardian about a problem
    - Dealing with a discipline issue
    - Making copies of the handouts you will need for the next day's lesson
    - Writing a brief reflection on the day's instruction
    - Making sure that the equipment and materials for the next day are ready

- **Step Three:** After you have determined the urgent tasks that need to be accomplished, look at the list of tasks again to determine the ones that can be accomplished with a brief delay of a day or two. It is always a good idea to get the more troublesome ones out of the way first. Examples of this type of task could include:
    - Recording or posting grades
    - Sending home positive notes for students
    - Giving feedback on assignments (Be sure to stagger this so that the feedback is timely and meaningful.)
    - Making copies of next week's handouts
    - Creating a test to be given next week

- Making daily plans for the next week and beyond
- Making sure you have enough supplies for next week's instruction

- **Step Four:** A fourth step in prioritizing the tasks in your workload involves determining the ones that are necessary to do but that do not need to be done for several days or could even be tasks that are optional. Examples of this type of task could include:

  - Creating a new bulletin board
  - Adjusting an alternative assessment for a current unit of study
  - Searching for new project materials
  - Browsing for creative lesson plans online
  - Planning a field trip for next semester
  - Updating your digital documents or cleaning out a file drawer
  - Sharing resources with a colleague for a new unit of study

- **Step Five:** After you have jotted down your tasks and identified their urgency level, go through the list and number them in the order that you intend to accomplish them. Figure 2.1 features a sample list to guide you.

To help prioritize your professional tasks, you can also adapt Teacher Worksheet 2.1 to meet your needs.

Today's Tasks

5. Make copies of Chapter 7 handouts

1. E-mail Joe Smith's mother

3. Make test for Chapter 6

4. Record Chapter 5 grades

2. Write today's reflection

Figure 2.1 Brainstorming a Task List

Prioritize Your Tasks

After you have brainstormed the tasks that you need to accomplish, you can use this worksheet to list them in the proper category so that you can manage your workload efficiently.

Tasks to Do Right Away	Tasks to Delay Briefly	Tasks That Can Wait
1.	1.	1.
2.	2.	2.
3.	3.	3.
4.	4.	4.
5.	5.	5.
6.	6.	6.
7.	7.	7.
8.	8.	8.
9.	9.	9.
10.	10.	10.

A Teacher's To-Do List

Many teachers also like to use a more structured daily to-do list to manage all the tasks that they need to complete each day. A template, such as the one shown in Teacher Worksheet 2.2, not only allows you to manage your tasks but also serves as an informal record of each day's work if you keep them on file. Teacher Worksheet 2.3 is a weekly reminder list you can use to assess how well you are doing each week.

A to-do list is such an invaluable tool that is hard to imagine a successful teacher who does not use one for time and task management. The best way to use a to-do list effectively is to create it the day before you will need it—preferably before you leave school for the day. If you do this, when you arrive at school the next morning, you will be able to start your day with a quick review of the things that need to be accomplished.

TEACHER WORKSHEET 2.2

A Teacher's Daily To-Do List

Here are some of the tasks that many teachers have to manage successfully each day. Use this list to plan how to manage your daily responsibilities.

Date: _____

Phone calls concerning students:

Student	Parent or Guardian	Phone Number	Reason

Other phone calls or contacts:

_____

_____

Conferences:

Student	What	When	Where	Outcome

Other meetings:

_____

_____

(continued on next page)

(continued from previous page)

After-school or extra duty responsibilities:

_____

_____

_____

_____

_____

Items to duplicate:

_____

_____

_____

_____

_____

Lesson plans or projects to complete:

_____

_____

_____

_____

_____

Notes, reminders, and errands:

_____

_____

_____

_____

_____

Checklist of a Teacher's Weekly Reminders

Although not every teacher's weekly reminder list will be the same, there are some tasks that almost every teacher should consider doing on a weekly basis. Use this checklist to assess how well you are doing each week. The more items you can check off, the more productive you will be.

1. _____ Plan active, fun-filled learning experiences for your students.
2. _____ Look ahead and design lesson plans as far in advance as you can.
3. _____ Find relevant online materials to include in lessons.
4. _____ Plan how you will provide remedial instruction.
5. _____ Plan how you will enrich instruction.
6. _____ Use formative assessments to check your students' progress at least twice.
7. _____ Run off materials for upcoming lessons.
8. _____ Return graded papers so that students have timely feedback.
9. _____ Record all grades for the week.
10. _____ Send home progress reports.
11. _____ Send a positive note home with at least five students.
12. _____ Hold a recap session so that students can review the week's learning.
13. _____ Celebrate student successes.
14. _____ Tidy the classroom and ready it for the next week's activities.
15. _____ Update your class web page.
16. _____ File handouts and other materials that are no longer needed.
17. _____ Reflect on your effectiveness as a teacher.
18. _____ Collect data on a classroom issue and decide how to use this information effectively.
19. _____ Teach or reinforce at least one study skill.
20. _____ Make sure your classroom policies are as transparent as possible.

Quick Tips for Maximizing the Time You Have at School

Learning to use the time that you have available to you while you are at school will not only make your school day easier and more pleasant but also your personal life because being productive at school will reduce the amount of work that you have to accomplish at home. Here are some quick tips to help you maximize the time that you have at school:

- When you have complicated tasks to do, divide them into smaller pieces with specific deadlines for each one.
- Write yourself reminders. Teachers have too much to do to keep everything straight without reminders. Set reminders on your phone or send yourself reminder e-mails or texts when you have important deadlines if handwritten ones don't work as well for you.
- If a task will take less than three minutes, do it right away.
- Use either a digital or paper calendar as a planner. Record tasks, appointments, and other information you'll need to remember as you plan your workdays. Don't just plan for the day but also for the week, for the month, for the semester, and for the year.
- Refuse politely when someone asks you to give time you cannot spare.
- Follow the old business rule: touch each sheet of paper only once.
- Keep your keys and your badge (if your district has issued you one) in the same location each day.
- Deal efficiently with mail. Act immediately on items that require a written response. Throw away or recycle junk mail. File catalogs for later use.
- Set up equipment early in case there are problems.
- Don't arrive too early or too late to meetings or duty assignments.
- Delegate as much as you can. Even very young students can accomplish many routine tasks, such as putting up posters or keeping the supply area clean.
- Have an up-to-date set of emergency lesson plans ready—just in case.

Further, you should learn to use small blocks of time wisely. You will be surprised at how much you can accomplish in a short amount of time if you stay focused. In fifteen minutes, you can

- Grade the objective portion of a set of test papers
- Update your class web page or blog
- Create a review sheet
- Answer e-mail
- Create warm-up exercises for the entire week

I think what surprised me the most as a new teacher was trying to manage my time. I am very good at time management and thought it would be a piece of cake. I was wrong. I felt prepared to teach my subject, but once the real work began to happen, I had to figure out a way to still go on walks, watch TV, and hang out with friends. It took time, but I was able to prioritize life and work.

Jessica Statz, 19 years' experience

In ten minutes, you can

- Call students' parents or guardians
- Write a lesson plan
- Grade some essay questions
- Average grades and post them
- Check homework papers

In five minutes, you can

- Create a dynamic closing exercise
- Write a positive note and send it home with a student
- Use the hole punch on a set of papers
- Write a positive comment on at least five papers
- Review key points in a lesson with a brief multimedia presentation

In three minutes, you can

- Record grades
- Drill your students with PowerPoint games
- Put stickers on a set of papers
- Praise a class for good behavior
- Have students write an evaluation of the day's lesson

In one minute, you can

- Erase the board
- Display an image related to the day's lesson
- Have students tidy the room
- Recognize the student of the day or week
- Write an inspirational message on the board

How Teachers Sabotage Their Time Management Strategies

Although there are far more tasks to be done than any teacher can ever manage to complete in a school day, if you just look around your building, you will find that there are excellent teachers who are so well prepared that they seem to radiate a calm energy. Unlike their stressed-out colleagues, they don't allow poor time management to disrupt their school days. To avoid the stress caused by this self-sabotage, it is important to be aware of the bad time management habits that you may have. Here is a quick list of some of the most common mistakes that can cause wasted time at work:

- Falling behind in grading, planning, and other predictable routine paperwork chores
- Attempting to cram instead of dividing a project into smaller, more manageable parts and doing each one systematically
- Trying to do everything yourself instead of asking for help or delegating tasks
- Neglecting to plan and prioritize your work
- Giving in to distractions when researching or working online
- Spending planning period time chatting with colleagues instead of accomplishing necessary tasks
- Being distracted by classroom concerns and other problems instead of resolving them
- Disregarding the importance of using a planner, a calendar, or other scheduling strategies
- Ignoring small problems until they become more difficult to resolve
- Checking e-mail all day long instead of at planned times
- Declining to use reminders, such as a to-do list or digital notifications

How to Minimize the Time You Spend Working at Home

In addition to the general increase in productivity that can result from sound time management strategies, there are four actions that you can take right away to lessen the amount of time that you spend doing schoolwork at home:

- **Action One:** Focus at school. Think of every minute at school as usable work time. Even five-minute blocks of time while you are waiting for a meeting to begin, for example, can be productive if you choose. Try your best to do schoolwork at school instead of at home. There are many apps designed to help you stay focused during the day. A user-friendly app that you may want to explore is Focus Booster (www .focusboosterapp.com). This app allows users to focus for twenty-five minutes at a time and then take a five-minute break. It is particularly useful for boosting planning period productivity.
- **Action Two:** Don't take all your papers home each day. Just take home a manageable number—only what you can grade in one hour, for instance. At home, set a timer and stop when the time you have planned for working is over. Dragging home so much work that you can't possibly complete it all will only distress you.

- **Action Three:** When you do take papers home, try to work on them as soon after you arrive home as possible. It's not always possible, but waiting until after dinner to begin working means that you will be exhausted after a long day instead of at your peak of productivity.

- **Action Four:** Set aside time for relaxation, no matter how much schoolwork you need to do. There is no virtue in allowing schoolwork to consume an entire weekend. Plan when you are going to work and plan when you are going to take time to just be yourself.

Planning Period Productivity

Teachers who use their planning periods effectively understand the importance of prudently mapping out how they will use almost every minute of the time. Without this careful attention to time management, planning period minutes can quickly vanish.

A productive planning period does not happen by accident. Setting routines for your planning period will allow you to take control of your time at school and add the consistency that is needed for task management. You can set aside specific days for certain tasks, such as grading, planning, or other routine work, for example. The key to a productive planning period is to deliberately decide how you will use the time instead of just letting it happen.

In addition to a lack of planning, another planning period time-robber is making several trips away from your classroom or planning area. It's tempting to wander around getting a snack, checking your mailbox, or chatting with colleagues. If you plan the trips you need to make during your planning period—to confer with an administrator, to the copy room, and to return a library book, for example—you will find that making one trip with several quick stops is much more efficient than if you were to make several trips.

Although every minute of your planning period should be organized for maximum productivity, don't neglect to build in a few quick minutes of mindful relaxation. Taking the time to breathe deeply, decompress, and focus on peaceful thoughts instead of a stressful school day will refresh your spirit and make it easier to manage the rest of the day.

A final strategy for using every minute of your planning period productively is to have the materials you need handy. Having everything ready at the start of your planning period will save you valuable time and allow you to use the time effectively.

During my first year, I wish I had planned ahead more. It's amazing how many times you feel a little overwhelmed when you think you've carved out time in the school day but then a million little things (parent e-mail, administrator wants to touch base, fellow teacher has a question, the copier calls it a day on you when you need that reading for the kids) pop up, and suddenly you're scrambling when you thought you had it all under control. I've got so many memories of having that "I got this" feeling turning to "I could have lined this up in twenty minutes yesterday!"

Kevin Healy, 11 years' experience

Create Handouts and Other Instructional Resources Quickly

One of the most labor-intensive responsibilities that any teacher has is the creation of instructional materials. Although this is often one of the most pleasant teacher tasks, it can also be time consuming, especially for novice teachers. When you create handouts and other materials, focus on the big picture of what you are trying to accomplish instead of getting bogged down in the details. To save valuable time while you work on this task, try some of these quick tips:

- Follow the advice you have probably heard already: don't reinvent the wheel. Adapt handouts and other materials prepared by others: your colleagues in your building, in your district, or even online.

- Although you want handouts to be as user-friendly and error-free as possible, you will soon find that you will tweak most of the materials you create before using them again. With that in mind, try not to be a perfectionist.

- Many teachers find it especially tempting to spend too much time creating presentations, such as PowerPoints or Prezis. It's hard to resist searching too long for the perfect graphic or font to make a point. However, the time spent adjusting a presentation that is already serviceable is not time that is well spent.

- As with all other facets of time management, it's important to be aware of how you are spending your time when you create handouts and other materials. Be disciplined about how much time you allow for creating handouts and instructional resources. Set a timer and stick to your plan.

Online Bookmarking Sites

It is annoying to find an incredibly helpful website only to lose it within a click or two. Futilely trying to relocate a site that appealed to you earlier is not only vexing but also a waste of time. Because of the abundance of online resources available for teachers, bookmarking websites are useful tools for teachers who research materials online frequently.

These websites allow users to organize their online bookmarks in such a way that the information they are looking for is easy to retrieve. In short, they are a valuable component of any time management plan because they can make it easy to access information quickly.

Here is one technique that many teachers have found useful when using a bookmarking site: when you create a bookmark, name it as specifically as possible so that you can quickly access the information you saved. A bookmark tagged "Lesson Plans" is not as easy to use as a board labeled "Fourth-Grade Science Assessments," for example. Although there are many different bookmarking sites, the ones in this list are particularly useful for teachers:

- **Diigo (www.diigo.com).** Diigo allows users to tag and bookmark websites. It also allows users to highlight information on those websites and to annotate them with digital sticky notes before storing them. Another valuable feature is that users can collaborate with others as they share bookmarks.

- **eduClipper (https://educlipper.net).** eduClipper allows users to create clipboards of resources that can then be shared with colleagues or can remain private. Designed as a social learning platform, eduClipper makes it easy for teachers to create portfolios for students as well as for their own use.

- **Livebinders (www.livebinders.com).** LiveBinders allows users to create digital portfolios of bookmarked sites as well as to upload various kinds of documents—from handouts to presentations to surveys. Each binder can be shared with colleagues or, if desired, remain private.

- **Pinterest (www.pinterest.com).** Pinterest allows users to create personal boards and to pin useful sites as well as to follow others' boards. Pinterest will also curate searches and suggest sites—a particularly useful feature.

Paperwork: Ten Thousand Documents and Counting

One of the most stressful aspects of a teaching career is the pressure caused by a heavy load of paperwork. Like many other professionals, teachers must successfully manage an ever-growing quantity of documents—both electronic and hard copies. In the last few decades, the amount of paperwork for all educators has multiplied because of changing initiatives, legal responsibilities, and the ease of electronic communication.

During just one school year, the average teacher will have to handle more than ten thousand student papers. Add to that the proliferation of e-mails, notices, directives, printouts, purchase orders, letters, forms, catalogs, and publications a teacher receives each day, and the amount of paperwork can be overwhelming. You can learn to stay ahead of paperwork by creating your own systems for managing those documents, whether they are in digital or paper format.

Each teacher's organizational scheme is as unique as that teacher, but successful schemes are those that are easy to set up, simple to maintain, and logical enough to make it easy to find the documents that you need quickly. An organized paperwork management plan will allow you to store documents that you do not need quick access to as well as to easily find the ones that you do need. Spending the time to create a commonsense system of managing your professional documents is well worth the effort because it will prevent the frustration you will feel as you waste time searching futilely for a misplaced document.

In the information that follows, you will learn about the various documents you will have to manage, how to organize both paper and electronic files, how to organize paperwork related to student information, how to grade student work efficiently, and finally, how to set up a professional binder.

Professional Documents You Need to Manage

Although each teacher will have specific paperwork responsibilities, there are some important documents that all teachers have in common. To create a system for organizing them for quick access, it is important to start with an idea of the documents that you will have to work with all year. Here, in brief, are some of the documents that you will have to manage efficiently:

Grading

- Your grade book
- Student papers to be graded
- Graded student papers
- Sample student papers to assess long-term progress

Professional Business

- Your teaching portfolio items
- Your faculty handbook
- Your parent or guardian conference notes and log
- Teachers' meeting notes
- Peer observations of you and the observations you make of others
- Your evaluation
- Your reflections
- Complimentary notes from parents or guardians, students, or colleagues

Instructional Concerns

- State and district curriculum guidelines
- Unit plans
- Daily plans
- Copies of the syllabi for each grading period
- Collaborative team minutes or notes
- Reference materials for future lessons
- Strategies and activities to incorporate into lessons
- Ideas for motivating students
- Extra handouts for students
- Makeup work for students
- Tests, quizzes, and other assessments
- Handouts for the current unit of study

Classroom Routines and Management

- Seating charts
- Student rosters
- Information related to class rules and consequences
- Information about discipline issues, such as incident reports or anecdotal notes

- Templates for routine business, such as hall passes, lunch counts, or notes home
- Reward or certificate templates
- Bulletin board ideas or materials
- Exit or entrance slips and topics

Student Information

- Student contact information
- Student inventories
- Student assessment data
- Attendance data
- Contact logs for meetings and phone calls
- Important e-mails from parents or guardians

Confidential Documents to Be Kept in a Secure Location

- All documents (including e-mails and conference notes) related to a student's IEP
- 504 Plan forms
- All documents related to student health issues
- Discipline referrals

What to Keep and What to Discard

During a year when so much of your work experience is new, having difficulty with something as seemingly uncomplicated as knowing which documents to keep and which to discard can be frustrating. Although some of these documents will be in paper format, if you can store work electronically, you will save paper and space. The types of documents teachers need to manage may vary widely depending on the grade or grades they teach, but you can adapt these lists to help you make decisions about the materials and papers you should keep.

DOCUMENTS TO KEEP UNTIL THE START OF THE NEXT SCHOOL YEAR

These documents are the ones that you should store for future reference. Many teachers have even been asked to produce such documents as attendance records or parent or guardian contact logs to justify an end-of-course grade.

- Save your grades for each grading period as well as the end of the year.
- Keep all attendance data records.

- Keep all parent or guardian contact logs.
- Keep all accident reports.
- Keep all discipline referrals, detention notices, and student behavior contracts.
- If you have sent home papers for parents or guardians to sign, keep them on file. This practice applies to progress reports, informal notes, grade sheets, and any other signed papers. Keep the documents you have collected in each student's individual folder.
- Don't throw away any information about curriculum guidelines in your state and local districts. Keep it handy and refer to it often.
- Don't throw away course calendars and syllabus information.
- Maintain a file of old tests and quizzes to draw from in future terms.
- If you give examinations, you should keep not only a master copy and a key but also student copies. If a grade is challenged, you will need to produce the test paper.
- Save copies of each handout that you want to reuse in the future.
- Keep your lesson plans. Annotated unit plans will be particularly useful when you begin to plan new units in the future.
- Keep all papers related to your own professional observations and evaluations.
- Save your personal reflections or discussion group notes to review in the future.
- Set up your teaching portfolio (see Section One) and save the items to be included in it.
- Be sure to hang on to any complimentary notes you have received. They will help remind you why you are a teacher on tough days.
- Save e-mails about students who require special consideration because of such concerns as illness, family problems, or learning disabilities.

DOCUMENTS YOU CAN SAFELY DISCARD AT THE END OF EACH SEMESTER

These documents are generally ones that you will not need in the future. Although they may have served a valuable purpose during the semester, saving too many documents will only add clutter to your paper and electronic files, making them hard to manage.

- Dispose of meeting notes or reminders that you have already acted on.
- Clear out routine e-mails about school business or daily tasks.
- Remove archived electronic and paper files that you no longer find relevant for lesson planning.
- Discard student classwork or homework papers that you may have saved instead of sending them home with students.

Organizing Paper File Storage

You will need to set up a filing system for the paperwork you must deal with each day. If you have a system in place before the term begins, you will save yourself much frustration and time later. Setting up a file cabinet is not a difficult task, but it does require planning and effort.

- **Step One:** Once you have a file cabinet, clean it out and lubricate any stuck drawers.

- **Step Two:** Go searching for file folders. Begin your search by letting it be known that you can use any folders that anyone in your building is about to toss out.

- **Step Three:** If your school has allotted money for you to spend on supplies, be sure to spend some of it on materials for your file cabinet. Purchase hanging file frames and hanging files for as many drawers as your budget permits. In addition to hanging files, you will need file folders, labels, and permanent markers.

- **Step Four:** Set aside one file drawer for student business. Here you will keep student information, progress reports, report cards, copies of parent or guardian correspondence, and other paperwork related to students. You should be able to lock this drawer to protect confidential records.

- **Step Five:** Set aside another file drawer for general business. Here you will store information for substitutes, hall passes, detention forms, and other general paperwork.

- **Step Six:** In the other drawers, file such materials as unit plans, handouts, tests, and paperwork related to your curriculum either in alphabetical order or in the order that you will cover them.

- **Step Seven:** After you have completed the basic steps in setting up your filing system, implement the following refinements, which will make your system much more efficient and easy to use:
  - Label the front of each drawer in large, bold letters so that you can tell at a glance what is inside.
  - File materials according to subject. Make a special effort to maintain orderly files.
  - Label everything. If you can color-code your labels, it will be even easier to find what you need quickly.
  - Stagger the tabbed labels on hanging files and the file folders within them so that you can see what is in the file drawer at a glance.

Three-Ring Binders

One particularly useful way to store important papers, especially those relating to instruction, is to use three-ring binders. Three-ring binders are a useful way to organize and store information because their convenience makes them adaptable for any grade level or content area. Here are some tips for using three-ring binders efficiently:

- Many teachers find that it is more productive to store documents by units or topics rather than by trying to cram documents for an entire grading period into one binder. Several smaller, well-labeled binders may be a better choice than a large one crammed with papers.

- There are many inexpensive ways to obtain the binders that you need. One is to purchase them at discount stores. Another way is to ask parents or guardians to donate gently used ones. Colleagues may also have extra binders that they are willing to share.

- When purchasing a binder, take the time to make sure that the rings close securely. If you have a binder with rings that do not close properly, it's usually easy to repair them quickly with a pair of pliers.

- Regardless of the subject matter of the documents in a binder, take the time to organize them internally with clearly labeled dividers so that you do not have to flip through the entire binder to find what you are looking for.

- Using clear plastic sheets or binder sleeves for documents is also a good idea for at least some of your documents. It's more secure to file smaller, irregularly shaped documents or documents with lots of sticky notes on them inside a sleeve.

Managing Digital File Storage

Failing to create a workable system for managing your electronic files can cost you hours of frustrated searching for misplaced, mislabeled, or lost documents. With just a bit of planning, you can design a scheme for managing your electronic files so that they are quick and easy to access. Here's how:

- Use a consistent method for naming files that will make it easy to understand what each file contains without having to open it. Many teachers find that it is helpful also to include a date in the file name. For example, "Ch 2 Quiz 2018" is an excellent title, whereas "Ch 2" is not. Be sure that the names you give files are professional in tone—just in case you need to share with a colleague.

- Group like things together in folders. For example, place all videos related to a unit of study in a folder labeled in such a way that you can quickly find the video you need. Try to be as specific as possible when you name a folder.

- Create subfolders inside the bigger folders that you have for documents. For example, for a unit on *Romeo and Juliet*, the main folder could be labeled *Romeo and Juliet*. The subfolders would have such topics as "Shakespeare's Life," "Elizabethan Theater," "Act I," "Act II," "Formative Assessments," "Enrichment Activities," "Reading Questions," and so on. Try not to have layers of subfolders. A main folder with several subfolders inside is much easier to search than subfolders stored in subfolders inside a main folder.

- Place documents in folders as you work on them. If you create folders for each unit at the start of that unit and file things promptly, you will find it easy to avoid having to sort through unorganized files.

- Be selective about what you save electronically, just as you would be with paper copies. Periodically purge your folders of files that you no longer find useful. Clutter just makes it difficult to find files when you need them.

RESOURCES FOR STORING DIGITAL DOCUMENTS

Because it's important not to lose your work, you should store your files in several different places. Your school district will probably have a network address assigned for you to use to store school documents. You can also use portable memory storage devices, such as flash drives. In addition, you may want to explore keeping digital files stored in the cloud as well. There are several free options for securely saving digital work in the cloud. Here are three of the most common ones:

- Dropbox (www.dropbox.com)
- Evernote (https://evernote.com)
- Google Drive (www.google.com/drive)

How to Organize and Manage Student Information

In addition to the many other documents you will have to preserve, the information about your students that comes to you from a variety of sources throughout the term is also something you must manage. Although there are numerous ways to manage this information, many teachers have found that the following simple approach works well because it is easy to maintain:

Paper Documents

- **Step One:** Set aside space in a lockable desk or file drawer.
- **Step Two:** Create a folder for each student and arrange the folders alphabetically.
- **Step Three:** Promptly file every piece of information you receive about a student. Date each item. Place new papers behind other items in a file folder so you don't have to shuffle through all of them to find one. If you don't have a dedicated folder ready, avoid putting papers into messy piles and use an in-box instead.

Electronic Documents

- Follow the same general procedure for electronic documents as for paper ones. Create an electronic folder for each student as well. Store all documents relating to each student in the appropriate folder.

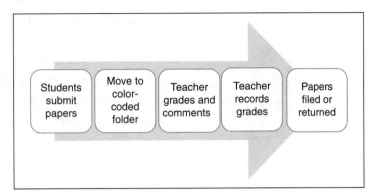

Figure 2.2 Consistent Paper Flow

Develop a Consistent Paper Flow for Student Papers

When students turn in their work, the sheer number of papers can make it difficult to keep them organized enough for you to deal with later. To eliminate problems and to streamline the way you mange student paperwork, establish a consistent paper flow for them (see Figure 2.2). Here is one that works for many teachers:

- **Step One:** Have students place papers in a designated area, such as a bin or a tray. If you provide a highlighter near where students are to turn in their work, they can highlight their names before submitting them. This will eliminate the problem of no-name papers.
- **Step Two:** Move them to a color-coded folder for each subject or class period to be graded. Color coding will make it easier to keep them organized.
- **Step Three:** Grade them.
- **Step Four:** Record the grades.
- **Step Five:** File the papers or return them to students.

Grading Student Work

Although all professionals may have to cope with too much paperwork, the largest and most stressful part of a teacher's paperwork responsibility is unique: student papers that require grading. Grading papers is a complex task that is never easy. It is not only one of the most time-consuming tasks for any teacher but also can be a major cause of stress if you succumb to the combination of tedium caused by too many papers and frustration at repeated errors.

Always keep in mind that your goal in grading papers is not only to find errors but also to improve student learning. As you grade, ask yourself, "What can I do to help this student?" when you come across error-filled papers. This will move you beyond frustration to working toward a solution to the lack of understanding that caused the errors.

Successfully learning to grade student work quickly and efficiently so that you can have the work-life balance that you need takes time, planning, and persistent practice, but it is

Find what works for you. This may take some time, but try new systems until you find a way that works best for you and optimizes your time.

Jared Sronce, 6 years' experience

an achievable goal. In the list that follows, you will find several suggestions that you can adjust to meet the needs of your own teaching practice. Although not all of them may work for your classroom, try to adapt as many as you can so that you do not have to spend hours and hours grading student work.

How to Grade Papers Quickly and Well

Learning to manage your responsibilities regarding grading papers efficiently will allow you to give your students the productive and timely feedback that they need to learn. Here are some tips to help you cope with the papers that you have to grade this term:

- Stagger due dates if you teach more than one class or have lots of papers coming in from various assignments. If possible, try to consider your own work schedule before setting a final due date for longer assignments, such as projects and essays.

- When you make assignments with more than one part, consider grading each part separately. For example, instead of grading all the parts of an essay at once, have students turn in their outlines to be graded first. Then evaluate each student's rough draft and offer suggestions before grading the final essay. Although this practice does spread an assignment over several days, the positive results and reduced stress are worth it.

- Be prepared when you have papers to grade: have a quiet work place, marking pens, rubrics, and answer keys ready so that you do not have to waste time getting organized.

- Remove as many distractions as possible when you begin grading. Temporarily turn off social media notifications and other electronic distractions. Close your classroom door or move to a quiet place to work.

- Do not try to grade stacks and stacks of papers in one sitting. Divide the work into smaller batches and tackle these in a systematic manner. Grading in focused bursts of concentrated effort with breaks in between is an efficient way to grade quickly.

- If you are grading at home, try to use your biological clock to grade when you are most alert.

- Reward yourself when you have finished grading an onerous set of papers. This will encourage you to stay focused.

- Make sure that the directions for each assignment are very clear. (See Section Four for help with this.) Explicit directions will eliminate many student errors.

- Before students submit their assignments, ask them to trade papers and review one another's work. A quick edit from a classmate could eliminate many of the less significant errors, such as typos.

- Create very specific checklists or rubrics that guide students as they complete assignments. This allows students to know what they must do to succeed.

- If you are not sure that your grading policies and techniques are as useful as you would like them to be, ask a mentor to review a paper or two with you before you grade an entire set.

- Don't grade everything your students produce. Some teachers find it easier to grade only part of an assignment—spot-checking for patterns of errors. Still others ask students to submit an example of their best work in a series of assignments. Formative assessments should not be graded at all.

- It is far better to focus on a few skills in each assignment rather than on every mistake that students make. Focused grading will allow you to concentrate on what's important and to determine the areas of strengths and weaknesses in student mastery.

- Don't cover papers with comments—one of the easiest mistakes to make. Instead, focus on a blend of positive comments and comments about what needs improvement. Limit yourself to three or four comments, if possible. If you need to make more comments, consider holding a conference with the student instead.

- Don't focus only on the errors that your students have made. Use a highlighter to point out the parts of their assignments that they did particularly well. Students not only appreciate the kindness in this action but also learn a great deal more from your positive comments than from a sea of red ink.

- Create a method of correcting student work that is simple for your students to understand and then use it consistently. Using the same proofreading marks on every assignment, for example, will make it easy for students to understand their mistakes. Post these marks online and on the board and make sure each student has a copy.

- When you grade quizzes and tests, grade the same page on every quiz or test in the stack before moving on to the next page.

- Make the answer sheets that your students use for quizzes and tests easy to grade. Allow plenty of white space and room for students to write so that you can read their responses quickly.

- It's often productive to review several papers before starting the grading process to get a basic idea of the general strengths and weaknesses of the work. This could save you time later as you decide what you will need to reteach.

Grading Electronic Work

Once the learning curve of the program used to collect and respond to electronic submissions from students is mastered, many teachers find that it is easier, more efficient, and quicker to grade electronic work than paper submissions. One especially popular difference is that it is easier to make meaningful comments electronically instead of having to rewrite them by hand over and over.

Another advantage of grading electronically is that you do not have to carry stacks of work home. Instead, you can grade anywhere you have a device. Another advantage is that you can grade student work in collaboration with a colleague, such as a co-teacher, with ease. Although you will want to follow the same general policies for grading electronic work as you do for paper submissions, there are some specific differences to consider. When grading electronic work, take care to

- Teach students the file-labeling protocol that they should use to label their work. It is crucial for students to make sure that their names appear on the files so that you do not have to search for them.

- Have a list of student e-mail addresses in advance of the first assignment. Using a class roster to record student e-mail addresses is an efficient way to keep this information handy. If you have a digital roster, you can also have students quickly type in their e-mail addresses during class. In addition, you can have students send you an introductory e-mail at the start of the term so that you can capture their addresses early on.

- Attend workshops and other help sessions offered at your school or in your district to learn how to use the programs that are endorsed by your school system.

- Arrange to work with a teacher buddy or two, especially at first, to share tips and techniques for maximum ease of grading and efficiency.

- Be explicit about the directions for posting times. Because the work can be submitted outside school hours, make sure that students know exactly when it is due. Be clear about what constitutes late work and what, if any, penalties there will be for late submissions.

- Spend plenty of time making sure students know how to submit their work. Arrange for a few practice submissions in advance of the first assignment due date. This not only will make it easier for students to submit their work with confidence but also will reduce the number of students who claim posting issues as a reason for late or missing work.

RESOURCES FOR ELECTRONIC GRADING

Although most teachers who accept electronic work from students will opt for a program used by other teachers in their district, there are many options for teachers who want to use electronic grading programs without district mandates. Be sure to check with your supervisors first to ensure that the program that you want to use is one that is approved by your district. Once you have that permission, you may want to explore using one of these programs:

- **Dropbox (www.dropbox.com).** This program allows users to store student work not in the cloud but on a computer where it can be accessed easily anywhere.

- **Google Docs (www.google.com/docs).** Widely used in thousands of school districts, Google Docs makes it easy for students to create and share their work. It's also a program that is user-friendly for teachers who want to respond to students' digital work.
- **Turnitin (http://turnitin.com).** This program not only makes it easy to check for plagiarism but also gives feedback to students.
- **Phrase Express (www.phraseexpress.com).** Phrase Express makes it easy to make meaningful comments on student work with automated responses generated by individual teachers.

How to Create a Useful Professional Binder

One of the most useful professional tools that you can have is a simple collection of the papers that you use most often. Putting these documents in a sturdy three-ring binder makes them immediately accessible. Many teachers also divide their binders into easy-to-use sections for various topics, such as recording grades and other assessment data, instructional planning, student information, or professional business.

When you set up your professional binder, your purpose is to have the documents that you use every day in a convenient place and not stored away in a file cabinet. Although every teacher's binder is a very personal set of documents, dependent on the needs of the teacher and the types of courses and students that teacher has to manage, there are some items that are almost indispensable in any teacher's binder. Here is a list of some of the documents that you may find to be useful additions to your professional binder:

- Class rosters
- Seating charts
- Your professional goals
- Your daily to-do lists
- Meeting notes
- A school year calendar
- An outline of the instructional plan for the year, semester, or grading period
- Unit plans
- Daily lesson plans
- A list of frequently used comments and proofreading marks
- Grading reminders, such as due dates or grading scales
- A copy of Bloom's Taxonomy
- A list of Gardner's multiple intelligences (to help with differentiation)
- Lists of instructional activities to refer to energize lessons

- Lists of activities to use at the start and end of class as well as during transitions
- A list of ideas for integrating technology into instruction
- A list of formative assessment ideas
- A list of classroom chores for students to manage

Questions to Discuss with Colleagues

Sharing ideas with colleagues is a helpful way to devise solutions to some of the problems that you must manage successfully at school. Here you will find several topics to open discussions with colleagues about successful instructional practices:

1. You should maximize how efficiently you use your planning period each day. What can you do to ensure that you don't waste valuable time?

2. You are spending long hours each weekend trying to get caught up on grading papers, even though you know this is not the best way to manage them. How can you become more efficient at how you manage grading paperwork?

3. You must share classrooms with other teachers. You have no private place to work because you share an office with other teachers. Their personal conversations make it difficult for you to use your planning period efficiently. To whom can you turn for help? What should you do?

4. What keeps teachers from being productive at school? How can you overcome these problems so that you don't have to take as much paperwork home?

5. What are your five most important daily tasks at school? Are you managing them as efficiently as possible? If not, what can you do to improve the way that you manage them?

Topics to Discuss with a Mentor

Although the topics that new teachers need to discuss with a mentor vary from teacher to teacher and from school to school, there are some that most first-year teachers should be comfortable discussing with a mentor or a trusted colleague. You should ask your mentor about these topics from this section:

- Suggestions for creating instructional materials quickly and efficiently
- How to obtain the basic supplies you need
- Suggestions for obtaining the extra materials and supplies that you would like for your classroom
- Suggestions for how to be as productive and well organized as possible
- Suggestions for managing the flow of documents that you are responsible for

Reflection Questions to Guide Your Thinking

1. What skills do you currently possess when it comes to being an efficient teacher? How can you capitalize on your strengths, and how can you overcome your weaknesses?

2. What supplies do you and your students still need for the rest of the term? What can you do to make sure that you will have everything? Who can help you with this?

3. How organized is your classroom at this point in the school term? What do you still need to accomplish? How can your colleagues help you?

4. Correctly organizing your file cabinet and your electronic files is a necessary chore that you will benefit from all year. What techniques have you employed to make sure your system is efficient and easy to use?

5. What are you most confident about regarding your document management? Are you confident that you will be able to successfully manage the documents that you will need to maintain all year? What do you need to adjust to be as efficient as possible?

SECTION THREE

Collaborate with Colleagues in Your School Community

Schools, even small ones, are complex organizations with an ever-changing mixture of administrative assistants, custodians, nurses, counselors, coaches, paraprofessionals, administrators, social workers, and police liaison officers as well as teachers, students, and students' families. Because of this complexity and the enormous power of collaboration, teachers in the twenty-first century are expected to work effectively with all members of their school community, whether that collaboration is something as simple as an informal sharing of ideas over lunch or working together on structured teams.

Research studies show that teachers who view themselves as valued members of a school community can transform their classroom practice. How? The most significant indicator of any group's potential for success is the ability to work together in focused harmony.

Just what does it take to work well with others? In general, teachers who collaborate effectively treat everyone in their work community with courtesy, behave as professionals, and commit themselves to the good of the students in their school. They view themselves as belonging to a network of other supportive professionals who comprise the larger school community and whose actions are thoughtful and professional.

One of the biggest challenges facing new teachers is learning how to manage the responsibilities expected of collaborative teams as well as learning how to establish themselves as trustworthy faculty members. In this section, you will learn how you can be a well-regarded member of the wider school community as well as how to be an effective member of a collaborative team.

Establish Your Professional Reputation

At the basis of successful collaboration lies the perceptions that others will have of you. Amid trying to set up a classroom, getting to know students, and figuring out how to plan engaging instruction, it's easy to overlook the importance of something as nebulous as establishing a professional reputation. Without a reputation as a competent, serious, and capable educator, however, it will be difficult to work well with your colleagues or to become the effective teacher you want to be. One of the best ways to begin to establish your reputation is to pay attention to the expectations that others will have of you.

No matter where you teach, there are some universal expectations for education professionals that you should strive to meet. When your colleagues see you working diligently to be the kind of teacher that they expect you to be, you will earn not only their respect but also their support. Use Teacher Worksheet 3.1 to examine how well you are already meeting expectations. The results can then guide your efforts to become a well-respected professional.

TEACHER WORKSHEET 3.1

How Well Do You Meet Expectations?

Rate how well you meet the expectations of your colleagues in this list by ranking yourself on a scale of 1 to 3. A rank of 1 means that you still need to work on the expectation, and a rank of 3 means that you have mastered it. A ranking of 2 means that you have almost mastered it but not quite.

At this point in your education career, colleagues expect that you

1. _____ Are courteous and cooperative
2. _____ Are willing to share ideas in meetings as well as listen carefully to the ideas of others
3. _____ Work toward shared goals
4. _____ Are understanding and supportive
5. _____ Conduct yourself as a professional
6. _____ Ask for help when necessary
7. _____ Are quick to offer help when you can
8. _____ Work for the good of everyone in your school
9. _____ Clean up after yourself
10. _____ Focus on school business while you are at school
11. _____ Are on time for everything
12. _____ Keep your promises
13. _____ Value their experience
14. _____ Are willing to do your share of extra duties
15. _____ Communicate openly and professionally
16. _____ Are interested in others but not in gossip
17. _____ Admit when you're not sure of something
18. _____ Have a sense of humor
19. _____ Are open to new ideas
20. _____ Keep trying to improve your professional skills

Finding Your Place in Your New School Community

As a new teacher, you will find that it is sometimes tempting to jump in immediately to offer suggestions about problems that you notice at your new school. Even though your ideas may be sound ones and you may be completely correct in your assessment of the issues, if you have not yet established your reputation as a serious professional, it is likely that your suggestions will fall on deaf ears.

Until you have had the opportunity to get to know your colleagues and to let them get to know you as a dedicated and knowledgeable collaborator, a wise course of action is to take note of things that you would like to improve but to delay acting on them until you have a team of coworkers behind you all the way.

As a teacher, you are also expected to uphold the values of your community—to live up to the high standards that your students, colleagues, and community have for its professional educators. The rewards of a reputation for professionalism are significant. Collaboration with your colleagues as well as with the parents and guardians of your students will be much easier. You will find yourself working in a supportive environment with others who value your contributions and who trust you to do the right thing.

Another easy mistake to make when you are new to a school is to share too much about yourself. Oversharing about your personal life at work tends to make others uncomfortable. It is far better to stick to professional topics or to ask questions instead. Before you reveal anything about your personal life, ask yourself, "Would I be comfortable revealing this if a school board member were in the room?"

It's also important to keep your promises at school. Because this is so important, be very careful not to make promises you cannot keep. You may find that it is so tempting to agree to sponsor a club or chaperone a field trip or take on other extra duties that you find yourself overcommitted. Take your time. Say no when necessary and ease into your new responsibilities.

Remember, you have been hired because you are a competent professional who was better than everyone else who applied. Be confident about what you can offer, and never be afraid to share your opinions at meetings or one-on-one with more experienced teachers—just don't be pushy or rude about it. It is all about mutual respect. Create a balance between tried-and-true methods and the new creative ideas you want to incorporate.

Jay O'Rourke, 2+ years' experience

Finally, do not talk about students when you are away from school. When you do this, you violate their privacy and your professional ethics. Take special care not to rehash a disagreeable incident. Discussing your school's problems around people who are not involved is not acceptable. You will only spread ill will about your school (and yourself) if you do so.

Fitting in at a new school takes time and patience as well as a commitment to the well-being of everyone at that school. If you focus on your primary responsibility—your students—it will not be long before your coworkers will begin to trust your judgment and to take what you have to offer with the seriousness it deserves.

Fifteen Quick Tips for Making a Good Impression at School

In addition to the more general things that you can do to fit into your new school, there are some very specific things that you can do immediately that will make a good impression on your colleagues:

1. Be visible. Don't hide out in your room during lunch. Be in the hall between classes. Stay after school. Be a recognizable figure around school.

2. Be dependable. Show up on time for meetings and have a pen and paper ready to take notes. Don't miss school. Pick up trash you find in the hall. Clean up after yourself.

3. Listen more than you speak. Ask questions and be genuinely interested in the answers. You not only will make a good impression but also will learn a great deal.

4. Be courteous to all. Smile. Have a friendly greeting for everyone you meet. Offer to carry heavy packages. Be respectful of colleagues' time.

5. Ask for help. No one expects a new teacher to know everything. Take advantage of that goodwill and ask questions. It is better to ask than to make avoidable mistakes.

6. Dress the part. Come to school dressed with the same degree of formality as everyone else. Your appearance should signify that you are a professional with a serious approach to your responsibilities.

7. Never be late. Especially don't be late to class or to a duty assignment where someone will have to give up personal time to cover for you.

8. Keep your classroom tidy. Although it does not have to be Pinterest perfect, your classroom should reflect your concern for making a safe and productive learning environment for your students.

9. Follow school rules and procedures. Few things will frustrate your colleagues more quickly than if you decide not to abide by the same rules or procedures that govern everyone else in the building.

10. Be positive. Even though you may have had a tough day at school, there are plenty of positive moments to focus on. Projecting a positive, can-do attitude will make it easier for colleagues to offer help when you need it.

11. Be serious about your work. Teaching is serious business. Even though you want to have fun with students and enjoy the school day, be sure to let others know that you take the responsibilities of your work seriously.

12. Help out. As a new teacher, you have skills that your older colleagues may not. Offer to help with software or be quick to cover a class when a substitute teacher is delayed. Use your strengths to make a positive difference for your colleagues.

13. Project confidence. No one wants to babysit a colleague who appears frightened or unsure all the time. Stay calm. Act as if you can succeed and soon you will.

A simple suggestion: don't stay in your room during lunch. Eat in a common area so that you get to know your colleagues. They are your greatest resource.

Michael A. Barrs, 32 years' experience

14. Put in the time and effort to plan engaging instruction. When it becomes evident that your students are busy learning and that you are prepared for every class, your colleagues will respect your work ethic.

15. Do your best to maintain an orderly classroom. When your colleagues pass your classroom, they will be impressed if they see students who are clearly on task. They will be less than impressed if they see a room filled with unruly and disrespectful students.

When Personal and Professional Lives Collide: Social Media

Few things can ruin a teacher's professional reputation and affect the way your colleagues regard you more quickly than indiscreet content on a social media site. Teachers have been fired for imprudent private postings, photos, comments, or even tags that followed them into their professional lives. Although you do have the right to a life beyond the walls of your school, the nature of social media tends to blur the lines between private and public life. Because of this, it is wise to protect your professional reputation from the fallout that can happen with injudicious personal online content. Here are some tips for making sure that your social media presence will not cause problems:

- You cannot be too cautious about your social media activity and the regulations that govern it. Familiarize yourself with your school district's guidelines for social media and take care to follow them carefully.

- Keep the distinction between your personal accounts and your professional ones very clear. Do not allow students or their families to friend or follow you on a personal account that you use to communicate with friends and family.

- Many teachers have social media accounts for professional use only—class Twitter pages, for example. Use this type of account for your professional life instead of a personal one.

- If you do communicate with students online, be sure to use school accounts instead of personal ones. Using a school e-mail address offers protection because you have no expectation of privacy there and so can't easily be accused of inappropriate behavior that you did not commit.

- Be careful about what you say to students online, and be clear about the tone and subjects that you find acceptable from them in return. Use this as a quick guide: if content would be inappropriate in a classroom setting, it is also inappropriate online.

- Avoid browsing students' accounts, even when you have access to them. For example, if students are expected to comment on Twitter for homework, don't scrutinize your students' other tweets or follow links that they may have posted.

- If you have a website or blog or other shared sites yourself, be aware that you are personally responsible for the content you produce.
- Be careful to check the privacy settings on all your social media sites periodically to make sure that they are truly private.
- Be sensible—do not write about your students or your school district. Never mention students by name. Be especially careful not to post photos of students.
- Be very careful about the groups that you join. Make sure that each one is appropriate for an education professional to join.
- It is not wise to complain about your job, your school, or your colleagues online. Even private posts do not always remain private online. If you feel the need to complain, talk to a mentor or trusted colleague in person.
- Avoid references and photos that present you in an unfavorable way: drinking, profanity, drug use, gang activity, provocative dress, or any illegal activity. Even if your posts are meant to be in jest, they can (and probably will) be misconstrued.
- When you identify your place of employment in a profile, do not give specifics about your school. If you must, give general information such as "middle school math teacher."
- Never use your school's location in a geo tag. Doing so will make it very easy for students and others who you may not want to see your private posts to find you.
- Monitor your own online presence carefully. Be aware when someone posts content about you by setting up a Google Alert (www.google.com/alerts) for references to your name online.
- Ask your friends to be mindful of any unflattering or potentially compromising photo in which you may be tagged. Remove any that you can find yourself.

The Surprising Importance of Perfect Attendance

Even though it may seem surprising that your absence from school could have a negative effect on your colleagues as well as on your students, a teacher's absence really does affect the entire school. Your colleagues may have to give up a planning period to cover for you or print and deliver your plans or even help the substitute teacher manage your students' behavior. To work well with everyone in your school, enhance your professional reputation, and lessen the negative impacts of your absence, be prepared for a time when you may have to miss school.

What to Do When You Have to Miss School

Although you should not attend school if you are ill, there are plenty of times when you may be tempted to miss a day of school when you are not really sick, just as when you were a student yourself. Be careful not to abuse your district's leave policy. If nothing else, you can never be sure when you will need to use the sick days you should have saved. A serious illness or an accident can erode years of banked leave time. Try to save those days for when you really need them.

Although it is always better for you to attend class, there are several actions that you can take to mitigate the negative effects of your absence: inform the right people, leave good lesson plans, and provide essential information for your substitute.

Inform the Right People

- Contact the people who are responsible for hiring a substitute teacher for you. Try to do this as quickly as you can so that they can hire the most competent sub for you.
- Call a colleague and ask for assistance. Ask that person to look in on your class during the day and to make sure the substitute knows what to do.
- Contact an administrator. Ask the administrator to look in on your classes from time to time throughout the day.
- If you think your students will not take advantage of the situation, you should tell them that you are going to be out. Use this time to ask for their cooperation and to talk about any problems that may arise with a substitute teacher. Stress the importance of maintaining the daily routine, even when you are not there.

Leave Good Lesson Plans

- You should not ask a substitute teacher to interpret lesson plans from your plan book. Instead, give a class-by-class description of what you want your students to do.
- Base your plans on written work that your students can do independently. Write out clear directions on the work itself so that students can complete it without having to talk with others or ask the substitute to interpret.
- Let your students know that they are not just doing busywork, but that it has an instructional purpose. Make sure they know that the sub will collect the work at the end of class.
- If the work involves handouts, photocopy them in advance and label them so that the substitute can find them quickly. Don't ask a substitute to photocopy for you.
- A common complaint that substitute teachers have is that teachers do not leave enough work for students to do. You should plan more work for your students than you would expect them to do if you were there. In addition, it would be helpful to provide a list of five to ten activities that students can choose from if they finish their work early.

Provide Essential Information for Your Substitute

- In addition to lesson plans, you should leave a well-organized three-ring binder of information for your sub. Because most of this information is not as apt to change as your daily plans, you can make up this folder early in the year and update it as often as necessary. Your sub binder should include the following items:

- Detailed lesson plans specifically designed for a substitute teacher to follow

- An updated seating chart for each class. Some teachers take photographs of their students as they sit in their assigned seats to serve as a helpful seating chart. This eliminates many behavior problems because the sub will know where students are supposed to sit and will have names to go with faces.

- An up-to-date class roster

- Attendance procedures that you want your sub to follow

- Your daily schedule

- The names of helpful students

- The names and room numbers of helpful colleagues

- A notepad and pen for notes to you about the day

- Class rules, routines, and procedures

- Where to find supplies and extra texts

- A map of the school

- Your e-mail address or phone number

- Fire drill or other emergency information

- Information about students with special needs or medical issues

- Blank referral forms just in case the substitute encounters a serious student problem

- Extra work for students to do if they finish everything else

Collaborate Successfully with the Support Staff

As a new teacher, you will have to learn many new faces and names as quickly as possible. Although it is sensible to learn the names of other faculty members first, it is a mistake to think that they are your only colleagues. A school community is composed of many different people in many different positions. Each of them deserves your cooperation and respect. Here is a brief list of just some of the actions that you can take right away to treat all staff members as colleagues:

- Develop professional relationships with other staff members. Learn the

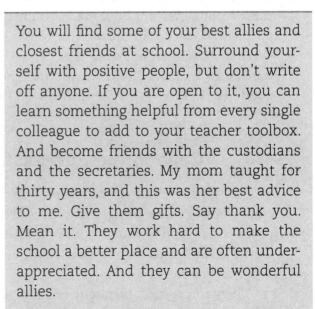

You will find some of your best allies and closest friends at school. Surround yourself with positive people, but don't write off anyone. If you are open to it, you can learn something helpful from every single colleague to add to your teacher toolbox. And become friends with the custodians and the secretaries. My mom taught for thirty years, and this was her best advice to me. Give them gifts. Say thank you. Mean it. They work hard to make the school a better place and are often underappreciated. And they can be wonderful allies.

Jennifer Burns, 13 years' experience

roles that various people play in your school and how they contribute to the overall picture. By doing this, you will be able to be supportive when they need your help.

- Learn the names of the support personnel in your school as quickly as possible. Greet each by name when you meet. Treat each person in the building with the same courtesy that you would like to receive.

- Encourage your students to respect the work of support personnel by modeling that respect yourself. Speak courteously to the cafeteria, clerical, and custodial workers as well as to other staff. Make sure that your students leave their work areas clean. Let them see you picking up trash in the hall.

- Never make a disparaging comment about the work of support staff members when you are with students. This courtesy means that you should go as far as avoiding making unkind remarks about the food served in the cafeteria, the media ordered by the school librarian, or the computer glitches that technicians can't solve quickly.

- Respect your colleagues' time, equipment, and other resources. For example, if the school secretary asks you not to tie up a phone line, respect that request, even though you may have a very important call to make.

Follow the Chain of Command

To work well with your supervisors and other staff members, you must know and follow the chain of command at your school. Few things annoy other employees as much as a person who does not have enough respect for others to follow the chain of command when things are not going well.

Not following the chain of command may win you a momentary victory, but it will be a hollow one. For example, if you have requested certain repairs to your classroom and these repairs have not been made, you may be tempted to speak to the principal about this problem. If you do this instead of speaking with the custodian in charge of your classroom, you may have been unfair to that person. There may be a good reason for the incomplete repairs. As a rule of thumb, if you need additional assistance in solving a problem, it is a good idea to talk with a mentor instead of ignoring the chain of command.

Collaborate Successfully with Administrators

The supervisory staff in your school district and in your school building depend on all employees to make things run smoothly. Although it is only natural that there will be problems, it is up to you to work well with your supervisors. Having a positive relationship with the administrators at your school means that you will be less stressed, more productive, and happier at work.

There is a specific hierarchy of supervision at any school. It is likely that you report to a department head, lead teacher, or grade-level leader who serves as a liaison between staff members and administrators. Assistant principals make up the next level. At the top of the hierarchy in your school is the principal, who is the instructional leader of your building. At the district level, your supervisors may differ in their titles but will include curriculum coordinators and assistant superintendents who report to their supervisor, the superintendent of schools. The hierarchy does not end there. The school board supervises all employees, including the superintendent.

If you want to establish productive relationships with your supervisors, you should take positive action. Don't hope that no one will notice you because you are a first-year teacher. In fact, you are particularly noticeable just because you are a first-year teacher. Here are some suggestions to establish a positive working relationship with your supervisors:

- Behave in a professional manner. This will win the support of administrators because it makes their jobs easier. In addition, if you maintain a solid reputation, it is easier for them to support you when you make mistakes.

- Take the time to familiarize yourself with the information in your faculty manual or handbook. This will help you avoid mistakes that may lead to negative interactions with your supervisors.

- Remember that administrators are responsible for the entire school and that you are responsible for only a very small part of it. If you can maintain this point of view, you'll find it easier to understand some of the policies you might otherwise find confusing.

- Think before you voice public criticism. Accept the fact that although you are not always going to agree with the decisions and actions of the administrators with whom you work, public criticism of their actions might seriously damage your professional reputation.

- Don't threaten to send your students to the office instead of resolving the problem through other more successful methods of discipline. Maintain control of your classroom so that when you send a student out of class, the action will have meaning for students as well as for administrators.

- Remember to be professional in your dealings with administrators. Always present a calm and competent image, not one of a furious teacher who lacks self-control. Regardless of your personal feelings toward a supervisor, always model respect.

- When you make a mistake, be truthful in discussing it with your supervisors. If you can do this before they find out the bad news from someone else, you should do so. Don't ever try to hide problems. Ask for help instead.

- Be positive. Sharing good news or taking a positive stance when problems occur will make it easier for an administrator to help you when you really need it. Constant complaints eventually fall on deaf ears.

- Share your successes with your supervisors. Help them create positive public relations for your school by letting them know about noteworthy news pertaining to your students.

Learn How to Collaborate as a Member of a Team

Even at the very start of your career, you can expect to belong to several different types of collaborative teams, such as vertical teams, grade-level teams, department committees, and procedure or policymaking groups—each one with its own purpose. This purpose can cover a wide range of activities—from solving problems or determining best practices to something as broad as sharing new information.

In the pages that follow, you can learn some of the skills, attitudes, and qualities that you need to develop to become a good team member as well as the behaviors that will help you get the most out of meetings and work through potential conflicts with team members.

Professional Behavior during Meetings

Seldom will you have a week without at least one meeting during the school year. At particularly busy times of the term, you will find daily conferences are the norm. With so much of your time spent in various types of meetings, it is only sensible to make sure that your behavior is such that you will not only present yourself as a competent member of the team but also that your collaboration skills are productive and professional. Here is a list of the behaviors that will make it easier for you to work well with your colleagues:

- Refrain from side talking. Although it is tempting to chat with someone sitting nearby, doing so will make it harder for you (and the people around you) to listen to the person leading the meeting.

- Focus on the business at hand during meetings. You will probably see colleagues grading papers, checking e-mail, and shuffling through briefcases. Try not to be one of those. Instead, pay attention. Take notes. Spend the time listening and learning and not being distracted.

- Unless the meeting is one that requires you to work on a device, it is courteous to silence your phone, put the lid down on a laptop, and stop using a tablet. If you are taking notes on a device, make it obvious to nearby colleagues that you are not checking e-mail or social media.

- Be on time. Coming in late is not only intrusive and rude but also presents you as less than professional. Set reminders to make sure that you know when and where a meeting is to be so that you arrive on time.

- Be prepared. If you were directed to have completed a reading or prepared a document before the meeting, do so. Being unprepared for a meeting is a waste of everyone's time.

- Take notes. Although you should not be so intent on capturing every word that you miss the big ideas in a meeting, taking notes will help you stay focused and allow you to take in the content under discussion.

- Be respectful of a group leader or speaker. Be engaged. Be courteous. Be especially careful to allow speakers to finish before you respond.

- Be an active listener as you consider others' viewpoints. Stop trying to talk; instead, really listen to your colleagues.

- Seek clarification during meetings if you are not sure of what has been said. Ask intelligent questions to avoid misunderstanding.

- Be aware of your body language. Make it a point to appear calm and engaged when others are speaking.

- Be a dependable team member. Honor your commitments, and be honest about your abilities, time constraints, and skills.

- Be positive. Negativity makes any undertaking harder to accomplish. Begin by focusing on the accomplishments and strengths of your colleagues.

- Pick your battles. Save your time and energy for the important issues at school instead of worrying about the less important ones.

- Be straightforward (but tactful) with what you say. Talking in generalities or around a subject will confuse and irritate others.

- When you are assigned follow-up activities, complete them. You will learn from the effort you put into them.

- Don't waste your colleagues' time with questions or suggestions that pertain only to you or a small group. Focus on items that are for the good of the whole group instead.

How to Handle Professional Disagreements

Professional disagreements are part of any school environment where many people are working diligently to help students. Because of the need for productive collaboration in twenty-first-century schools and because professional disagreements are so stressful, it is important to learn how to handle them well. If you find yourself in a conflict, try these suggestions to resolve it:

- Curriculum issues constitute a frequent area of disagreement. If you are involved in a curriculum dispute, refer to your state's guidelines and standards. All instruction must satisfy those requirements, even if you have colleagues who think differently.

- Instead of just reacting to a problem, respond by taking a problem-solving approach to try to work out a solution. Deciding to resolve a problem, instead of ignoring it or lashing out in anger, is a productive and professional approach.

- Think about how you may have contributed to the problem instead of blaming others. Make sure that you are not overreacting or misreading the situation. In the hurried pace of a school day, it is very easy to misread another's intentions or reactions.

- Refuse to act in kind if the other person has been rude or uncooperative. Try to be as open-minded, respectful, and tolerant as possible.

Understand that everyone has their own styles and also their own struggles. Teaching is not just a job. It is a very personal thing. The last thing you want to do is to insult another teacher or to make them feel that what they are doing is not right just because it may be different.

Mary Landis, 22 years' experience

- Sometimes, when you need to collaborate closely on a potentially contentious matter, agree to disagree. Not all solutions are simple ones.
- Resist the urge to vent about a conflict with colleagues. Limit its negative impact by involving as few people as possible.

Be Guided by These Helpful Attitudes about Collaboration

Successful collaboration is a crucial part of any school setting. Here are some useful suggestions for being the best team member you can be:

- Be patient. Feeling frustrated about meetings does not make them go away. Although not every meeting will be as productive as you would like, most of them will be.
- Everyone on a team has a responsibility to make it an effective team.
- Even though the details are necessary in solving problems collaboratively, it's important to keep the big picture of what you are trying to accomplish in mind.
- Sharing ideas works best when everyone's ideas are considered respectfully.
- An inclusive and encouraging approach is not only pleasant but also a productive way to work with others.
- Asking respectful and thoughtful questions is a positive way to refine ideas and to stay on track.
- Remember that issues are what's important in a meeting and not petty differences with people.

Questions to Discuss with Colleagues

Sharing ideas with colleagues is a helpful way to devise solutions to some of the problems that you must manage successfully at school. Here you will find several topics to open discussions with colleagues about successful instructional practices:

1. Your school has a strict policy on the instructional materials that can be photocopied and distributed to students. Your supervisor keeps rejecting your handouts. How can you solve this problem?

2. A supervisor assigns you an extracurricular task that you can't possibly do well. You want to be regarded as a team player at your new school, but you know you can't adequately fulfill this responsibility. What should you do?

3. You've been assigned to work closely with a teacher whose philosophy of education is very different from yours. In fact, you are uncomfortable working with this colleague. How can you handle this situation in a productive and diplomatic way?

4. You are having such a busy day that you forget to attend your assigned afternoon bus duty. Your duty partners are clearly not pleased about this. What should you do to manage this situation successfully?

5. You find that you must miss a day of school. What can you do to make the day a productive one for the substitute teacher as well as for your students?

Topics to Discuss with a Mentor

Although the topics that new teachers need to discuss with a mentor vary from teacher to teacher and from school to school, there are some that most first-year teachers should be comfortable discussing with a mentor or a trusted colleague. You should ask your mentor about these topics from this section:

- Faculty and staff dress code policies
- District policies for staff social media use
- Procedures for obtaining substitute teachers
- The specific chain of command for your school
- The responsibilities of various administrators and other staff members

Reflection Questions to Guide Your Thinking

1. What skills do you already possess that make it easier for you to work with the various groups at your school? How can you enhance these skills to help you become a valued coworker to those around you?

2. How does learning to work well with supervisors and colleagues affect a teacher's ability to maintain a productive classroom? Identify teachers at your school who work well with their colleagues and supervisors. What can you learn from them?

3. What other strategies can you can use to adapt to your school's culture? What difficulties can you anticipate while learning to adapt? How can you overcome these difficulties?

4. How are the various types of meetings at your school different from other meetings that you are used to? How can you make the time you spend in meetings and conferences as productive as possible?

5. Are you comfortable with the way you are currently managing your social media? What steps can you take to ensure your privacy and to maintain a professional image in your school and community?

SECTION FOUR

Become a Capable Classroom Leader

Many successful people will readily admit that their achievements have been shaped by an overwhelming passion, such as succeeding in business or winning athletic competitions. Education professionals are like those other successful people in that they are also passion-driven, but unlike many of those others, educators are not guided by just one passion but by three. A career in education demands that we feel passionately about the subject matter that we teach, that we have an intense interest in teaching, and, most important, that we are passionate about helping our students. The result? A richly rewarding sense of fulfillment and purpose that few other professions can equal.

Many experienced teachers will also admit that they initially chose a career in education because of their passion for their subject matter. Think of the teachers in your own past who made potentially dull topics come alive for you because of their enthusiasm for even the smallest details of the content. As a student yourself, your school career may have been shaped by one of these intriguing teachers, whose expansive background knowledge made math class the high point of your day, ancient history come alive for you, or the intricacies of a foreign language fascinating topics to debate with classmates.

Just as important as a passion for subject matter, a passion for the process of pedagogy is crucial for educators. Because teachers spend so much time designing and delivering instruction and because of the continual advances in our knowledge of how students learn best, it only makes sense that excellent teachers work diligently to improve the way they offer instruction.

And finally, it is impossible to find an excellent teacher—a capable classroom leader—who does not have a passion for helping students. Excellent teachers tend to see students as intriguing and worthwhile people who can achieve academic and behavioral success. Excellent teachers enjoy being with students and trying to figure out how to reach and teach them. Of all three of the passions that drive teachers, this one is the most transformative because it is also the one that is most evident to students.

As you work through the material in this section, consider how you are driven by your passions. Don't lose the fresh enthusiasm that brought you to a career in education, but rather, use it to learn and grow along with your students. When you do, you will become one of those memorable educators who don't just teach; you will make a difference.

Capable Classroom Leaders Communicate Their Beliefs

You have enormous power over the lives of your students. In fact, you can make the students in your classroom into successful scholars, or you can make those same students into academic failures. Your beliefs about your students form a self-fulfilling prophecy.

The self-fulfilling prophecy begins with the expectations you have about your students. These expectations are your unconscious as well as your conscious attitudes about your students' ability to succeed. You communicate those expectations to your students in many subtle ways—for example, through your body language, by the assignments you make, in the language you use, and through how much time you spend with individual students.

Because humans tend to behave as they are treated, your students will react to the way you communicate your expectations. If students believe that you do not think them capable of hard work, they will not deliver it. Students are often more capable than their teachers believe them to be. If you motivate your students to do their best, they will strive to live up to your expectations. If you think highly of your students, they will tend to behave better for you than they do for teachers who obviously do not enjoy being with them.

If you believe that the students in your class are capable of good behavior and academic success, then your students are highly likely to behave well and strive for success. Because the power of your personal beliefs about teaching is so important, don't hesitate. Be open with your students about your beliefs in their capacity to succeed. Be explicit in your support. When you communicate openly with your students about the confidence you have in them, you will help them become the successful students you want them to be.

> I'm consistent, I'm fair, and I'm available. Students like the fact that I'm predictable and that they can count on me.
>
> *Margaret R. Scheirer, 12 years' experience*

What Are Your Fundamental Beliefs about Teaching?

One often-asked question of teaching candidates at job interviews involves asking them to explain their philosophy of teaching. Even though there is never enough time to answer this question adequately in an interview setting, it is still an important question to consider. Although they may be aware of the latest research, effective teachers don't just thoughtlessly spin from one educational trend to another. To be effective at leading a classroom, they select the best options for their students based on their own fundamental beliefs about teaching.

As you develop your classroom leadership skills, a good place to begin is to examine your own beliefs about what is most important to you as an educator. In Teacher Worksheet 4.1, you will be able to examine and evaluate some of the most prevalent beliefs that educators hold about teaching to enhance your own teaching practices.

What Are Your Fundamental Beliefs about Teaching?

As you read each of the following statements about teaching, consider its importance to your classroom practice. Then jot down some quick thoughts about how the belief and its importance to you affects your classroom leadership. What are the implications of this belief, and what next steps are necessary to improve your classroom leadership?

Belief Statement	How This Belief Affects My Classroom Leadership	Implications/ Next Steps
A class functions best when there is a sense of community among students and between students and teacher.		
My role is to facilitate learning, not to be the sole disseminator of information.		
I accept responsibility for the success of my students.		
All students have an equal right to learn, but not all of them learn in the same way.		
I value the opportunity to serve as a role model for my students.		
High expectations are necessary for the success of all students.		
A diverse student population strengthens a classroom.		
There are many paths to the successful mastery of material or acquisition of skills.		
Students and their needs come first in my classroom.		
Students should be given appropriate autonomy and taught to make good decisions about their learning.		
It's more effective to motivate students through positive methods than through punishment.		

The Three Components of Classroom Leadership

In the following pages, you will find information about the three essential components of classroom leadership: developing your front-of-the-classroom persona, elevating your role as a supportive teacher, and controlling the flow of class time. As you work through this section, you will be able to understand the importance of a teacher who makes deliberate and informed decisions that can have a profoundly positive effect on student learning. The information you find here is designed to guide your thinking about how you present yourself to your students.

To begin, it's wise to reflect on your current strengths at leading a class and to build on those strengths. Teacher Worksheet 4.2 is designed to guide your thinking about your strengths.

Assess and Use Your Strengths
as a Classroom Leader

In the list here, you will be able to identify the positive teacher traits that you already have. Circle all that apply to you.

- Dependable
- Forgiving
- Compassionate
- Self-controlled
- Curious
- Organized
- Flexible

- Humorous
- Resourceful
- Enthusiastic
- Positive
- Trustworthy
- Dedicated
- Friendly

- Knowledgeable
- Tolerant
- Sympathetic
- Confident
- Sensible
- Cooperative
- Courteous

After you have determined some of your strengths, think about their application to the three components of classroom leadership. How can you use the strengths that you circled to enhance each component?

Your Front-of-the-Class Persona	Your Role as a Supportive Teacher	Your Control of Class Time

Your Front-of-the-Class Persona

The first of the three essential components of classroom leadership involves the way you present yourself as a teacher—your front-of-the-class persona. Although some critics have objected to the idea that teachers should "perform" for their students, it does make sense that the way you behave—your mannerisms, your voice, your posture—in front of a crowd of energetic students is very different from the way you behave in quieter settings, such as eating lunch with colleagues or hanging out with friends and family.

Effective teachers are aware that it is important to deliberately create a persona for themselves if they are to be the capable classroom leaders that their students need. Obviously, it would be a disservice to you and to your students if the persona you present to them is not authentic. Although you should not assume a false role, you should think about the way you want your students to view you as their teacher. Here are some of the characteristics that you may want to consider as you determine how to present yourself to your students:

- Professional: From the way you greet students to the way you dress to the arrangement of the furniture in the room, you signal to your students that you are professional in your approach to your responsibilities. Your actions should indicate that you are a trained, knowledgeable, and confident educator.

- Enthusiastic: You should project an energetic enthusiasm for your subject matter, for the day's instructional activities, and, most important, for your students' academic success. Your enthusiasm will ignite your students' enthusiasm.

- Focused: Having a focused approach to the way you instruct your students will make it easier for them to concentrate on learning because you will serve as a role model. Strive to be as prepared and organized as possible before class begins so that you can focus on teaching while you are with your students.

- Inclusive: When you ensure that every student is involved in the lesson and that you care about their success, you send a powerful message to your students. The way you move around your classroom, your body language, and the way you speak with all students combine to help students feel they are part of a classroom community. Just as you should make your classroom into an inviting place for your students, so should your persona be inviting.

- Positive: Of all the traits that you should consider as you develop your front-of-the-class persona, being positive is the most important. If you want your students to be positive about learning, about their class, about you, and about their ability to succeed, then you must first make your own positive attitude about them explicit. If you are a cranky

> I wish my students knew how much I focus on their learning when I am not in the classroom. I wish their parents knew that thoughts of how to make their children's learning successful consume much of my downtime.
>
> *Deborah McManaway, 23 years' experience*

and negative teacher, then you can expect your students to reflect that undesirable approach to their schoolwork. Fortunately, the alternative is also true: when you project a positive expectation that your students will succeed at what you ask of them, then you are highly likely to encourage them to persist when they meet challenges.

As you read the following information, you will be able to learn more about the various options you have in your efforts to become the effective teacher that your students need.

Use Body Language to Your Advantage

Some experts estimate that as much as half of what we communicate is done through the way we move our bodies. Paying attention to the nonverbal messages you send can make a significant difference in your relationship with students. In general, most students are often acutely tuned in to their teacher's body language. For example, when your students first enter the classroom, their initial action is to look for their teacher. Think about how reassuring and empowering it is for a student when that teacher has a courteous greeting and a welcoming smile. Smiling at students—to let them know that you are glad to see them—does not require a great deal of time or effort, but it can make a significant difference in the classroom climate right from the start of class.

Think of your body language as another element of your leadership—one that is silently at work every minute you are with students. It's important that your body language signals that you are at ease and confident. Your students will find it difficult to trust a teacher who sits behind a desk all class or who won't make eye contact or whose voice can barely be heard. They will also find it difficult to trust a teacher who shouts or who appears agitated at the slightest provocation.

Make sure, too, that the body language signals that you send match your verbal ones. For example, if you must force yourself to hide a smile while reprimanding a student, then that student will not take you seriously. If you frown while praising a class, then you will only confuse students. To avoid sending mixed signals such as these, the following are some nonverbal signals you should avoid:

- Snapping fingers at a student
- Jabbing a finger at a student's chest to make a point
- Ignoring students who fall asleep in class
- Staying seated all class period
- Chewing gum or eating in front of students
- Speaking too rapidly, too loudly, or in a monotone
- Leaning away from students
- Avoiding eye contact with certain students
- Pointing at students

- Laughing while delivering a serious message
- Turning your back while a student is speaking to you
- Slamming doors, books, or anything
- Rolling your eyes as if in disgust
- Sharing "knowing looks" with other students when someone is having trouble with an answer
- Talking on and on while ignoring body language signals from students
- Using a sarcastic tone
- Throwing anything at students, even in jest
- Tapping fingers to show impatience with students
- Putting your hands too close to a student's face, violating his or her personal space
- Standing with your hands on your hips, obviously impatient or angry
- Not responding to a student's answer to a question or when a student speaks to you

Capable teachers also pay close attention to nonverbal cues from their students. You need to add some pizzazz to your instructional activities if you notice that your students are doing any of the following:

- Watching the clock
- Looking confused
- Staring off into space
- Talking to someone sitting nearby
- Refusing to look at you
- Putting their heads down on their desks to sleep
- Doing homework for another class
- Asking to go to their lockers, the restroom, or the nurse
- Tying and retying their shoes
- Sighing loudly and rolling their eyes

Use Your Teacher Voice

One of the most important tools in your classroom leadership toolbox is your voice. Your voice is one of the first things that students notice about you. If you are not sure of what to do, quick-witted students can pick up the hesitation in your voice and move off task. Conversely, a confident voice can convey information in such a no-nonsense fashion that it can convince a roomful of rowdy students that you mean business.

When you take a deliberate approach to using your voice effectively, there are several things to consider. First, think about how you can use different volumes effectively. One of the most important tips that veteran teachers can share with you is that shouting to be heard is never effective. If you want a class to listen to you, catch their attention and then slowly lower the volume of your voice. If you really want to make students pay attention, a dramatic stage whisper works wonders.

Another way to make sure to use your voice effectively is to match your tone to your purpose. Teachers who do not use a serious tone when the situation warrants it can confuse students who quickly pick up on the discrepancy between the tone of voice their teacher is using and the seriousness of the moment.

You may recall teachers in your past who had unfortunate verbal mannerisms—repeating "you know"; clearing their throat; or using annoying filler words, such as "like." If you suspect that you may have a potentially distracting verbal mannerism, one of the best ways to be certain is to record yourself and then listen critically. You can also ask for honest feedback from colleagues or from your students.

A final way to modulate your voice to make it a more effective teaching tool is to vary the speed at which you speak. Teachers who talk very quickly or in a slow monotone in front of the class are not tuned in to their audience. Remember that when you are in class, you should not be in the same conversational mode that you would use with your friends. Instead, use your voice to make it easy for your students to understand you.

How to Make a Point Students Will Remember

Although there are many creative techniques to help your students remember the main points of what you say to them, you will have to plan and prepare to make each technique successful. Successful teachers often experiment with a variety of approaches to help their students find success. The following techniques are some you can use, modify, or combine to help your students stay alert and interested in a lesson:

- Help your students make a personal connection to the lesson. They should be able to identify with the material under study. One easy way to do this is to include the interests, hobbies, experiences, or cultures of your students when creating worksheets or questions.

- Include visual elements. Use media. Show film clips. Hold up objects. Do demonstrations. To make the visual elements of a lesson even more engaging, include student interaction, such as having student-made media presentations or student-led demonstrations.

- Invite guest speakers to talk to your students. Hearing a community leader talk about the importance of local government, for example, can reinforce the points you are trying to make about this topic.

- Hide items related to the lesson in a large box. Ask students to guess what the items could be. As you open the box, have students explain or predict the significance of each item as it relates to the day's lesson.

- Play music that fits the lesson of the day and ask students to explain how it applies to the lesson.
- Display a statement that you want your students to recall. Guarantee that they will do so by immediately playing a video clip that supports it.
- Surprise students with a bit of theater. This not only will make your lesson enjoyable but also will make it one your students will recall for a long time. Say something outrageously startling and interesting, stage a reenactment, wear a costume, or (even more fun) have your students wear costumes.
- Tell students in advance the specific number of facts they will learn during a presentation. As you cover each one, mark it off, resulting in a countdown of the facts.
- Stop periodically to review notes by calling on students to share what they have learned. Keep at it until all the points of the day's lesson have been mentioned.
- Stop and ask students to share their notes with a partner so that they can fill in any missing information.
- Hand each student two sets of ten cards. On each card from one set, have the first part of a fact from the presentation. On each card from the other set, have the second part of the fact. As the lesson progresses, students can match the cards from the two sets based on the information they are learning.
- Ask students to complete a graphic organizer as they listen.
- Stop periodically and ask students for a quick recap of what they have learned so far.
- Give students a bank of key words, dates, or other items to use in their notes.
- Put ten words from the lesson on a handout. Ask students to mark them off as they encounter them.

Set the Stage

Before you begin a presentation, set the stage by previewing the topic in such a way that students will want to know more about what you have planned for them. If you begin in a dull way, many of your students will quickly tune out. However, if you incorporate one or more of these preview techniques, your students will be motivated to pay attention:

- Post a motto, slogan, or other catchy phrase related to the lesson in a conspicuous spot and ask students to comment on it.
- Display and talk about an unusual object related to the lesson.
- Make a provocative statement and ask students to respond to it.
- Read part of a passage to the class. Be sure to stop reading at an exciting part of the text. Finish the passage later in your presentation.
- Pass out a handout with missing parts. Your students can fill in the missing information as they listen.

- Do a demonstration and then ask students to explain what they observed.

- Take a poll of your students on some aspect of the topic. A useful online tool for this is Poll Everywhere (www.polleverywhere.com).

- Pose a problem for students to decipher. Work out the various steps in solving the problem as you present material. To make it even more engaging, ask students to predict solutions or next steps as you present.

How to Catch Your Students' Attention

Few things can be as frustrating for a teacher as being ignored, and yet it happens in classroom after classroom, day after day. Instead of trying to talk when your students are not ready to listen, wait until you have everyone's attention. Arrange a signal with students so that they know that they are supposed to stop what they are doing and listen. If you teach older students, a simple signal, such as "May I have your attention, please?" spoken while you are at the front of the class obviously waiting for their attention, is often effective. For younger students, a variety of signals may be more useful. Some of the most popular and effective signals include these:

- Stand in front of the class and begin a series of actions that you want students to copy: touching your nose, putting your hands on your hips, and so on. Once they are copying your actions, you have their attention.

- Teach your students to hold up a hand and to stop talking when they see you holding up yours.

- Count backward from ten.

- Say, "One, two, three, freeze!"

- Have a class call and response, such as the popular "Hocus, pocus, everybody focus" or "One, two, three, eyes on me." You can find many more engaging call-and-response ideas at Angela Watson's helpful site, The Cornerstone for Teachers (https://thecornerstoneforteachers.com/50-fun-call-and-response-ideas-to-get-students-attention).

- Display an online timer or a clock and count down until students are paying attention. To find intriguing timers that your students will like, go to Online-Stopwatch .com (www.online-stopwatch.com/classroom-timers).

- Play a song that students like so that they know they must be ready to pay attention at the end of it.

- Establish a rhythmic clapping pattern that students will follow once you start.

- Have a bell on your desk so that students can stop working and focus as soon as they hear it.

Finally, be aware of your audience. Students do not have long attention spans. They become restless after just a few minutes. Break up activities and allow brain breaks periodically to help them to stay on track. Don't get so caught up in your lesson that you forget that even the best-planned lesson is useless if no one is listening.

The Right Spot at the Right Time

It is very difficult to be a capable classroom leader if you do not move around your classroom. Students will be aware that you are not monitoring their behavior and will attempt to take advantage of the gaps in your attention to misbehave. Just moving around the classroom is not enough, however. It is important to be at the right spot at the right time during the flow of your lesson.

Many teachers find it helpful to position their desks at the back or on the sides of the classroom so that all students have an unimpeded view of the front of the room. This works well if the board is in the front. Not only do your students have a clear view of the board but also when your desk is in the back or on the sides, you will be able to unobtrusively observe your students. If you place a chair beside your desk facing away from the class and toward you, you will also be able to have a quiet conference with a student without disturbing others.

It is also important to choose just the right place in the room where you can deliver directions or speak to the whole group. Usually, the front of the classroom works best for this. If you move to the same spot every time you call for the attention of the group, students will soon learn to anticipate this and to focus on you when you are in that area.

Many teachers also find that using a clipboard to jot notes as they walk around the room makes it easier to leave their desk area. Moving around the room without the risk of tripping will be possible once you help students understand the need to stow their book bags out of the aisle.

Doug Lemov, author of the landmark book *Teach Like a Champion 2.0* (published by Jossey-Bass in 2015), as well as several other highly regarded and very helpful books about classroom leadership, suggests that teachers use a technique called Pastore's Perch when monitoring students. With this technique, teachers can broaden their view of the class simply by moving to the front corner of a classroom when scanning to make sure that everyone is on task. By moving just a few steps away from the center of the room to a front corner, a teacher's view of the class widens dramatically. This just-right spot makes it much easier to observe students.

Finally, it's helpful to move around while deciding where to position yourself at various times during class. Can everyone see you? Can you observe everyone? Can students see the board or the area where you have information projected? When you need to speak to students privately, can you do so while still facing the rest of the class?

Teach with Purpose

One trait that all effective classroom leaders share is the ability to help students understand the purpose for their hard work. If you find your students questioning why they must complete an assignment, you have failed in one of your most important tasks:

making students aware of the benefits of the instruction they are receiving. Students often do not automatically understand the connection between sitting for hours at an uncomfortable desk and the successful lives they envision for themselves when they are adults. You must help them make these connections. Preempt your students' doubts by making it clear why they need to know what you are teaching them. Here's how:

- Put the benefits of the lesson on the board so that students will know them right away.

- Tell students how their lives will be better when they know the material you intend to teach. Focus on why students need to know the information right now as well as why they will need it in the future.

- Begin a unit by connecting it to previous learning so that students can see a progression of knowledge and skills in their schooling. Be very specific. Say, "At the end of class today, you will be able to _____" or "You need to know this because _____."

- Take the time every now and then to ask students to tell you why they need to know the information you are presenting. Make a list of their ideas and post it in a conspicuous spot.

- Draw connections between what your students are doing now in your class and the work they will be doing later in the term.

Teach Your Students to Follow Directions

Effective teachers realize the importance of making sure that students know how to follow directions. Students who know how to follow directions are likely to remain engaged and busy all class. As the leader of your classroom, it is up to you to make sure that your students receive explicit directions delivered in ways that they can understand.

When students know what to do and how to do it well, confusion vanishes. Although they may still not be sure of the information in the material, at least they do know what is expected of them. The potential for failure and disruption is lessened considerably. Here are some things to keep in mind when you design and deliver directions to students:

- Make following directions well an important part of the culture of your classroom. Talk about this every day. Work on it until your students see that following directions is not only something their teacher thinks is important but also a necessary life skill.

- Expect and command attention. When you are ready to go over written or oral directions, expect your students to stop what they are doing and to pay attention to you from the beginning of your explanation to the end.

- Seek clarification. Ask students to rephrase directions until you are sure everyone knows what to do.

- Ask students to focus when you read test directions. When you are giving a test, teach students to read the directions on the test with you. They should not be trying to complete the first page as you explain the directions on the last page.

- Be alert to impatient, anxious students. Don't be fooled by students who inform you that they know what to do. These impatient students may just want to get started and do not always have a clear understanding of the assignment.

Guidelines for Giving Written Directions Successfully

- Check for understanding by asking students to restate or clarify the directions and by monitoring students' work after they begin the assignment.

- Make sure your directions satisfy the objectives of your lesson. This will help students understand the big picture behind the assignment.

- Express directions in the form of logical steps students should accomplish to complete the assignment. List and number the steps in the order you want students to complete them.

- Keep each statement brief. For example, try "Write your answers on your test paper" instead of "Be sure to put all that lined notebook paper you have on your desk away because I want you to write just on the test."

- Take the time to go over directions orally with students. This is especially important on tests where there may be several sections with different directions for each one.

Guidelines for Giving Verbal Directions Successfully

Before Class Begins

- Write the instructions where students can read them as you review them orally: on the board, on slips of paper for each student, on a computer display, or on a large piece of bulletin board paper.

- Word each step simply and positively. For example, "Turn to page 117" is a well-expressed direction. "Turn to page 117 and begin about halfway down the page—you don't need to read the top of the page" is not as easy to follow.

During Class Instruction

- Call for your students' attention by using the same signal every time. Something as simple as "May I have your attention, please?" is enough to let your students know to listen to you.

- Wait until all students have stopped what they are doing and can look at you. Take as long as you need to allow students to focus their attention on you and to ensure they are no longer opening their books, rummaging in their book bags, or trying to borrow a pencil.

- Check for understanding by asking a student to restate the directions. If necessary, ask several students to clarify and explain until everyone is clear about what to do.

After You Have Given Instructions

- Stay on your feet to circulate and monitor students to see that they are starting the work correctly.

- If you see that several students are having trouble, do not hesitate to stop class and clarify for everyone.

Your Role as a Supportive Teacher

The second component of capable classroom leadership, being a supportive teacher, would seem to be inherent to the task of being an educator. Being a supportive teacher, however, is far more than just saying, "Good job!" when students appear to be on the right track. Being a supportive teacher goes beyond rote encouragement to challenge your students to work hard, persist when things are difficult, and assume responsibility for their work, their effort, and their success. Supportive teachers show students that mistakes are just another way to learn and that it is okay to take risks as they work to meet their teacher's high expectations for academic achievement.

Hold Students Accountable for Their Own Success

Just as it is important to be empathetic and kind to your students, it is just as imperative to hold them accountable for their own success. Setting high standards is simple. Holding students accountable for their success is not.

No matter how difficult it may be, however, holding students accountable as they work to meet their teacher's high standards is critical to the positive learning climate in any classroom. When a supportive teacher is involved with hardworking students, the classroom climate becomes what we want for our students and for our own satisfaction. To be an effective classroom leader, you must convey to your students that they can achieve success through their own effort and hard work. Here are some suggestions for how you can hold your students accountable:

- Teach your students how to do their work. Students should be taught the study skills they need to reach the standards you have for them.

- Involve parents or guardians as often as it takes for you to create an effective team of caring adults who want to help a child succeed.

- Create a wide variety of fair assessments. Employ as many effective ways to evaluate student progress as you can to meet the needs and abilities of your students.

- Call on every student every day. Allow no student to be invisible in your classroom.

- Return graded papers promptly so that students know what they should do to improve.

- Make sure your feedback on assignments is geared to helping students correct their errors and improve their performance.

- When students have completed an assignment, give them another one to begin right away or allow them to choose among acceptable alternatives.

- Consistently enforce class rules, policies, and procedures. Your expectations should be clear.

- Refuse to allow your students to sleep or to do homework for other classes in your class. They should be doing your work in your class.

- Make it clear that you expect 100 percent accuracy in student work. Some students will aim to just get by with a minimum of work unless you encourage them to do otherwise.

- Be very specific about your criteria for success on an assignment so that students have a clear idea of what is expected before they begin to work. Advance rubrics are always a good idea.

- Plan the procedures you want your students to follow in case they don't have their materials or textbooks in class. Don't allow students to get away with not working because they don't have materials.

- When you are moving around the room to monitor activity, ask your students to underline the answers they think are correct and to circle the ones that puzzle them so that you can work together to make sure they understand their assignment.

- If you find that some of your students are reluctant to complete their assignments on schedule, contact their parents or guardians. If students know that their progress is being monitored at home as well as in class, they usually perform better.

- When students miss the answer to a question, ask them to write the correct answer on their papers.

- Make neatness an important component of the work in your classroom. You don't have to be extremely picky, but you should expect students to turn in neat work.

The Importance of Helping Students Make Good Decisions

The gamut of decisions that today's students must make is not only tough but also sometimes unforgiving. Sometimes it seems that the hardest decisions must be made by those students who are poorly equipped to manage the task. The impact of students who make poor decisions for themselves can be devastating on a classroom.

There are many nonthreatening opportunities to help students make good decisions, and there are many advantages to giving students safe options as often as possible. Here are just a few of them:

- When teachers allow students opportunities to make choices and then discuss the consequences of those choices, they teach them to think about the actions they take.

- Options increase students' problem-solving abilities while reducing the need for time-consuming and unpleasant power struggles.
- Giving students choices can allow them to share ideas while working toward a common goal—a skill they will need as good employees when they are adults.
- Allowing students frequent options indicates that their teachers value their opinions, respect their uniqueness, and have faith in their ability to succeed.

You do not have to lose control of your class while you help students make good decisions. The best way to promote sound decision making is to give students a limited range of choices. For example, instead of saying, "Do you want homework tonight?" try "Do you need to do exercise three or exercise four for extra practice at home tonight?" Here are some other safe ways to begin thinking about how you can give your students options:

- "You may be excused from the room three times this month. How can you use those passes wisely?"
- "Do you need to do this now, or can it wait a few minutes?"
- "Do you need more practice on this, or should we count the next activity for a grade?"
- "What would be a better way to express that?"
- "In what order do you want to answer these questions?"
- "You have ten minutes left. Please choose one of these activities to complete."
- "There are five questions for you. Answer any three of them."

Help Students Develop a Growth Mindset

When students and teachers believe that success is achievable only by those individuals with innate capabilities, such as being intelligent or talented in some way, their mindset is said to be *fixed*. When students and teachers have the mindset that success is possible through such qualities as work, effort, and persistence, this attitude is a *growth mindset*.

First identified in 2006 by Stanford psychologist and researcher Dr. Carol Dweck in her book *Mindset: The New Psychology of Success* published by Random House, the importance of a growth mindset in students has revolutionized classroom practice. The spread of the growth mindset movement has been swift and exponential, in part because it confirms what experienced teachers have recognized for years: if students do not believe in their ability to succeed, then they will not succeed.

Along with that self-evident truth is an equally important one: teachers also need a growth mindset. If students are to become high achievers, they need a teacher whose foundational belief is that students have the capacity to learn and achieve.

As a classroom teacher, the growth mindset movement will have weighty implications for your teaching practice as you work to figure out how to help your students avoid a fixed mindset and to develop the attitudes that make up a growth mindset instead. Here are some of the most important concepts that compose the growth mindset movement:

- Generic praise, although kind, is not helpful to students. Expressions such as "You are a superstar!" or "You are so smart!" do little to encourage students to master challenging work. Instead, because the praise centers on innate qualities, generic praise such as this promotes a fixed mindset.

- Instead of generic praise, specific feedback is a crucial tool for teachers who want to help their students seek challenges. Feedback should be specific, timely, focused on problem-solving processes, and recognize the importance of effort in increasing self-confidence.

- The celebration of effort, hard work, and persistence is a key element of a growth mindset. Students who recognize the importance of these three traits in their academic success are more likely to welcome challenges. Teachers should arrange opportunities to celebrate these traits in addition to recognizing academic success.

- Mistakes are viewed as valuable assets to learning. Students with a growth mindset do not fear mistakes as students with a fixed mindset do. Teachers should make sure that students are aware that mistakes are a normal, expected, and necessary part of learning.

- Deliberate practice, wherein students focus on the parts of an assignment where they have not mastered the material and deliberately practice improving those weaknesses, is an important part of the learning process because it is specific and focused to help students gain mastery.

- Students need to be mindful of the strategies and processes that they use to arrive at answers because this awareness enables them to apply those strategies and processes in other ways.

- *Yet.* With this one word, students can begin to transform their thinking from a fixed mindset to a growth mindset. A negative statement such as "I don't know how to do this" becomes a positive declaration of intent when a student can change it to "I don't know how to do this *yet*." Bulletin boards, class mottoes, posters—in a classroom where students are learning to develop a growth mindset, the word *yet* is often displayed in various forms.

Here are some specific strategies that you can use to promote a growth mindset among your students:

- Explicitly teach the terms *growth mindset* and *fixed mindset* so that you and your students have a common vocabulary for discussing work habits and other classroom issues.

- Ask students to review one another's work to offer constructive criticism. Constructive criticism is key in helping students understand how to do their work well. It is often easier for a student to hear constructive criticism from a classmate than from a teacher.

- Have students plan their work before they begin instead of just diving in. Ask them to predict how long it will take or where they can find help if they need it.
- After students complete an assignment, hold a debriefing session where they can share their ideas about what went well as they worked and where they struggled. Sharing these ideas with classmates can build confidence.

Because of the widespread adoption of the growth mindset concept, there are countless articles and books about it. One of the most reliable sources of information for exploring the idea of the growth mindset further is Mindset Works (www.mindsetworks.com). At this site maintained by Dweck and her staff, you will be able to learn more about her research and how the growth mindset culture can help your students become self-disciplined learners.

Celebrate Mistakes in Your Classroom

One of the most positive results of the growth mindset movement is the understanding that teachers now have about how to help students view mistakes as an important step in the learning process. In the past, when students made mistakes as they learned, their attitude about them often shut down their effort. The shift from thinking about mistakes as failure to regarding them as valuable tools in the learning process can have a positive effect on your classroom practice. Here is how to encourage this in your classroom:

- Analyze common mistakes in a whole-class discussion. When trying to change how your students view mistakes, a good place to begin is to make analyzing common mistakes on an assignment part of a whole-group discussion. Once students see that their classmates have made the same mistakes that they have, it will be easier for them to move forward. Not only is it comforting for students to know that they are not alone in their mistakes but also sharing information about them is a useful way for students to correct their errors.
- Focus on strategies. Another way to celebrate mistakes is to ask students to discuss the strategies that they used while working on an assignment. They can share their strategies with a partner or a small group as well with the larger group or one-on-one with you. Discussing strategies allows students to see beyond the problem itself to understand the bigger picture of how to use various strategies.
- Ask students to examine *why* they made a mistake. Asking students to consider why they made the mistakes they did is also useful because it helps students understand the connection between their effort and their mistake. It's important for students to realize the difference between a mistake made because they did not fully understand a concept and one made because they were in a hurry to finish the assignment, for example.

- Look at the specific information involved in a mistake. Reframing the mistake in specific terms will also allow students to understand more about it. Instead of saying, "I see you missed the third question" while working with a student, if you say, "I see that you missed the third question. Do you think you understand the information it's asking?," you will help students move past the specific missed question to the information involved. When students can look beyond just the mistakes they made to understand the concepts that they don't understand, they have a better idea of what they do and do not know instead of just a count of their mistakes.

- View mistakes as a public service for the rest of the class. When a student makes a mistake in front of peers, instead of making a harsh judgment, thank the student for making that mistake. Mention that it is one that classmates probably made and that others will now understand the information better because of that student's mistake (and bravery in sharing with the rest of the class).

Motivation: A Daily Requirement for All Students

Even though your school district may require you to use a detailed lesson plan template for daily instructional planning, the chances are good that one of the most important parts of a lesson will not be included on that template: motivation. Too often we think about the outcomes that we want for our students and the activities that we want them to do without considering the specific ways that we should encourage them to want to do their work. Capable classroom leaders know that to be the supportive teacher that their students need, they should consistently include motivational techniques as part of every lesson plan.

How to Use Extrinsic Motivation Effectively

Researchers classify the various ways that we attempt to motivate students as either extrinsic motivation or intrinsic motivation. Extrinsic motivation is the type of positive reinforcement that offers external or tangible rewards to students as behavioral motivators. There are two categories of external rewards: activities that students find enjoyable and desirable items that students receive.

Extrinsic motivation is a controversial practice because its effects do not appear to be as long-lasting as those of intrinsic motivation. Students tend to be too focused on the reward being offered rather than on the successful mastery of the material. Other problems with extrinsic motivation include some teachers' tendency to overuse it and the high monetary expense for teachers who attempt to be fair and offer many students tangible rewards.

Despite these negatives, however, extrinsic motivation can play a valuable role in motivating students to succeed. Its greatest advantage is that it makes an immediate connection between the reward being offered and the work students are expected to complete.

If you choose to use various types of extrinsic rewards in your class, keep in mind that they work best when students know about them in advance of the work and can anticipate earning them. Take care to offer extrinsic rewards only occasionally so that they are novel enough to be coveted by students.

TANGIBLE REWARDS STUDENTS ENJOY

You do not have to spend a fortune on rewards for your students. The most effective rewards are activities that students enjoy. Instead of shopping for stickers or other prizes, offer students some of these free rewards:

- Time to play an educational online game
- Being team captain or group leader
- Time to work on a puzzle or other enjoyable activity
- Bookmarks made by other students
- A walk for the entire class
- Having their names displayed on a wall of fame
- Having their work displayed
- Watching video clips
- Using the library during free time
- Having a decorated desk
- Being the "Student of the Week"
- Sitting in a special desk or chair
- Borrowing a book from the classroom library
- Time for independent reading
- Encouraging notes on their work
- A positive note from you to take home
- Having you call a parent or guardian with a positive message

Why You Should Not Use Food as a Reward

For many years, educators used candy, snacks, and other treats to encourage students to do their work and behave well. Recently, however, educators have begun to realize that using food as a reward is not a sound practice. Here's why you should not offer food treats to your students:

- Childhood obesity is a national epidemic. As caring adult role models, teachers have a responsibility to help students stay healthy.
- Using food as a reward contradicts the information about fitness that students learn in health or nutrition classes.

- When teachers offer candy and other snacks to students, they make life more difficult for students who do not want to overeat.

- You may have students with serious medical conditions, such as diabetes or food allergies.

- When you reward students with food, you establish a connection between food and behavior that can lead to problems later in life.

- Parents often object to food as a reward because it may undermine the values about nutrition that they are trying to teach their children.

Make Sure Intrinsic Motivation Is a Classroom Constant

Intrinsic motivation is an incentive to work that is satisfying in itself. Although extrinsic motivation can be effective in boosting students' self-confidence and their desire to do well, intrinsic motivation is a more effective way to create fundamental change in student effort and achievement.

There are countless ways to harness the power of intrinsic motivation in every assignment. For example, many students enjoy being able to use recently acquired knowledge in new ways or to engage in a community event related to the work at hand. It does not take long to determine that students are far more engaged in activities that encourage them to discover, inquire, or play rather than to just listen passively to a teacher lecturing.

Thoughtful teachers find ways to increase the intrinsic motivation in assignments by considering how they can make assignments appealing to their students. To do this, offer assignments that provide novelty and an unexpected departure from routine activities, such as:

- Writing on anything other than lined paper
- Watching short videos
- Listening to music that matches the day's assignment
- Completing only the odd or even problems in an assignment
- Creating their own quizzes, worksheets, games, or puzzles
- Communicating only through notes instead of conversation
- Making three-dimensional graphic organizers
- Taking mini field trips within the school
- Role-playing
- Sharing personal reactions to their work
- Playing games
- Discussing paradoxes or odd facts or unusual images
- Determining what unlike things could have in common

- Solving brainteasers
- Drawing inferences from interesting case studies
- Exploring an unusual artifact
- Examining a photograph for incongruities
- Using manipulatives
- Finding hidden facts or clues
- Earning a silly reward or bragging rights
- Getting up and moving around the class
- Racing the clock
- Racing another team in the class
- Making a movie or audio recording
- Performing in a class skit
- Making a Prezi or PowerPoint presentation
- Tweeting an opinion or fact about the lesson
- Making a stick figure sketch
- Working with simulation problems
- Defending or refuting a point in a class debate

Make Success Visible

One of the most productive ways to motivate students is to make their success visible. A classroom environment in which student engagement is valued and student success is celebrated is a positive one in which students thrive. There are different ways to make your students' success visible. Here are just a few of the methods of visually encouraging student success that you can adapt for your classroom:

- Using stickers on student papers
- Rubber-stamping student work with positive messages
- Writing positive notes to students on their papers
- Sending home positive notes or e-mails to parents or guardians
- Using buzzwords, such as "Woo-hoo!," in unison as class shout-outs
- Using a class hand signal, such as a thumbs-up, to acknowledge success
- Displaying photographs of students with their good work as well as the work itself
- Holding brief recognition ceremonies periodically
- Setting aside a special section on a bulletin board as a display area for student work
- Awarding certificates for such qualities as persistence and dedication
- Creating large bulletin board graphs to chart the success of an entire class

Control the Flow of Class Time

The third component of capable classroom leadership is one that teachers can control: class time. You have door-to-door control over the ways your students use the all-too-few hours they spend with you in your classroom. You can allow students to have nothing productive to do for much of the time they spend with you, or you can arrange to have students engaged in a variety of learning tasks while developing a positive attitude about their academic responsibilities.

You Control the Time Your Students Have with You

Sometimes it will seem that such interruptions as intercom announcements, commotions in the halls, or unruly students disrupt your class much too often. Just as other teachers do, you will have to find ways to cope successfully with these obvious disturbances as well as with many more subtle disruptions of your class routines.

If you do not control the use of time in your classroom, what are the consequences? If you waste only two minutes of your students' day—a few seconds at the opening of class, a distraction or two, a lost handout, maybe even a minute of free time at the end of class—over the course of a typical school year, those two minutes a day will add up to more than six hours of lost instruction. That's an entire school day.

The results of misused instructional time can be grim. Teachers who do not use class time wisely experience far more discipline problems than teachers who make use of every minute. Students who waste class time are less able to succeed academically. Discipline problems and academic failures not only make a teacher's workday unpleasant but also can eventually lead to burnout.

What can you do to avoid the hazards of wasted class time? Start by making a commitment to yourself and to your students that you will teach them during every minute that they are with you.

How Teachers Waste Classroom Time

One way to use class time to the best advantage is to be aware of how easy it is to waste it. Some of the ways that teachers misuse class time include the following:

- Teaching lessons that are not relevant or interesting to students
- Not having clear procedures for student activities
- Not using the first few minutes of class effectively
- Allowing students to goof off for the last few minutes of class
- Not intervening quickly enough to keep problems manageable
- Confusing digressions from their topic with teachable moments
- Neglecting to set up equipment in advance

- Not establishing routines for daily classroom procedures
- Not double-checking links for websites students will need to use
- Calling roll instead of quickly checking attendance with a seating chart
- Not enforcing a reasonable policy for leaving the classroom
- Not providing assistance for students without materials
- Allowing students to decide when class is over
- Not determining students' prior knowledge of new material
- Assigning an inappropriate amount of work
- Giving confusing directions
- Making poor transitions between activities
- Giving homework that is only busywork

If you recognize that you could be guilty of any of these poor decisions, rest assured that it is possible to change that bad habit with awareness, planning, and effort. In Teacher Worksheet 4.3, you can reflect on your current teaching practice and how well you use the class time that is allotted to you and your students.

TEACHER WORKSHEET 4.3

How Well Do You Use Class Time?

To determine how well you use class time at this point in your teaching career, use the self-assessment that follows. Place a check mark in the column that best fits your time use for each statement. The actions listed in the first column are positive ones that all teachers should cultivate. If you mark the actions in the other two columns, you should consider how to improve your use of class time.

	I Always Do This	I Sometimes Do This	I Don't Do This
I expect students to begin working on established class routines as soon as they enter the classroom.			
My students can pick up handouts and other materials as they enter class.			
My students follow a predictable routine for the end of class.			
I delegate as many chores as appropriate given the age and ability levels of my students.			
I provide small pencil sharpeners at various places around the room.			
When I show videos, I show only the most relevant clips.			
When groups need to pick up materials, only one student picks them up for the entire group.			
When students need to pick up various types of materials, I avoid long lines and congestion by placing the materials in various stations around the room.			
I make a point of testing equipment before students arrive to make sure that it is in working order.			
I give directions verbally one time while students follow along with written or posted copies.			

(continued on next page)

(continued from previous page)

	I Always Do This	I Sometimes Do This	I Don't Do This
I have extra pencils and paper available for students who lack supplies.			
I always have a backup plan in case a lesson does not work well.			
I design lessons to meet state and district objectives.			
I offer brain breaks at regular intervals so that students find it easy to remain on task.			
My students and I stop periodically during a lesson to review and recap.			
I routinely use a timer to help students focus.			
I realize that all students can have trouble transitioning from one topic to another and adjust my plans accordingly.			
I use formative assessments to determine my students' readiness for a unit of study.			
I teach my students how to keep their notes and other materials in order so that they can find them quickly.			
I make a few extra copies of handouts so that students who have lost theirs can begin right away.			

Use the Principles of Effective Classroom Time Management

Learning to use class time wisely is a skill that will take effort, patience, and practice to acquire; however, the rewards are well worth the effort. You and your students will benefit every day from classes that run smoothly. You can eventually gather many tips from your colleagues and learn even more from your own classroom experiences; until then, you can start with these general principles for using class time wisely:

- Reduce distractions. Look around your classroom for things that might distract your students. Some obvious sources of distractions might be windows, desks too close together, doorways, pencil sharpeners, trash cans, screen savers, too many posters or banners, graffiti, or—the most enticing one of all—other students.

- Raise student awareness. Your students need to learn that time is important in your class. This doesn't mean that you should rush them through their tasks, but you should discuss the importance of using class time wisely, making sure that your students understand that you expect them to work productively.

- Establish routines. If you have routines for daily activities in your class, your students will save minutes each day and hours each week instead of wasting time because they don't know what to do.

- Monitor constantly. Monitoring your students instead of sitting at your desk will allow you to help students while their problems are still manageable.

- Be very organized. If your students must wait while you find your textbook or a handout, that is a poor use of their time. Make it a point to be so organized that you will be able to keep yourself and your students on task.

- Take a door-to-door approach. Engage students in learning from the time they enter your classroom until the time they leave. Many teachers make the mistake of thinking that students need a few minutes of free time at the start of class and at the end of class to relax. Although students do need time at both ends of class to make effective transitions, they do not need free time to do this. Instead, give them interesting activities that relate to the day's lesson.

- Use small blocks of time. Just as you can accomplish many of your own tasks with brief bits of concentrated effort, so can your students. If you have only five minutes until dismissal, refuse to allow students to do nothing just because it will take too long to get them working on a new assignment. Instead, use this time and other snippets of time in class to review or to teach a new fact.

- Teach to an objective. If you teach a subject that you enjoy personally, it is tempting to spend more time on certain topics than the curriculum dictates. Stick to your plan so that your students won't be shortchanged on other topics.

- Assign enough work. If students finish a task, there should be another waiting for them. For example, students who sit around after a test waiting for others to finish before going on to the next activity are obviously wasting time. Always make sure that your students know what they are supposed to do after they finish their current assignment.

How to Handle Interruptions

Many teachers feel frustrated when their carefully planned lesson is interrupted by a fire drill, a class visitor, or even too many students who need to sharpen pencils. The best defense you have against losing instructional time to interruptions is delivering an interesting lesson. Students who are fully engaged in meaningful and interesting work would rather stay on task than pay attention to yet another classmate sharpening a pencil. You can minimize the negative effects of interruptions by meeting three goals:

- **Goal One:** Prevent as many interruptions as you can. Some teachers find that putting a sign on the door, such as "Learning in Progress—Please Do Not Disturb," serves as a gentle reminder to those visitors whose business may not be urgent. Others work with colleagues whose classrooms are nearby so that one teacher does not schedule a noisy class activity on the same day that another has planned a test or other quiet activity. Work with your colleagues in a similar fashion to solve problems when you can.

- **Goal Two:** Minimize the disruption caused by an interruption. Although you can prevent many interruptions during your school day, some are unavoidable. For example, you cannot prevent the interruption caused by a message from the office requesting a student for an early dismissal. In such situations, your goal must be to keep the other students on task. If you remind yourself that your goal is to minimize the disturbance, you are likely to create a solution to the problem.

- **Goal Three:** Prepare for predictable interruptions. Having a plan in place for unavoidable, predictable interruptions will give you confidence, and your students will behave better because you will know what to do in almost any situation. When you make plans for predictable interruptions, keep the solutions simple so that your students will be able to respond appropriately when interruptions occur. Here is a list of some of the predictable interruptions that teachers must handle successfully so that you can plan how you will manage each one:
  - A student does not have supplies or materials
  - Students ask to leave the class to use the restroom, see the nurse, or go to their lockers
  - Students need to listen to intercom announcements
  - A visitor asks to speak with you
  - A computer doesn't work properly
  - Students leave class early or arrive late
  - Students need to sharpen pencils, staple papers, or dispose of trash

- A student from another class asks to speak with one of your students
- There is a commotion in the hallway or another classroom

How to Handle Student Requests to Leave the Classroom

Making good decisions about allowing a student to leave the classroom is not always easy, no matter how much teaching experience you have. Consider the following guidelines as you begin to formulate your policy on leaving class:

- Do not allow more than one or two students to leave at one time.
- Do not refuse to allow students to go to the restroom or to the clinic. Use your best judgment about other requests.
- If a student seems to be making too many requests to leave the classroom, speak privately with him or her about the problem. If this does not work, call a parent or guardian. If there is a problem, the parent or guardian can apprise you of it. If there is not a problem, enlist that person's help in keeping the student focused and in class. Often, just knowing that you take the problem seriously enough to call home will convince students to make fewer requests.
- When you send students out of the room, make sure whenever possible that an adult will supervise them. You are responsible for your students until another adult assumes that responsibility.
- Never allow students to leave the building without contacting an administrator first. Older students may wish to retrieve items that they have left in their cars, but school parking lots can provide opportunities for violence and other misbehavior.
- When it is necessary, refuse requests in a polite but firm manner. Instead of brusquely refusing, try one of these phrases:
  - Can you wait a few minutes?
  - Have you finished your work?
  - Let me check to see whether _____ is in the _____ office.
  - Can you do that right after class?
- By using a hall pass such as the one in Sample 4.1, you will be able to keep track of your students. Having a hall pass procedure for leaving the classroom also sends the message to your students that you take their absences seriously.

Keeping Track of Students Who Leave the Classroom

Because you will need to keep track of students who are out of your class, you should have a sign-out sheet as well as hall passes. A sign-out sheet can take many forms. You can post

Sample 4.1
Hall Pass

Student name: _____ Date: _____

Time out: _____ Time returned: _____

_____ Restroom

_____ Guidance office

_____ Locker

_____ Library

_____ Clinic

_____ Media center

_____ Water fountain

_____ Principal's office

_____ Classroom

_____ Other: _____

Teacher signature: _____

a sheet for students to fill out as they leave, have them sign out on a computer, or maintain a class logbook. Having a sign-out sheet, such as the one in Teacher Worksheet 4.4, will make it easier for you to keep accurate records of when your students leave your class and where they go.

Student Sign-Out Sheet

Student Name	Date	Destination	Time Out	Time Returned

Use Time Wisely by Pacing Instruction Well

Pacing instruction is the art of making sure that you assign just the right amount of meaningful work to keep students engaged in learning activities all class long. Pacing instruction well is not a skill that is easy to master because the dramatic variations in students' readiness levels, preferred learning styles, processing speeds, and work habits make it difficult to design assignments that all students will finish at the same time.

Although pacing instruction for maximum learning is a skill that usually requires experience to master, the guidelines that follow can make it easier for you to design instruction that will keep students engaged in learning for the entire class period:

- Provide plenty of early assistance so that those students who need help completing assignments do not fall behind other students.

- Use a mixture of whole-group, small-group, and individual instruction to manage the pace of assignments.

- Consider providing high-interest enrichment and remedial activities for students to work on when they complete their basic assignments. Offering attractive optional assignments will engage students constructively.

- Post a list of activities for students who finish their work early. Suggested activities might include starting homework early, working at a learning center, playing online games for review, reading a library book, working with another student on an extra project, or organizing notebooks.

- Provide directions in the form of checklists for students to follow as they complete their work so that they can plan for themselves how to accomplish their assignments.

- Always have the next assignment ready for those students who complete their work early. Allowing students who finish other work early to begin their homework in class is a reasonable use of their time if they know how to complete the work.

Learning how to manage classroom time is a developed skill. The better you know the content and how you want to teach it, the better idea you'll have of how long it will take to implement. I still haven't fully mastered this, and it is now my third year of teaching, but here are some things that helped: wearing a watch, setting a timer when I was lecturing so I knew when to stop, and taking a flipped classroom approach and having students do some independent learning at home.

Jay O'Rourke, 2+ years' experience

The First Ten Minutes of Class

Inefficient teachers overlook the potential power of the opening minutes of class. Often, if students are quiet enough and if there are many pressing demands on a teacher's time at that moment, more than ten minutes can vanish before class starts. It's no wonder that students are tardy to class; they have little reason to be on time.

You can use the first ten minutes to get your class off to a great start, or you can choose to waste this time. The first minutes set the tone for the rest of the class. If you are prepared for class and have taught your students an opening routine, they can use this brief time to make mental and emotional transitions from the last class or subject and prepare to focus on learning new material. You should establish a comfortable and predictable routine for the opening of class. Here is a simple opening routine that many teachers follow and that you can adapt to meet the needs of your class:

- **Step One:** Greet each student as he or she enters the class. You can hand out any papers you need to distribute. You can also answer questions, collect attendance notes, and check the emotional states of your students. Your students will appreciate that you care enough to stand at the door to greet them.

- **Step Two:** Have students go immediately to their respective seats. You will avoid many problems if you strictly enforce this part of the routine. Students who wander around the room while you are busy at the door can cause problems that will last throughout class. Furthermore, students will often carry problems from earlier in the day into your room. By insisting that your students take a seat right away, you will help focus their energy on your class and on learning.

- **Step Three:** Have students check the board for a predictable opening exercise. The opening exercise gives them time to settle down, organize their materials, and shift mental gears to what is going to happen in class. Your message on the board might include directions such as these:

Today's Tasks

1. Open your textbook to page 23.
2. Please get out a pen and paper.
3. Copy tonight's homework assignment into your planner.
4. Place last night's homework on your desk.
5. Read the objectives for today's classwork.

- **Step Four:** Have students complete an introductory or warm-up activity. The activity should arouse curiosity and relate the day's new learning to previous knowledge. It should be interesting yet simple enough for students to complete independently. The activity will thus increase their confidence so that they are even more interested in the day's lesson.

Use your creativity and your knowledge of your students to design activities that they will enjoy as they look forward to the day's lesson. For example, ask students to do one of the following activities or modify one to suit your students' needs. Students can

- Work with classmates to combine puzzle pieces containing information about the material being studied.

- Survey classmates to gather reactions to a quotation related to the day's lesson.
- Complete a graphic organizer. A site with many easy-to-use organizers is maintained by Education Oasis (www.educationoasis.com/curriculum/graphic_organizers.htm).
- Display their homework for classmates to evaluate with colored dots. (See Section Nine for more ideas on how to use colored dots.)
- Work with classmates to skim the day's reading and make group predictions.
- Listen to music associated with the lesson. A good site to explore the various types of music you can use for this purpose is Freeplay Music (http://freeplaymusic.com).
- Work with a partner to solve a problem related to the lesson.
- Respond to an intriguing, open-ended question.
- Make a one-minute presentation on a topic that interests the entire class.
- Work with classmates to share ideas about their homework or previous learning.
- List what they already know about the day's lesson.
- Skim the day's reading materials and predict what they will learn.
- Solve a brainteaser. BrainBashers (www.brainbashers.com) is an excellent site to search for brainteasers. Managed by British mathematician Kevin Stone, it features thousands of games, riddles, puzzles, and illusions.
- List three reasons to study the day's topic.
- With another student, combine information from notes.
- Watch a video clip and write about it. You can find thousands of short audio or video versions of historical events as well as clips from movies and television broadcasts at American Rhetoric (www.americanrhetoric.com).

As you can see, there are countless ways to open class with a predictable routine that your students will enjoy. Use Teacher Worksheet 4.5 as a template to make interesting and beneficial plans for the start of each class.

TEACHER WORKSHEET 4.5

Plans for Starting Class Effectively

With just a bit of careful planning, you can make the opening minutes of your class a productive time that sets a positive tone. Use this worksheet to ensure that the first few minutes of class are ones that you and your students will find useful.

Lesson topic: _____ Date: _____

Handouts to be distributed:

_____

_____

_____

_____

Routine procedures posted:

_____

_____

_____

_____

Day's agenda for students:

_____

_____

_____

_____

Activity to open class:

_____

_____

_____

_____

Materials needed:

_____

_____

Time needed: _____

Productive Transitions

Because your students are accustomed to the fast-paced action of modern life, they may lose interest in a lesson that seems to last too long. Experienced teachers create a positive learning environment by designing lessons around several brief activities. Although having several activities is sensible, it requires transitions that encourage students to be productive between activities.

Transitions are difficult to manage well because they require students to do three things in a very brief amount of time: mentally close out one task, prepare for the next one, and refocus their mental energy on a new topic. Fortunately, a wise first-year teacher can do several things to help students handle transitions effectively. Here's how:

- Design activities that flow naturally from one to the next, requiring a minimum of large-group instruction from you. Sequencing instruction in this way encourages students to manage their own learning.

- Try using a kitchen timer to set a time limit for a change in activities. When students know that they have only a minute or two to switch from one activity to another, they are more likely to move quickly.

Make transitions productive by providing your students with activities that will convert useless waiting time into learning opportunities. Using small blocks of time to engage your students in active thinking and learning can be enjoyable for both you and your students. You can use these activities as they are, or you can adapt, adjust, or add information to them to create others that will keep your students involved in productive learning throughout class. Ask students to

- Justify the rules for _____.
- Apply the information in the lesson to a real-life situation.
- Match words and meanings.
- Create a to-do list for a project or other activity.
- Complete a word sort.
- Read a brief newspaper article and respond to it.
- Create a time line of _____.
- Fill in the blanks in a brief outline.
- Put a series of events in chronological order.
- Practice the process of elimination on the answers to some sample standardized test questions.
- Paraphrase information.
- Respond to a humorous cartoon. A good source of cartoons appropriate for students is Today's Cartoon by Randy Glasbergen (www.glasbergen.com).

- Respond to a picture. You can search the millions of images at Google Images (https://images.google.com).
- Review information with a partner.
- List important facts from the last few days of class.
- Explain why the day's lesson is useful.
- Recall facts from the last lesson.
- Answer trivia questions related to the lesson.
- Write a key term on a scrap of paper and pass that scrap to a classmate, who then has to explain it.
- Circle or highlight key words in their notes or reading.
- Make quick flash cards to review vocabulary.
- Read the opening paragraphs from an assigned reading and tell a partner what they learned from the reading.
- Brainstorm a list of ten important concepts from the lesson.
- Describe an object in the room in twenty-five words.
- Draw a concept from the lesson.
- Scan the text to find _____.
- Go to a learning center and _____.
- Classify groups of words.
- Create relationships among the vocabulary terms in the lesson.
- Quiz themselves on the words on a word wall.

> I came right out of the military and would let individuals know to the last second how late she or he was: two minutes and forty-three seconds. They hadn't heard that before, and I didn't know any different. Time was precious in the military, and I felt that way about their instructional time, too. They actually got a kick out of it—or forgave me.
>
> *Laura Moore, 18 years' experience*

- Follow specific directions to star, underline, or circle certain words in a passage.
- Create a cause-and-effect web about an event in the lesson.
- Make a Venn diagram illustrating a concept or relationship in the lesson.
- Write a question about the lesson they will study tomorrow.
- Decide how and when they will complete their homework assignment.
- Find three dissimilar objects and describe what they have in common.

The Last Ten Minutes of Class

You have two goals for the end of class: to have students who are reluctant to leave and to have students retain the information you have just taught them. The last ten minutes of class are the ideal time to accomplish both goals.

The routine you create for the end of class should be predictable but also one that students can look forward to. Here is a simple two-step plan for the end of class that you can follow to make sure that the last few minutes of your class are as productive as all the rest:

- **Step One:** Do an eight-minute closing exercise. Use this brief period to help students retain information by reviewing what you have just taught and by looking ahead to what they will be learning next. Here are some activities that you can adopt or adapt to end your class on a positive note:
  - Have students individually list several things that they have just learned. Have them share this list with a classmate or with the entire group.
  - Ask students to predict what they will learn next.
  - Ask students to predict the meaning of the key terms for the next part of the unit.
  - Have students write a quick explanation of the most interesting aspect of the day's lesson.
  - Hold a quick review, vocabulary practice, or spelling bee.
  - Ask students to explain the directions for their homework. Be sure to ask them to estimate how long it should take them to complete the assignment successfully.
  - Unveil a final thought for the day that you have hidden under a sheet of paper that was taped to the board earlier in the day.
  - Give your students a brief text passage to read and ask them to comment on it.
  - Show students a relevant cartoon or illustration for a quick discussion or recap.
  - Assign an exit slip activity.
- **Step Two:** Implement the two-minute dismissal. After the closing exercise, you should allow two minutes for your students to prepare to be dismissed at your signal. During this time, they should have a routine to follow that includes the following activities:
  - Disposing of trash
  - Stowing away books and materials
  - Checking to make sure they don't leave anything behind

During the last two minutes of class, you should move to the door so that you can speak to students as they leave. This will prevent any last-minute misbehavior and show your students that they have a teacher who cares about them. You should not allow students to congregate at the door or to jump up and bolt when the bell rings. Insist that you will dismiss class and that they should wait for your signal. You should not detain students after the bell has rung. See Teacher Worksheet 4.6 for plans to help you end class effectively.

TEACHER WORKSHEET 4.6

Plans for Ending Class Effectively

Lesson topic: _____ Date: _____

First Eight Minutes

Review activity:

_____
_____
_____
_____
_____

Homework discussion and clarification:

_____
_____
_____
_____
_____

Prediction activity:

_____
_____
_____
_____
_____

Reflection on the day's learning activity:

_____
_____
_____
_____
_____

Last Two Minutes

Students clean their work areas and gather their belongings to prepare to exit. Students exit on a dismissal signal from you.

How to Use Any Time Left at the End of Class

Sometimes, despite your best efforts, there may be a few minutes left at the end of class. Although many teachers may be tempted to allow students to just sit and wait for the bell to signal the end of class, you should consider how you and your students can benefit from these tiny gifts of free time. With just a bit of preparation and planning, you can use even these short moments to connect with your students. In addition to using any of the activities mentioned earlier in this section, here are some ideas for you to consider:

- Show a short video from an inspirational segment on TeacherTube (http:// teachertube.com) or YouTube. (www.youtube.com).
- Keep a list of riddles or jokes to read so that your students can leave class smiling. A good source for this is Riddles.com (www.riddles.com).
- Conduct a quick informal survey. Ask students their opinions about school events, sports, songs, or just about anything that they are interested in outside of school.
- Ask students each to state something new that they have learned during the class or the week.
- Ask students to share their favorites—favorite colors, foods, music, sports teams, _____.
- Ask students to share their pet peeves.
- Ask students their opinions about a class problem.
- Read a biographical paragraph or story to inspire your students.
- Ask students to tell you something that surprised or confused them on the first day of school or when they were younger.

Questions to Discuss with Colleagues

Sharing ideas with colleagues is a helpful way to devise solutions to some of the problems that you must manage successfully at school. Here you will find several topics to open discussions with colleagues about successful instructional practices:

1. Your students continue to talk while you are talking. You have warned them several times but to no avail. What can you do to get their attention focused on you instead of on chatting with one another?

2. Your students are not as accepting of one another's mistakes as you would like for them to be. What can you do to keep them from snickering when a classmate makes a mistake in front of the others?

3. You've noticed that once students finish an assignment or test, they all seem to ask to be excused. What can you do to stop this parade so that only those students who really need to leave class are excused?

4. You have several students who are not motivated by the prospect of making good grades. What should you do to motivate these students to fulfill their academic potential? Who can help you with this? How can you learn more about how to motivate each student?

5. Even though you know the first ten minutes of class are crucial in setting the tone for the rest of it, your students are slow to settle down. They chat and walk around the room and are obviously not in a hurry to get to work. What can you do to make the first ten minutes of your class productive?

Topics to Discuss with a Mentor

Although the topics that new teachers need to discuss with a mentor vary from teacher to teacher and from school to school, there are some that most first-year teachers should be comfortable discussing with a mentor or a trusted colleague. You should ask your mentor about these topics from this section:

- Suggestions for the first and last few minutes of class
- How to show your positive feelings for your students
- How to cope with some of the predictable interruptions at your school
- Suggestions for delivering effective instructions
- Suggestions for improving your classroom leadership skills

Reflection Questions to Guide Your Thinking

1. Think about the ways that you may unintentionally waste your students' time. How guilty are you? What can you do to avoid misuse of instructional time?

2. How effective do you think you are at being a capable classroom leader at this point in your career? What are your weaknesses? What are your strengths? How can you use your strengths to overcome your weaknesses?

3. What is your policy concerning students' leaving the room? What is your school's policy? Are you satisfied with your policy? If not, who can help you with this?

4. Which of the activities in this section would work well with your students? How can you organize them so that you have a quick list of activities at hand when you need to plan instruction?

5. The beginning and end of class are times you can use to your students' advantage. What routines do you have planned to open and close class on a positive and productive note?

SECTION FIVE

Start the School Year Productively

One of the most important aspects of creating the productive classroom environment that you want for your students involves getting the school year off to a great start from the first day onward. Your goal for the start of school is simple: your students should look forward to the rest of the school year because they feel comfortable with you and with their classmates. To achieve this goal, you can use many different strategies. In the rest of this section, you will find some of these strategies divided into four categories: getting ready for a great year, managing the first day, establishing positive relationships, and managing the first week of school.

Get Ready for a Great School Year

Getting ready for a great school year starts before your students ever enter your classroom. In the days leading up to the first day of class, two of the most important tasks that you will have to manage are getting the physical space of your classroom set up and making sure that you present yourself as a confident and competent professional at your school's open house.

Because there are so many tasks that all teachers must complete in the few weeks and days before the beginning of a school term, it is very easy to be overwhelmed. The time line that follows will help you prioritize your responsibilities and avoid being overwhelmed with too much to do in too little time.

A Month before the Term Begins

- Shop the back-to-school sales for supplies.
- Make sure that your wardrobe reflects your professional status.
- Order any supplies your district has allocated money for.

- Gather the other supplies you may need.
- Begin searching online for information about the subjects you will teach.
- Download your district's calendar for the school year.
- Download your state and district curriculum guides.
- Pick up teachers' editions and supplementary materials.
- Begin reading and studying course materials.
- Create your professional goals. (See Section One for help with this.)
- Plan how you will manage the stress that will accompany the changes that you will experience as you start your new career. (See Section One as well as the end of this section for advice on stress management.)

Three Weeks before the Term Begins

- Create a general course overview for the year.
- Join at least one professional organization.
- Start investigating helpful websites and bloggers for advice and encouragement.
- Create broad unit plans for the first grading period.

Two Weeks before the Term Begins

- Make sure that the equipment in your room is in working order.
- Create your class rules and procedures. (See Section Eleven for further information.)
- Put together information for substitute teachers in case you need them.
- Put your classroom in order.
- Set up your desk and files.

One Week before the Term Begins

- Obtain the school forms you will need, such as hall passes or lunch counts.
- Work with a mentor to find answers to your procedural questions.
- Create procedures for daily routines, such as taking attendance, passing out papers, or taking a lunch count.
- Prepare a letter to introduce yourself to parents or guardians. (See Sample 5.1 for a letter template you can adjust to meet your needs.)
- Write out your first two weeks of daily lesson plans. (See Section Nine for tips on writing lesson plans.)
- Prepare a list of alternate plans to use just in case a lesson doesn't work.
- Study your class rosters to learn your students' names.

- Create seating charts.
- Familiarize yourself with the software programs you will be expected to use for class business, such as attendance or grades, during the school year.

The Day before School Starts

- Finish any last-minute tasks.
- Ask any last-minute questions.
- Exercise, eat well, and get enough rest.
- Plan how you will to manage your work-related stress.
- Pack your materials the night before so that you can start the day confidently.

Classroom Safety Issues

As you begin creating the classroom space you want for your students, it's important to remember that maintaining classroom safety is one of the most important tasks that we have. After all, the well-being of a classroom full of students depends on our diligence. It's a good idea for you, as a new teacher, to learn about school safety by following your district's safety procedures, observing other teachers, asking questions, and using common sense. Follow these suggestions to make your classroom secure for you and for your students:

- Check classroom windows and screens to be sure they are in good working condition.
- Check all outlets. When you do plug in equipment, make sure all electrical cords are secure.
- Keep your classroom as clean as you can to reduce the spread of contagious diseases.
- Use only cleaning supplies that meet your school's policies and are not harmful to students.
- If possible, teach with your door closed. You will minimize disruptions from outside your classroom.
- Don't keep matches, sharp scissors, or other potentially harmful items where your students can take them.
- Discourage your students from taking such items as staplers from your desk. Instead, provide materials just for their use in another part of the room and teach students to respect your property.
- If your classroom is not in use, keep it locked. No room should be left unattended.
- Make it easy for students to move about. Space desks carefully, and don't block the exits to your classroom.

- Stabilize all bookcases and other tall pieces of equipment so that they can't tip over. Make sure all objects on them are also placed securely.

- Keep your personal belongings, confidential documents, and any money that you collect during the day securely locked out of sight.

- Never give a student keys to your classroom or car.

- Learn your school's procedures for such emergencies as fire drills, disaster drills, or intruders in the building.

- When students say that they are feeling unwell, take the matter seriously.

- Don't use hard candy as a reward or treat. It is too easy for students to choke on it.

- Never leave your students unsupervised.

- Report suspected weapons or potential acts of violence immediately.

- Be aware of the procedures you are to follow to assist your students who have a chronic illness.

- If you suspect that a student has been abused, act at once.

- Make your classroom as orderly as possible. Teach and enforce your rules and procedures until everyone understands what you expect of them.

- Monitor your students at all times. Be especially careful when they are working together on activities that require lots of movement.

- Take a stand against bullying in your classroom. Make it easy for students to talk to you if they are the victims of bullies.

- When students leave the room with a hall pass, be alert to when they return. You are responsible for their safety.

- Make it clear that you will not tolerate racial, cultural, or other prejudices.

Evaluate Your Classroom

When you go to your classroom for the first time, you will be able to save time if you work efficiently to plan how you want to set it up.

- You will save time if you take a digital camera, paper, pencil, and a tape measure with you on your first visit.

- Photograph the room thoroughly so that you can make plans when you are not at school.

- Measure storage areas, windows, shelves, bulletin boards, interactive boards, and whiteboards.

- Locate the electrical outlets, telephone jacks, and other electronic connections. Look for equipment and furniture that needs repair or that could pose safety concerns.

- Survey the room for items or areas that have the potential to distract your students.

- Count the student desks, tables, chairs, and computers to determine if you have enough for your students. Make note of any necessary repairs.
- Survey the room to make sure you have these essential classroom items:
  - Keys to the door and any lockable cabinets
  - Cables for computers and other electronic equipment
  - Extension cords
  - Emergency procedures booklet/equipment
  - Operating instructions for the heating and cooling systems
  - Windows and blinds that are clean and in good repair
  - An American flag on display
  - At least one pencil sharpener
  - A clock
  - Sufficient lighting
  - Bookshelves
  - A desk and chair for the teacher
  - Empty and usable file cabinets
  - A trash container
  - A recycle bin
  - A computer for the teacher to use
  - A classroom phone
  - An intercom system

Prepare Your Classroom for Students

Your students will thrive in an environment in which you take their needs seriously and in which they feel valued. When you create a classroom that invites students to join in a learning community, you are reaching out to your students in a tangible way. An inviting classroom sends a clear message to your students that they are important to you—that you approve of them.

Creating a safe and welcoming place where students can comfortably work together is worth the hard work and energy it takes to complete such tasks as shoving furniture, taping down cords, and decorating bulletin boards. Preparing a classroom does take time, however. Plan to spend several hours in your room while you are setting it up.

One of the best choices for a teacher who wants to create an inviting classroom is to make the classroom reflect the interests and concerns of the students, not those of the teacher. Too often, teachers make the mistake of decorating their classroom beautifully but with items that appeal to their own tastes instead of their students'. With creativity and careful planning, it is possible to create a welcoming classroom without spending a great deal of money. Here are some suggestions that will help you get started:

Use the Entire Room

- Decorate your classroom with student work. Students feel a sense of ownership and pride in a classroom where their work is displayed. Be sure to display everyone's work. If you hang only the best work, students might feel that you are playing favorites, which, of course, would be harmful to the class environment. You can display all sorts of student work, not just creative projects or A papers. Have students list facts on bright note cards, and then post them near the door as a review. Post drawings, notes, sketches—anything that shows how much you value your students' efforts. Students will enjoy seeing a changing display of things they have created far more than purchased posters.

- Set aside an area for class business. You can keep your students informed and involved by posting such items as assignments, due dates, school announcements, and other shared business. Your students should participate in keeping this area up to date, if they are old enough to do so.

- Set aside an area for tracking progress. If you have class competitions, students should see the results displayed. For example, if you want to improve the way your students complete homework assignments, create poster-size bar graphs to record each day's results. Making progress visible is a powerful way to keep students on the right path.

- Set aside an area for motivation. Students could illustrate words of wisdom from the Internet, books they have read, or song lyrics. Consider using a giant graphic of brainstormed mottoes for success to remind students how much you care about their future.

- Create areas where students can work with enrichment and remediation materials. Use trays, baskets, large envelopes, or rolling carts to store materials for students to use after they have finished their assignments. In this area, you could include a variety of items that interest your students, such as books, puzzles, art supplies, or manipulatives.

Create Quick and Effective Bulletin Boards

Try these simple tricks to make the bulletin boards in your classroom effective connection builders:

- Use wrapping paper as a background. Staple it into place at the start of the term and you will not have to replace it the rest of the year.

- Borders can be as simple as strips of construction paper, or they can be more creative. Cut out borders from old newspapers, magazines, wrapping paper, or even maps.

- Save time when you print out the messages you need to display using a large font, and cut out the letters.

- Use adhesive-backed hooks to hang three dimensional objects.

- Many websites have helpful tips for using the bulletin boards in your room to connect with your students. In particular, you can use the following sites to search for good ideas to adapt for your students:

  - **Kathy Schrock's Guide to Everything (www.schrockguide.net/bulletin-boards.html).** Here teachers can find a comprehensive list of sites, images, and books devoted to bulletin boards.

  - **Pinterest (www.pinterest.com).** The most popular site for bulletin board ideas of all types, on Pinterest you can find bulletin board ideas for almost every grade level or subject.

  - **The Teacher's Corner (www.theteacherscorner.net).** This award-winning site offers many seasonally themed bulletin board ideas as well as bulletin board ideas of general interest.

TRAFFIC FLOW CONSIDERATIONS

Traffic flow in a classroom is more important than many novice teachers realize when they are getting ready for the school year. For example, if you place your trash can near the door, the stapler on your desk at the back of the room, and a tray to collect completed work near the front, students will wander all over your room just to throw away trash, staple their papers, and turn in their work.

Carefully consider the routine activities your students will perform before you set up your room so that you can minimize distractions and interruptions. Some of these routine activities could include:

- Entering class
- Checking the calendar
- Checking the clock
- Using hand sanitizer
- Checking the board
- Passing in papers
- Speaking with you privately
- Using a computer
- Picking up supplies
- Disposing of trash
- Sharpening pencils
- Using a stapler

Seating Arrangements That Work at the Start of the Term

Arranging student desks so that your students can focus on their work is important for their success. During the year, you will probably change the desk arrangement several times or even provide flexible seating. Until you get to know your students and have helped them settle into the routines and expectations that you have for the class, it is a good idea to keep your seating arrangements as manageable as possible. To arrange student desks for an optimum effect, keep these pointers in mind:

- Arrange desks so that you can see every student's face. Every student should also be able to see you with no difficulty.
- Retain the ability to move freely around the room.
- Keep desks away from attractive graffiti spots, such as bulletin boards, window ledges, or walls.
- Avoid placing desks near distractions, such as a pencil sharpener or a computer monitor with an interesting screen.

THREE COMMON STUDENT DESK ARRANGEMENTS

Although there seems to be an endless number of ways to arrange student desks, there are three common ones that many teachers find particularly effective in helping students stay on task all class long.

Traditional Rows

Many teachers begin the year with desks in traditional rows. The desks can either be in horizontal or vertical rows. In both arrangements, students face the board and not one another. This sends the message that you want your students to focus their attention on you and not on classmates.

Traditional rows at the start of the year also make it easy for you to learn your students' names. The traditional row configuration allows you to see every student and for the students to see you as you work from the front of the classroom. Many teachers who routinely use other desk arrangements often move their students into traditional rows for testing to reduce the possibility of cheating.

Whole-Group Horseshoe

In this configuration, the students on the two sides of a horseshoe face one another, while the students seated in the connecting row at the back of the horseshoe face the front of the classroom. This arrangement is suitable for class discussions because it encourages students to talk with one another.

Pairs or Triads

Seating students in permanent pairs or triads makes it very easy for them to work together. This configuration facilitates the formation of collaborative study groups because students grow to depend on and support their group partners. It is ideal for allowing students to be able to work together as well as getting them to focus on you when appropriate.

The Why and How of Seating Charts

No matter how old your students are, seating charts are necessary. Seating charts solve many problems and prevent many more. If you use a seating chart, here's how you and your students will benefit:

- Students from the same neighborhood will not choose to only sit next to one another, avoiding what might have been an obvious ethnic separation.
- Timid students will have the same seating opportunities that aggressive ones do.
- Students will not argue with one another over which desk belongs to whom.
- Unmotivated students can be moved from the back of the room to a place where you can more easily engage them in lessons or offer assistance.
- Easily distracted students can be seated in a place where it will be easier for them to stay on task.
- Students with special needs can sit in a location where their needs can be accommodated without calling attention to them.
- Students with medical problems can be accommodated as necessary.
- Taller students will not block the view of smaller ones.

Begin the school year with a preliminary seating chart that will make it easier for you to learn your students' names. In a few days, after you get to know your students, you should make up a seating chart based on other factors. Here's how:

- **Step One:** Begin by drawing a diagram of your room in which each desk is represented by a rectangle.
- **Step Two:** Using your class roster, pencil the names of your students on your diagram. Begin with the students who must sit in a certain area of the room due to medical issues or the terms of their IEP or 504 Plan.
- **Step Three:** After you have considered students with special needs, move on to the students who misbehave in their current seats. Place them where they can focus on you and their work rather than on having fun with their classmates.
- **Step Four:** Finally, move the rest of your students. Do your best to find each student a seat that will be comfortable for his or her size and temperament.

Flexible Seating

Although the idea of providing flexible seating options has customarily been more common in the younger grades than in secondary classrooms, it is a concept that is gaining in popularity in all grade levels as school districts recognize the importance of activity and student choice in promoting student achievement. In classrooms where there is a flexible seating arrangement, teachers create *student work spaces* in place of the traditional rows of student desks.

Just a quick search of online images for classrooms with flexible seating arrangements reveals the endless possibilities and variations available to teachers interested in flexible seating. In a typical classroom with flexible seating, you could find arrangements that include the following:

- Soft cushions, beanbags, and chairs of all types
- Worktables for students to share
- Cubbies and bins for shared materials as well as for individual student storage
- A small work space area for the teacher
- Rugs and carpets to delineate specific work areas
- Balance balls, wobble chairs, stools, and other options for student seating

Instead of being expected to sit quietly for long periods at a desk, students in classrooms where there is flexible seating can choose to sit, kneel, stand, lean, lie on the floor, or select another option their teacher designs for them. There are several unmistakable advantages to flexible seating arrangements in classrooms. In classrooms with flexible seating, students can

- Choose the work space that appeals to them
- Learn to make good choices about how to work efficiently
- Move around and be more active as they work
- Be comfortable instead of restrained as they learn
- Remain on task while working because they are engaged and focused

Although the benefits of flexible seating arrangements are unmistakable, there are some important negative aspects to consider, especially for first-year teachers:

- Other teachers may not be as open to change as you are and therefore not able to offer help and suggestions based on their experience.
- Switching from a traditional classroom arrangement where the furniture is already provided for you can create storage problems as you eliminate furniture.
- Your school district may not provide you with the funds to purchase the new equipment that you need, and the cost for many teachers (even those who are thrifty and inventive) can be significant.
- Classroom management problems may be an issue at first as you and your students adapt to new spaces and ways of thinking about how to work productively.
- Because many students with special needs require preferential seating, it is not always easy to provide those necessary accommodations.
- Flexible seating requires experimentation, tweaking, and careful planning at a time when you are already dealing with many other classroom issues, such as instructional planning, building positive relationships, and classroom management.

Despite these negatives, the advantages of flexible seating arrangements are unmistakable. If you decide to use flexible seating, here are a few suggestions to make the process a bit easier:

- Make changes very gradually and after careful consideration. Add in a shared work space. Provide a comfortable chair or two. As students adjust to these and as you learn how to manage them well, you can then make other changes.

- Safety should be a first concern. Furniture that has been purchased by a school district has been vetted for safety issues, while furniture you purchase has not. Some districts do not allow teachers to use classroom furniture that has not been purchased by the district. Check with your supervisors about the changes that you are planning to make before you begin implementing them.

- Expect to rethink classroom management. Different spaces require different behavior. What was unacceptable behavior in a traditional space may not be unacceptable in a space where there is more student movement and interaction.

- Continue to make your classroom as transparent as possible. Make sure your supervisors and the parents or guardians of your students are kept apprised of the changes you make in your classroom.

- Consider assigning spaces and rotating students through the different options at first to reduce student conflicts (they are likely to argue over seating choices), to expose students to the various work spaces, and to reduce student anxiety about having to compete with classmates for spaces.

- Help students make sound decisions about how and where they are most comfortable working. Student choice still requires teacher guidance.

- Students with special needs, IEPs, 504 Plans, or other accommodations that require preferential seating need options that allow for those accommodations. You cannot disregard this when planning new arrangements.

- Enlist other teachers who may want to create flexible seating arrangements in their classrooms so that you can share ideas and resources.

- Don't overspend your own funds. Instead, be patient and look for bargains. If you are committed to flexible seating, work with your district to fund your classroom changes instead of paying for them yourself.

Welcome Your Students to a New Year

When you begin planning for the first day or the first week of a new school year, you will probably focus your efforts on classroom management and instructional activities. Although these are crucial to the success of your students, making your students feel welcomed in your classroom is just as important. When students feel that they are valued and included, they will find it easier to cooperate, to work, and to learn.

Fortunately, there are many ways to make students of all ages feel that they welcomed at school:

- Play music as they enter the room. An excellent source for music for your classroom is Pandora (www.pandora.com). At Pandora's website, you will be able to browse musical genres that will appeal to students. You can use instrumental or classical music or even music with lyrics suitable for school.
- Make sure that every student is quickly seated in the right spot with as little confusion as possible.
- Smile at individuals and at the entire group.
- When students enter the room, have an interesting activity for them to do right away.
- If students do not have school supplies, lend them what they need without fuss.
- Make sure students know the names of several of their classmates by the end of class.
- Having students interact with classmates on the first day sends a positive message about the importance of teamwork in your class.
- If you need transitions between activities, consider showing a motivational or intriguing PowerPoint or movie clip.
- Talk to your students about how you are nervous and that you predict that they are as well. Discuss your shared anxieties.
- If students will be moving to other classrooms, make sure everyone knows where to go. Passing out school maps and assigning buddies to find other classrooms are both good ideas.
- Wear a name tag. If appropriate, ask students to wear name tags as well for at least part of class.
- Ask for their advice on solving a classroom problem, such as how to store materials or remember the schedule for the next day.
- Make sure you are organized and prepared for class so that you can focus on helping your students.
- Assign buddies to students who may be new to the school.
- If students have a written assignment, provide the paper. Odd shapes and colors are always more fun for students than lined paper.
- Compliment the group throughout class and especially at the end.

How to Hold a Successful Open House

Your school district will probably arrange several opportunities for parents or guardians and teachers to meet during the school year. You may have "Meet Your Teacher Day" before school starts so that parents or guardians and students can introduce themselves to you.

Some parents or guardians may just stop by your classroom to introduce themselves, especially at the start of the term or if their children have special needs. Although these opportunities are helpful to students, parents or guardians, and teachers who want to work well together, they don't have the impact of an open house. During an open house, parents or guardians can come to school to meet their children's teachers. In some places, this event is referred to as "Back to School Night." No matter which name your district uses, this meeting can generate goodwill for you all year long. However stressed you may feel about an open house, it is your chance to connect with parents or guardians positively and professionally. It is an effective way to build a strong team of support for your students and an excellent opportunity to generate the goodwill that will sustain you in the days ahead, particularly when some of your students need extra help and guidance. In the following pages, you will find information designed to help you manage an open house successfully. You will learn a few general guidelines, what to include in your presentation, and how to inspire confidence. You will also find a suggested time line as you prepare to meet the families of your students.

A Few General Guidelines

- At an open house, expect to meet many parents or guardians. The number will vary with your school population and how successfully your school district has promoted the event.

- Prepare to give a brief presentation that will probably be five to fifteen minutes long, depending on your school's schedule.

- Avoid talking about specific students and their concerns; instead, you will need to set up appointments for later with parents or guardians who want to discuss their children or your class policies in more detail.

- Clean up your classroom. Parents or guardians want to see a spotless room that shows that you are a well-organized professional and in control of your environment. You may not be able to do anything about graffiti from previous years, but you should make the room as attractive and clean as possible.

- Plan and practice your presentation. This is not the time to try your skill at winging it.

- Start collecting student work on the first day of class and display it on the walls of your classroom. Parents or guardians enjoy seeing their child's work on display, no matter how old the child.

- Prepare a handout with general information about the course, your homework policy, important dates, classroom policies, and your contact information.

- Have copies of course materials available.

- Prepare a sign-up sheet and place it near the door. Include a column for students' names as well as one for adults' names so that you will be able to match parents or guardians to their children.

- Dress in your professional best to present yourself as a competent educator.

What to Include in Your Presentation

- Introduce the general topics and skills you will cover in class before the end of the term. Give a quick overview so that parents or guardians will not be surprised about what their children are learning. Explain your class rules, policies, and procedures.

- Inform parents or guardians of any major assignments and approximately when these will be assigned. Parents or guardians should have warning about such projects as major term papers, class trips, or science fairs.

- Ask parents or guardians to contact you if a problem arises. Make sure you give out your school voice mail number, e-mail, and phone number so that parents or guardians can contact you if a problem arises.

How to Inspire Confidence

- Meet parents or guardians at the door. Pleasantly greet any latecomers.

- Begin your presentation promptly. Be upbeat, enthusiastic, and positive.

- Be very careful not to mention any problems you have with specific students. Protect their privacy, and do not embarrass their parents or guardians.

- Plan to run out of time. Create a presentation that will last the entire time that you have allotted for it. If you open the floor for questions, you may run into a sticky situation in which parents or guardians can attack you for reasons you may not be prepared to defend in a large group.

- As parents or guardians enter your classroom, have them begin by completing Parent or Guardian Worksheet 5.1. Not only will you learn a great deal of useful information about your students but also their parents or guardians will appreciate the opportunity to tell you what they believe is important for you to know.

TIME LINE FOR A SUCCESSFUL OPEN HOUSE

Even though an open house lasts for only a short time, you will need to spend some time in advance of the event making sure that your presentation goes smoothly. To ensure that you use your time wisely, you can follow the time line provided here:

One Week in Advance

- Send home open house announcements if your school does not.
- Display student work.
- Begin preparing your presentation.
- Create and photocopy handouts.

Three Days Before

- Make up the electronic portion of your presentation if you plan to present a Power-Point or use some other electronic display.
- Create a sign-in sheet.

Two Days Before

- Begin practicing your presentation.

One Day Before

- Practice your presentation again; you cannot be too polished.
- Begin straightening your classroom.
- Get enough rest for the long day tomorrow.

On the Day of the Open House

- Dress professionally.
- Adopt a positive attitude.
- Tidy the classroom one final time.
- Make sure all equipment is working.
- Put the sign-in sheet near the door with a pencil nearby.
- Have textbooks, materials, and hand-outs ready.

Reach out to parents and guardians at the beginning of the year. As many as you can. Not all caregivers can attend Back to School Night. But establishing a positive relationship from the start can make a huge difference. I've sent personal thank-you notes to each parent or guardian who attended Back to School Night with an observation or two about his or her child. And then followed up with those who couldn't attend with the same. If you do this early enough, there is something encouraging to say to each family.

Jennifer Burns, 13 years' experience

Please Tell Me about Your Child

Please use the space here to tell me the information that I need to teach your child successfully. You should feel free to include past school experiences, medical issues, how your child learns best, or anything else that may help me be an effective teacher for your child.

_____

_____

_____

_____

_____

_____

_____

_____

_____

_____

_____

_____

_____

_____

_____

_____

_____

_____

_____

_____

_____

_____

_____

_____

_____

_____

_____

From *The First-Year Teacher's Survival Guide, 4th Edition*, by Julia G. Thompson. Copyright © 2018 by John Wiley & Sons, Inc. Reproduced by permission.

How to Manage the First Day

The first day of class can be an intimidating experience for students. They worry about many things on this day: if they will get lost trying to find the classroom, if they will have friendly classmates, if they will know what to do once class starts, and if their teacher will be approachable, just to name a few of their worries.

The first day of class can be intimidating for teachers, too. Not only will you meet your students for the first time but also it is probably the busiest day of the year for any teacher. You must get everyone settled in comfortably while managing the first-day paperwork and all the other pressing tasks that are required of classroom teachers. By using your imagination to put yourself in your students' places and by working to overcome your own anxieties to plan and deliver engaging instructional activities, you will be able to make the first day of class pleasantly memorable for you and your students.

Overcome Those First-Day Jitters

There are many things you can do to handle the jitters that beginning a new school term can cause in even the most self-assured teacher. The most stressful part of your day will probably be sometime in the first half hour of class, when you realize that your students are nervous, cooperative, pleasant, and *depending on you*. To calm yourself, try an assortment of tips and techniques from this list:

- Accept the fact that you will feel nervous and excited on the first day of school. Many veteran teachers do, too. Denying your concerns will not help you deal successfully with them.

- Boost your confidence by dressing well. Teachers traditionally dress up a bit on the first day—even the ones who slouched around in jeans before school started.

- Pack a good lunch and force yourself to eat it when lunchtime arrives. Avoid having too much caffeine at breakfast.

- Ride to work with a colleague, if you can. Carpooling on the first day will give you a chance to share your fears and to provide mutual support.

- Pack your book bag the night before and leave it by the door so that you can just grab it as you leave.

- Look over the list of your students' names one last time the night before school starts. You will feel more confident if you can pronounce them correctly.

- Plan more work than you believe your students can possibly accomplish—and then plan some more. It is truly terrifying to run out of work for your students on the very first day of school.

- Have extra supplies on hand so that every student can complete assignments with no trouble.

- Arrive early. You do not have to be so early that you help the custodians unlock the building, but you should be early enough that you do not feel rushed in finishing any last-minute chores.

- Remind yourself that the chances of major disruptions are slim on the first day of class; students tend to be on their very best behavior during the first few days of school.

What to Do on the First Day: Your Priorities

As you begin thinking about the first day of class, you should decide how to convince your students that you are the best teacher they will ever have. Your first-year jitters may be bad, but theirs are probably worse as they worry that they will not have a good teacher or a good year.

Because it is so important that the first day of school be an encouraging experience for your students, you must present yourself to your students in as positive a manner as possible. This will be easy for you if you focus your energy on the following six important priorities:

Priority One: Take Charge of Your Class

- Even if you are overcome with stage fright, you must conquer your personal feelings and pretend to be confident and self-assured. Sometimes, by pretending to be confident, you can begin to convince yourself that you are.

- Have a seating chart ready so that you can show students to their respective seats and get them started on their opening exercise at once. Have an assignment on the board, or give students a handout as they enter the room.

- Before the term begins, when you have made up your introduction, class rules, and expectations, consider having a friend record you presenting them. You can really have fun with this if you film your presentation at the beach, on a boat, or even in your own backyard. This will allow you to be creative and to make a polished presentation. When school starts, show the video and give your students a handout on the class expectations to fill in as they watch and listen. Showing a video instead of having to remember details on an already stressful day makes the day easier for you as well.

Priority Two: Calm Your Students' Fears

- Stand at the door of your classroom and welcome students to your class. Wear a bright name tag. Make sure to prominently display your name and room number so that students and their parents or guardians can be sure that they are in the right place.

- Smile. Look glad to see every student. Greet each one pleasantly, using his or her name if you can.

- Teach your first lesson as if it is the most important lesson you will teach all year. In many ways, it is. Your students should feel that they learned something interesting and that they will continue to learn something in your class every day.

Priority Three: Introduce Yourself

- Because you want the first day of class to go well and because you want to control the amount of speculation about you, the new teacher, you should introduce yourself so that students can start to connect with you. You should select the following information that would be most appropriate for your students:
  - How to spell your last name
  - Your title (Mr., Ms., Mrs., Dr.)
  - Where you went to college
  - Where you grew up
  - Why you are looking forward to working with them
  - The positive things you have heard about them
  - The positive things you have heard about the school
  - What your favorite subject was in school
  - Why you chose to be a teacher

Priority Four: Engage Your Students' Minds

- Design fast-paced, interesting instruction that will appeal to students with a variety of learning styles and engage their critical thinking skills. Solving puzzles, completing a challenge, quick writing assignments (if students can write), and other brief activities often work well.
- Consider a lesson that will allow you to assess your students' readiness levels as well as give them an overview of the skills they will learn or the material they will cover during the term. Make sure that the lesson is one that encourages them to be active and not just one that requires them to listen passively.

Priority Five: Begin to Teach the Class Routines

- Teaching acceptable school behavior is part of what teachers do and is certainly part of what students expect from their teachers. For example, when it is time for students to turn in the day's written assignment, take a minute to show them the procedure for passing in papers that you will expect them to follow all term.
- If students lack supplies to do the assignment, lend them what they need for class and gently remind them that they will need to have paper and a pencil in the future.
- Instead of harsh reprimands, stick to gentle reminders instead.

Priority Six: Begin to Build a Classroom Community

- Even on the first day of class, your students will view themselves as members of a classroom group. (See Section Six for more information on creating positive relationships.) You can enhance this natural tendency by using inclusive words, such as *our* or *us,* when referring to the class.

- Ask for their help in such routine tasks as passing out materials, tidying the room at the end of an activity, or helping one another.

How to Get Everyone in the Right Seat on the First Day of Class

Although having students sit in assigned seats on the first day of class is an excellent strategy for many reasons, it is not always easy to bring about. Your goal should be that students can quickly find their seats without confusion or embarrassment. Although this seems difficult at first, with just a bit of planning and preparation, it can be done so easily that all your students can be comfortably seated almost as soon as the bell to start class sounds. Here's how:

- **Step One:** Arrange the desks in your classroom in the configuration that you would like them to remain in for the first few days of class.

- **Step Two:** Number each desk. You can use a bright, easy-to-read label on a top corner of the desk or on the back of the chair, or you can write the number on the desk itself. If you write the number on the label instead of typing it, be sure to use a pen that does not smear.

- **Step Three:** Print out a roster of your students' names. If you do not want to use an alphabetical list, then use the roster to type a personalized list.

- **Step Four:** Go through any information about special needs or other requirements that you should take into consideration when assigning seats.

- **Step Five:** After you have decided where each student will sit, put the number of the assigned desk next to the student's name on the roster.

- **Step Six:** As students file into the classroom, meet them at the door. Ask them to find their names and seat numbers on the roster. They should then be able to walk to their desks without any hesitation.

If you teach students with special needs severe enough that this strategy would not be feasible, then consider having another teacher or adult help you seat those students on the first day of class. If your students are very young, they can still find their seats if you give them a colored shape (such as a star or a heart or a ball) and ask them to match it to the one on their desk. After everyone is settled, you can collect the shapes to reuse with other classes.

Activities for the First Day

In addition to an overview of the day's lesson and class expectations, your first day of class can include many other activities to engage students in meaningful work. Using the planning template in Teacher Worksheet 5.1. will make it easier for you to ensure that the first day of school will be a productive and positive one for your students. When you are trying to decide just what you want your students to do on the first day, consider some of these activities:

- Photograph students on the first day of class. This is a good way to begin your class scrapbook.

- Show examples of the supplies students need.

- Pass out colorful paper and ask students to write what they can contribute to make the class better for everyone. Display the papers in a giant collage.

- Issue textbooks or materials and supplies and have students skim through them, looking for items in a treasure hunt.

- Have students work with a partner, telling that person one thing that they can do well and one thing that they would like to learn how to do. Have partners introduce one another to the class by sharing this information.

- Ask students to write you a brief note, telling you three things you need to know about them so that you can teach them well.

- Place a large sheet of paper on the wall. Hand students old newspapers or magazines and have them tear out words and photos that describe their strengths, interests, and talents. Glue the photos and words in place to create an instant piece of art that will interest every student.

- Have students jot down what they already know about the subject you are teaching and then share this information with the class.

- Have students fill out the student information form in Student Worksheet 5.1.

- Give students handouts with questions directing them to find out what they have in common with their classmates. Some possible areas to explore are hometowns, hobbies, favorite movies, pets, and sports. Go beyond the obvious and include attitudes for success, goals, or other personal traits.

- Ask older students to recount a memory from their earlier first days of school.

- Have students write exit slips explaining what they learned in class on their first day.

Planning Template for the First Day

Although not all these items may be applicable to your class and to your students, this template can give you some idea of how to plan for your first day.

Opening welcome exercise (Time allotted: _____):

_____

_____

Supplies, materials, and books to be issued (Time allotted: _____):

_____

_____

Student information forms and inventories to be used (Time allotted: _____):

_____

_____

Rules, policies, and procedures (Time allotted: _____):

_____

_____

_____

_____

_____

_____

Introduction of self (Time allotted: _____):

_____

_____

Welcome activity (Time allotted: _____):

_____

_____

Forms to be sent home (Time allotted: _____):

_____

_____

(continued on next page)

From *The First-Year Teacher's Survival Guide, 4th Edition*, by Julia G. Thompson. Copyright © 2018 by John Wiley & Sons, Inc. Reproduced by permission.

(continued from previous page)

Fees to be collected (Time allotted: _____):

_____

_____

Activities to help students connect (Time allotted: _____):

_____

_____

Lesson (Time allotted: _____):

Teacher input:

_____

_____

_____

_____

_____

_____

Student activity:

_____

_____

_____

_____

_____

_____

Closing (Time allotted: _____):

_____

_____

_____

_____

_____

_____

_____

First-Day-of-School Welcome Packet

One of the best ways to get your students off to a good start is to provide each one with a folder containing the many papers he or she will need on the first day of school. Even though many students may come to school prepared to manage the numerous documents they will receive on the first day, some will not be prepared. It's wise to help all students organize their papers in a folder. Here are some suggestions for how to make that first-day-of-school packet appealing and helpful for all students in your class, no matter their grade level:

- Because the folders you send home filled with the various first-day forms and documents can then be used all year to organize individual student information, encourage your students to personalize their folders before they return them. This will also provide you with insight into their interests and skills. You can then use these folders all term to store each student's documents, such as notes from home or sample work.

- Sadly, not all students will see their parents or guardians after school on the first day of class, yet there will probably be many forms for parents or guardians to sign. If you allow students to return forms during the first few days of school instead of the next day, you will reduce their anxiety about not being able to complete this seemingly simple task.

- One good way to guarantee that students will return all the papers that need to be signed is to offer a small reward for those who do it within a few days.

- If you create a spreadsheet with a column for each form that needs to be returned and a row for each student, you will be able to check off the forms quickly as students return them.

WHAT YOU CAN INCLUDE IN STUDENT PACKETS

In addition to the various forms that your school will require you to send home, you may consider including these items:

- A student inventory of interests or even learning style preferences to learn more about each of your students.

- A parent or guardian inventory, such as the one in Parent or Guardian Worksheet 5.1 shown earlier in this section.

- An independent assignment for students to begin as soon as they find their seats. This can be a form to complete, a puzzle, an inventory, or any other activity that will engage their attention while you assist other students.

- You should also include a letter to parents or guardians, such as the one in Sample 5.1, that
  - Tells a bit about your experience in education
  - Gives information about how they can contact you

- Requests their support
- Explains the kinds of work they can expect to see their child doing all year
- Explains the grading scale
- Describes the supplies their child will need for class
- Explains your homework policy
- States the positive expectations you have for the year ahead

How to Establish Positive Relationships Right Away

As many veteran teachers would agree, the most important responsibility that any teacher has on the first day of school is to establish a positive relationship with students. No matter how exciting the lesson or well behaved your students are, if they leave dreading the rest of the year with you, then the first day of class was a failure.

Deliberately planning how to connect with your students and to help them connect with one another on the first day of class is a positive first step to take. In the information that follows, you will learn how to begin the process of connecting with your students. Although the information you'll find here deals with the start of school, you will find much more about building relationships in Section Six.

> One of my professors in an education class said that years after students leave school, they will not remember what information I taught them, but they *will* remember how I treated them. That has stuck with me, and I think about it every single day that I teach.
>
> *Betsy Jones, 12 years' experience*

Connect with Your Students on the First Day

Although the first day of class will seem to fly by in a haze of activity, connecting with students is still a priority. Savvy teachers know that they can't just set aside five minutes for this and then check it off their to-do lists. Instead, the activities that you use to build positive relationships with your students should be woven into the fabric of the day. Here are some straightforward strategies you can adapt for your classroom on the first day of school:

- Let your joy in being with your students show. Be enthusiastic, friendly, inclusive, and upbeat. If you are not glad to be there, your students will not be either.
- Use your class rosters to learn students' names as quickly as you can. Being able to call students by name will boost your confidence as well as help you connect.
- Plan an engaging activity that showcases an aspect of the subject material that your students will find intriguing. Allowing your enjoyment and interest to show as you present this material will make it easier for students to connect with you.
- Make a to-do list so that the paperwork that you must submit on the first day of class is organized efficiently and will not deflect your attention from your students.

Sample 5.1

Introductory Letter to Parents or Guardians

Dear Parents or Guardians,

Let me introduce myself. I am a graduate of _____ with a degree in _____, and I am looking forward to a new school term as your child's teacher. This year will be an exciting time for all of us. We will study _____ in preparation for the successful completion of the state's standardized tests next spring. I have planned many activities throughout the course of the year that are designed to help your child succeed academically, not only this year but also in the future.

Students and their parents or guardians are naturally curious about the amount and types of homework to be assigned this term. There will be homework assignments on _____ nights. You should expect to see your child spending _____ minutes reviewing, reading, working on projects, or studying. A copy of the weekly schedule will be given to each student to keep in his or her binder as well as posted on _____. In addition, students are expected to copy their assignments into their assignment notebooks at the start of class each day.

When you have questions or wish to talk with me about your child, please feel free to e-mail me at _____ or to call me at school. Our number is _____.

I am looking forward to working with my new students this year. I am also looking forward to meeting you and working with you to help your child succeed.

Best wishes,

_____

- Schedule brain breaks if the class is long enough that your students grow restless. Talk to students about how you use brain breaks to help them be successful students. (See Section Twelve for more information about brain breaks.)

- Keep any interventions and redirections as low key as possible. Spare students embarrassment on the first day of class.

- Greet your students at the door as they enter, and stand at the door to say goodbye and to wish them well as they leave.

Help Students Connect with One Another on the First Day

Although you can and should help students connect to one another all term long, it is not always easy to fit this in on the first day of school, even though it is one of your most important responsibilities. There is often not enough time to arrange for lengthy team-building activities. Instead, you can build in various short activities that help students learn a little about one another as a foundation for the team building that will take place all year. Here are a few brief connection activities to consider for the first day:

- Give students sticky notes, and have them write their names and a fact about themselves on the note. They are then to put the sticky note on themselves and to mingle for three minutes. At the end, post the notes so that everyone can read them.

- Ask students to line up by birthday month and day, by eye color, or by some other appropriate criteria.

- Ask students to mingle and to learn the first and last names of five classmates. After they have mingled, group students in pairs. They then need to teach those five names to their partners.

- Place students in a large circle and have a soft foam or inflatable beach ball ready. Ask students to toss the ball to a classmate who must say his or her name upon catching the ball. Continue around the circle until everyone has had a chance to speak.

- Assign students to work with a partner. Ask them to share three facts about themselves with their partners. They then move to join another set of two students, where each student will introduce his or her partner to the others.

- Do a quick survey of favorites by asking students to stand as soon as you say their favorites. You can call out foods, sports teams, colors, musicians, or other popular topics.

- Ask students to stand in groups of five. Ask them to learn the names of the students in their groups by playing a name chain game where they must correctly repeat everyone's names.

- Give students three minutes to prepare a thirty-second talk about something that is important to them. At the end of three minutes, ask them to join other students to form a three-person group. Time them as they give their talk to their groups.

- An ever-popular activity that students of all ages can enjoy is to write notes to their future selves. Pass out note cards, and ask students to record their names and their impressions of their first day. Collect them at the end of class, and place them in a container to be opened on the last day of class.

How to Help Your Students Look Forward to the Rest of the Year

One of the most important tasks that you have on the first day of class is to make sure that your students leave looking forward to the rest of the year. Even if the first day does not go as smoothly as you would like, don't worry. Most students are willing to be understanding of their teacher's missteps on the first day if you have made a sincere effort to connect with them and to ensure their well-being and ease. Here are several quick ways to make sure that your students leave your classroom looking forward to an enjoyable year ahead:

- Don't promise what you can't deliver, but if you are aware of special events and other interesting activities planned for your grade level or subject matter, tell students about them. Mention such activities as the field trips that they will take, guest speakers, or various class or schoolwide celebrations throughout the year.

- Tell students about the skills they will acquire as the year progresses. Show a future difficult problem or assignment and assure students that in just a little while they will find it easy.

- Reassure students that you will help them all year. Be explicit about the ways that you intend to help them succeed.

- Show students the readings, experiments, or problems that they will do so that they have some idea of what they will be learning as the year progresses. A quick demonstration is a terrific way to generate interest.

- Talk about the types of celebrations that you like to have for your students. Even talking about something as simple as a ten-minute video clip on Fridays (Movie Day!) will build anticipation.

- Teach students an unusual fact or technique related to your course so that they have something definite to say when a parent or guardian asks, "What did you learn today?"

Student Information Records

Although you will have access to a great deal of official information about your students, that information may not always be current or even easy to find. One way to make sure that the information that you have about your students is accurate and accessible is to ask students to complete a form such as Student Worksheet 5.1.

Because of its length, after you have allowed ten or fifteen minutes for it, you should consider having students take the form home in their welcome packets to complete. Do not be surprised if even older students do not know their personal contact information, such as their address. Many older students also have contact information stored in their phones and will ask if they can access it during class. Because this is a reasonable request, if your class is going smoothly and students seem to be cooperative, then you should consider allowing them to do this while in class.

Student Information Form

Your full name: _____

What you want me to call you: _____

Your home phone number: _____

Your e-mail address: _____

Your birthday: _____

Your student number: _____

Your age: _____

Your brothers' and sisters' names and ages:

_____

_____

What are your goals for the future?

_____

_____

What hobbies do you have?

_____

_____

What sports interest you?

_____

_____

Names of your parent(s) or guardian(s):

_____

_____

(continued on next page)

(continued from previous page)

Which parent or guardian would you like me to contact if I need to call home?

Mr., Mrs., Ms., Dr.: _____ First name: _____ Last name: _____

Please tell me the cell phone number, work phone number, and e-mail address of each of your parents or guardians.

Mother: _____

Cell phone: _____ Work phone: _____

E-mail address: _____

Father: _____

Cell phone: _____ Work phone: _____

E-mail address: _____

Guardian: _____

Cell phone: _____ Work phone: _____

E-mail address: _____

Guardian: _____

Cell phone: _____ Work phone: _____

E-mail address: _____

What is your address (street address, city, zip code)?

_____

_____

Learn Your Students' Names Quickly

Learning how to correctly pronounce and spell your students' names is one of the most important tasks you will have to master as the school term begins. Being able to call all your students by name is an important step in getting to know them as people and in managing your class.

The depth of resentment that mispronouncing or misspelling a student's name can cause is often surprising to first-year teachers. Although teachers may think of it as a small mistake, students tend to view teachers who do not call them by the right name as uncaring and insensitive.

Learning all your students' names on the first or second day of school is not very difficult. These quick tips will make it possible for you to go home on the first day of school confident that you know the students in your class well enough to get the term off to a good start:

- Put in some preliminary work. Organize your seating charts, study class rosters, and prepare name tags if you are going to use them.
- Make sure that your students sit in their assigned seats for the first few days so that you can quickly associate names with faces.
- If you have students fill out a student information form, when you read what your students have written, mentally match their faces to the information in front of you.
- While students are working on a written assignment, walk quietly around the room, checking the roster.
- Ask each student to say his or her name for you. Repeat it as you study the child's face. You can also use the recording feature of your phone to record students pronouncing their names.
- Mark pronunciation notes on your roll sheet. Also, make notes to help match names to students. For example, you can write "big smile" or "very tall" next to a student's name. These little clues will help you when you are struggling to recall a name on the second day of school.
- Take photos of your students in their assigned seats and then study the photos at home later to help you match names and faces.
- When you cannot recall a child's name, admit it, and ask for help. When you hear it again, write it down, repeat it, and try again until you can recall it.

How to Manage the First Week

The first week of school is probably the most stressful week of the entire school year. You not only will have to adjust to new routines and the uncertainties of your classroom responsibilities in front of an audience of curious students but also will have to help your students with their own adjustment as well. The intense paperwork load and the fast pace of each day, as well as the weighty responsibilities you must manage well, all combine to make this adjustment period a tough one. It helps to know what to expect during the first week and to have a plan in place to manage the new stresses in your professional life.

> Remember that in a twenty-day working month, fifteen days will be average. Three will be tops, but you will have two bad days. The longer you teach, the more days that are tops you will have.
>
> *Edward Gardner, 36 years' experience*

What You Can Expect during the First Week

The first week of a school term is filled with many changes and adjustments for teachers and students. Here are some of the things that you can expect and plan for during the first week of school:

- Students will have schedule changes. Even if you teach very young students in a small school, it is prudent to anticipate that students will be added to or removed from your class during the first week.

- Some students will have trouble finding their classrooms during the first week. This is a potentially embarrassing situation for any student that you can alleviate by standing at your classroom door and greeting students as they enter your room.

- At least a few of your students will not have supplies on the first day of school or even by the end of the week.

- You can expect to be surprised by how much your students will have forgotten from previous years. The lack of social skills can be particularly distressing until you get students accustomed to school manners again.

- Anxious students will act out in surprising ways until they can be assured that you are a good teacher with their best interests at heart.

- Your to-do list will be very long. All the tasks on it will be important ones with short deadlines.

- You will have to reach out to soothe anxious parents or guardians who worry about their children's potential for success in your class.

- You will have to work hard to keep up with your classroom keys and other important belongings that you are too stressed or distracted to put away with mindful deliberation.

- You will have to find time to eat, rest, exercise, and take care of your personal life during the first few weeks of school.

- Some of your colleagues will want to share unpleasant and unhelpful stories about your students. Avoid these sessions as tactfully as you can.

- You will find that it is hard to pace lessons correctly during the first few weeks of school because you are not familiar with your students and the way they work and learn.

- The administrators and other staff members at your school will have to adjust to last-minute changes in enrollment and teaching positions. You must pay attention to the many directions that will come your way with changes that affect the entire school.

- You will notice that your students will have wildly varying learning styles and levels of readiness.

- Your students will need your patient and persistent help in learning how to relate appropriately to one another and to you as well as how to adjust themselves to the routines of the class.

- At the end of the day, you will find it almost impossible to recall what you taught or said earlier in the day. Make a detailed lesson plan and follow it carefully.

- You will feel exhilarated and exhausted at the same time.

Have a Plan for Start-of-School Stress

During the first week of school, you will not be alone in needing to develop stress-relief strategies for the common and predictable problems that you and your colleagues will face. In the following chart, you will find some of the problems that you can anticipate and suggested strategies for managing the stress that accompanies each one:

Problem	Suggested Stress-Relief Strategy
You are overwhelmed by the newness of everything you are required to do.	Be patient. Time will take care of this.
There's too much paperwork, and it is all due right away.	Make a to-do list with due dates. Work steadily and efficiently to get it done.
You can't predict how well a lesson or activity will work because you don't know your students.	This will resolve itself as you give students interest and readiness inventories and get to know them better.
Some students have no supplies.	Lend them the materials they need until they can purchase school supplies.
You run out of lesson before you run out of class.	Have a simple extra or alternate lesson plan ready until you can learn to pace instruction correctly.
Students find it difficult to follow routines and procedures.	Patiently teach and reteach. Calmly and quietly enact your consequences until students stop testing the boundaries.

Problem	Suggested Stress-Relief Strategy
You find it difficult to attend to your personal life because you are exhausted and school looms large in your thinking.	Do your best to rest, exercise, and eat well. Soon you will have the work-life balance you need.
Students who were well behaved on the first day of class are not as well behaved at the end of the first week.	Calmly and quietly enact your consequences until students stop testing the boundaries. Focus on the positive behaviors in your class.
Your lesson plan was a disaster.	Be specific in your analysis. Spend time reflecting on what went well and where you could improve the lesson. Make the changes that you can right away.
You have so much to do that you worry that you will forget something important.	Make a to-do list and maintain a calendar to keep reminders of everything that you need to do right at your fingertips.
You are uncertain about what to do in situations where other teachers seem confident.	Don't give in to feelings of intimidation. Those confident teachers were first-year teachers once. Ask for help.

Questions to Discuss with Colleagues

Sharing ideas with colleagues is a helpful way to devise solutions to some of the problems that you must manage successfully at school. Here you will find several topics to open discussions with colleagues about successful instructional practices:

1. Several teachers have stopped by to tell you about the new students that you will have this year. Unfortunately, some of these teachers have told you stories that emphasize the negative sides of your new students. How can you deal with this information now, and how can you avoid this uncomfortable situation in the future?

2. Because there is so much paperwork at the start of the school term, it's difficult to keep up with it all. How can this responsibility be managed efficiently?

3. It's all too easy to feel exhausted and overwhelmed at the start of school. How can you cope with this stress so that you can enjoy being with your students?

4. Which strategies make it easier for you to get to know your new students? How can you find out about their interests and abilities so that you can begin to differentiate instruction?

5. What seating arrangements do the other teachers at your school use that would also work well in your classroom? What do you need to consider before moving students into new seating configurations?

Topics to Discuss with a Mentor

Although the topics that new teachers need to discuss with a mentor vary from teacher to teacher and from school to school, there are some that most first-year teachers should be comfortable discussing with a mentor or a trusted colleague. You should ask your mentor about these topics from this section:

- Suggestions for student seating arrangements
- How to manage stress at the start of a new school term
- How to help students have a positive first-day-of-school experience
- Suggestions for lesson plans and activities to introduce yourself to students
- Advice about helping students adjust to your class routines and expectations

Reflection Questions to Guide Your Thinking

1. What can you do to make sure the first day of school is productive for you and your students? What small things can you do to ensure that your students are comfortable and glad to be in your class?

2. What would you like your students to say about your class at the end of the first day? What specific steps can help you achieve this goal?

3. Which seating arrangements would work best at the start of the year for your students? How can you accommodate all students? Where can you learn more about how to arrange student seating? Who can help you with this?

4. How can you organize the information you gather about your students so that it is easily accessible all term? What can you do to ensure that all students return the forms that they need to take home?

5. How can you prioritize your tasks at the start of school so that you can be sure to manage them well? How can you plan instruction and your school day successfully?

SECTION SIX

Cultivate Positive Classroom Relationships

Positive classroom relationships are far more important than many teachers realize. Without a productive relationship with your students and their parents or guardians, no matter how well you have prepared instruction and planned classroom management, nothing will work well. Although these two relationships are crucial to the success of your students, positive relationships do not happen by chance.

You will have to be the one who reaches out to parents or guardians to make sure that they are confident in your ability to teach their children well. And it is up to you, as a classroom teacher, to patiently commit yourself to ensuring that your students are not only connected to you but also that they feel connected to their classmates.

If the demands of covering curriculum and your everyday responsibilities seem to be a better use of your time than relationship building, consider this: few teachers leave the profession because of daily responsibilities. Instead, many teachers who self-identify as burned out admit to significant stress due to poor classroom relationships.

In this section, you will first learn about the strategies that you can use to create that important positive relationship with the parents or guardians of your students. You will then learn how to forge the strong bonds that you need to work well with your students.

It's Necessary to Work Well with Parents or Guardians

Even though you may not see them, the parents or guardians of your students are in your classroom every day. As the primary caregivers of your students, they influence how your students think, feel, and react. If you work well with the parents or guardians of your students, not only will your job be easier but also your students will find it easier to do well in school.

Working well with parents or guardians creates a team of allied adults all trying to help students succeed in school. Interacting professionally is important, and many areas of this

> Parents have worked hard to get their children to you. They want the best for their children. And you want the best for your students. Work as partners.
>
> *Anna Aslin Cohen, 40 years' experience*

delicate relationship may require special attention. In the pages that follow, you will learn strategies to ensure that your interactions are as productive as possible. Interacting with your students and their families in a professional way in every situation is not always easy, but it will be worth the effort.

Develop a Positive Reputation among Parents or Guardians

You will be gossiped about. There is no escaping it. Whenever parents or guardians gather, they will discuss their children's school experiences and their teachers. Just as it is important to build a reputation for professionalism among your colleagues, it is important to have a positive reputation among parents or guardians.

The parents or guardians of your students will have some very specific expectations of you: to value their children, to teach the mandated material, to encourage achievement, and to work with them for the good of their children. Because these expectations are ones that could be reasonably asked of an educator, conducting yourself as a professional will allow you to build the reputation that you need to work well with parents or guardians. Be known as a teacher who can make the material so interesting that students talk about it at home. Be known as a teacher who always has the best interests of students at heart and who is willing to work with parents or guardians.

Although it is important to live up to expectations, there are three important caveats that you should consider as you work to build your reputation among the parents or guardians of your students. First, as a professional educator, you have a right to protect your privacy at home. Don't give out your home phone number. Keep your relationships businesslike. Second, be sure to return phone calls to parents or guardians as soon as possible. Make it a rule to call back within twenty-four hours. Respond to e-mails within that time frame as well. Third, never forget to treat your students with utmost respect. To you, a student may be a completely annoying headache, but to a parent or guardian, that student is a precious child and a beloved member of a family. Never lose sight of this; your professional reputation depends on it.

Prevent Miscommunication with a Transparent Classroom

One of the easiest ways to prevent miscommunication and to establish a positive relationship with the parents or guardians of your students is to make sure that your classroom is as transparent as possible. You can do this by providing easily accessible information about your students and their learning activities.

When you create a transparent classroom, you are not just a teacher who grudgingly shares test dates or other routine information with your students' families. Instead, actively solicit participation and support from everyone concerned. With today's technology, making sure that everyone knows firsthand what is happening in your class is easier than ever. Your students' parents or guardians expect to be kept informed about these topics:

- Class policies, rules, and consequences
- Beginning-of-the-year information
- Homework and major assignments
- Tests and other assessments
- Grading concerns
- Due dates
- Field trips
- Special projects
- Resources to help students learn
- Positive things about their children

One frequent complaint that parents or guardians have involves not being informed about homework assignments and important project due dates. Take extra care to make sure your homework policies are published in several different ways and that all due dates are announced well in advance. The parents or guardians of your students should not have to struggle to find out what their children's homework is and when work is due.

Another frequent complaint is that teachers wait too long before contacting a parent or guardian about a problem. When in doubt, make the phone call. It is far more effective to call home when a problem is small enough to be manageable than to wait until the situation is serious.

In the first two months of school, I set a goal of sending two positive e-mails a day to parents or guardians. Only two a day makes this achievable and more personal for each student. I found the results to be very positive, leading to much more effective communication later in the year. A great side effect was that I realized students were also very grateful. Getting a positive message from a teacher created good things for them at home. I now also integrate this into my teaching by trying, whenever possible, to send a positive e-mail when a student achieves something. I do this especially for a student who was struggling either academically or behaviorally in my classroom. The main lesson is that positive communication with home goes a long way to improve interaction with both students and parents.

Shelly Sambiase, 8 years' experience

Be Positive with Parents or Guardians

Being negative with the parents or guardians of your students will gain you nothing; in fact, it will make a resolution to any classroom problem very difficult. Although you may look to parents or guardians for support, they, in turn, are looking to you for help for their children. Working out solutions together requires a positive approach—a can-do attitude.

A positive atmosphere must begin with you. There are many ways to make positive contacts with the parents or guardians of your students. Although it may take time to follow through on these little actions, the benefits will compensate for the time you spend on them. Here are some ways you can create the positive atmosphere you want for your students:

- Have parents or guardians sign papers with good grades as well as bad ones.
- Compliment parents or guardians to other people. Do not hesitate to let students know that you think highly of their parents or guardians.
- Make it a habit to thank parents or guardians of your students for their support whenever you see them.
- After a parent or guardian has helped you with a problem, take the time to call or write a personal thank-you note.
- Call or e-mail parents or guardians with good news.
- If you have a school voice mail, record a positive message to parents or guardians.
- Send home a thank-you note after a conference.

One of the most effective ways to be positive with the parents or guardians of students at all grade levels is to send home positive messages as often as you can. Even the parents or guardians of older students will appreciate the effort you take to recognize their children's hard work and successes. Consider adapting Sample 6.1 to fit your needs.

Sample 6.1
Positive Message to Parents or Guardians

Although many formats can be used to notify parents or guardians of student achievements, it is best to keep your message simple. Adapt the format of this sample message for your own students.

To the Parents or Guardians of _____:

I am writing to let you know how pleased I am with your child's recent success in my class. You will be proud to know that

_____.

I know you are as proud of this effort and achievement as I am. Thank you for your support.

Sincerely,

_____

Assist Parents or Guardians Who Do Not Speak English

At some point in your career, whether you teach in a small town or in a large city, you will have to communicate with parents or guardians whose primary language is not English. This situation can be awkward and confusing for everyone if you are not prepared to offer assistance. Although it is likely that your school district made efforts to provide such assistance when the student enrolled, it is up to you to find a way to communicate effectively if you cannot find an adult interpreter.

One solution is to have students translate for their parents or guardians. This is effective if the student is trustworthy and old enough to handle the task. Another solution is to involve an older sibling of the student if that person is dependable.

You can also use technology to help with this problem. Many Internet sites are available to assist you in translating what you need to communicate to parents or guardians. Try visiting Google Translate (https://translate.google.com) the next time you need a translator. This site has a comprehensive catalog, is user-friendly, and takes just seconds to translate.

Make Telephone Calls with Confidence

Phoning parents or guardians when there is a problem is one of the unpleasant tasks teachers must do well. Even experienced teachers dread interacting with the occasional angry parent or guardian who makes phoning a student's home an upsetting experience. However, as disagreeable as this task can be, phoning a parent or guardian is a necessary action. There are several strategies you can adopt to make phoning home easier:

- Plan what you want to say and what information the parent or guardian needs to know so that you can work together to solve the problem.

- Find a phone at school from which you can make the call with at least some privacy and in a place where you are not likely to be interrupted. Don't use your personal phone for school business.

- Be sure to have a pen and any notes you have made about the situation with you.

- Don't hesitate to call a parent or guardian at work. However, be careful not to reveal too many details to the colleagues of the person you are calling. Protecting his or her privacy shows respect and engenders cooperation when you ask for help.

- If you call while a parent or guardian is at work, begin the conversation by asking, "Do you have a few minutes right now?" so that this person can set his or her work aside long enough to listen.

- Remember that the purpose of the phone call is not to allow you to vent your frustration but rather to enable you to solve a problem by working with the parent or guardian.

- Begin with a positive statement about the student and then say that you would like to enlist help in solving a problem: "I had a problem with Jim today, and I wonder if you could help me."

If the e-mail is longer than a sentence or two, call instead. If you feel that the e-mail won't go over well, call instead. Let the parents or guardians know that you are acting in the best interests of the kids and that everybody is on the same team—student, parent, teacher, and administration.

Jared Sronce, 6 years' experience

- Be very specific about the problem. Don't just say, "Jim is acting odd today." Try "Jim laughed out loud at inappropriate moments three times today and fell asleep right before lunch."
- After detailing the problem, state what you have done to correct it. Again, be very specific, and give the result of your actions.
- Pay attention while the parent or guardian explains what he or she knows about the situation. Make sure to listen carefully and to clarify any points you do not understand.
- Finish the call with a positive statement, expressing your appreciation that a solution has been devised.

Before you go on to your next task, document the call. Complete a contact documentation form (see Teacher Worksheet 6.1) so that you have a record of the conversation and what each party decided to do.

Conduct Successful Conferences with Parents or Guardians

Teachers who want to communicate well realize that parents or guardians want to be reassured that their children can succeed in school. Even if that is not what is happening at the moment, parents or guardians want teachers to work with them to help their children. A strong connection with your students' parents or guardians is achievable if you make sure that your goals for conferences are clear. Here are five goals you should have for every conference:

- **Goal One:** Parents or guardians should see you as a friendly and knowledgeable teacher who has their children's best interests at heart.
- **Goal Two:** Parents or guardians should feel an atmosphere of cooperation and support when they are meeting with you.
- **Goal Three:** Parents or guardians should leave a conference with all their questions answered and all the points they wanted to discuss covered.
- **Goal Four:** You as well as parents or guardians should share a sense of mutual respect and an understanding of one another's problems and viewpoints.
- **Goal Five:** Workable solutions to any problems should be agreed on, and everyone involved should work together to help the student.

Conferences with parents or guardians are much more involved than a quick chat after school. Successful conferences require planning and attention to detail before, during, and after the meeting. Use these guidelines to guarantee that the conferences you have this year are positive and productive:

Actions to Take before a Conference

- Make sure you have a clear purpose for the conference and a clear understanding of the outcome you would like.
- Plan the points you want to cover. Write them down.
- Gather samples of student work or other evidence you would like to use in the conference. Include progress reports and other information related to grades or behavior.
- Review cumulative records and report card information.
- Take notes on the student's strengths and weaknesses as well as any other special information you would like to present.
- Create a seating arrangement that will be comfortable for adults. Arrange chairs around a table or desks large enough for adults in a circle. Do not sit behind your desk.
- Make sure to provide a pen and paper for everyone.
- Make a neat "Do Not Disturb" sign; post it on your door so that you can meet without distractions.
- Meet the parents or guardians and escort them to your room.

Actions to Take during a Conference

- Be prepared to begin promptly. Do not make parents or guardians wait while you shuffle papers.
- Begin by expressing your appreciation that the parents or guardians have come to the conference. Try to establish a tone of goodwill and friendly cooperation as quickly as you can.
- Use language that will make the parents or guardians comfortable. Do not use educational jargon.
- Begin with positive remarks about the child. Talk about the student's aptitude, special talents, improvements, and potential. Focus on strengths, even if there is a serious problem. Never lose sight of the fact that the child is very important to his or her parents or guardians.
- State any problems in simple, factual terms. Express your desire to work with the parents or guardians for a successful resolution.
- Discuss specific examples of a problem. Show examples of work or give details about the student's behavior.

- Let the parents or guardians say what they need to say. It is always best to allow upset or angry parents or guardians to speak first. After the parents or guardians have had the opportunity to say everything they need to say, then—and only then—can they listen to you or begin to work on a solution to a problem.

- If you have discussed a problem previously, let the parents or guardians know of any improvement.

- If you want to solve a problem, give your full attention throughout the entire conference. Your nonverbal language is crucial for success. Be friendly and attentive.

- Don't try to outtalk the parents or guardians. You may make your point, but the parents or guardians will not listen to you. Do not give in to the temptation to interrupt.

- End the conference gracefully by recapping the points that you have covered.

- Determine what you will do to follow up on the conference and to keep in contact with the parents or guardians.

- Express appreciation again for their concern and the time they have spent with you in the conference.

Actions to Take after a Conference

- Immediately complete your notes, the documentary evidence of what was discussed, and the agreed-on decisions. Spend enough time on this so that your records are complete. Should you need to refer to this material later, you may not remember details accurately if your notes are not thorough.

- Write a quick note or e-mail thanking parents or guardians for their support now and in the future.

The Importance of Keeping Contact Records

By now you are probably convinced that you will spend your free hours at school documenting things you took for granted in your own student days. There are forms for just about every interaction you will have with your students, and you must complete each form accurately and promptly.

It is a sensible practice to keep accurate records of the times when you have contacted parents or guardians. Even the very best teacher could be asked to provide proof that he or she did all that could be done to help a student. Every year there are countless cases in which frustrated parents or guardians sue teachers in an attempt to find a simple cause for a complex problem. Although it may be upsetting to think that this could happen to a dedicated teacher, it does happen.

Fortunately, you can protect yourself with just a few minutes of planning and paperwork. You can enhance your professional reputation by being able to provide documentation that you have contacted parents or guardians appropriately. Keeping a record of home contacts does not have to be time consuming. Use or modify Teacher Worksheet 6.1, and keep plenty of copies on hand so that you can complete one each time you contact a student's parents or guardians. Fill out the form, and file it in a folder or binder with other paperwork you have kept for that student.

Home Contact Documentation Form

Student name: _____

Parent or guardian name(s): _____

Phone number: _____

Date and time of contact: _____

Type of contact:

_____ Phone call

_____ E-mail

_____ Letter

_____ Detention notice

_____ Home visit

_____ Informal meeting

_____ Meeting with administrator

_____ Meeting with counselor

_____ Other: _____

Person(s) initiating the contact: _____

Topics discussed:

_____

_____

_____

_____

Steps parent(s) or guardian(s) will take:

_____

_____

_____

Steps teacher will take:

_____

_____

_____

Additional notes and reflections:

_____

_____

_____

_____

_____

_____

_____

From *The First-Year Teacher's Survival Guide, 4th Edition*, by Julia G. Thompson. Copyright © 2018 by John Wiley & Sons, Inc. Reproduced by permission.

Why Some Parents or Guardians May Not Relate Well to You

As you gain experience, you will find that not all parents or guardians are supportive of you or the other teachers in your school. Although your first tendency may be to take this personally, if you understand their viewpoints, it will be easier for you to work together well. Here are just some of the many possible reasons for negative attitudes from home:

- Some parents or guardians may have had unpleasant experiences in school themselves.
- Their child may have told them something objectionable (although probably exaggerated or false) about you.
- One of your lessons may have contained information they find inappropriate.
- You may not have presented yourself as professionally as possible when you first met them.
- You may have allowed a problem to escalate by not contacting them as quickly as you should have.
- They may be reacting out of their own frustration with their child's behavior, particularly if the problem is a long-standing one.
- They may disagree with you about the appropriate consequences of their child's behavior.
- They may feel embarrassment at their child's behavior or lack of success.
- Their child may have had unsympathetic or unsupportive teachers in the past.
- Previous teachers may have reacted negatively to their efforts to parent their child.
- Your uncertainty and lack of confidence may be obvious.
- They may want to protect their child from potential embarrassment or punishment.

Helicopter Parents or Guardians

The term *helicopter parent* is one that describes a style of rearing children by parents or guardians who "hover" over their child, second-guessing every decision made by his or her teachers. Although there can be extreme cases of excessive involvement, experienced teachers have learned to appreciate parents or guardians who involve themselves in their child's education.

If you find yourself having to deal with helicopter parents or guardians, there are several actions you can take to ensure that the relationship you have with them is as beneficial as possible. Consider using some of the actions in the list that follows to ensure that the relationship you have with all parents or guardians is a constructive one:

- Adopt a positive attitude about your ability to cope successfully with this type of parent or guardian. Working together for the good of the student is an important enough endeavor to justify a special effort.

- Keep the channels of communication open. Having a transparent classroom can allay many concerns that parents or guardians may have about your class. Communicate often and be explicit about your expectations.

- Be very clear that you like and respect their children, and acknowledge their rights as parents or guardians.

- Try to prevent situations in which helicopter parents or guardians can react anxiously by taking extra care to follow your school and district policies and best practices.

- If you receive an unpleasant phone call or e-mail, don't forget that you are a professional, and respond in a professional way. Lashing out in frustration will only make the situation worse.

- Schedule a face-to-face conference and really listen. Their anxiety about their children may be relieved once they have had the opportunity to speak freely and have their concerns heard by a competent, caring professional.

- Although you should actively promote the importance of the student's taking appropriate individual responsibility for his or her own academic and behavioral success, try to accommodate as many requests as you reasonably can.

- Never stoop to putting the student in the middle of a battle between home and school or in a position in which he or she is made uncomfortable because of a disagreement between the significant adults in his or her life.

- Do not try to manage helicopter parents or guardians by yourself. Involve knowledgeable colleagues who may have had similar experiences and who may be willing to assist you. Counselors and administrators can also be invaluable sources of support when working with helicopter parents or guardians.

Unreasonable Requests

Although almost every contact you will have with a parent or guardian will be pleasant and productive, on rare occasions you may have to deal with unreasonable requests or reactions. When this happens, the situation can be unnerving and perplexing.

When you are a new teacher, it is not always easy to determine if parents or guardians are being unreasonable. For example, it is reasonable for them to request that you send home a daily behavior report in a student's planner or respond to a daily e-mail from home. These are reasonable requests because the student will have to take responsibility for giving you the planner, or the parent or guardian will have to take responsibility for remembering to send you an e-mail. It is unreasonable to expect you to remember to send a note home without being reminded or to initiate a daily e-mail.

Other requests that could be considered unreasonable might include being asked to offer extra credit to just one student, exempt a student from a standardized test or important project, or change the weight of an assignment for just one child. If a request or reaction from a parent or guardian seems unreasonable to you, there are some actions you should take right away:

- Do not act alone. Delay responding until you have time to think and to consult others. As soon as you can, consult a mentor, team members, or an administrator for advice.

- Try to be as compassionate and understanding as possible. You, as well as the parent or guardian, want what is best for the student. That can only happen if you are all in agreement and can work together.

- When you discuss the situation with the parent or guardian, be clear about what is reasonable and what is not. Try to work out a compromise when you can.

- Accept the idea that you will probably not win the parent or guardian over to your side of the conflict. You should attempt to calm the situation and to work with him or her to create reasonable accommodations instead.

Angry and Uncooperative Parents or Guardians

No matter how hard you try, parents or guardians will not always be as cooperative as you would like. The best way to avoid this situation is to intervene early, follow procedures and rules, maintain accurate records, present yourself as a professional, and keep parents or guardians informed about their child's progress.

If you find yourself in a confrontation with a hostile parent or guardian, it is up to you to assume control of the situation. The following steps can help you manage meetings so that they result in productive outcomes instead of heated words:

- Listen to what the angry parent or guardian has to say without trying to interrupt or correct him or her. Do not try to present your side of the disagreement until the parent or guardian has had an opportunity to express himself or herself.

- Show your interest by asking questions about specific details. A simple misunderstanding is often the cause of the problem.

- Make sure to restate the problem so that the other person can be reassured that you do understand. Try "I think you're saying _____."

- Explain the problem from your viewpoint as objectively as you can. Be specific about what was expected, what the child did that was not appropriate, and how you responded.

- Make it clear throughout the confrontation that you want to work with the parent or guardian for the child's welfare.

- Remain calm and professional.

- Remember that it will only harm you in the eyes of the parent or guardian and your supervisors if you act on your natural desire to justify your actions in a loud tone or to return insults.

- Do not accept threats or abuse from the parent or guardian. If, after you have sincerely tried to resolve a problem, the parent or guardian remains upset, suggest calling in an administrator to help.

- If you suspect that a parent or guardian plans to contact an administrator, make the contact first. It is never wise to allow your supervisors to be surprised with bad news. Instead, see an administrator, present your point of view, and ask for assistance.

Helping Students Learn to Work Well with You

It's up to us. Developing a positive relationship with your students is crucial to student success. Your students need to feel that they matter to you, that you like them, and that you enjoy being with them. Positive relationships are the cornerstone of an effective classroom.

Although positive teacher-student relationships are rewarding in countless ways, cultivating those relationships can be challenging. Many students may have difficulty developing stable attachments to the adults in their lives. Some students may also not have been taught the simple social skills that they need to bond appropriately with others and to succeed in school. In addition, significant cultural differences between school and home can also play a role in making it even more difficult for students to learn how to relate well to their teachers and to their classmates. In the rest of this section, you will explore how presenting yourself as a *warm demander* while using your personal strengths will make it possible for you to reach every student.

Be Yourself: Use Your Unique Strengths

One of the best things about being a teacher is that you have an opportunity to share yourself—your ideas, your interests, your way of approaching life—with a roomful of students who look to you as a model of how they should conduct themselves. Being an effective teacher forces you to present an authentic version of yourself to your classes; even very young students have uncanny ways of seeing through phonies.

Use your unique strengths as a guide to relate to your students. Are you naturally curious? Are you enthusiastic about your content? Do you have a great sense of humor? Take a few minutes every now and then to think about the personal strengths that you bring to your classroom practice and how you can use those strengths to connect with your students. One way to think about your strengths is to use Teacher Worksheet 6.2.

Reflect on Your Relationship-Building Strengths

Here you will find twelve statements that reflect the strengths of excellent classroom teachers who want to connect successfully with their students. As you read each statement, think about how it relates to your teaching practice. If a statement expresses a strength that you already have, place a check mark in the blank before it. You should then be able to see your relationship-building strengths and the areas where you could improve.

1. _____ I value the differences among my students.
2. _____ I think of myself as a strict but fair teacher.
3. _____ I have high expectations for all my students and help them meet those expectations.
4. _____ I believe courtesy is important for successful relationships.
5. _____ I believe it is important for students to feel that they belong.
6. _____ I want the atmosphere in my class to be one of mutual respect.
7. _____ I want each of my students to have a positive attitude about school.
8. _____ I find my students to be interesting as people as well as students.
9. _____ I want my classes to be dynamic and enjoyable.
10. _____ I want my students to find success attainable with effort and persistence.
11. _____ I encourage my students to cooperate with one another and with me.
12. _____ I believe my students are worthwhile people who can learn and succeed.

The Focus Should Be on Your Students

Teachers who have cultivated successful relationships with their students know that their students must come first. It's not always easy to be focused on teaching or students all class long, day after day. We all can experience legitimate distractions from time to time—an illness in our families or our own fatigue, for example.

However, those teachers who are so distracted that they do not pay enough attention to their students are not able to build successful classroom relationships simply because their attention is not on their students. The following questions may help you gauge the level of distraction you may be experiencing each school day. Once you are aware of any problems in this area, you may want to consider how to adjust the way that you interact with your students.

- Do you grade papers in class?
- Do you leave your cell phone on while you are supervising students?
- Do you find yourself without enough prepared handouts or other teaching materials?
- Do you check e-mail in class?
- Are you distracted during class by your family responsibilities?
- Are you distracted by routine paperwork chores, such as book counts, attendance forms, or parent contact documentation?
- Do you work on extracurricular activities, such as clubs or sports that you sponsor, while you are in class?
- Do you confer with other teachers during class time?
- Do you conduct personal business during class?

Be Clear about Your Role in Classroom Relationships

As a first-year teacher, you may struggle to determine the relationship you want to have with your students. How friendly should you be? What if your students don't like you? What if they won't listen to you? How strict is too strict? There are several decisions that you can make that will help you define your role:

- You should act in a mature manner all the time. This does not mean that you cannot have fun with your students; however, if having fun with your students means indulging in playful insults, then you are not acting in a mature manner. Being sarcastic or angry, playing favorites, and losing your temper are not only immature behaviors but also have the potential to destroy the relationships that you want to build.

- You should show that you care about your students. Your students want you to like them and to approve of them, even when they misbehave. It is crucial that your students feel that they are important to you and that you care about their welfare. Do not be afraid to let your students know you are interested in how they think and feel.

- You should have a thorough knowledge of your subject matter. Knowing your subject matter may not seem to have much to do with developing a successful relationship with your students, but it does. If you are not prepared for class, you won't be able to focus on your students. The worst result of inadequate knowledge of your subject matter is that your students will lose respect for you and no longer trust your judgment.

- You should take command of the class. If you do not assume a leadership role in your class, others will. Relationships will suffer as students try to dominate one another. Although you should not be overbearing, you should be in command of the class. You can and should allow your students as many options and as strong a voice in the class as possible, but never lose sight of your role as the classroom leader. Your students won't.

- You should maintain a certain emotional distance from your students. Being a teacher is much more than being a friend to your students; they have peers for friends. You are a teacher and not a peer. The emotional distance you keep between yourself and your students will enable you to make choices based on what students need instead of on what they want.

The Limits of Your Responsibility to Your Students

It is easy to become too involved in helping students when it is obvious that they need more than just classroom instruction to be successful. As teachers, we are in a caring profession that values service and encourages us to help the whole child. It's impossible to just stand by when our students struggle with hunger, homelessness, or any other serious issue that makes it difficult for them to learn. We should help. After all, our students depend on us to keep them safe from harm.

Although it is essential that we help our students, it is important that we do so in a professional manner so that success is more likely. Think of yourself as a key player in getting help for your students. Once you become aware of a student's need, you should act promptly.

Remember, too, that you are part of a team of caring professionals who are all trained to assist students. Never take it upon yourself to act alone to solve student problems. Instead, involve counselors, administrators, school resource officers, school nurses, social workers, and other appropriate personnel as quickly as you can.

Although you were trained as a classroom teacher, your colleagues in specialized fields will have access to resources and support that you do not. Their assistance and support can be more extensive and better suited to student needs than any help you can offer. If you have students who are struggling with any of the issues in the following list, act quickly to contact other professionals to seek their help:

- Pregnancy
- Bullying

- Neighborhood threats
- Mental health issues
- Suicide threats or attempts
- Emotional, verbal, or sexual abuse
- Substance abuse issues
- Serious family problems
- Gang involvement
- Sexual orientation issues
- Attempts or threats to run away
- Chronic illness or injury
- A need for eyeglasses, a hearing aid, or other adaptive technology
- Hunger
- Homelessness

Connect and Lead: Become a Warm Demander

You have probably been given lots of advice since your friends and family first discovered your interest in an education career. Although some of the advice you may have heard is not particularly useful—"Don't smile until Thanksgiving," for example—one especially helpful bit of advice that you may have been given is to be "friendly but firm." On the surface, being friendly and being firm don't seem to be strategies that work well together, but they do.

In fact, teachers whose approach to student relationships is both friendly and firm tend to be the most effective teachers in any school. The term for their approach in relating well to their students is called being a *warm demander*. First identified by educator and researcher Judith Kleinfield in a 1975 article, "Effective Teachers of Eskimo and Indian Students" in *School Review*, the term refers to the unique combination of a teacher's personal warmth regarding students with a highly structured environment in which student achievement is not only the focus but also expected.

On the one hand, sometimes new teachers can hesitate to be demanding or strict because they fear that their students will regard them as mean. When students describe a teacher as being mean, they usually describe a teacher who is unduly harsh or who singles them out for unpredictable humiliations. No one wants to be regarded as a mean teacher. After all, being mean is the antithesis of our purpose as educators.

On the other hand, teachers who are warm demanders make it clear to their students that they find them capable of academic and behavioral success and that they enjoy being with their students. They also have a highly structured classroom environment in which students are expected to work hard and to comply with classroom policies, procedures, and rules. They are those beloved strict teachers who can make even the most disruptive students sit up straight and turn in their homework on time. It is the combination of a teacher's personal warmth toward students with an unassailable approach to classroom management that makes it possible for teachers who are warm demanders to be compelling classroom leaders.

In the rest of this section, you will explore the techniques that you can use to develop your own skills as a warm demander. You will first learn about the various ways that you can project your positive concern for your students as you develop your *warm* qualities and then discover more about how be a *demander* to create the classroom atmosphere in which all students are expected to perform their best.

The *Warm* Qualities of an Effective Teacher

Many educators find it almost effortless to develop the qualities that make up the *warm* component of being a warm demander. After all, a love of children is often one of the driving forces behind education as a career choice. However, it is equally important that teachers have a growth mindset regarding their students. (See more about the growth mindset in Section Four.) Teachers who want to have a strong connection with their students must believe that their students are capable of school success.

With this attitude as a strong basis, the other strategies that teachers can use to connect with their students can be successful. Here you will find a list of some of the strategies that you can adopt as you work to improve the way that you build rapport and project your concern for your students. Teachers who have highly developed personal warmth toward their students

- Take a proactive and positive approach to classroom management
- Offer timely and specific feedback so that students can improve quickly instead of repeating mistakes
- Ask students to share in solving classroom problems when appropriate
- Promote trusting relationships with and among students
- Use positive body language when engaging with students
- Scaffold instruction for student achievement
- Use student mistakes as a learning tool
- Treat all students with courtesy and respect
- View discipline issues as problems with solutions
- Create an inclusive environment where students feel a sense of belonging
- Connect personally with students as individuals
- Are familiar with students' backgrounds, home lives, and cultures
- Are sympathetic and empathetic when students experience personal problems
- Move about the room frequently to offer assistance and engage with students
- Are aware of student learning styles and preferences and use them to plan instruction

Students can touch your heart. I came in to school even though I was sick. I had to sit down during my lesson. A student went to the vending machine and bought me a Coke and told me that Coke always made her feel better when she was sick.

Mary Landis, 22 years' experience

Although these strategies are ones that will allow you to project a sense of caring and concern about your students, they are also strategies that can improve your instructional practices in general. When students know that their teachers care about their well-being and can see them as individuals, the synergistic effect of these strategies can empower students to succeed.

How to Be a Likeable Teacher

Somewhere in your academic past, you probably had a teacher who you liked a great deal. You looked forward to that teacher's class for lots of different reasons but mainly because of how that teacher made you feel about yourself:

- You knew that you could ask for help without embarrassment.
- You felt intelligent and capable.
- You were confident that the teacher was your ally and watched out for you.
- You felt that you mattered to that teacher.

You can make your students feel the same about you. Working at being a likeable teacher is a worthwhile expenditure of your time when you are considering how to cultivate positive relationships with your students. After all, who would want to have a relationship with a grumpy teacher who makes it clear that the student is just an annoying part of the school day? You can avoid the grumpy teacher phenomenon by increasing your likeability factor.

When you work to increase your likeability factor, the most important step is to first make a conscious decision to be upbeat, cheerful, and positive. Here are some easy tips that will make your students glad that you are their teacher:

- Remember that the class is about your students and not about you. Be careful not to overpower your students with your knowledge or authority. Instead, be gentle and inclusive in your approach.
- Smile.
- Overwhelm your students with niceness.
- Share a joke or a silly rhyme or saying. Create a "Joke of the Week" where everyone can laugh together.
- At the end of class, ask students to tell you what went well or what they did right.
- Arrange for students to help one another. Provide opportunities for peer tutoring or even groups to help other groups.

- When students make good choices, praise them for the maturity it takes to make a hard decision.

- Tell your students what you like about them. Make it a point to compliment them whenever you can. Compliment individuals, small groups, teams, pairs—the entire class.

- Show that you have a sense of humor. Share a laugh with your students whenever you can. Playing together and laughing together will make school fun for everyone.

- When you speak with students, lean toward them slightly. Let your body language indicate that you are interested and accessible.

- When you see a student trying to improve, speak privately to that student to let him or her know that you noticed and are pleased.

- Take the time to reveal a little bit about yourself. For example, a brief story about a silly mistake you made or how you learned a lesson the hard way will make you much more accessible and appealing to your students than if you are always right.

- Ask questions and wait expectantly for answers. Let your body language signal that you are interested in the responses that you may receive.

- Use inclusive pronouns such as *we, our,* or *us* instead of ones that exclude students from ownership in the class.

- Use a kind voice when you speak with your students.

- Stress the things that you and your students have in common: goals, dreams, and beliefs.

- Maintain a birthday calendar for your students. Celebrate birthdays with birthday messages on the board.

- Attend school events. If your students play a sport or perform in a concert, go and watch them to show your appreciation for their hard work.

- Use good manners when you deal with your students and insist that they do the same.

- When students confide in you, follow up. For example, if students told you that they were worried about a test in another class, take the time to ask about how they did.

- Ask about a student's family. If you know someone is ill, show your concern.

- Speak to every student each day.

- Write notes to your students. Use plenty of stickers, and write positive comments on their papers.

- Pay attention to your students' health. If students need to go to the clinic, send them. When students miss several days because of illness, call to see how they are doing or send a get-well card or message. Be prompt in sending work to the student's home if appropriate.

- Use this sentence to convey your concern: "What can I do to help you?"

- Talk with students when you notice a change in their behavior. For example, if a normally serious student is neglecting his or her work, find out why.

- Include everyone in every activity. Students notice when their teachers let shy students or students that others perceive of as not capable off the hook. Be gentle, but be inclusive.

- Get your students up and moving. Sitting at a desk day after day will not only bore them but also make the emotional distance between teacher and students greater.

- Provide opportunities for students to share their opinions and beliefs with you and with one another in a nonthreatening way.

- Be empathetic and sympathetic. Acknowledge when a student is having a bad day.

- Take advantage of as many opportunities as you can to interact with your students on a one-to-one or personal level. Ask about their hobbies, problems, or families—whatever it takes to connect.

- Be fair. Few things destroy a relationship between teacher and student faster than a student's suspicion that he or she is being treated unfairly.

- Be tactfully honest. Students know when they are being lied to, and those lies will destroy the relationship you may want to build.

- Show respect for your students as well as for their families, neighborhoods, and cultures.

- Use your students' names frequently and with a gentle tone of voice.

- Be relaxed. Take a few deep breaths and focus on your students. Stressed-out teachers tend to transmit that negativity to their students, who will in turn respond negatively.

- Make frequent eye contact with everyone when you address the whole group.

- Laugh at yourself. When you show that you have a bit of self-awareness of your own foibles, you show students how to laugh at themselves, too.

- Be aware of the gestures you make. Do they indicate that you are open and friendly or the opposite?

- Be the first one to admit when you have made a mistake.

- Use such real-world technology tools as cell phones or social media sites when appropriate. By encouraging students to use the tools with which they are already familiar, you acknowledge their importance to your students.

- When you point at a student, do so with your hand palm up instead of using a closed fist with your index finger extended.

- Keep disruptions to a minimum whenever you can so that the potential for relationship damage is also minimized. All students will judge your performance when you have to manage a misbehaving classmate.

- Pay attention to the emotions behind your students' words. When you know your students well enough to be sensitive to their feelings, you will find it easier to relate well to them.

Verbal Immediacy

The words you use when you speak with your students constitute one of the most important ways you have of creating a strong bond with them. Kind words spoken in a gentle voice make it much easier for your students to connect with you. If you say something unkind to a student, it will hurt even more than an insult from a peer because it is from someone the student should be able to count on. Simply put, *verbal immediacy* is the sum of all the verbal interactions that you have with your students that draw them to you. Calling students by name, sharing classroom jokes, greeting them at the door, and even using a friendly voice all serve to create an atmosphere in which you and your students are connected in positive ways.

There are very few rules about how you should speak to your students. The age and maturity levels of your students will guide how you speak. For example, it is usually a serious offense for a teacher in an elementary classroom to tell students to shut up. In a high school classroom, this phrase is not as serious; it is merely rude. You should avoid using it, however, because there are more effective ways to ask students to stop talking.

The one language mistake you should never make is to swear when you are with your students. When you do this, you cross the line of what is acceptable and what is not. If you are ever tempted to swear around your students, remember that teachers have been fired for swearing at students.

If a word slips out, you should immediately apologize to your students, let them know that you are embarrassed, apologize again, and then continue with instruction. After your class is over, you should speak with a supervisor and explain your side of the situation as soon as you can and certainly before your supervisor hears about it from an angry parent or guardian.

Although swear words are clearly not something you should say around students, there are other language issues to which you should also pay attention. Make sure your own words are ones that help your students and do not hurt them. Never make negative or insulting remarks about any student's

- Race
- Gender
- Religion
- Family
- Friends
- Nationality
- Clothing
- Neighborhood
- Body size
- Sexual orientation
- Disability
- Age
- Appearance

Take an interest in what's going on in your students' lives. Ask them about their weekends, their sports teams, their trips, their goals, their classes, their clubs, and their hobbies. The more you ask, the more they share, and the more comfortable everyone is with one another. These little conversations go a long way in letting students know that you care about them, and once those relationships are established, students will buy wholeheartedly into your teaching, guidance, and leadership.

Jeff Vande Sande, 2 years' experience

You should also make a point of using "I" messages whenever you can. "I" messages are statements that use such words as *I, we, us,* or *our* instead of *you.* For example, instead of the harsh "You'd better pay attention," a teacher can say, "I'd like for you to please pay attention now." "You're too noisy" becomes "We all need to be quiet so that everyone can hear," and "You're doing that all wrong!" can become "I think I can help you with that."

With these simple changes, the statements are no longer accusatory, harsh in tone, or insulting. The language points out a problem but does not put anyone on the defensive. "I" messages work because they state a problem without blaming the student. This, in turn, creates a focus on a solution and not on an error the child has made.

A Long-Term Process: Get to Know Your Students

Warm demanders realize that getting to know their students is vital to establishing the positive connection that they want to have with them. Although you may want to connect with your students right away, it takes time not only to build the necessary rapport but also to gather as much information as you can. Even if your class size is small, you will have students with various quirks, life experiences, and personalities to try to decipher, and that cannot be done in a hurry.

Another reason that it takes time to learn about your students is that every day will bring new maturity and growth. Interests will develop or evolve, and life experiences will create change. Even though this can be challenging, learning about your students is one of the most rewarding aspects of your teaching practice. Here are just some of the ways that you can learn about your students:

- Review your students' records. Be sure to follow the correct procedures and confidentiality regulations. You may want to jot quick notes on each student as you scan his or her information.

- Make a point of observing your students as they interact with one another. Who appears to be shy? Who is a peacemaker? Who is generous? You can learn a great deal about them simply by being mindful of their interactions with one another.

- When you make a positive phone call home, you have an opportunity to ask questions. Likewise, when you send home an introductory letter, you can add a section asking parents or guardians to tell you about their children. (See Section Five for a sample letter for this.)

- Your students' previous teachers may be another good source of information. One drawback of this method is that you may sometimes get information that is not completely objective and that may bias your view of a student.

- Learning preferences inventories are excellent ways to discover more about your students as learners. You can find more information about these in Section Eight.

- One of the best ways to get to know your students and to help them get to know one another is to use icebreakers. As you watch students interact with one another, you will learn a great deal about them. In addition, icebreakers will give your students an opportunity to learn to value one another's contributions to the class. Try these icebreaker strategies to learn more about your students:

  - Have students work in pairs or triads to fill out information forms about one another. Include questions that will cause them to learn interesting and unusual details, such as their favorite performers or athletes or pet peeves.

  - Pass around a large calendar on which each student can record his or her birthday. Also consider having students mark their birthplace on a large map.

  - Play "Would You Rather?" with your students. In this quick game, you call out a question with two answer choices. Examples include "Would you rather be famous or be rich?" or "Would you rather have a dog or a cat as a pet?" Students can indicate their choice in a variety of ways, such as standing, raising hands, or moving to a designated area of the room.

  - Hand students half sheets of paper and ask them to write three interesting things about themselves without stating their names or obvious characteristics. Have students ball up the sheets before dropping them into a large container. Shake the container to scramble the balled-up sheets. Distribute them randomly to each student. Give students three minutes to try to match their classmates with the information.

  - Put students in pairs. Give each pair a blank Venn diagram; have them chart how they are alike and how they are different. After the initial pairs have completed the diagram, each pair should then join another pair and create another Venn diagram that shows how the pairs are alike and different.

  - Have each student create a time line of his or her life. If you let students use large sheets of bulletin board paper and bright markers, you will be able to decorate your classroom with work that students will find fascinating.

  - Have students group themselves according to birthday, eye color, favorite sports teams, favorite music, or other common interests.

  - Check out the many icebreaker websites. One that is particularly helpful for classroom use is Youth Group Games (www.jubed.com/search/ice-breaker).

  - Ask your students to list five things they do well. You will be surprised at how difficult this is for many students; too often, students focus on their weaknesses, not on their strengths.

- Give each student an object and ask what he or she has in common with it. When your students present their findings to the class, you will learn a lot about them as they reveal how they are like paper clips, bookmarks, tissue boxes, or other common classroom items.

- Put your students into pairs and have them determine seven things they have in common. Insist that they go beyond the obvious to discuss such topics as shared experiences, attitudes, aspirations, or other appealing topics.

- You can also learn a great deal about your students from brief writing assignments in which students respond to quick questions. Here are fifty suggestions for topics in the form of statements to be completed by students that you could use at any time of the term:.

  1. When I am grown up, I want to _____.
  2. My favorite things to do at home are _____.
  3. My special friends are _____.
  4. My favorite things to do at school are _____.
  5. The subjects I do best in are _____.
  6. The subjects I need help in are _____.
  7. If I could change anything about school, it would be _____.
  8. I am looking forward to learning about _____.
  9. I like it when my teachers _____.
  10. I would like to know more about _____.
  11. I am happiest when I am _____.
  12. My closest friends are _____.
  13. One thing people don't know about me is _____.
  14. A skill I have is _____.
  15. A person I admire is _____ because _____.
  16. Something I would like to learn to do better is _____.
  17. My previous teachers would tell you this about me _____.
  18. I am proud of myself when I _____.
  19. My greatest asset is _____.
  20. I am an expert on _____.
  21. I have trouble dealing with _____.
  22. My favorite class is _____.
  23. The most influential person in my life is _____ because _____.
  24. It was difficult for me to learn _____.
  25. It was easy for me to learn _____.
  26. Three words that describe my personality are _____.

27. One lesson I had to learn the hard way is _____.
28. I am optimistic about _____.
29. I am pessimistic about _____.
30. If I could do anything right now, I would _____.
31. If I had ten dollars, I would _____.
32. When I do poorly on a test, I _____.
33. When I do well on a test, I _____.
34. I tried hard to learn _____.
35. If I were five years older, I _____.
36. I am most proud of _____.
37. The hardest thing I ever did was _____.
38. At home, I have these rules: _____.
39. If I were a teacher, I would _____.
40. I would like to visit _____.
41. Not many people know _____.
42. I always laugh when _____.
43. I wish teachers would _____.
44. I deserve a trophy for _____.
45. I feel needed when _____.
46. Something I value in a friend is _____.
47. The best advice I've ever received is _____.
48. My favorite day of the week is _____.
49. I worry about _____.
50. I handle stress by _____.

Create a Positive Group Identity

All classes have an identity—a class chemistry that permeates almost everything they do all day long. One of the most important responsibilities of a warm demander is to help entire classes view themselves as uniquely capable. When classes assume a positive identity, they tend to reinforce one another's good behaviors and work together well. The opposite is also true. Once a group starts to think of itself in a negative way, it is almost impossible to change the group's self-perception into a positive one.

When you make a conscious effort to praise and reinforce your class's positive group attributes, you will promote the group's desirable behaviors and extinguish the group's negative ones. Even difficult classes can have positive attributes. If a group is very talkative, for example, you can put a positive twist on it and praise the students for their sociability.

To create a positive group image, you must identify and reinforce positive attributes. Here's how:

- **Step One:** If you learn that your class has a negative self-image, let students know that you disagree with it.

- **Step Two:** Observe two things about your class: how your students interact with one another and with you and how they do their work. Find at least one positive attribute that you can reinforce.

- **Step Three:** Think of a positive label or two for each class and use these labels frequently. Students in each of your classes should believe that their class has a special place in your heart. Here are a few positive labels your students should hear you use at the start of the year:
  - Caring
  - Motivated
  - Intelligent
  - Focused
  - Prepared
  - Successful
  - Friendly
  - Polite
  - Accurate
  - Family
  - Efficient
  - Reasonable
  - Adaptable
  - Reflective
  - Adventurous
  - Energetic
  - Creative
  - Studious
  - Realistic
  - Cooperative
  - Industrious
  - Likable
  - Helpful
  - Open-minded
  - Dependable

- Ingenious
- Determined
- Thoughtful
- Punctual
- Fun-loving
- Curious
- Generous
- Kind
- Inventive
- Tolerant
- Unique

Create a Sense of Belonging to the Whole Group

Just as it is necessary to create connections that bind students to you and to one another, it is also important for them to feel that they belong to a special community. As you work with your class to create a whole-group positive identity, encourage a sense of belonging to the entire group. Here are some suggestions to help students learn to see themselves as part of a positive classroom community:

- Celebrate improvements that they have made as a class: settling down quickly, leaving their work areas tidy, or scoring well on assessments, for example.

- Make it easy for the group to speak with you about concerns. Have students elect student ambassadors to represent them when necessary. For example, the class may want to change a due date for a major project. Instead of each student nagging you, they can talk to their ambassadors, who will formally present their request for you to consider. Their voice is heard, and you do not have to listen to endless complaints.

- Set class goals for them to achieve. Although academic goals are always helpful, nonacademic ones are as well. If there is a charity drive at your school, for example, your students can set goals for how they contribute as a group.

- Celebrate successes. Even minor celebrations can build a sense of unity among students.

- Have class mottoes, code words, handshakes, and other rituals.

- At the end of a unit of study, have a showcase where students can share their best work with their peers.

- Directly teach the cooperation skills necessary for a peaceful classroom.

- Have the group create a class code of conduct that they can use as a guide for their behavior decisions.

Hold Class Meetings

Long associated with primary and elementary classrooms, class meetings have become a staple in many secondary classrooms as well. Class meetings are useful and versatile: you can hold them as often as you like, for as long as you like, with whatever rules you establish, and on any topic. In fact, they are so advantageous that classroom circles are an essential element of the restorative justice movement. (See Section Thirteen for more information about restorative justice.)

For a warm demander, however, class meetings not only offer a strategic way to get to know students but also opportunities for students to interact in positive ways. When you hold class meetings that involve topics that are of interest to students, such as how to study effectively or other issues specific to your school or classroom, then you show your students that you are interested in them as individuals. Because of the inclusive nature of class meetings, students also learn to view themselves as part of a classroom community. Here are several quick tips for conducting successful class meetings:

- Keep it manageable. Hold a carefully planned meeting about a specific topic lasting no more than ten minutes once a week.

- Have a purpose for the meeting. Is it to discuss discipline issues? To allow students to express opinions about a schoolwide topic? To create community?

- Have a specific topic in mind and allow students to think about the topic by having them jot their ideas down before the meeting begins. This will build the necessary confidence students need to be comfortable speaking to the group.

- Arrange the seating so that students can all see one another.

- Spend time before the first meeting talking about the importance of tolerance of and respect for other students' beliefs.

- Make the rules for no side talking and respectful listening clear before the first meeting. This will help ensure that meetings are successful and students will be respectful and focused on the topic.

- Control who speaks with a token, such as a talking piece that students can pass around. The only person who can speak is the person with the token.

- Keep the pace of the meeting brisk. Set a timer at the start so that students are aware of the time limit.

- Consider class meetings that do not involve the whole group. Instead, divide the class in half or into thirds to have mini meetings. Starting each week with mini meetings where students can share personal information with a small group of peers is a useful way to encourage connections among students.

- Holding a brief meeting at the end of the week is also a positive way for students to recap their learning, review main ideas, and look ahead to the next week's assignments. This is also a good way for students to end a unit of study.

Help Students Learn to Relate Well to One Another

To create the connections that are necessary for a productive classroom environment, warm demanders know that when students feel that they are valued members of a group, the results can be remarkable. When they do not feel this connection with their peers, such problems as inattention and disrespect can dominate the classroom.

Warm demanders know that when students are in conflict with one another, learning suffers, so they actively work to manage the problems that may be hindering relationships. They promote the values that can make it easier for students to avoid conflicts: respect for one another's views, tolerance of one another's differences, and willingness to work together for the mutual good of their classmates. Warm demanders also make time to help students learn to work well as part of a community of learners by removing the barriers to peer acceptance that make it difficult for students to work together and by teaching the social skills that will make a classroom environment productive.

REMOVE BARRIERS TO PEER ACCEPTANCE

What are some of the most common barriers to social acceptance in school? Many students could feel excluded because they do not know their classmates. It is a mistake to assume that students know one another well. Even students who have attended school together for several years may not know much about their classmates.

Another barrier is that your students may live in different neighborhoods. If you teach in a school where students may live at a distance or come from different neighborhoods, it is likely that they have not had many opportunities to interact with one another outside of school.

Perhaps the greatest barrier that you will have to help your students overcome is the perception that they may not have much in common with a classmate whom they do not know well. With effort and persistence, you can help students discover their commonalities so that they can learn to accept and support one another. Use the tips in the list that follows to guide you as you work to help students remove the barriers to peer acceptance:

- Make sure that each student's strengths are well known to the rest of the class.
- If a student has an unpleasant history of failure or misbehavior, make it clear that it is time for a fresh start.
- Show your students the correct ways to interact with one another. They need plenty of models and monitoring until they have learned to cooperate productively.
- Let each student shine. Every student should believe that he or she is really your favorite.
- Be sensitive to the differences that divide your students and to the potential for conflict that those differences can cause.

- Make it a point to recognize students who work well with others. Whenever possible, praise the entire class for its cooperative attitude.

- Encourage students to share experiences and personal information about their families, cultures, dreams, and goals while working together or in class meetings.

- Make it very easy for students to understand class routines and procedures and to follow directions well. Students who know what to do are less likely to make embarrassing mistakes for which they can be teased or excluded later.

- Be careful that you model appropriate behavior, thereby encouraging your students to do the same. Don't give in to the temptation of losing your patience when a student blunders in front of classmates. Your actions could set that student up for social exclusion later.

TEACH SOCIAL SKILLS

As a warm demander, one of the most important expectations that you can have for your students is that they treat one another with respect and courtesy. You must not only teach your students the social skills they require to function well in your class but also enforce those skills by insisting on courteous behavior. Here are a few suggestions for teaching social skills in your class:

- Make sure that everyone understands which behaviors are courteous and which are not. Not all your students mean to be rude when they shout insults at one another, interrupt, or put their heads down on their desks when you are talking. Social rules, particularly those in schools, vary widely. Some teachers tolerate behavior that other teachers find offensive. This confuses students of all ages. Be direct and specific about what you expect. Here is a list of some of the social skills that are helpful in any classroom. All students should

  - Use an appropriate volume when talking

  - Not interrupt others unnecessarily

  - Use "please," "excuse me," and "thank you" when speaking with one another and the teacher

  - Try to control angry outbursts or other unpleasant comments

  - Ask permission before taking something that belongs to someone else

  - Refrain from using inappropriate language, such as profanity or insults

  - Drop used tissues in the trash

  - Stay upright in their seats unless they are ill

  - Not clutter the aisles with their personal belongings

  - Slip quietly into class when tardy or when returning from being excused so as not to disturb others

  - Raise their hands as a signal for attention and then wait to be called on

- Show that they are attentive by looking at a speaker
- Clean up their work areas
- Respect others' values, outlooks, and life experiences
- Address one another and the teacher by using appropriate names

- Notice and praise students when you see courtesy in action. This is especially important at the start of a term when students are still unsure of their boundaries. When you see a student or a group of students being courteous, take notice. Point it out so that everyone else can see what you mean when you talk about being polite.

- Exploit the power of peer pressure. You can steer students in the right direction by insisting that everyone in the class treat one another courteously. When this happens, discourteous students will see that there is no peer support for bad behavior. Soon they will police themselves.

- Encourage students to accept one another's differences. Encouraging students to be tolerant of one another can eliminate many negative behaviors in class. You can do this by modeling acceptance and respect for each of your students, particularly the ones who struggle with social skills. Gentle persistence is key to helping those students.

- Model courteous behavior. Rules are useless if you do not model the behavior you want from your students. If you are rude to your students, you can be sure that they will be rude to you and possibly to one another. Each day you have hundreds of opportunities to show your students how to be polite. Take advantage of each one. Being able to show that you are a courteous person is a powerful teacher tool.

The *Demander* Qualities of an Effective Teacher

Just as the *warm* qualities of an educator who is a warm demander come almost effortlessly to caring teachers, so do the three most important *demander* qualities: being explicit about expectations, being consistently focused on learning, and being firm in the enforcement of classroom policies, procedures, and rules. These three key qualities, in combination with a warm relationship with students, make successful learning attainable.

Explicit expectations make the boundaries of acceptable behavior clear for students so that they can begin to self-regulate their behavior. Warm demanders spell out exactly how and why students are to perform classroom procedures and how they will benefit from following routines and policies. Their expectations for exemplary work habits and effort are nonnegotiable.

The second demander quality, being consistently focused on learning, sets a straightforward tone for students: they are expected to work toward mastery of material and to acquire the skills they need for school success. Warm demander teachers have extensive content knowledge, a clear idea of learning outcomes, and well-planned instructional activities. Because they tend to be highly organized, warm demander teachers can focus on the learning needs of their students and the best ways to help them acquire knowledge and develop skills. Warm demanders also offer different paths to mastery and sufficient

R-E-S-P-E-C-T. This may sound like a cliché, but it couldn't be truer. Nagging usually falls on deaf ears, but if students respect you, they will bend over backward for you. Develop a rapport with your students, and strive to be more than just the teacher who is *liked* by everyone. Strive to be both liked *and* respected. It doesn't have to be one or the other. That's the relationship you should strive to develop with your students. Get them to the point where they never want to let you down, and you'll see the results, both academically and behaviorally.

Jay O'Rourke, 2+ years' experience

scaffolding so that students can learn. Teachers and students in a warm demander's classroom work together. Mistakes are celebrated. There is a growth mindset. In fact, one of the chief characteristics of warm demanders is that they insist on student effort and persistence—the keystone of a growth mindset.

The third quality of a warm demander, being firm in the enforcement of classroom policies, procedures, and rules, is possible because the teacher has taken the time to build rapport, earn student respect, and create a positive class environment. The particulars of classroom management have been decided upon with both positive and negative consequences in place. Misbehavior is either treated proactively or with care to protect student dignity and to help misbehaving students move forward. When a student misbehaves, a warm demander treats the misbehavior as a problem with a solution, calmly uses redirection strategies, and enacts appropriate consequences.

Call on Students Equitably

Being a warm demander in the way that you conduct class discussions or elicit whole-group responses requires that you call on all students if you are to hold them accountable for their learning and effort. Many teachers hesitate to call on students who don't appear to know the right answer to a question under discussion out of kindness. They do not want to embarrass students who may not be prepared to answer. The problem with this kind-hearted approach is that it encourages students to not engage fully in the material because they know that they will not be called on. Although the goal of calling on each student every class period is a reasonable and productive one, it is not always easy to do along with all the other management tasks that you are responsible for at the same time. There are several ways to handle this so that you can call on your students equitably.

Some teachers print out a student roster or create a list of student names. As they call on students, they place a check beside their names to indicate that they have already responded.

Another technique that many teachers use is to write each student's name on a note card and then shuffle them into one stack. As students respond, the teacher creates a separate stack of note cards for those students. Once the original stack has been depleted, shuffle and begin again. A similar technique is to write each student's name on a Popsicle stick. As the discussion progresses, the teacher can then separate the popsicle sticks with the names of students who have been called on with those who have not.

If you want to use an online resource that students enjoy seeing in action, try using a random name generator, such as the one at ABCya.com (www.abcya.com/random_name_picker.htm) or Class Tools (www.classtools.net/random-name-picker).

Whichever method you use, keep in mind that if you are going to be a no-nonsense but caring teacher when calling on students, you must call on them equitably. Don't hesitate out of kindness. Instead, help students who don't know the answer understand that mistakes are an acceptable part of learning. Develop a system of calling on students that works well for you and put it into action.

Hold the Entire Class Accountable for One Another

As you work with individual students, holding them accountable for their own success and effort is a relatively simple task, but it is not enough to make a positive difference. (See Section Four for more information about holding students accountable.) Warm demanders know that it is also important that students learn to work together to help one another succeed both as individuals and as a community. Classroom projects, such as growing windowsill plants, keeping supplies in order, or passing out papers, are all tasks that not only help students bond with one another but also learn to be accountable to the group. Delegate as much as your students can reasonably handle. Here are some ways that you can help your students be accountable to one another. In classrooms where students are accountable to one another, students

- Manage daily classroom tasks, such as recycling or keeping the board clean
- Help one another clean up their work areas at the end of class
- Find ways to make class more enjoyable, such as suggesting video clips or music stations
- Remind one another of homework assignments
- Share study tips to work more efficiently
- Maintain a class scrapbook
- Take responsibility for distributing supplies and other materials during class
- Maintain a class blog, web page, or online study group
- Peer edit one another's work before turning it in
- Tutor one another
- Help one another follow classroom policies, procedures, and rules
- Study together
- Remind one another of important due dates
- Help new students become part of the class
- Share notes and other study resources
- Maintain bulletin boards, posted class calendars, and other displays

- Set and work to achieve goals as a class
- Gather handouts for absent students
- Take notes and text them to absent classmates
- Keep a class logbook. You will find a form in Student Worksheet 6.1 that you can adjust to meet the needs of your students. Either ask students to sign up or assign them to do the task of being the class recorder for the day. Pairs of students sitting near one another often manage the task easily, as they can take turns recording the class business. Keep the pages in a three-ring binder for absent students to check when they return to class or for a record of class events.

STUDENT WORKSHEET 6.1

Class Log Page

Day of the week and date: _____

Student reporter: _____

Here's what happened today in class: _____

Homework assignments and due dates:

_____
_____
_____
_____

Handouts you need to pick up:

_____
_____
_____
_____

Class activities:

_____
_____
_____
_____
_____
_____

Work turned in:

_____
_____
_____
_____

Questions to Discuss with Colleagues

Sharing ideas with colleagues is a helpful way to devise solutions to some of the problems that you must manage successfully at school. Here you will find several topics to open discussions with colleagues about successful instructional practices:

1. A parent objects to a book that you have assigned for your entire class to read, even though you obtained administrative approval to use this particular work. How should you handle this situation?

2. During a conference, the parents of an unruly student blame you for their child's misbehavior. What are some of the mistakes you should avoid as you attempt to solve this problem? Who can offer assistance with this issue? What should you do?

3. Some of your students are from nonnuclear families. You want to make sure that you treat their families courteously. What are some of the steps you can take to guarantee that your relationship is positive, beneficial, and respectful?

4. At the beginning of the school year, you gather a great deal of information about your students and their families. How can you organize this information so that you have ready access to it all year?

5. Your students leave the class a mess every day—candy wrappers, trash, and personal materials have been thrown around the room. How can you encourage them to clean up after themselves and to take responsibility for leaving the classroom tidy?

Topics to Discuss with a Mentor

Although the topics that new teachers need to discuss with a mentor vary from teacher to teacher and from school to school, there are some that most first-year teachers should be comfortable discussing with a mentor or a trusted colleague. You should ask your mentor about these topics from this section:

- How to gather and organize information about your students
- How to manage unpleasant interactions with parents or guardians
- Suggestions for helping students relate well to one another
- Suggestions for having high expectations for your students
- Advice on how to find the right balance of warmth and caring for your students

Reflection Questions to Guide Your Thinking

1. You notice that at certain times of the school day, you tend to be more negative than positive with your students in general. What can you do to increase the positive interactions you have with students while still maintaining an orderly classroom?

2. What are you already doing to be a teacher who is a warm demander? What aspects of how you present yourself would you like to improve?

3. How can you show that you care about students while maintaining a respectful emotional distance? Which of your students need more care and understanding at this point in the year than others?

4. What have you observed another teacher doing to forge a positive connection with his or her students' parents or guardians? How can you improve the way that you relate to parents or guardians?

5. What did you do to help your students be successful this week? How do you know they were successful? How did your students react to your actions?

SECTION SEVEN

Meet the Needs of All Students

On the first day of class with your new students, the day will probably zoom past in an exciting blur of new faces and responsibilities. Because you don't know your new students yet, it's tempting to overlook the unique qualities of each. For most teachers, however, those unique qualities are an enjoyable and rewarding challenge. It takes a great deal of creativity, compassion, and insight to meet the needs of every student.

In the past, teachers tended to aim instruction at some sort of imaginary midway point and hope that most students could learn what was expected of them somehow. Educators now realize that having a narrow, academic-based view of their responsibilities was not meeting the needs of every student. An approach to students without consideration for other critical factors in their lives, such as their communities, their families, their health, their learning preferences, or their overall safety, has been unsuccessful in school after school.

Thankfully, this method has been replaced by researched-based approaches that acknowledge the importance of individualized instruction in making the content accessible to all learners. Today's teachers take student differences into consideration when designing instruction and making classroom management decisions.

In the rest of this section, you will learn about some of the initiatives that are changing classroom practice and about how you can reach and teach all your students, including those students who will need extra support from a caring and knowledgeable teacher.

The Whole Child Movement and Its Implications for Your Classroom

The Association for Supervision and Curriculum Development (ASCD), in cooperation with a host of global partners, launched the Whole Child Initiative to support a wide-ranging and inclusive approach to educating all students. The Whole Child Initiative takes the stance that students deserve an environment where they can thrive because they feel safe and are treated as worthwhile individuals whose social, emotional, and physical health needs are addressed.

As a twenty-first-century educator, you should learn as much as you can about the whole child approach to education. Your district or school may make it a priority and offer in-service training because it is a child-centered, caring approach to improving student learning outcomes. In addition to attending local training and working with other educators in your school, here are three excellent resources to help you learn more about how you can include the principles of the whole child approach in your own teaching practice:

- **Association for Supervision and Curriculum Development (ASCD) (www .ascd.org/whole-child.aspx).** A leader in the whole child approach to education, at the ASCD site, you can find a great deal of useful information about the movement and about how you can incorporate the approach into your classroom.

- **Educate the Whole Child (www.educatethewholechild.org).** This site offers a comprehensive view of the whole child approach as well as a wealth of links to articles and resources for educators.

- **The Whole Child (www.wholechildeducation.org).** Here you can learn more about the Whole Child Initiative's scope and history as well as professional development opportunities.

As you learn more about the whole child approach, you will realize that it incorporates many of the best practices that you already have in place in your classroom. Here is a quick list of just some of the ways that you may already be including the principles of the Whole Child Initiative in your classroom. In classrooms where the needs of the whole child are considered, teachers

I wish my students knew how much I legitimately care about them. As a teacher, I *want* them to succeed in whatever way possible; it doesn't have to look like an A. For some students, success looks like improving from a D to a C, and I want them to know that that's okay and that I'm proud of them regardless. There have been countless commutes back to my home at the end of a school day when I reflect and ask, "Did I do enough for student XYZ today?" I wish they could see that side of me as well.

Jay O'Rourke, 2+ years' experience

- Create an inclusive environment where learning goals and activities are transparent to students and parents or guardians
- Model respect for students' cultures and expect that students will also demonstrate respect for one another's cultures
- Differentiate instruction so that the learning needs of all students can be met
- Create a classroom environment where students are safe both physically and emotionally
- Use the mandated curriculum guides provided by their state and district to ensure that the curriculum content is appropriate and relevant for students

- Address the needs of students who need help in strengthening their basic academic skills so that they can learn at an appropriate rate

- Pay attention to the physical, mental, and emotional needs of their students so that they can be healthy

- Maintain an orderly classroom environment where students work together with their teacher and classmates in a purposeful, positive way

- Promote a growth mindset in their students so that they can rise to the challenges of school and daily life

- Connect with their students as caring adults who are concerned about the well-being and success of individual students

How to Include Social Emotional Learning in Daily Classroom Life

Social emotional learning (SEL) is another powerful approach that focuses on the whole child instead of just on academics. Social emotional learning is just what its name implies: learning the emotional skills to handle life and its challenges. For many students, SEL at school enables them to mature and grow through self-awareness and self-regulation. With its emphasis on forming positive and appropriate relationships with others, SEL can make your classroom run more smoothly as well as benefit individual students.

SEL programs vary greatly from school to school because there is such a rich source of material to cover and because students of various ages process the different aspects of SEL at different stages of their development. The social skills that are appropriate to teach young students would not be appropriate in older ones, for example.

If your school district has adopted the SEL initiative, you may be offered in-service training, just as you would have received whole child approach training. This would be particularly helpful to you because it would allow you to make decisions about content and process in collaboration with your colleagues. Although many schools adopt a school- or district-wide program to include SEL in classrooms, yours may not. If you are interested in this intriguing movement, here are two useful resources for learning more about SEL:

- **Collaborative for Academic Social Emotional Learning (CASEL) (www.casel .org).** At the CASEL site, you can learn the basics of SEL and how to incorporate it into your classroom. There are links to various research projects, articles, and practical advice for teachers.

- **Responsive Classroom (www.responsiveclassroom.org).** Here you can find a great deal of useful information about how to help students learn in general and about how to integrate SEL into your classroom. At the home page, use "social emotional learning" as a search term to access the many resources Responsive Classroom offers.

If your school does not have a SEL program in place, you may want to adopt some of the more helpful ideas for your classroom practice. Here are some to consider as you learn more about SEL and how it can improve student learning and well-being. A teacher in a classroom where there is at least an informal SEL program in place

- Helps students connect with one another through shared activities, collaborative learning, class meetings, and team-building activities and icebreakers
- Actively works to build a class community where students have positive relationships with one another and feel a sense of connection to the whole group
- Teaches students to appreciate differences in their classmates' cultures and in global cultures
- Models the social skills students should learn and use
- Helps students appreciate the value of giving to others by encouraging classroom service projects
- Celebrates mistakes and works to make the classroom a risk-free environment
- Helps students learn to resolve conflicts in productive, positive ways
- Teaches students how to set, work for, and achieve goals
- Recognizes the importance of such qualities as determination and persistence
- Teaches students how to work together peacefully and productively

Establish a Risk-Free Environment

No one wants to be embarrassed in front of an entire class, but your students will make mistakes, and sometimes those mistakes will be very public and result in embarrassment. Insightful teachers know that they must take the time to show students how to move past their embarrassment and to learn from their mistakes. Insightful teachers also know that it is their responsibility to establish a classroom environment where ridicule is not acceptable.

Students who are comfortable tend to have teachers who value kindness and cooperation and who make the importance of both traits part of the behavioral expectations for the class. In short, these teachers have made it possible for students to be comfortable enough to take a risk—to try something new without fear of failure or embarrassment.

One of the most intimidating parts of any school day for students involves being called on in class. In review sessions, class discussions, or any activity where students are asked to respond verbally, there is a potential for an awkward moment when a student is wrong in front of peers. To help students avoid being intimidated, here are a few general tips for creating a risk-free environment that you can use when calling on students in class:

- Be open about the mistakes you make yourself. Model how to react appropriately when you are wrong.
- Encourage students to write out their answers before speaking. This will give them time to think as well as to engage fully with the material.

- Make it clear that if students speak to you in advance, you will not call on them.

- When a student is struggling with an answer, here's how you can make the situation easier:

  - Ask if he or she would like to get suggestions or advice from a classmate.

  - Tell students that it is okay to say, "I am not sure, but _____."

  - Ask if he or she would like to opt out or take a pass on the question.

  - Tell the student to give his or her best guess.

  - Offer to come back to the student later.

  - Ask for clarification by saying, "Did I hear you say _____?"

  - Say, "Almost. Can you add a bit more?"

  - Ask another student to tell you what is correct about the answer but then to add to it.

> Many kids have a story that will break your heart. The kids who are the loudest and toughest are often really the most fragile. And you will probably never learn their stories. Continue to offer them opportunities, and connect them with resources. You may get through to them and you may not. It is easy to feel like they are trying to make things difficult for you. But really, they are hurting.
>
> *Jennifer Burns, 13 years' experience*

Create a Culturally Responsive Classroom

One of the most enduring strengths of the public school system in America is the variety of cultures that meet peacefully in thousands of classrooms each day. In classroom after classroom, students of all different races and cultural backgrounds study together. At a time when school systems are scrutinized and criticized from many sides, classroom diversity is one of our nation's greatest assets.

Although some people try to define culture in ethnic or racial terms, a broader definition is more accurate. Every person belongs to a variety of cultural groups delineated by such features as geography, age, economics, gender, religion, interests, or education level. If you ignore the cultural differences among your students, you will create strife and tension. Conversely, if you choose to accept and celebrate those differences, you will find your students' cultures to be a rich resource for your class.

Teach your students to value their differences. When you do this, you are creating a truly global classroom. By expanding students' appreciation of one another, you are showing them how to appreciate the rest of the world. Although the topic of a culturally responsive classroom requires extensive investigation, here are some general guidelines you can use to begin to incorporate the many cultures in your classroom into a successful and unified community:

- Be aware that your attitudes are influenced by your own culture. If your students' cultures are different from yours, you should strive to be sensitive to the differences in attitudes that you may have and of your own implicit bias regarding culture, race, and ethnicity.

- Expose your students to a wide variety of cultures throughout the term. This exposure will enable them to be more tolerant of one another's differences. Instructional materials should incorporate multicultural information and approaches whenever possible.

- Make discussing the cultures in your class an important part of what you and your students do together. You can manage a few minutes every now and then for an informal discussion without losing valuable instructional time.

- Because cultural differences can sometimes lead to misunderstandings, be alert to the potential for student conflict so that you can prevent or minimize it.

- Be very clear about your behavior expectations so that the classroom culture you create can serve to guide student actions and interactions.

- Make it obvious that you appreciate and value your students' cultures. Activities that allow students to learn about their classmates' cultures can include marking birthplaces on a large map; creating a word wall of expressions, such as *thank you* or *please,* in other languages; and having students post photos or images from their cultures on a bulletin board or class web page.

- Accept that the concerns of a parent or guardian who is not part of your culture may be different from the concerns that you have. If you are sensitive to potential differences when you speak with family members, you will find yourself asking questions that can help you determine what their goals for their child are before you attempt to impose your own beliefs.

- Stress to students the importance of an open-minded attitude about people whose beliefs or lifestyles are different from theirs. Make sure you model that tolerance yourself.

- Promote activities that will increase your students' self-esteem. Students who are self-confident are not as likely to taunt others to feel good about themselves.

- Because different cultures stress different ways of learning, you should design instruction that offers a variety of differentiated strategies that students can use to access the material. You should also offer as much appropriate scaffolding as possible to all students who need it.

- If students learn racism or intolerance at home, know that you will have a very difficult time stopping it in class. Your first step in combating intolerant attitudes should be to make your position of tolerance very clear to your students through what you say and do.

RESOURCES THAT CAN HELP YOU PROMOTE CULTURAL SENSITIVITY

There are many different resources to help you and your students learn to appreciate diverse cultures. In this list, you will find two websites with extensive resources for teachers as well as an intriguing and helpful book designed to help you understand the need for cultural awareness:

- **National Education Association (NEA) (www.nea.org/tools/diversity-toolkit .html).** In NEA's extensive toolkit, you will find a wealth of advice and useful information about how to create and manage a diverse classroom.

- **International Education and Resource Network (https://iearn.org).** At this well-known site, you can find lesson ideas, resources, and materials to create an inclusive classroom and promote social justice.

- One of the most thought-provoking and informative books on the topic of culturally responsive classrooms is *For White Folks Who Teach in the Hood and the Rest of Y'all Too: Reality Pedagogy and Urban Education* by Dr. Christopher Emdin (Beacon Press 2017).

There are many easy-to-use online resources available to help teachers who want to include learning projects that will appeal to students while exposing them to a variety of different cultures. Browse the options at these sites to make the best decisions possible about the types of projects that you would like to use to involve your students in authentic learning activities that will not only connect them to other classrooms around the globe but also help them to see the value in the diversity of cultures that populate their world:

- **ePals (www.epals.com).** At the easy-to-navigate ePals site, teachers and students can collaborate with other teachers and students from over two hundred countries in authentic learning projects. You can join other classrooms in projects that are already in progress, or you can design your own project and ask other classrooms to join in.

- **Skype in the Classroom (https://education.microsoft.com/skype-in-the-classroom).** Skype in the Classroom is a community of teachers who are working together to create Skype lessons and connect K–12 classrooms globally through free Skype video, audio, and texting.

Integrate Mindfulness to Support Students

As the whole child approach grows in popularity, so too does the power of mindfulness as a way for students to take care of themselves emotionally. Mindfulness is simply the act of being present in the moment and remaining calm and focused. Such mindfulness practices as guided imagery, self-reflection, or deliberate breathing techniques have long been a part of school life.

In classrooms where teachers and students practice mindfulness, many students report that they are better able to focus and learn. Because of the deliberate slowing down required to stop and breathe deeply or to practice meditation, mindful classrooms tend to be places where students are more self-aware of their reactions and have coping mechanisms in place to manage their feelings. Thus, misbehavior and conflicts are often reduced.

There are many ways to incorporate mindfulness into your classroom that do not take time away from instruction. For example, a brain break where students watch a brief calming video or participate in a guided imagery exercise could take only a few minutes and would leave students refreshed. Another effective technique is to create a class mindfulness motto and have students repeat it during brain breaks. Although there are many resources available to teachers who are interested in including at least some mindfulness strategies into their classrooms, one excellent place to begin is Pinterest (www.pinterest .com). Here, by using the search term "classroom mindfulness," you can find dozens of ideas for incorporating mindfulness techniques for students of all ages. Yet another excellent resource is the website Mindful (www.mindful.org), where you will be able to learn general information about mindfulness and how you can use it to help students and yourself manage stress.

Students Who Need Special Care

Perhaps the basic responsibility that all educators must fulfill is to meet the needs of each of their students. One of the great joys that you will experience as a teacher will happen when, after working diligently with a student to overcome a learning issue, that student finally achieves success. At that moment, all your effort, persistence, and patience will have been worth it.

Although every student deserves the best from you, there are some students who require more attention and care from you than others. In the following pages, you will learn about how to help some of these special populations. From students with attention disorders and 504 Plans to students with special needs or behavior disorders, these students require the very best skills, knowledge, and understanding from their teachers. Although each section is necessarily brief, it is designed to provide an overview of the students who need special care, some general suggestions to work productively with them, and resources to learn more.

> Kids are kids. They are not small adults. They are young. They get to learn. They get to fail. They get to succeed. You get to be their support and cheerleading section.
>
> *Anna Aslin Cohen, 40 years' experience*

Students with Attention Disorders

Students with attention deficit disorder (ADD) or attention deficit/hyperactivity disorder (ADHD) usually require intervention from supportive adults to be academically successful.

If you are a general education teacher, a special education teacher or a counselor will probably talk to you at the beginning of the term about your students with attention disorders. That teacher will suggest appropriate accommodations and will review each student's individualized education program (IEP) or 504 Plan with you.

To learn more about how you can help students with attention disorders, search the Internet, beginning with the websites of the Attention Deficit Disorder Association (www.add.org) and Children and Adults with Attention-Deficit/Hyperactivity Disorder (www.chadd.org). These helpful sites offer many practical tips, links to other sites, articles on a variety of issues pertaining to attention disorders, and information on legal issues of concern regarding students with attention disorders. In addition to your own research, here are some general guidelines to assist you in teaching students with ADD or ADHD:

- Enlist assistance from other professionals and from the parents and guardians of students with ADD or ADHD. These people can be an excellent source of support and advice as you work together to assist students.

- Teach school success skills. Students with ADD or ADHD have not always mastered effective school-related skills, such as taking notes or following directions. Take the time to show them how to accomplish some of the tasks that other students find easy.

- Clearly define classroom procedures for students with ADD or ADHD to help them stay on task. They will benefit from seeing as well as hearing directions and other information.

- Monitor students with attention disorders unobtrusively by placing them near you. You should also seat them with their backs to other students so that they will be less easily distracted. Other distractions to consider are doors, windows, computer screens, pencil sharpeners, and high-traffic areas.

- Give students with attention disorders extra assistance during transition times; it is not always easy for them to adjust to a change.

- When you give directions, be sure to give them one step at a time. Because students with attention disorders tend to be easily overwhelmed by large tasks and need guidance in planning how to accomplish their work, you should help students understand that each task is a sequence of smaller steps.

- Photocopy parts of a text that students may find particularly difficult, then highlight key parts. Using this text as an example, show your students with ADD or ADHD how they can do the same thing themselves to focus on important information in the text.

- Offer alternative auditory modes of learning. Students with attention disorders usually do well when they can listen to an audiotape of a text as they read the selection; the soundtrack helps keep them focused on the text.

- Encourage computer use. Using a computer is a skill that students with ADD or ADHD often find helpful because it enables them to work quickly and competently, thus making it easier for them to stay on task because much of the tedium they associate with written work has been removed.

- Review frequently so that students with attention disorders have the basic skills and facts mastered before you move on to the next topic.

At-Risk Students

At-risk students are those who are likely to drop out of school instead of graduating. Like most students, their future success depends on their getting as much education as they can. Although there are many promising programs and a great deal of support available for students who are at risk in this way, too many students still drop out of school. Students can be at risk for dropping out for many reasons. Here are just a few of the possible contributing factors:

- Family problems
- Poor academic skills
- Substance abuse
- Pregnancy
- Emotional problems
- Chronic peer conflicts
- Repeated failure in school
- Inadequate supervision by parents or guardians
- Undiagnosed learning problems
- Chronic illness

At-risk students depend on their teachers to help them stay in school. Although the strategies listed here will benefit all your students, it is especially important for you to reach out to those who are at risk. Adapt the following ideas to meet the needs of your at-risk students:

- Be persistent in your efforts to motivate at-risk students. Do not hesitate to let them know you plan to keep them in school as long as you possibly can.
- Spend time helping your students establish life goals so that they can see a larger purpose for staying in school. Without a purpose for learning, a student who wants to drop out may see school as an exercise in futility.
- Set small goals that will help students reach a larger one. If you can get them in the habit of achieving at least one small goal each day, they can build on this pattern of success.
- Involve students in cooperative learning activities. Feeling connected to their classmates empowers and supports students who may be considering quitting school.
- Invite guest speakers or older students to talk with younger ones about the importance of staying in school.

- Ask open-ended questions so that at-risk students can attempt giving answers without fear of failure or embarrassment.

- Be generous with praise and attention. Your kind words may often be the only ones your at-risk students will hear all day.

- Seek assistance from support personnel and family members. It takes many determined adults to change a student's mind once he or she has decided to drop out.

- Check on students when they are absent. Call home. Show your concern.

- Create situations in which at-risk students can be successful. Perhaps they can tutor younger students, mediate peer conflicts, or help you with classroom chores. Focus on their strengths.

- Tailor activities to students' preferred learning styles. When the work seems too difficult, at-risk students can often be successful if the their teacher uses another modality to teach the material they need to know.

- Connect to at-risk students in a positive way. Make sure that they understand that they are important to you and to their classmates.

To learn more about at-risk students, begin with the National Center for School Engagement (http://schoolengagement.org). At this site, you can learn more about the reasons students are truant or drop out of school and how to help them stay in school.

LGBTQ Students

Headlines about students who identify as LGBTQ (Lesbian, Gay, Bisexual, Transgender, and Questioning) and the statistics that accompany them are as disturbing as they are sad. LGBTQ students are overwhelmingly more prone to commit suicide than their straight classmates. LGBTQ students of all ages also report a relentless barrage of harassment that begins as early as preschool and never stops. It is our responsibility as professionals to offer support and encouragement to all our students, including those who struggle as much as LGBTQ students are forced to.

As a caring educator, you can take many actions to support the students in your class who may be LGBTQ. One good place to start is to educate yourself about LGBTQ students and their very real struggles in regard to their education. A good resource for this is provided by Human Rights Watch (www.hrw.org), an organization that offers a wealth of information about the plight of LGBTQ students as part of its mission to defend and protect human rights around the world. The organization's report *Hatred in the Hallways* outlines the difficulties that many LGBTQ students face in school and offers suggestions concerning how educators can support this population in the classroom.

In addition to educating yourself, there are some commonsense actions you can take to assist the LGBTQ students at your school:

- Be a role model of acceptance and support for all your students, including LGBTQ students.

- If an LGBTQ student confides in you, respect his or her privacy, if possible. If it is not possible for you to do so—for example, if he or she has been sexually abused or bullied—inform the student before he or she confides in you further.

- Encourage and support diversity programs at your school and in the community. Diversity does not only mean culture, skin color, or ethnicity but also includes sexual orientation.

- Take action when you hear name-calling, harassment, or other types of bullying. Many schools have a clearly defined antidiscrimination policy to address bullying. Enforce it.

- Be aware of harmful stereotypes and the common slurs that students can use against their LGBTQ peers so that you can combat them effectively.

Students Who Are Not Native Speakers of English

In recent years, the number of students for whom English is not their native language has greatly increased in many U.S. schools. The cultural diversity these students bring enriches our classrooms, even as it presents a perplexing problem for teachers who do not speak their students' native languages. With sensitivity, courtesy, and insight, you can help your students who primarily speak a minority language. Here are some strategies that should make this process easier for you and these students:

- Keep in mind that students who speak little English not only have to learn the content that your other students must learn but also have to learn it in a foreign language.

- Make a point of learning to pronounce the names of these students correctly. Insist that your other students do so, too.

- Be aware of cultural differences and sensitive issues. For example, in many cultures it is rude to maintain eye contact.

- Give as many directions as you can in writing as well as orally.

- Label items in your classroom to help students learn simple words.

- Keep resources on your students' cultures on hand for other students to read. Library books and Internet sites are good sources of such material.

- Arrange for your students to interact. Students who can communicate with one another about their work tend to be successful. It is also easier for students to learn English if other students engage them in conversation as much as possible.

- Use a variety of learning styles to help your students master content as well as a new language. Graphic organizers and other useful study devices will help students who are learning English.

- Encourage students to read aloud to you whenever it is appropriate. Be careful that your corrections of English learners are helpful and not overwhelming.

- Set realistic expectations for your students who speak little English. They are not going to be able to do as much work as your other students if the work involves intensive interaction with a text because it will take them longer just to figure out the language.

- Don't rush to answer questions or to fill in words when students are struggling to think through their responses. You must be patient and supportive if you want your students to learn successfully.

- Find bilingual dictionaries in the languages that your students speak. Encourage them to use the relevant bilingual dictionary frequently. Model its use yourself.

- Use audiotapes and other technology appropriate to the age and ability levels of your students. Students benefit from both seeing and hearing the language.

Although there are many resources available to help you work well with your students who are not native speakers of English, there are three that are particularly helpful:

- **Dave's ESL Cafe (www.eslcafe.com).** This excellent site offers a wealth of useful information, resources, links, activities, and insights into teaching students who are not proficient in English.

- **Internet Polyglot (www.internetpolyglot.com).** Here you can find interactive games and instructional activities to help students who are not English language learners as well as help with translating into many different languages.

- **Larry Ferlazzo,** a prolific writer and blogger, is also an English teacher at Luther Burbank High School in Sacramento, California. Ferlazzo offers an incredible wealth of valuable materials—many geared to helping English language learners— in his many books, syndicated columns, blog, work with BAM Radio and Edutopia, and daily RSS feeds. To access the resources Ferlazzo offers, use his name, "Larry Ferlazzo," as a search term to discover an abundance of resources for your classroom

Students Who Are Underachievers

Few students go through their school years without having moments when they could have done better. Occasional underachievement is to be expected, but this behavior becomes challenging when it is the overriding pattern in a student's school life.

Chronic underachievement is a problem for students of many ages and capabilities. Their parents or guardians are often quick to reveal that their children are either lazy or just don't try hard enough. The students often label themselves in these negative ways, too. As you begin to work with underachieving students, you may find yourself calling their parents or guardians often, and you will find yourself frustrated when no punishment you can devise solves the problem. In fact, many underachievers accept punishment as their due.

Chronic underachievement is not just a bad habit. It is often an elaborate defense mechanism that students adopt to protect themselves from their anxiety about failing. Underachieving students often have successful, highly goal-oriented parents who are very involved in their lives. Parents of underachievers often spend lots of energy trying to understand and help their children.

The problem compounds itself when underachievers are gifted students. These students must live up to their parents' high expectations and their own exacting standards. They opt for certain failure instead of trying and possibly failing. The contrast between their potential and what they achieve is frustrating for everyone who works with them. Working with underachieving students can be made less frustrating with a combination of these strategies:

- Accept that these students' shortcomings are not the result of laziness, even though they may see themselves as lazy and worthless. Their anxiety often paralyzes them.

- Work with parents and guidance counselors to help underachievers, but be aware that overinvolvement can sometimes increase a student's anxiety.

- Strive to make assignments so appealing that all students will want to do their work. Underachievers need extra motivation. They seldom find the work intrinsically interesting.

- Don't expect your underachieving students to be more than briefly motivated by their own success. Too often, after a successful school experience, underachievers will stop putting forth any effort—a situation that frustrates their family and teachers.

- Work out a plan with these students and their parents or guardians to guarantee that work will be turned in to you on time. Underachievers often do not turn in work, even when they have completed it. Consider accepting digital assignments whenever feasible.

- Use a checklist to show students how to accomplish their assignments. Underachievers need assistance in establishing their priorities so that they can work with purpose.

- Teach study skills, time management, and organization strategies so that the work will not be burdensome for an underachieving student who is easily overwhelmed by school tasks.

- Be matter of fact about assignments. Expect students to do them, and offer extra help and encouragement where necessary. If you allow your anger to show, or if you reprimand underachieving students harshly for not completing the work, they will have difficulty finishing it.

- Be positive and supportive as you encourage effort and the attempts to work. One of the most effective strategies is to bolster self-esteem in your underachievers.

- Offer help soon after you give an assignment in class. For many underachievers, the hardest part of an assignment is getting started. They may make several beginnings before giving up.

- Be aware that underachievers seldom ask for help. Be proactive in offering assistance.

- Offer frequent and unobtrusive encouragement. Underachievers often have a perfectionist approach to their studies that results in incomplete work—the opposite of what they wanted to accomplish.

- Don't allow students to give you such excuses as "I am just lazy" or "I never do well in math." Most underachievers passively accept criticism from the disappointed adults in their lives. They tend to use the negative labels to excuse themselves from not working.

- Form a close connection with underachieving students whenever you can. If they feel that you are counting on them, they have more incentive to work than if you indicate that you do not care if they do their work.

- Boost students' self-esteem by encouraging them to tutor students who are less able. Underachievers often will help other students when they will not help themselves.

Students Living in Poverty

Millions of school-age students in America live in poverty. You don't have to teach in a blighted urban area or a depressed rural region to teach students who are from a poor family. The lives of poor students are often very different from those of their more affluent peers. They cannot look forward to presents at Christmas or on their birthdays. Back-to-school shopping is not an exciting time of new clothes and school supplies. Even small outlays of money are significant to students living in poverty; a locker fee, a soft drink for a class party, or a fee for a field trip may be out of their reach. In addition, because they do not wear the same fashionable clothes as their peers, poor students are often the targets of ridicule.

Economically disadvantaged students have a very difficult time succeeding in school. One of the most unfortunate results of their economic struggles is that students who live in poverty often drop out of school, choosing a low-paying job to pay for the small luxuries they have been denied instead of an education. Despite the bleak outlook for many of these students, you can do a great deal to make school a meaningful haven for them. You can help your students who live in poverty by implementing some of these suggestions:

- When you suspect that your students are taunting their disadvantaged peers, act quickly to stop the harassment.

- If you want poor students to connect their book learning with real-life situations, spend time adding to their worldly experiences by involving them in such activities as field trips or internships. Students who live in poverty may not have been exposed to such broadening experiences as family vacations, trips to museums, or even eating in restaurants.

- Listen to your disadvantaged students. They need a strong relationship with a trustworthy adult if they are to succeed.

- Work to boost the self-esteem of students who live in poverty by praising their school success instead of what they own.

> I had a student visit my snack drawer every day. I found out that he was saving his school breakfast and lunch to take home to his little sister because they had very little to no food in the house. I made sure that my snack drawer was always full for him.
>
> *Deborah McManaway, 23 years' experience*

- Keep your expectations for poor students high. Poverty does not mean ignorance.
- Don't make comments about your students' clothes or belongings unless they are in violation of the dress code.
- Take the time to explain the rationale for rules and procedures in your classroom. Students who live in poverty may not always know the correct behaviors for school situations. At home, they may function under a different set of social rules.

- Be careful about the school supplies you expect students to purchase. Keep your requirements as simple as you can for all students.
- Arrange a bank of shared supplies for your students to borrow when they are temporarily out of materials for class.
- Do not require costly activities. For example, if you ask students to pay for a field trip, some of them will not be able to go because of the cost.
- If you notice that a student does not have lunch money, check to make sure that a free lunch is an option for that child.
- Be very sensitive to the potential for embarrassment in even small requests for or comments about money that you make. For example, if you jokingly remark, "There's no such thing as a free lunch," you could embarrass your low-income students.
- Make it clear that you value all your students for their character and not for their possessions.

For more information on how to help your economically disadvantaged students, visit aha!Process (www.ahaprocess.com), an organization founded by Ruby Payne, a leading expert on the effects of generational poverty on students. Her book *A Framework for Understanding Poverty*, first published in 1996 by aha!Process, is significant because it explains how the silent culture clash between students and teachers in classrooms has a harmful effect on students.

Other helpful resources are offered by the National Education Association (www.nea.org). Use "children of poverty" as a search term on the home page to access dozens of helpful articles.

Students with Autism Spectrum Disorders

One of the most encouraging results of neurological and educational research in recent years is that educators not only are more knowledgeable about the various types of disorders falling under the heading of autism spectrum disorders (ASD) that may affect their students but also now know more about how to help these students. ASD can be loosely defined as developmental disorders that can include autism, Asperger's syndrome, Rett syndrome, and others. Although individuals with ASD can have very different characteristics from one other, often these disorders can cause difficulties with social and communication skills, aversion to change and difficulty with transitions, atypical responses to sensory stimuli, and sometimes repetitive behaviors.

As a teacher, you are very likely to have students with ASD in your classes, even if you do not work exclusively with students with special needs. To make learning attainable for students with ASD, the first step you must take is to educate yourself about the types of disorders that your students may have. One of the best resources to help you with this is the National Institute of Child Health and Human Development (www.nichd.nih.gov). At this division of the National Institutes of Health that deals with children's health, browse the "Health & Research" tab to learn more about ASD and to access links to even more resources.

You can also learn more at the site maintained by the Autism Society (www.autism-society.org). This large grassroots advocacy organization has many different chapters across the United States. At this site, you can find specific resources as well as links to more help.

In addition to learning as much as you can about ASD, it is also very important that you learn as much as possible about the individual students with ASD in your class. To do this, you should first reach out to the parents and guardians of your students, who can then inform you of the best ways to help their children. As with parents and guardians of all your students, a strong partnership between your classroom and your students' families is an excellent way to help your students. You should also take the time to consult with previous teachers your students may have had as well as any records your school holds. By educating yourself about ASD in general and about your students in particular, you will be in a better position to make success attainable for them. Here is a list of some other useful strategies to help your ASD students:

- Make your classroom as inclusive and welcoming as possible. This may mean educating other students about ASD so that they know the most appropriate ways to interact with all their classmates. Consider creating peer buddies to help students with ASD. Both the buddy and the student with ASD will benefit from such interactions.

- Be extra diligent about documentation and record keeping for your students with ASD. This will enable you to be able to work well with their parents or guardians as well as with other professionals who work with these students.

- Create a well-organized classroom where students with ASD, who can sometimes be overwhelmed by stimuli, can feel comfortable. Avoid clutter and overdecoration whenever you can. If possible, establish an area of the room where students who are feeling stressed can go for quiet time and recovery.

- Provide visual cues to help students stay on task and focused. Calendars, charts, and other informational cues are often helpful for students with ASD. Further, graphic organizers can help students master academic work.

- Plan daily routines that students can follow independently. This makes the school day more manageable for students with ASD, especially because transition times are often difficult periods for them.

- Plan how you are going to manage the behavior challenges that students with ASD can present. Ask yourself which behaviors you can ignore and which ones you must deal with. Promote and encourage positive behaviors.

Gifted Students

Gifted students are usually both fun and difficult to teach. When a lesson interests a gifted child, he or she will take the lesson far beyond the boundaries of the material. Gifted students are also challenging to teach. They are impatient with topics they don't perceive as interesting, and they can be especially impatient with teachers and peers whom they perceive to be less than capable. To learn more about teaching gifted students, consult some of the many books and websites that other teachers have found valuable. Two helpful sites are listed here:

- **National Association for Gifted Children (www.nagc.org).** At this site, you will find excellent resources for educators: links to websites with advice for those who teach students with high potential, research articles, and helpful information about teaching gifted children.
- **TeachersFirst (www.teachersfirst.com/gifted.cfm).** At TeachersFirst, you can access reading lists; strategies for teachers; links to other websites, including interactive online sites; booklists for students; and information on how to modify instruction to appeal to multiple intelligences.

When you have gifted students in your class, you will need to modify the content of the material, the learning process, or both to accommodate their needs. Use or adapt the guidelines that follow to help your gifted students be successful:

- Allow students to have a strong voice in how they will accomplish their goals. Gifted students are often self-directed learners. Take this characteristic into consideration when you modify the process of learning.
- Set a rapid pace for instruction. Gifted students quickly grow bored with the slower pace of undifferentiated instruction.
- Focus on having students use higher-level thinking skills throughout a unit of study; gifted students quickly master the recall and comprehension levels of assignments.
- Use technology as often as you can. Your gifted students are likely to become proficient at accessing resources on the Internet with just a bit of guidance from you.
- Encourage student input in the selection of material. You may have a general unit of study, but allow students to study the details that most interest them.
- Focus on depth of content rather than on quantity. For example, having students read three excellent books on a topic of study is better than asking them to read five books of lesser quality.

- Although allowing gifted students to serve as peer tutors is acceptable, be careful not to overuse this technique. It reinforces what they already know, but it doesn't provide enrichment of their own skills in the subject they are tutoring past a certain point.
- Work closely with the parents and guardians of gifted students so that you can fulfill each child's needs and reduce gifted learners' frustration when lessons don't appeal to their abilities or learning styles.

Children of Trauma

According to the National Child Traumatic Stress Network, one-quarter of all students will experience a traumatic event before the age of sixteen. There are many ways that students in twenty-first-century classrooms can experience trauma: a divorce in the family, the loss of a family member or friend, witnessing violence, abuse, neglect, or being a refugee. The hardships that students can undergo are sadly endless.

Perhaps the most supportive action that you can take with a student who has been traumatized is to be aware of the problem and to act in as supportive a manner as possible. For example, you may notice that a normally well-behaved student is having trouble focusing or working cooperatively with classmates. If you ignore the situation, the student will not receive the help and support he or she needs. If, instead of ignoring the problem, you take the time to talk with the student and to listen carefully, you may learn the cause of the problem and be able to offer the appropriate support.

Be aware that you will have children of trauma in your class. Take the time to learn about them, and you have a better chance of not only working well with them but also being part of the healing process that they need. A particularly helpful site to learn more about what you can do to connect with and support these students is the National Child Traumatic Stress Network (http://nctsnet.org). Their toolkit offers a great deal of useful information and links to other helpful sites.

Reluctant Learners

If you think back to your own school days, it may help you to understand the students in your class who are reluctant learners. All of us have been reluctant learners at one time or another. We, too, did not feel like doing our homework or paying attention or working with others in a group. The difference in being an occasionally reluctant learner and one who never wants to work, however, is serious. When students don't do their schoolwork, they lose their ability to stay apace with their classmates. Over even a brief period, they fall behind and then find other, even less acceptable ways to amuse themselves in our classes.

There are many resources available for teachers who want to work well with reluctant learners. One very helpful site for learning how to work with reluctant learners is found by using "reluctant learners" as a search term at Mindshift (https://ww2.kqed.org /mindshift).

Here are just a few brief ideas to successfully turn around students who are reluctant learners:

- Strive to determine the causes of the child's reluctance. Too often teachers view a student as lazy or react in anger instead of taking a problem-solving approach.
- Try not to overwhelm the reluctant student with a large amount of practice work.
- Teach students efficient shortcuts that can take the tedium out of assignments.
- Offer instruction that appeals to various learning styles.
- If you notice that students are not working, ask them to tell you what they already know. Often this will encourage them to continue.
- Offer help to those students who feel that their work must be perfect before they turn it in.
- Stress the practical value of what they are learning.
- Provide an authentic audience as often as possible.
- Build student confidence. Students who feel capable will try harder than those who don't.
- Stress the relationship between effort and outcome.
- Appeal to their interests, sense of fun, and competitive natures whenever you can.
- Involve them in authentic, cooperative projects that offer help to others less fortunate.
- Involve them in work that requires cooperative learning, technology, inquiry, critical thinking, or open-ended questions.

Impulsive Students

Students with this learning problem are easy to recognize in any classroom. They are usually the ones soaking up all the negative attention. Impulsive students may act before thinking. They may spend too much time in an unproductive attempt to get organized at the beginning of an assignment. The floor around their desks may be littered with piles of balled-up paper that has been hastily scribbled on and discarded.

These students disturb others by calling out answers without regard to whether they are right or wrong. These are the students who seem to live frantic lives in a state of near crisis. Every request to leave the room is an emergency. Every bad grade is a sure sign they are going to fail the entire course. Undone homework—a constant problem—is someone else's fault. They are fidgety and forgetful and their own worst enemies.

Impulsive students require the utmost in patient firmness from their teachers. With the help of sympathetic teachers and other adults, these students can be transformed into well-behaved and successful students. If you have one of these students, consider trying some of the strategies suggested here to help them develop self-discipline and to work productively:

- Replace their negative behaviors with more appropriate ones. Teach the correct behavior to follow in your class for the various times when impulsive students seem to have the most trouble staying focused. For example, be firm about expecting these students to remain seated while you are speaking to the entire class.

- Be very specific about what is and what is not acceptable behavior. Begin consistent reinforcement as soon as you do this. If you are not consistent, you will only confuse impulsive students.

- Don't accept excuses that are clearly inappropriate. Impulsive students need to be sure of the boundaries of acceptable and unacceptable behavior. Be concrete and specific.

- Make sure they see their assignments as small steps that lead to something bigger and that these small steps need to be accomplished one at a time.

- Use plenty of positive reinforcement to build confidence and to reassure impulsive students that they are on the right track. They need positive attention to replace the negative attention they have been used to receiving.

- Impulsive students also usually respond well to a behavior contract because it is very specific about what they will be expected to do.

A helpful site for learning how to deal with impulsive students is sponsored by Understood (www.understood.org). At Understood, use "impulsive students" as a search term to learn more.

Students with Oppositional Defiant Disorder

ODD (oppositional defiant disorder) students are those students who persistently display these characteristics: anger, irritability, refusal to compromise, refusal to follow directions or rules, vindictiveness, and testing of limits. In a classroom, even one ODD student can create chaos. Although there is no cure for the disorder, there are several things teachers can do to work successfully with these stress-inducing students. Here are a few suggestions that may help you cope with the ODD students in your classroom:

- Start each day with a fresh and positive attitude and encourage the ODD student to do the same. Carrying a negative attitude over from the previous day will not help you or the student resolve the present day's issues.

- Figure out ways to manage your own stress levels. If any students are going to create stress for you, the ODD students will. Be proactive in thinking through how you will manage your frustration.

- Be very explicit in establishing the boundaries for behavior in your classroom. ODD students are known for testing limits. If there are gray areas instead of clearly defined limits, expect misbehavior.

- When reprimanding any student, and particularly an ODD one, use a very calm and matter-of-fact tone.

- Never threaten. Just state the consequences that you are willing to enact.

- Avoid power struggles and don't allow yourself to be dragged into arguments. Instead, be explicit in your directions and expectations. (For more information about classroom power struggles, see Section Fourteen.)

- ODD students misbehave most often when a teacher is permissive or inconsistent. Be fair, firm, and friendly, but do not consider "just this once" with ODD students.

- Help ODD students who have misbehaved save their dignity by speaking to them about the problem in private, away from the embarrassment of having other students overhear. This is especially excruciating for the ODD student.

- Do not delay acting on a misbehavior once a transgression has occurred. Put the consequence into effect at once.

- State all directions in a positive manner to avoid the escalation of a power struggle. Redirect as often as you can. For example, instead of "Stop doing that" say, "Please go to your seat."

- Offer limited choices in a two-step format. For example, you can say, "You can either begin working now, or you will have to do it during recess. It's up to you." The key is to calmly offer the ODD student valid choices.

Two helpful sites for dealing with ODD students are found at Intervention Central (www.interventioncentral.org) and Difficult Students (www.difficultstudents.com). At both sites, you can find practical resources, materials, and advice about how to support ODD students.

Students Who Fall through the Cracks

Teachers use the term *fall through the cracks* to describe students who struggle to succeed academically but who do not qualify for special services. There are far more of these students in classrooms than many inexperienced educators could anticipate given the extensive testing that most students undergo. Experienced teachers, however, are sadly all too familiar with the difficulties faced by students who fall through the cracks.

It is not always easy to identify students who fall through the cracks until you really get to know them as individuals. They tend to struggle in school for years, just barely missing the qualifying deficits for special needs qualifications, but with many of the same negative behaviors and failures that identified students have. Too often students who fall through the cracks present themselves as lazy or uncaring. If you suspect that you have students in this category, there is a great deal that you can do to support them.

First, discover as much as you can about their learning styles and their school history as well as their home situation. Talk to past teachers and parents or guardians. Study permanent records. Look at test score data. Observe their work habits. Do all that you can to understand the barriers to success for these students.

These students, like their classmates, benefit from differentiated instruction. Being able to use their strengths to overcome weaknesses in learning is rewarding and motivating for students who fall through the cracks.

Many of the same accommodations, such as preferential seating, copies of notes, and audio texts, that are helpful to students who have qualified for special education or 504 services are also appropriate for these students. Offer them freely as differentiation methods.

> *Never* tell a parent you have not read the paperwork (504, IEP, etc.) for his or her child. You should read everything before the school year starts *and* review everything before any parent meeting.
>
> *Margaret R. Scheirer, 12 years' experience*

It is also important to not give up on students who fall through the cracks. Even though they may not have qualified for special services, there is clearly an undiagnosed need for support that you, as a caring teacher, can provide.

For more information on how you can help students whom you suspect of falling through the cracks, visit the website maintained by We Are Teachers (www.weareteachers .com/low-performing-students-tactics).

Students with 504 Plans

A 504 Plan is a legally binding document that protects students who have a documented physical, emotional, or mental disability that limits their ability to learn. Students with 504 Plans are those whose disabilities do not need to be addressed by a teacher specifically trained to teach special education students. Instead, students with 504 Plans have needs that can be addressed with modifications by a general education teacher.

Students with 504 Plans might have any number of issues that affect their ability to succeed in school: ADD or ADHD, chronic illness, anger management problems, or impaired vision or hearing; or they might be obese or be confined to a wheelchair—just to name a few. Although these students do not qualify for special education programs, their 504 Plans spell out special accommodations they must receive. The accommodations in a 504 Plan may include various types of assistance, such as extra time on assignments, an extra set of textbooks, classrooms that are wheelchair accessible, or preferential seating.

When the school term begins, you will receive copies of the 504 Plans for your students. You may also meet with the 504 Plan administrator for your school to discuss each plan and what your specific responsibilities are. Although each 504 Plan is unique because it is tailored to the needs of the child it protects, typical accommodations that you might see include the following:

- Preferential seating
- Extended time on assignments

- Extra books or materials
- Reduced practice time
- Frequent contact with parents or guardians
- Early notification of parents or guardians when problems arise
- Written copies of notes presented orally
- Assistance with organization skills

You must follow 504 Plans exactly. 504 Plans are different from other school documents in that if you fail to follow them, the parents or guardians of the child have the right to sue not only the school district but also the classroom teacher. Even if you are personally uncomfortable with an accommodation, you must make that accommodation.

A useful site for learning how to successfully help students with 504 Plans is sponsored by Understood (www.understood.org). At the site, use "504 plans" as a search term to learn more.

Students with Special Needs

Special needs is a very broad term that encompasses a wide range of disabilities and conditions. Students with special needs will be the treasures of your first year as a teacher when you learn to work with them successfully.

In years past, most teachers did not see students with special needs in their classes. These students were segregated in special classrooms or centers, where they had little contact with the general school population. This practice ended with the passage of Public Law 94–142, which mandated that children be educated in the "least restrictive environment." Because of this law, students who have special needs are now frequently part of ordinary school life.

The Internet provides a great deal of information about students with special needs. To learn more about this topic, try these websites:

- **Council for Exceptional Children (www.cec.sped.org).** This site is the "voice and vision of special education." It offers current information on trends, online courses, information about national and local policies, guidelines for various types of exceptionalities, and an excellent overview of the field.

- **LD OnLine (www.ldonline.org).** This site advertises itself as the world's largest website for students with learning disabilities and attention disorders. It offers advice on motivation, an excellent glossary of educational terms, many practical strategies, information about social skills for students with learning disabilities, and an online forum.

- **Learning Disabilities Association of America (LDA) (www.ldaamerica.org).** In existence since 1963, the LDA offers current strategies for handling such practical concerns as homework policies and test accommodations. The informative site offers a great deal of support for teachers who have students with specific learning disabilities.

You can expect to have many types of students with special needs in your classes, from students who need only a slight accommodation to help them learn to students with severe disabilities. How successfully you handle this challenge will depend on your attitude. Along with having a positive attitude, the following general strategies can guide you as you teach your students with special needs:

- Accept your students' limitations and help them overcome them. Although some teachers think students with disabilities that are not as obvious as others just need to try harder, trying very hard is not enough to create success for many of these students.

- Be proactive in dealing with students with special needs. Make sure you understand their specific disabilities and the required accommodations.

- Give your best when teaching students with special needs. They deserve your best effort. When you take this view, you will be in a good position to help them. Expect to work closely with the special education teachers assigned to help you modify your instruction to meet the needs of every learner in your class.

- Accept responsibility for your students' success. Don't anticipate extensive additional training on how to help your students with special needs. Continue to educate yourself about how to work well with these students by reading professional literature, researching relevant websites, attending workshops, and observing special education teachers as they teach.

- Be sensitive to the needs of each student and anticipate them whenever you can. For example, be sure to seat students with special needs where they can see and hear you without distractions.

- Use the resources available to you. Study students' permanent records to understand the instructional strategies that have worked well in past school years. As soon as possible, contact the special education teachers who are working with your students with special needs so that you can learn the specific strategies that will help them learn successfully. Some of the other adults who can help you learn about your students are parents and guardians, the school nurse, counselors, and current or previous teachers.

- Talk with each student with special needs about his or her concerns. Make it easy for these students to communicate with you. Even young children can tell you when they learn best and what activities help them master the material.

INSTRUCTIONAL STRATEGIES FOR STUDENTS WITH SPECIAL NEEDS

The following are some helpful ideas for teaching students with special needs. Because students' needs vary, not all the ideas will be appropriate for every one of these students, but you can adapt them to fit your needs.

- Limit the materials you ask students with special needs to manage at any given time. They should have only the materials necessary for the successful completion of a lesson on their desks.

- Limit the number of practice items. For example, instead of assigning fifteen drill sentences, ask students to complete ten before checking for mastery.

- Consider each student's learning style preferences when you create assignments. When you can, modify the assignment to better fit his or her needs. If you can provide alternative materials, do so.

- Be sure to provide prompt feedback when a student with special needs completes an assignment.

- Limit the amount of written work that you assign to students with special needs.

- Offer a variety of activities. Change the pace several times in each class so that students will find it easy to stay on task.

- Structure your classroom routines so that students can predict what they will be expected to do. Go over the daily objectives at the start of the class, and offer students a checklist to keep them on task all day.

- Be generous with your praise when your students with special needs do something well.

- Give very clear directions. Ask students with special needs to restate what you want them to do. On written work, use bold type or other eye-catching design elements to distinguish the directions from the rest of the text.

- Offer collaborative learning opportunities often. Working with other students often reinforces learning, gives students with special needs a chance to interact in a positive way with classmates, and tends to build their confidence as learners.

- Help your students with special needs understand their progress. Set small, achievable goals, and celebrate together when students reach them.

COLLABORATING WITH SPECIAL EDUCATION TEACHERS

When students with special needs began to be included in all classrooms, special education teachers and general education teachers formed teams to help students who required special accommodations. The unique features of this type of collaboration are that frequently both teachers are present in the classroom at the same time and they take joint responsibility for the education of all students in their class.

These collaborative teams of teachers face an important challenge: sharing the duties of the class so that they have common goals for delivering instruction, assessing progress, and managing behavior. Successful collaboration is likely if team teachers see themselves as equal partners who are actively engaged in all parts of the teaching process.

The general education teacher's responsibilities usually include the following:

- Creating activities to teach the content
- Finding and adapting resource material for all students
- Delivering effective instruction
- Meeting the curriculum requirements of all students

The special education teacher's responsibilities usually include the following:

- Adapting material to meet the needs of students with special needs
- Adapting activities to match the learning styles of students with special needs
- Modifying assessments
- Meeting the curriculum requirements of students with special needs

What makes it possible for two teachers with different educational backgrounds to work together in a successful collaboration? The primary requirement for a positive working relationship is a commitment on the part of both teachers to work together for the common good of their students. Both teachers should also agree to

- Plan lessons together
- Follow the same classroom management procedures
- Discuss controversial class events in civil tones and in privacy
- Assume equal responsibility for what happens in class
- Present a united front to students
- Share resource materials
- Schedule time to work together on a regular basis

Strengthen the Skills That Can Make a Difference for Your Students

Sometimes it is easy to assume that students already have the basic skills they need to do well in school—until their struggles make it obvious that they need help. It is especially easy to believe this if you teach older students. You may assume that their earlier teachers taught them the school success skills that they need in your class. This is not always the case. The skills that students need in each class and in each grade level can vary widely. It is up to you to help students learn the specific skills that they will need to access the material in your curriculum.

Although it is necessary for you to help students develop the specific skills that they will need to succeed, there are some basic school success skills that all students need. In the remaining pages of this section, you will learn about some of these skills and how you can help your students learn to develop them. The skills that all students need are basic skills in reading, writing, vocabulary acquisition, digital media, listening, and distraction management.

READING SKILLS

Many reading experts agree on an important guideline for teaching reading skills: no single approach works for all students. Instead, instruction in reading skills tends to change as students progress in their education. Students, especially those who are beginning to learn to read, need instruction in phonics. Trained reading teachers usually perform this instruction. Older students benefit from instruction in the other aspects of reading. Any teacher, even one who works with older students in other content areas, can and should work with students to improve all areas of reading.

Even though you may teach older students or a subject, such as advanced math, in which reading is not required as frequently as it is in an elementary classroom, it is still your responsibility to work with your students to help them become better readers. If reading is, indeed, the primary learning tool for all students, then working to increase your students' reading skills is a responsibility you cannot ignore. In the list that follows, you will find some easy-to-implement strategies to help students improve their reading skills regardless of their age or the content of the course:

- Be positive with struggling readers. In time, with increased instruction and support from all teachers, students can improve their reading skills.

- Try a variety of activities to teach reading skills. Appealing to students' learning style preferences is essential, regardless of their age.

- Activate any prior knowledge your students may have or provide enough background information for students to make connections between the material and their own experiences.

- Employ real-life, informational texts in your classes when appropriate.

- Read aloud to students as they follow along in a text. Poor readers often are not exposed to rich oral language at home.

- Prepare students for successful reading of an assignment with activities before, during, and after the assignment.

- Work with the families of students who struggle with reading. Many times, parents, guardians, and other family members are willing to be supportive but do not know what to do. A partnership between classroom and home is an important source of support for struggling readers.

- Teach students how to determine the purpose of assigned reading and to adapt their rate and method of reading accordingly.

- Include activities to help students comprehend the information in the text. Using a variety of techniques, such as graphic organizers and collaboration with peers, will help students derive meaning from their assignments.

Resources for teaching reading skills include the following helpful sites:

- **International Literacy Association (www.literacyworldwide.org).** The International Literacy Association is an influential organization of literacy professionals. At their website, you will find extensive information about literacy issues as well as specific links to resources devoted to reading and reading issues at all grade levels.

- **Reading Is Fundamental (www.rif.org).** This organization focuses on young children. It offers advice, tips, lesson plans, book-based activities, web resources, and daily activities for young readers.

- **ReadWriteThink (www.readwritethink.org).** At this site, the International Literacy Association and the National Council of Teachers of English, two powerful organizations involved with school literacy, offer thousands of links to resources for teachers who want to help their students improve their literacy skills.

WRITING SKILLS

Many research studies have traced the effectiveness of writing as a learning tool in all subjects and in all grade levels. The results of this work are clear: every teacher teaches writing. All teachers teach writing by modeling language when speaking with students, when writing for students, and when asking them to write.

Along with modeling good language skills, you should teach writing skills and hold students accountable for their writing. You don't have to be an English teacher, a grammar expert, or a veteran teacher to teach your students to write well. Here are some effective and painless ways to help your students become effective writers:

- Encourage your students to use a dictionary and a thesaurus. If your students have ready access to the Internet, encourage them to use an electronic resource, such as Dictionary.com (www.dictionary.com).

- When students ask, "Does spelling count?," say, "Yes. How can I help you spell a word?"

- Encourage students to use the writing process whenever possible. When you ask students to write even brief essays, encourage them to plan or prewrite their answers, write a rough draft, edit and revise that draft, and create a final copy to turn in to you.

- Encourage students to catch your errors. When you make a mistake, acknowledge it and correct yourself, showing students that correctness is not something that ends when class is over.

- Circle obvious errors on papers. You don't need to circle each one or use elaborate editing marks. You should not correct the mistake yourself; instead, just make students aware of a mistake by circling it and asking them to make a correction.

- Because students tend to write the way they talk, speak Standard English around your students and expect them to speak it, too.

- Model good writing for your students. Proofread your own work.

- Offer lots of writing opportunities for your students. You can do this on tests and quizzes as well as in daily informal assignments and projects, such as reports.

Here are some resources for you to help your students with writing skills:

- **Achieve the Core (https://achievethecore.org).** At this site you can find many valuable resources to help students improve their writing skills by using "writing" as a search term.

- **National Writing Project (www.nwp.org).** At the National Writing Project site, you can find helpful advice, books, articles, links to other sites, and many other different resources pertaining to writing instruction.

- **Teaching That Makes Sense (www.ttms.org).** At this information-packed site, teachers can access a wealth of general materials about teaching writing as well as learn about specific activities and strategies.

VOCABULARY ACQUISITION SKILLS

For all students, from emergent readers to graduating seniors, vocabulary acquisition is an important skill area. In fact, it is a lifelong process for all of us. You can teach students new words and their concepts in two primary ways.

The first way that many students learn new words is through new experiences. When you take your students on a field trip, show them a video clip, sing a silly song with them, or involve them in other activities that are new and different, you expand their language skills. Such activities broaden their world and give them a real-life context in which to apply the new vocabulary words to which they are exposed.

The second significant way that students learn new words is through reading. The more reading experiences a student has, the more language he or she will acquire. However, if students are not capable or independent readers functioning at grade level, it will be very difficult for them to acquire new words from reading without help. Therefore, their teachers need to assist them in learning new words. Here are some basic actions you should take when teaching students new vocabulary words:

- Teach students to associate words with other material. Build connections between words they are studying in your class and words or concepts they have learned previously or in other contexts.

- Present vocabulary words many times and in different ways. Present the words before you teach a lesson so that students can understand them and, in turn, comprehend the text. As your students study the material, take care to go over the words again. Finally, at the end of a unit of study, review the vocabulary so that students can lock in their learning.

- Make connections with other content areas. If students can take words from your class and use them in another context, you have been successful. Help students make this connection by asking them how they could use a word or a form of a word you are studying in other ways.

- Take the tedium out of finding meanings. Derive meanings together. When students formulate their own definitions, they tend to remember those meanings far better than the ones they look up in a dictionary.

- When you present a list of words before a lesson, ask students to anticipate what the words might mean in the context of the lesson.

- Because students need to hear new words, always spend time pronouncing the words under study with students. This technique is particularly helpful to auditory learners, and it assists everyone in making the words part of their spoken vocabulary.

- Show students how to use context clues. For example, you could ask students to read a passage and find three words that have the same definition. You could also have a mini discussion in which you ask students how they figured out a word's meaning from the text.

- Expose students to a variety of words. It is not enough for poor readers to just see and hear the words in a textbook if they are going to improve their reading skills. They need to see and hear the words associated with real-life occupations, technology, academics, current events, and other aspects of everyday life. Often, students who are poor readers are often not exposed to these words at home.

- Raise your students' awareness of the words around them. Use games, activities, discussions, varied readings, and other strategies to help your students pay attention to the words they encounter each day.

- Model good vocabulary acquisition skills. Let students see you looking up words in a dictionary or taking care to use the correct synonym when you write sentences on the board. When you teach students whose families are not well educated or whose families do not speak English as a first language, it is especially important to model good vocabulary acquisition skills often.

DIGITAL MEDIA SKILLS

Because our students, like us, are inundated with an overwhelming amount of information from a multitude of reliable and not-so-reliable sources, it is imperative that we teach them how to manage the information that comes to them and that they will themselves produce in our increasingly digital world.

Media literacy is not just the ability to use various pieces of hardware or the newest software products, although both skills are covered in the broad sense of the term. Instead, working toward media literacy means that our students will develop the skills and knowledge they will need to become discriminating and informed global citizens. Our students not only will have access to the vast streams of media available to them through social media, phones, televisions, radio stations, the Internet, and other technology-dependent ways to communicate but also will be able to understand what they receive and send.

As a classroom teacher, you should make helping your students become media literate one of your priorities. You will not be able to do this in just a few lessons, even if you teach high-achieving older students. Instead, a more sensible approach is to integrate media literacy lessons into appropriate instructional activities. For example, if your students are required to bring articles on current events to share with the class, one of the skills that you should teach in advance of the assignment is how to find reliable sources. By frequently asking students to evaluate and analyze sources, information, and even images or advertisements, you will help your students develop their media literacy skills. Other ways to help your students become informed digital consumers and producers can include these activities:

- Expose your students to appropriate guided online activities as often as possible. For example, ask students to work together as a team to explore a site and then report back to other teams about the information they found as well as how it was presented and the information's reliability.
- Ask students to find examples of information targeted at specific audiences and then to provide evidence to support their findings.
- Encourage your students to make informed decisions on a variety of topics by having them research topics that are of personal interest to them and then share their ideas with their classmates.
- Ask students to create digital products, such as class web pages, blogs, or multimedia presentations. Have them examine their own choices in terms of their products' suitability or purpose.
- Ask students to compare and contrast articles, cartoons, illustrations, or other digital materials on the same topic.
- Provide opportunities for students to share their ideas about current events or information that is related to a topic under study so that they can determine if their ideas arise from valid sources or not.

Here are some excellent resources on the topic of teaching media literacy skills:

- **Center for Media Literacy (www.medialit.org).** Here you can learn about media literacy by reading numerous articles, incorporating the suggestions in the site's "Best Practices" section, and reviewing the many useful free resources of various types to engage and instruct your students.
- **National Association for Media Literacy Education (NAMLE) (http://namle .net).** This useful site offers many helpful resources for teaching media literacy to students of all ages.

LISTENING SKILLS

Good listening skills are crucial for academic success for students of all ages. Listening well is something anyone can learn to do over time and with practice. Fortunately, creative teachers can find many ways to help their students improve their listening skills. For example, you could read aloud from a short news article each day and then quiz your students about what they heard. Or you could have students enact a real-life scenario, such as making a complaint, and then ask the student audience to recount what they heard.

The key is to offer many practice opportunities appropriate to the ages and interests of your students. You can also help your students become good listeners by teaching what it means to be an active listener who pays attention. Here are some tips to help you teach your students to be active listeners:

- Talk with your students about the importance of maintaining an open mind when someone is speaking. They should listen closely to their teachers and classmates and not quit listening when they disagree with what they hear.

- Teach students to listen for the key topics under discussion, an important skill for students who take an active role in their learning.

- Teach your students to generate questions as they listen to you but to hold their questions until you call for them.

- Play a gentle classroom game in which you ask students to respond every time they hear you say a certain word. For example, they could tap their desks every time they hear you say "book." The competitive nature of this game will keep students alert.

- If students are not sure whether they have understood the main points of a presentation, ask whether they can summarize it. If they can summarize what they've heard, then they are competent in active listening.

- Find a simple drawing of a person, object, or scene and describe it to your students in vivid detail as they attempt to draw it from your description. You could even have pairs of students speak as well as draw to reinforce the idea of attentive listening.

- Stress the importance of looking at the person speaking. Often when students are not looking at the teacher, they can tune out.

Here is an excellent website for teachers who want to help their students improve their listening skills:

- **Teaching Ideas (www.teachingideas.co.uk).** A British primary school teacher, Mark Werner, manages this site. Although many of the ideas are for teachers of younger children, the site has hundreds of useful games, activities, and teaching suggestions for all teachers.

DISTRACTION MANAGEMENT SKILLS

It is no secret that our students are distracted. They reflect the easily sidetracked society around them. Few people can resist the lure of an intriguing online video, funny meme, or social media update. Although adults self-regulate their distractions, it is not always easy for students to know how to manage the many temptations that can entice them away from their schoolwork. Caring teachers can help their students strengthen their ability to remain focused instead of distracted while doing schoolwork. Here are several suggestions that you can adapt for your classes to help students learn to work with focus and to fight their tendency to be distracted:

- Make distraction management a whole-group project. Have students brainstorm ideas and strategies that are helpful for coping with distractions and then share with the group. They can also share helpful productivity and time management apps that make it easier for them to stay focused.

- Have students share their advice about what you can do to create a classroom environment that encourages focused work. Display student-made posters or other reminders to make students mindful of the issue. When they can be part of the solution, students will have greater buy-in.

- Use a timer to help students complete work within a specific time frame. This will raise awareness of the importance of staying on task.

- When there are several tasks that students must accomplish, have students prioritize them so that they will know how to accomplish their work on time.

- Manage electronic distractions, such as cell phones in your classroom, so that students will not give in to temptation. (There is more information about how to manage student cell phone use in Section Fourteen.)

- As students are working on assignments, schedule brain breaks so that they can stay on task. Discuss how this would be effective for them at home as well.

- Consider having students play brain games as an anchor activity. Although there are hundreds of computer games that can help students improve their focus, take care to select games that are appropriate for your students and for school. One good source for enjoyable free educational brain games is National Geographic (http://channel.nationalgeographic.com/brain-games).

Questions to Discuss with Colleagues

Sharing ideas with colleagues is a helpful way to devise solutions to some of the problems that you must manage successfully at school. Here you will find several topics to open discussions with colleagues about successful instructional practices:

1. Several of your students require preferential seating. How can you arrange the furniture in your classroom so that the needs of all your students can be met?

2. You believe that one of your students is hyperactive and has an attention deficit disorder, but her parents refuse to consider the possibility. What can you do to help this student be a successful learner?

3. You have a student who turns in poorly done work on a regular basis, even though you have made your standards clear. What is your goal? What do you do?

4. You suspect that one of your students is falling through the cracks. What can you do to help this student keep from failing? How do you gather data? Who can help you with this?

5. You have bilingual students who refuse to speak the language required by your school. How do you encourage them to use the language of the school? What do you do?

Topics to Discuss with a Mentor

Although the topics that new teachers need to discuss with a mentor vary from teacher to teacher and from school to school, there are some that most first-year teachers should be comfortable discussing with a mentor or a trusted colleague. You should ask your mentor about these topics from this section:

- How to manage accommodations for students with 504 Plans
- Advice about how to cope with a student who is classified as ODD
- How to incorporate mindfulness practices into your classroom practice
- Advice for working well with a teaching partner
- How to support students who appear to have undiagnosed learning problems

Reflection Questions to Guide Your Thinking

1. What do you anticipate as your biggest challenge in dealing with the differences among your students? What can you do to meet this challenge? Where can you find assistance?

2. What do you already know about your students who may need special care and support? How do your supervisors expect you to help these students? How do the students themselves expect you to help them? Who at your school can help you learn the best ways to help these students?

3. What strengths do you have that will help you meet the diverse needs of your students? How can you use your strengths to help all the students in your class reach their full potential?

4. Who is struggling academically or behaviorally in your class? What should your attitude toward these students be? What schoolwide programs can help the struggling students in your class? What can you do to help them stay in school and be successful?

5. How can you create the kind of classroom environment where all students, regardless of their learning needs, can feel comfortable, valued, and supported? What are you already doing to create this environment? How can you improve?

SECTION EIGHT

Adapt Instruction through Differentiated Instruction

Whether our students are active or calm, energetic or quiet, focused or off task, our classrooms are complex communities composed of students whose differences and how well we accommodate those differences can determine the success or failure of the entire class.

In this section, you will learn some of the basics of differentiating instruction so that your students can learn and achieve. You will learn how to create a classroom environment conducive to differentiated instructional activities, the key strategies of differentiation, how to use formative assessments, how to manage feedback, how to plan for differentiated instruction, and how to manage a classroom where differentiation activities are in place.

Differentiated Instruction Supports All Learners

In twenty-first-century classrooms, the shift from one-size-fits-all instruction to differentiation is solidly under way. Teachers who intentionally differentiate instruction treat their students as individuals with varied learning characteristics instead of treating all students as if they had the same learning strengths and weakness, the same readiness levels, or the same learning preferences.

Differentiated instruction is effective because it meets students at their various readiness levels and then offers instruction in sync with their learning needs. It is also effective because the focus on appealing assignments that encourage self-efficacy engages students in productive learning instead of misbehavior.

Because instruction in a differentiated classroom takes a proactive stance toward learning differences among students, the main components of classroom instruction—content, process, and product—can all be adjusted to promote learning. Formative assessments are also a key element in helping teachers design and adjust instructional activities.

At its most basic level, differentiating instruction is being fair to all students. It means creating many paths to access that material so that students of different abilities, interests, or needs experience appropriate ways to learn. Everyone has a chance to succeed when teachers differentiate.

Misperceptions about Differentiated Instruction

As a new teacher, differentiating instruction can be intimidating because there seems to be an overwhelming amount of work just to deliver a lesson. Differentiated instruction requires careful planning, but it is a manageable task and certainly worth the effort. As you learn to differentiate instruction for your students, you may hear comments from your colleagues who are not as forward thinking as you are and who may not fully understand the importance of differentiation. Here are some of the common misperceptions you may hear:

> In the 1960s, a student was placed in my general mechanics class because he could not read. I asked him what he liked to do. He said he liked to mess with motors. He had taken his diesel tractor motor out and put it in an old pickup truck. This is what he drove to school. In the spring, the motor went back in the tractor for spring plowing. Other teachers had told me this boy was dumb.
>
> *Edward Gardner, 36 years' experience*

- Differentiated instruction requires individual lesson plans for each student.
- It is impossible to cover the content because differentiation takes too long.
- All formative assessments need to be graded.
- It's okay to use differentiation for enrichment but not for remediation or instruction.
- It's impossible to stay organized when you differentiate instruction.

Don't give up on differentiating instruction for your students. After all, thousands of your colleagues routinely differentiate instruction to help their students succeed. Instead, start small and systematically develop a repertoire of ideas, strategies, and activities that can make differentiation an accepted part of your classroom practice.

"How Can I Possibly Meet Everyone's Needs?"

It is daunting to try to teach a roomful of students who come from different cultures and who have varied learning preferences, maturity levels, interests, and abilities. It can seem confusing at first to work out the best methods to differentiate instruction, but it is not difficult to meet the needs of the learners in your classroom.

The trick to success is simple: rotate every student through a variety of task types. You will strengthen weak areas and allow students to enjoy their preferences. Not all students are visual learners, for example, but many students are, and they will benefit from being able to use their learning style preferences. At the same time, the auditory and kinesthetic learners in your class will be able to strengthen an area of weakness as they work through tasks that would normally appeal mainly to visual learners. Rotating students through a variety of tasks makes accommodating the needs of every learner a reasonable and achievable endeavor.

There are some other methods that will enable you to use differentiation to meet the needs of all your learners. In the list that follows, you will discover some basic guidelines to use as you offer differentiated instruction:

- Always begin with your district's standards. No activity, no matter how exciting it may be, is useful if it does not serve to move your students' knowledge and skills forward toward mastering a specific learning objective.

- Use as much data as you can to adopt a prescriptive approach to instruction. Think of the data you gather as a means to help you teach rather than as a way to find out what your students didn't learn.

- Emphasize quality of thought rather than the size of the workload. If a student has mastered how to solve a certain type of problem, for example, don't continue to assign more of the same kind of problem. Instead, offer alternative problem types or allow the student to move ahead.

- Focus on student growth instead of grades. One way to do this is to have students self-assess several times within a unit of study. Teach students to reflect and then evaluate themselves if you want them to become self-disciplined learners.

- Everyone needs variety, teamwork, and hand-on activities. Offer opportunities for these whenever possible.

- Plan for quiet work days. Not every class has to be a lively experience. You do not have to be "on" every day, and neither do your students. Allow time for students to work steadily on assignments that are engaging but not necessarily thrilling.

- Take advantage of every technology resource that you can. You'll find a list of useful resources later in this section.

- Be flexible. Always have a backup plan ready. You will need it.

- Have explicit directions for all activities. Provide specific procedures for those students who need clarification. The more comfortable students are with the procedures they are to follow when doing their work, the easier it will be for them to be successful.

- Provide a balance between teacher-assigned work and student-selected work. Allow students as much choice as is appropriate and reasonable to manage.

- Proceed at a pace that is comfortable for you. It is better to be cautious than to have an out-of-control classroom.

Create a Classroom Environment
That Supports Differentiation

Because differentiation can be a much more productive experience than just assigning some optional activities occasionally, it is necessary to create a classroom environment that supports the differentiated activities that you have designed for your students.

There are two aspects to this environment: the physical space and the community within that space.

In a differentiated classroom, the physical space needs to be set up so that students can move around easily as they go from task to task. Students should be able to move quickly and easily into group configurations. Supplies and materials also should be easily accessible so that students don't waste time wandering around looking for what they need. Students need an area where directions for various activities and information about learning styles are posted so that they can refer to them as needed. In short, the room needs to be arranged so that students can focus on their work because they are comfortable in their physical environment.

A strong sense of community is also an essential part of differentiated instruction because it enables students to take the risks necessary to try new, challenging activities and to work well with their peers. In an environment that supports differentiation, classroom management policies, procedures, and rules are firmly in place so that students can operate in a safe and familiar framework. Student learning differences are acknowledged and appreciated. The teacher is a warm demander who makes it clear that he or she appreciates students and enjoys being with them while at the same time holds them accountable for persistent effort, good behavior, and appropriate work habits.

Use Growth Mindset Principles to Support Differentiation

One of the chief characteristics inherent in the growth mindset movement is that it empowers students by encouraging them to believe in their own capabilities. Differentiated instruction has the same effect on students because it encourages them to become self-aware and to use their strengths to overcome their learning deficiencies. Persistence and acceptance of mistakes are expected when differentiating instruction as well as when encouraging students to develop a growth mindset.

Because of the complementary nature of both approaches to teaching and learning, the methods that you use to encourage students to develop a growth mindset can also be used as you differentiate instruction. Specific feedback, positivity, the recognition of hard work and effort, and a celebration of mistakes are just some of the components of the growth mindset movement that can make differentiation work well in your classroom.

Key Strategies for Differentiation

Successful differentiated instruction involves the use of several key strategies to modify instruction. These strategies form the bedrock of the choices that informed teachers make when they design and deliver differentiated instruction activities for their students. In the pages that follow, you will be able to explore these strategies as you learn how to use differentiated instruction in your teaching practice.

STRATEGY ONE: INDIVIDUALIZED INSTRUCTION

Although differentiated instruction does not demand a separate lesson plan for each student, instruction should be tailored to meet the specific needs of individual students. Even though this may seem difficult at first, with a bit of planning and effort, individualized instruction can be managed without hassle.

To provide instruction that is customized for different students, it is first necessary to get to know those students very well. Although the techniques for getting to know your students discussed in Section Six can also be used when differentiating instruction, there are three other student qualities that you need to explore when determining how to adjust instruction: student readiness, student interests, and student learning preferences.

Student Readiness

Student readiness refers to a student's current level of knowledge or skills regarding the material in a unit of study. Having an accurate picture of student readiness is important because it is the first difference that you must consider in differentiating instruction. Prior knowledge of the material and a connection to it will influence a student's readiness to access the content, so it is helpful to determine both before planning how to differentiate instruction. Students who have a great deal of prior knowledge of the material should be offered a different entry point to it from those students who need extra support in building background before beginning the unit. Readiness can be determined by various formative assessments, such as brainstorming what students already know, one-minute papers, surveys, or exit slips.

Student Interests

The interests that students already have when they arrive in your classroom can be powerful motivators. When students have an opportunity to learn more about a topic that they are already familiar with, they deepen their knowledge and connection to upcoming related content. Students who are curious about an impending topic are usually willing to persist in learning about related topics because they can see the connections among them. For example, when students are interested in a certain sport, they may be willing to learn more about related topic, such as its history, the equipment required to play it, the safety regulations that govern it, and notable players.

There are many ways for you to learn about your students' interests throughout a school term. During class meetings (see Section Six for more information about class meetings), you can ask students to share their interests, or you can have students interview one another about their interests and share that information with the class. You can also pass out note cards and ask students to write their names on one side and their interests on the other. Perhaps the most powerful way that you can learn about your students' interests, however, is to be a good listener. Students share their ideas with one another and with their teachers in every class period. Make a point of attending carefully to what they share so that you can add an extra layer of engagement to instruction.

Student Learning Preferences

Partly because of our increased knowledge about how the brain works and partly because of the growing acceptance of the benefits of differentiated instruction, thoughtful educators are using student learning preferences to make informed decisions about differentiation. Research shows that we all have learning styles that we prefer to use when faced with a learning task. Although there are many different learning styles that can be applied to classroom use, it is impossible to design instruction to appeal to all of them. Most teachers adapt instruction based on these three learning styles: visual, auditory, and kinesthetic. These three learning preferences can be adapted easily to both whole-group or individual instruction. They also can be paired with other learning preferences, such as students who find studying by themselves more effective than those students who enjoy collaboration with others.

To learn about your students' learning styles, you can create your own simple questionnaire or survey that would be appropriate for the age and skill levels of your students. Just ask students to select statements that apply to them, such as the following:

- I learn best when I work on assignments with classmates.
- I like to work in a quiet area where it is easier for me to focus.
- I like to listen to music when I study.
- I enjoy making sketches, diagrams, and graphic organizers.
- It is easier for me to learn something when I can see a model of it.
- I like to watch videos about the subjects I am studying.
- Having a buddy to study with makes it easier for me to learn.
- Class discussions help me remember important information.

You can also search for a learning styles inventory online. There are dozens of them—just use "learning styles inventory" or "multiple intelligences inventory" as search terms to find inventories that would be suitable for your students. Two particularly useful interactive surveys can be found at LdPride (www.ldpride.net) and Edutopia (www.edutopia.org/multiple-intelligences-assessment).

As you gather data about learning preferences, keep in mind that they are not absolute choices. Students could be both kinesthetic and visual learners, for example. Instead of labeling a student as only one type of learner, it is helpful to determine a ranking of their preferences from the dominant preference to the least important one.

It may be useful to create a visual snapshot of the learning preferences in your classroom. One way to do this would be to create a pie chart and to place students' names in the area that corresponds with their dominant preferences. You can use Figure 8.1 as a guide to creating one for your classes. It could also be helpful to make a large one, have students put their names on the slice corresponding to their preferences, and post it for everyone to see.

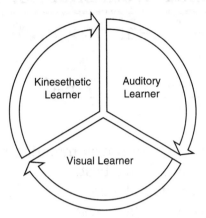

Figure 8.1 Learning Preferences Chart

Once you have determined your students' readiness, interests, and learning preferences, you will need to organize that information in such a way that it is easily accessible when you design differentiated activities. One way to do this is to maintain a learning profile document for each student—a quick snapshot of unique learning characteristics. This document can be completed by the teacher or by students and their parents or guardians. Once it is completed, you will have useful data at your fingertips to consider when you make differentiation decisions. You can use Teacher Worksheet 8.1 as a template, or you can adjust it to meet your needs.

Student Learning Profile

Student name: _____ Date: _____

Learning Styles

Please rank the ways that you prefer to learn new material in this order:

Place a 3 in the blank before the way you like best.

Place a 2 in the blank before the way you like next.

Place a 1 in the blank before the way you like least.

_____ Auditory learning (I learn best by hearing.)

_____ Visual learning (I learn best by seeing.)

_____ Kinesthetic learning (I learn best by doing.)

_____ Combination of learning styles _____ and _____

Additional notes or explanation of learning styles:

_____

School Work Habits

I would describe my school work habits as:

_____

Interests

My interests include:

_____

School Experience

My favorite subject is _____ because: _____

_____

My least favorite subject is _____ because: _____

_____

Strengths and Weaknesses

My strengths as a student include:

_____

My weaknesses as a student include:

_____

I learn best when I:

_____

My goals in life are:

_____

From *The First-Year Teacher's Survival Guide, 4th Edition*, by Julia G. Thompson. Copyright © 2018 by John Wiley & Sons, Inc. Reproduced by permission.

STRATEGY TWO: FLEXIBLE GROUPING

Flexible groups are purposeful collaborative groups that allow students to be appropriately challenged and help you avoid labeling a student's readiness or skill level as unchanging. During a school term, your students should work as members of many different groups, depending on the task and content. It is important to permit movement among groups because interests and skills change as students move from one topic to another.

Flexible grouping also has other advantages in a differentiated classroom: it allows for a variety of ways to match students to necessary tasks; makes it easier for you to observe and assess students; and, most important, allows you to assign appropriate instructional activities to meet each student's learning needs. What types of flexible groups are possible in a differentiated classroom?

- Readiness level groups
- Homogeneous ability groups
- Heterogeneous ability groups
- Interest groups
- Learning preferences groups
- Impromptu study or discussion groups
- Just about any type of group that you think would benefit your students

Here's a quick way to group students according to a specific trait. In this example, students are grouped according to learning preference.

- **Step One:** Use colored index cards to color-code your students' learning preferences, assigning a different color to each learning preference: auditory, visual, and kinesthetic.
- **Step Two:** Write each student's name on a card that corresponds with his or her learning preference.
- **Step Three:** Arrange the cards into three stacks according to color.
- **Step Four:** If you want to group students with others who have the same learning preferences, you would use the three stacks of index cards as your baseline groups, keeping students with the same learning preferences together. To create groups with a balance of learning preferences, take cards from each stack to create new stacks combining all three colors. These combined stacks represent balanced groups where students with different learning preferences work together.

STRATEGY THREE: TRANSPARENT LEARNING FOR STUDENTS

There should be no surprises when it comes to student learning. If students are to benefit fully from differentiated instruction, they must participate fully in the process. Unless this is an explicit expectation, students will not become the confident, self-disciplined learners that we want them to be.

Students should be involved during the process of differentiating instruction as is appropriate for their age, maturity level, and ability. Here is a quick list of some of the ways that their learning can be made transparent for students during differentiated instruction. Students should

- Understand the purpose for learning the material under study
- Understand the essential information or skills that they are expected to master in each unit of study
- Be aware of their learning preferences and how to implement various strategies to use those preferences fully
- Use feedback to improve their work
- Understand how to demonstrate mastery
- Be aware of their progress as they work through the material
- Reflect periodically on the work and their work habits

STRATEGY FOUR: STUDENT REFLECTION

If students are to work efficiently and to learn what they are supposed to learn, then they should be encouraged to reflect systematically on their learning. When students can think about the strategies that work best for them, about how they go about their work, about their progress, and about their goals, they are more likely to remain engaged and on task because their effort is relevant and meaningful.

Reflection moves students toward being self-directed learners because it makes it possible for them to understand the purpose for their work. Reflection can also make students aware of the patterns in their work habits, see the connections between ideas, and help them develop solutions to the problems they may experience while learning.

Reflection may not come naturally to all students. It is up to you to set the expectation that serious thought is required when students reflect by modeling how you want their reflection to be done. It is also important that you set aside time for students to reflect frequently so that they have time to think while they are in the moment. As you begin to think about how to include student reflection in your classroom, here are some quick ways to begin. To reflect on their learning, students can

- Keep a reflection journal in a dedicated section of their student binders or in a notebook
- Color-code their work, with one color representing material that they know well, another color representing material with which they are somewhat comfortable, and a third color representing material that they need help with
- Record problems that they experienced and how they solved them
- Talk with peers about what worked and what did not

- Keep a record of the highpoints of the day, the week, or the unit
- Write an explanation of their thinking process on various questions. They can include an explanation of what they should have been thinking as well as what guided them to answer the way that they did.
- Describe their response to feedback and the effectiveness of their response
- Write a brief reflection of their work on a sticky note and share it with others by posting it on a designated area of the board
- Write an entrance or exit slip about their class work
- Predict problems that they still may have with the material and possible solutions
- Rate their day's learning on a scale of one to ten, with a brief explanation of the rating
- Brainstorm as many ideas as possible about the day's lesson for three minutes and then look for patterns in the brainstorm
- Explain to partners what they will do differently on the next assignment, how they prepared for this one, and what they learned from their work
- Assess their readiness to move on to new material. If they are not ready, ask them what their next steps should be.

STRATEGY FIVE: RESPECTFUL TASKS

Respectful tasks are ones that recognize and honor individual students' learning differences. When designing respectful tasks, teachers should pay attention to the readiness level of each student and offer all students opportunities to learn according to their own readiness levels. Teachers who design respectful tasks do so with the intention that all tasks should be equally interesting, important, and engaging. Teachers should ensure not only that each task is appropriate and fair but also that they have taken a proactive approach in determining how best to accommodate student needs. When you set about creating respectful tasks, consider these questions:

- Will the task be appropriate for students' differing readiness levels?
- Will the task include student interests so that it is intrinsically appealing?
- Will the task allow students to use their learning style preferences?
- Will the task help students master the material?
- Will the task be one that is practical and easy to manage?

Although there are any number of assignment types that you can offer students, a beneficial way to stay organized and to work efficiently is to keep handy an ongoing list of the activities that appeal to your students. Many teachers find it helpful to store such a list in their professional binders. (See Section Two for more information about professional binders.) Here is a list of just some of the many activities that you could use to differentiate instruction for your students:

- Agendas: Students are offered individualized personal checklists of work to complete within a set time—usually a week or so. Although students may have some assignments in common, agendas allow for differentiation by offering work that is less or more challenging while appealing to diverse learning style preferences.

- Alphabet boxes: Students are given a grid of squares with a letter of the alphabet in each square. They then brainstorm to recall words, ideas, and concepts related to a unit. For example, in an alphabet box for a unit on global warming, a student would write "Polar bears endangered" in the *P* box, "Ozone" in the *O* box, and so on for every letter.

- Artifact boxes: Items from a unit of study are displayed in a box for students to use to analyze and predict information. An artifact box may be used for enrichment, teaching, or remediation.

- Audio materials: For students who are auditory learners, audio materials offer another approach to learning. Students listen to recorded materials as they read or instead of reading. Audio materials can be used to study, review, or introduce information as well as in many other ways.

- Case studies: Students investigate real-life situations through reports, articles, and other observations. They complete their investigations in cooperative groups.

- Chalk talks: Five students go to the board and stand so that they cannot see one another's writing. The teacher calls out a topic and has everyone in the class write about it for one minute. Students discuss the work of the five chalk writers and compare it to the work of their classmates.

- Choice boards: With a choice board, students are given a menu of possible tasks to accomplish. This is a structured way to allow for student choice.

- Chunking: Assignments are broken into smaller, more manageable parts, with structured directions offered for each part.

- Dialectical journals: Students write two-column notes about information they read or hear about. In one column, they are given or select a topic to write about, and in the other, they write a response to the topic.

- Hot Potato: Similar to the Tingo Tango game later in this list, each student has a note card with a question about the lesson on it. Learners trade their cards as quickly as possible for thirty seconds. When time is called, each student will have to answer the question on his or her card either in writing or orally.

- Interactive bookmarks: Students use premade bookmarks specific to a unit of material to record notes, answer questions, define words, and make observations as they read.

- Jigsaws: Students in a group divide the material to be studied into various sections. Each group member becomes an expert on his or her section and teaches it to the others.

- Learning circles: Students gather to discuss a reading passage in depth. The concept can be applied to reading of all sorts and to working out common problems in math or science courses.

- Manipulatives: Hands-on activities can be used to help students in all disciplines learn. From science labs to word sorts, manipulatives benefit the tactile learner in that he or she can associate movement and the material to be learned.

- Mini lessons: Students are given brief lessons designed to target specific areas for remediation or enrichment.

- Note checks: Students review and highlight one another's notes.

- Online collaboration: Students work together to create and post blogs or to collaborate with other students on activities involving podcasts, virtual projects, tweets, or wikis.

- Open-ended problems: Students solve open-ended problems periodically throughout a unit of study. For example, during a unit about the American Revolution, students might be asked to view portraits of the leaders of the day and to make predictions about their social status based on clues in the paintings.

- Paper discussions: Small groups of students are seated in circles. Each group is handed a sheet of paper, and one student in each group writes a response to a question or idea pertaining to a topic. That student then passes the sheet to the next student, who adds to the response and passes it to the next student, and so on as quickly as possible in a specified time limit.

- Roundtables: Students discuss their work by sitting in a circle and taking turns. This works best if they have had time to write questions, concerns, or responses to a question first.

- Sticky note note-taking: Students write brief notes on sticky notes as they work or read.

- Student observations: Students watch video clips or live demonstrations and then record and share their observations.

- Task cards: Because of the various activities possible in one differentiated class period, students read explicit directions for an activity instead of hearing a quick flurry of verbal directions. They can then refer to the directions as class progresses.

- Tingo Tango: Students stand in a circle rapidly passing a soft foam ball or beach ball around the circle as the teacher repeatedly says, "Tingo." At random intervals, the teacher says, "Tango" instead of "Tingo." The student holding the ball at that point must answer a question or call out a fact.

- Vocabulary charades: Students work in triads to act out vocabulary words and definitions. This also works well for reviewing key terms and facts in a unit of study.

- Write-pair-shares: In a write-pair-share, students write a response to a question. They then share their response with a partner first and with the entire group afterward.

STRATEGY SIX: TIERED INSTRUCTION

Tiered instruction is made possible when teachers evaluate their students and then use the data they collect to provide a different tier of instruction for each student. The most common types of tiers offer instruction to students on these three levels: students who do not know the concept or who do not have the skill, students who have some understanding of the concept or skill, and students who have mastered and understand the concept or skill.

Tiered instruction is an extremely flexible strategy. Every aspect of a lesson can be categorized into one of the three tiers. Teachers can differentiate process, content, and product into the three tiers, for example. Other opportunities to create tiered instruction can include in-class assignments, homework, learning stations, and even assessments. In the example of one set of possible tiers that follows, you can see just how adaptable this strategy can be:

I create groups of three to four students with a variety of strengths, whether it be organization, content knowledge, communication skills, and so on. I make sure the students know what I think they could add to the group so that they gain confidence to give advice in those areas. They get five to ten minutes of class time to work on an assigned task, such as organizing time or study strategies. It's the group's job to look out for one another if one is absent or encourage and help the other group members if they are struggling. This can be magical in some classes and mildly helpful in others, depending on class chemistry, but when it works, it can really benefit so many areas of your class.

Shelly Sambiase, 8 years' experience

For Struggling Students

- The teacher introduces vocabulary words.
- Students read with learning buddies.
- Students use guided questions to aid comprehension.
- Students use a word bank.

For Students Who May Just Need Practice

- Students read a text independently.
- Students take notes on the text independently.

For Advanced Students

- Students determine the parts of the topic they would like to explore further.
- Students do independent research about the topic using several sources.

If you would like to begin using tiered instruction in your classroom, the process is not complicated. Follow these steps for successful implementation of this key strategy:

- **Step One:** Identify the standards or concepts and skills you want students to learn.
- **Step Two:** Collect data to determine if students have the background necessary to be successful with the lesson.
- **Step Three:** Assess students' readiness, interests, and learning profiles.
- **Step Four:** Create an activity that is focused on the standard or concept and skills of the lesson.
- **Step Five:** Adjust the activity to provide tiers of difficulty that will lead all students to be successful. Think of ways to make it more accessible for struggling students and then how to provide enrichment activities for students who may have mastered the material quickly.

When using tiered instruction, these guidelines will assist you with wise decisions that can help your students learn:

- The material that students need to learn must remain constant, but tiered instruction allows for different pathways to access that material.
- Although it is possible to have any number of tiers, keeping the number to two or three is manageable, especially when you first start using this strategy.
- Tiered instruction does not dumb down the material but instead offers a different way to learn it. The assignments in each tier should not only be respectful but also include higher-level thinking skills.

STRATEGY SEVEN: FORMATIVE ASSESSMENT

Formative assessments are quick snapshots of the progress of student learning and powerful tools for examining the way your students learn because they allow you to make informed, prescriptive decisions about the content and process of instruction. These assessments tend to be informal and brief. They can take a wide variety of forms, depending on the age and ability levels of the students as well as the subject matter being taught. Frequent formative assessments and careful analysis of the data they yield will make it easy for you to focus your efforts on the instructional practices that will be most effective for your students.

Frequent formative assessments can provide continual information about what your students know, what they don't know, and how you can adjust instruction to help every learner in your classroom succeed. For example, if several students missed the same question on a quiz, take a closer look at the quiz and how you designed and delivered the instruction leading up to it. As you reflect on the information, you could ask yourself how you can help students improve their work habits and how you can improve the way you deliver instruction.

As you gather this data, you should consider how you are going to organize it for maximum efficiency. Some of your notes about the information that you gather from formative assessments may just be brief reminders, while the other data you gather may be more extensive. To help manage the data from formative assessments, consider using a tracking form such as the one in Teacher Worksheet 8.2. To track data on this form, quickly record students' names in the first column. In the second column, record the formative assessment that you used and the date of that assessment. In the third column, record the implications or insights that you gained from the assessment.

TEACHER WORKSHEET 8.2

Tracking Formative Assessment Data

Unit of study: _____

Skills: _____

Formative Assessment _____ Date _____

Student	Implications of Data

Types of Formative Assessments

Just about any assignment or activity can serve as a formative assessment if it is used to collect data that will not only inform but also influence instruction. Because many formative assessments tend to be brief, they are easy to use frequently without losing instructional time.

Although formative assessments are flexible and easy to use, it is still necessary to select an assessment that will provide the targeted data that you need. For example, as a quick formative assessment during a review of math strategies, you may ask students to give thumbs-up or thumbs-down signals as they rate their own knowledge. Although this will yield data, it is not as reliable as a quick quiz because students may not be aware of the gaps in their understanding that a quiz could reveal. As you get to know your students and their strengths and weaknesses, selecting the most effective formative assessments will become a straightforward process.

To learn as much as you can about your students' progress and then use what you learn to adjust instruction, try some of the suggestions for different types of formative assessments that follow. Ask students to

- Answer brief multiple-choice questions
- Answer brief true-or-false questions
- Complete practice problems
- Label or draw maps or diagrams
- Listen to a peer's explanation of the material and rate it for accuracy
- Put items in order of importance
- Complete a brief cloze procedure
- Take a quiz created by a classmate
- List ten things they learned
- Match right answers to corresponding questions
- Place items in chronological order
- Create an analogy comparing new information to something they are familiar with
- Rank their knowledge about the lesson on a scale of one to five, with a reason for their ranking
- Complete self-evaluations
- Teach a concept to a partner
- Create a "Three Truths and a Lie" activity about the lesson and get a classmate to find the lie
- Evaluate or edit a peer's work
- Answer an open-ended question
- Complete a word sort
- Write a question that they still have and get the answer from three classmates
- Brainstorm for two minutes to recall information

- Write a one-minute summary
- Use a checklist to check off the skills that they have mastered
- Make a quick sketch of three of the main ideas covered in the lesson
- Restate material in fewer than fifty words
- List three key words, two interesting ideas, and one remaining question
- Complete or make graphic organizers
- Restate definitions
- Make an entry on a graffiti wall related to the topic
- Meet with the teacher in a mini conference
- Meet with teammates in mini conferences
- Have students write one comment and one question about the lesson
- Predict three things that other students may find confusing
- Complete a brief crossword puzzle about the lesson
- Make a Venn diagram about the material
- Make flash cards related to the information
- Generate their own quizzes
- Determine what was the clearest point in the lesson and the muddiest point
- Write a brief outline of the main points in the material
- Classify material into categories
- Take a group quiz
- Give different examples for new information
- View photographs related to the material and write captions for them

How to Gather Baseline Data before Beginning a Unit of Study

A necessary type of formative assessment that will yield valuable information is one that allows you to determine your students' level of knowledge before they begin a unit of study. Collecting baseline data will allow you not only to design differentiated instruction activities and adjust the pace of learning as the unit proceeds but also to track student learning because you will have a clear starting point. Here are some suggested formative assessments that are particularly useful for gathering baseline data:

- Give students a list of statements related to the unit and ask them to determine if they are true or false. Alternatively, you can ask students to agree or disagree with statements about the work.
- Ask students to predict the meaning of the vocabulary terms they will be studying.

> Never assume that kids are coming to you with certain skills or knowledge. Students of every level are entering your classroom with deficits in writing, studying, executive functioning skills, and more. Assess them on skills that are important to their success, and if they need help, then teach them—think aloud so that they understand the process, allow them to practice these skills, and encourage them to reflect.
>
> *Jennifer Burns, 13 years' experience*

- Have students write a two-minute paper in which they tell you what they know about the upcoming material.
- Ask the entire class questions about the material and observe how many students can answer the questions correctly.
- Give students a Know/Want to Know/Learned chart and ask them to fill it out with what they know.
- Have students share ideas and brainstorm what they know about the topic together.
- Hold a class discussion in which you ask general questions about the material and observe your students' reactions and answers.
- Give students a list of items pertaining to the topic and ask them to rate or rank them.

A Useful Formative Assessment Strategy: Exit Slips

Exit slips have been around for a long time because of their powerful appeal to students and teachers alike. As a method of assessing student learning, exit slips are effective for a variety of reasons. They are brief, focused on the day's learning, and easy for students to manage and for you to evaluate. Further, they can offer specific information about what students need to be successful. Another important aspect of exit slips is that they encourage students to be reflective about their own learning and to determine their own strengths and areas in need of improvement.

One quick way to have students complete exit slips is to ask them to complete a problem or set of problems or to answer a set of questions directly related to the day's work. True-or-false statements, multiple-choice questions, or even brief short-answer questions can all work well as exit slips. The responses to these do not need to be graded but rather quickly appraised to see where changes need to be made for the next day's lesson.

Two popular exit ticket activities that can yield valuable data are to ask students to relate the information in the day's lesson to the essential question for the unit by writing a quick response and to use 3-2-1 slips, whereby students are asked to write three things they learned, two things they found particularly interesting, and one thing they are still confused about.

You can also ask your students to finish some of these sentence starters as a way for you to gather information as they leave the classroom:

- I was surprised when _____.
- I'm beginning to wonder _____.
- I think I will _____.

- I still need help with _____.
- I would have liked _____.
- Now I understand _____.
- In class tomorrow, I will _____.
- Today was valuable to me because _____.
- The easiest part of class today was _____.
- The hardest part of class today was _____.
- Because I need help with _____, I will _____.
- Today I changed the way I _____ because _____.
- Class would be more interesting if _____.
- I can be more successful in this class if I _____.

Formative Assessment Digital Resources

Because of their brief nature and because of the need for fast feedback, digital resources to help you assess student work can be time-savers. Here is a list of some of the most efficient and easiest-to-use digital resources. All were free at the time of publication.

- **Animoto (https://animoto.com).** Students can make quick thirty-second videos to share with classmates.
- **ForAllRubrics (www.forallrubrics.com).** This versatile site allows teachers to create rubrics, access student work, and print or share results. It is user-friendly, and the badge feature is particularly appealing to students.
- **Kahoot! (https://kahoot.com).** Kahoot! allows students to give instant responses and to play various classroom games as they collaborate with one another.
- **Piazza (https://piazza.com).** Piazza is an app that encourages collaborative responses, polling, teacher responses, and much more.
- **Plickers (https://plickers.com).** Plickers is a quick and easy way for students to respond to questions using only one device instead of requiring each student to have one.
- **Quizlet (www.quizlet.com).** At Quizlet, students can create flash cards and play study games.
- **Socrative (www.socrative.com).** You can use the Socrative app for different purposes, but it's especially useful for quick responses from students who are also online.
- **TodaysMeet (https://todaysmeet.com).** Here your students can hold online discussions and share ideas with one another and even with students in other classrooms and schools.
- **Triventy (www.triventy.com).** Students can take teacher-generated online quizzes. It can also be used for class surveys.

STRATEGY EIGHT: EFFECTIVE FEEDBACK

One of the most useful benefits of formative assessment occurs when teachers respond to student performance on an assessment with appropriate and helpful feedback. Unlike the response that happens during a summative assessment where teachers assign grades that reflect how well students mastered the material, formative assessment feedback serves an entirely different purpose: helping students move forward with their learning. A test of the effectiveness of feedback is this: after receiving feedback, students should have a clear idea of what they are supposed to do to improve their work. To accomplish this, there are certain attributes that effective feedback must have. To be effective, feedback

- Must be timely. The faster students can learn how well they are managing an assignment, the better. When there is a delay in feedback, there will be a delay in learning, as students waste valuable time waiting to learn how to proceed.
- Should not be critical, judgmental, or harsh. Because the goal of formative assessment feedback is to help students improve, the tone should be pleasant and friendly.
- Should be brief and to the point. Overwhelming students with too much information is not helpful because it does not provide a focused way of improving. Students who have to wade through too many comments and suggestions lose sight of what it is they are supposed to accomplish. Be concise. Be clear.
- Is geared to help students improve. Instead of flat evaluative statements, to be effective, feedback should offer help, support, and suggestions. Instead of a statement such as "You need to spend more time on this!," a more productive comment would be "Have you considered adding more supporting details to your second paragraph?" or "I suggest that you review your notes before trying the next set of problems."

STRATEGY NINE: PLANNED IMPLEMENTATION OF FEEDBACK

It is not enough just to give students useful feedback; you must build in the time that they need to implement the suggestions that you offered. Although the time required for this will vary from student to student and from assignment to assignment, it is necessary to plan a routine that you want students to follow as soon as they receive feedback. Some things to consider as you develop the routine that you want students to follow can include how to demonstrate that they have implemented the suggestions, when students are to do this work, how they can get the help they need, and how to accomplish their remaining tasks without feeling that they need to rush through the implementation of feedback suggestions.

STRATEGY TEN: STUDENT CHOICE

When students have a choice in the activities that they are assigned, engagement increases. Helping students learn to make sensible choices about the activities that will serve them best will be richly rewarded as students mature throughout a school term. Offering the opportunity to choose among a limited but attractive array of assignments encourages students to think about their learning needs and goals.

Although there are countless ways to offer students choices when differentiating instruction, one of the easiest to manage is to give students a choice board. A choice board is usually a group of nine tasks that students can choose from as they work, although the choices may be expanded or reduced to meet the needs of different classes. To make it easy for students to complete a choice board, give a copy of the choice board to students and ask them to mark off assignments as they complete them. Although the number of assignments that you ask students to complete can vary, asking students to complete four or five of the tasks is reasonable.

The most effective choice boards offer assignments that are equally engaging and difficult. Creating tasks that appeal to different learning styles will allow students to work comfortably using their preferred learning styles while strengthening their learning weaknesses. In the choice board shown in Sample 8.1, you can find assignments that will appeal to student learning preferences.

Sample 8.1
Choice Board for a Unit of Study on a Book

Write a summary.	Make a diagram of the plot.	Make a book jacket of the most exciting part of the book so far.
Record yourself as you read the three most interesting passages out loud.	Take a quick quiz on the most important plot events so far.	Sketch three of the main characters interacting with one another.
Make a videotape of you and some of your classmates acting out a scene from the book.	Take a quick quiz on the most important plot events so far.	Make a booklet of the words and their meanings that were new to you so far in this book.

STRATEGY ELEVEN: ANCHOR ACTIVITIES

Anchor activities are independent, ongoing activities that students may work on at any time when they have completed their primary assignments or when the teacher is busy with other students. Anchor activities serve two very important purposes: they help with classroom management, and they promote learning.

Difficulties with classroom management are often cited as a concern by those teachers who are attempting to differentiate instruction for the first time. Anchor activities make classroom management easier because they engage students in structured and engaging instructional activities without having to interrupt the work that the teacher may be doing with other students.

Anchor activities also promote learning because they allow students to remain focused on learning during classroom downtime. Because anchor activities are instructional, they can be used in conjunction with current or past units of study, or they can be activities of general interest, such as a cross-disciplinary project, independent research, or online review games.

Teachers who use anchor activities often find that such activities are most successful when the expectations for academic work and behavior are explicit, when students know that their work is meaningful and will be assessed, and when students are offered choices. It is helpful to explain the purpose of anchor activities so that students understand that they are not optional but will help them learn. Be clear in modeling the routines and procedures that you expect students to follow so that they can work with confidence and without disruption.

Although anchor activities can be related to the unit of study that your students are working on, they can also be broad based. Students will find anchor activities that are connected to their individual interests particularly engaging, especially if they have input into the creation of the activities. Although you will want to take your students' learning needs into consideration, here are some suggestions for engaging anchor activities that you can adapt for your classroom use:

> A student touched my heart when I received a correspondence from a college adviser letting me know one of his student advisees wrote an essay about how I touched her life and made her want to go into teaching. She is now an English teacher in my same county.
>
> *Jessica Statz, 19 years' experience*

- Reading independently
- Completing creative writing projects
- Using or making flashcards
- Playing online games
- Completing puzzles
- Visiting a virtual reality museum or other site
- Working with classmates on a class blog, web page, or scrapbook

- Reflecting on learning
- Maintaining a binder or portfolio
- Completing vocabulary work
- Solving a problem of the day
- Working at a learning center
- Making multimedia presentations
- Reviewing with a partner
- Completing art projects

How to Plan for Differentiation

Until differentiation becomes a classroom norm for you and your students, you may feel unsure of how to plan instruction. It can be intimidating to determine how to fit all the parts of a differentiated lesson into the mental template that you may have for a daily lesson plan. A productive way to manage this is to look over the following time line of a differentiated lesson and decide how you can plan for each part. Once you have this in place, you can then determine how to include these steps into the daily flow of instruction in your classroom.

- **Step One:** Use your state, district, and school curriculum standards to determine the objectives and essential knowledge.

- **Step Two:** Determine how much time is needed. Will the lesson cover one day? Two? Longer?

- **Step Three:** Administer pre-assessments to determine student readiness.

- **Step Four:** Use data from pre-assessments to determine tasks. You will also determine flexible groups and tiers at this point in your planning if they are to be included in the lesson.

- **Step Five:** Deliver whole-group instruction about the material and review or reinforce the procedures and routines students should follow.

- **Step Six:** Move students to their differentiated tasks, making sure that each student has a clear idea of how to complete the work and how to signal for help when needed.

- **Step Seven:** Provide formative assessments so that students can check their understanding. Provide quick feedback and allow time for students to implement improvements.

- **Step Eight:** Reteach if necessary. Students who have mastered the material move to anchor activities.

- **Step Nine:** Provide time for students to reflect on their learning.

- **Step Ten:** Spend time yourself reflecting on the effectiveness of the lesson. How can you improve it? What would you do again?

A Planning Checklist for Differentiation

You can use this checklist to think through a differentiated activity to meet the learning needs of your students. As you work through the questions in the first part of the checklist, you should be able to determine how you can effectively differentiate the activity. After you have completed this part, use Part II to guide your thinking further.

Part I: Looking at the Big Picture

After you formulate an answer for each of these questions, place a check mark in the blank beside it.

1. _____ What needs do you hope to serve by including the activity in your instruction?

2. _____ Which learning styles will your activity appeal to?

3. _____ What materials and resources will you need?

4. _____ How much time do you anticipate will be needed?

5. _____ What preparation is necessary before you use this activity in your instruction?

6. _____ Which routines or procedures do you need to establish or reinforce?

7. _____ What problems can you anticipate? How can you prevent or solve them?

8. _____ How will you gather data before and during the activity?

9. _____ How will you deliver feedback to students?

10. _____ How will students implement feedback suggestions?

11. _____ What will the products of the activity be? At what stages will these products be assessed?

12. _____ How will you know if the strategy is successful?

(continued on next page)

From *The First-Year Teacher's Survival Guide, 4th Edition*, by Julia G. Thompson. Copyright © 2018 by John Wiley & Sons, Inc. Reproduced by permission.

(continued from previous page)

Part II: A Time Line for a Differentiated Lesson Plan

As you complete each step of the process for creating a differentiated lesson plan, place a check mark in the blank.

1. _____ Use your state, district, and school curriculum standards to determine the objectives and essential knowledge.

2. _____ Determine how much time is needed. Will the lesson cover one day? Two?

3. _____ Administer pre-assessments to determine student readiness.

4. _____ Use data from pre-assessments to determine tasks. You will also determine flexible groups and tiers at this point in your planning if they are to be included in the lesson.

5. _____ Deliver whole-group instruction about the material and review or reinforce the procedures and routines students should follow.

6. _____ Move students to their differentiated tasks, making sure that each student has a clear idea of how to complete the work and how to signal for help when needed.

7. _____ Allow time for quick formative assessments so that students can check their understanding. Provide quick feedback and allow time for students to implement it.

8. _____ Reteach if necessary. Students who have mastered the material move to anchor activities.

9. _____ Provide time for students to reflect on their learning.

10. _____ Spend time yourself reflecting on the effectiveness of the lesson. How can you improve it? What would you do again?

More Differentiated Instruction Planning

After you have worked through the information in the time line and in Teacher Worksheet 8.3, you can use the template in Teacher Worksheet 8.4 to be precise about how you plan for differentiated instruction.

TEACHER WORKSHEET 8.4

Individualized Instruction Planning Template

To ensure that your plans for differentiated instruction are on the right track, you can use this template to design instruction that will meet the needs of all your learners.

Lesson topic: _____   Dates: _____

Concepts and essential questions:

_____

_____

_____

_____

Outcomes, objectives, and goals:

_____

_____

_____

_____

Learning style preferences (circle the preference[s] that the lesson is designed to appeal to): Visual   Auditory   Kinesthetic

Preliminary assessment activities:

_____

_____

_____

_____

Estimated time needed: _____

Direct instruction activities:

_____

_____

_____

_____

Estimated time needed: _____

(continued on next page)

(continued from previous page)
Differentiation Strategies

Respectful tasks:

_____
_____
_____
_____

Flexible groups:

_____
_____
_____
_____

Tiered instruction:

_____
_____
_____
_____

Estimated time needed for all strategies: _____

Formative assessments:

_____
_____
_____
_____

Estimated time needed: _____

Implementing feedback:

_____
_____
_____
_____

Estimated time needed: _____

Anchor activities:

_____
_____
_____
_____

From *The First-Year Teacher's Survival Guide, 4th Edition*, by Julia G. Thompson. Copyright © 2018 by John Wiley & Sons, Inc. Reproduced by permission.

Classroom Management Strategies for Differentiation

It's reasonable to wonder just how you are going to manage a classroom in which students are engaged in different activities. For example, what is the rest of the class going to be doing when you are helping a small group of students? Although the management challenges of a differentiated classroom can be difficult at first, once your students are accustomed to the routines and expectations for their class, they will remain on task because the work will be engaging. Here are some management tips that can make creating a differentiated classroom a workable solution to how you will accommodate the needs of all your students:

- Encourage classroom ownership and a sense of shared responsibility for the success of the entire class. Ask students to self-reflect, make informed decisions for the good of the group, articulate their learning goals, and help one another be successful.
- Appoint student experts who can help their peers.
- Have clear written directions for all activities so that students know what to do. Many teachers find that checklists and daily agendas are effective in making assignments and expectations clear.
- Establish clear time lines for assignments so that students know that they are expected to produce work within a set time. This will help everyone stay focused.
- Post a list of procedures for those students who finish early. Provide plenty of high-interest anchor activities for these students.
- Use signals to control noise—even good noise can get too loud sometimes.
- Establish class routines for turning in work, passing out materials, moving to groups, and so on.
- Keep the pace brisk, businesslike, and purposeful.

Response to Intervention

In the broadest sense, Response to Intervention (RTI) is a form of differentiated instruction in that it offers modifications to content, process, and product to help students master curriculum material. Although RTI is a highly successful program in many schools, it differs from classroom differentiation in a significant way: RTI is a schoolwide intervention framework instead of differentiation delivered by an individual teacher.

Similar to other types of differentiated instruction, RTI offers a tiered approach to interventions. In the first tier, students are instructed by a general education teacher using solid, classroom-tested strategies, including differentiated instruction. Ongoing data collection through a variety of assessments is used to help determine the needs of all students in the class.

Students who, according to the collected data, are not mastering the content or acquiring the necessary skills required by the curriculum are moved to the second tier of instruction. Students in the second tier continue to remain in their general education classroom and receive the same instruction as their classmates. In addition, however, students in the second tier also receive more intensive instruction targeted to help them overcome their learning difficulties. Such instruction is usually delivered in small-group format, in learning centers, and even by an additional staff member. After a specified time, if students in the second tier have mastered the material, they then move back to the first tier of instruction. If they are still experiencing difficulties, they move to the third tier.

> I never give up on any student, regardless of his or her grade, level of effort, and so on. I also make it clear to each student, over and over, that I'm not giving up, no matter what.
>
> *Margaret R. Scheirer, 12 years' experience*

Students in the third tier receive instruction that is more intensive and individualized than that offered in the first two tiers. Often a specialist or a special education teacher provides this instruction on an individual basis, although the general education teacher can still be involved. Instruction is specifically targeted to assist individual students. Ongoing assessments at this level continue to play an important role, as students may be referred to a screening committee that will consider them for eligibility for special education services.

Although there may be experts at your school who are already involved in an RTI program and who can assist you in learning more about it, there are also two very good websites where you can access much more information:

- **Center on Response to Intervention (www.rti4success.org).** At this carefully researched and maintained site, nationally recognized experts offer resources and advice to help schools implement RTI programs successfully.
- **Intervention Central (www.interventioncentral.org).** Here you can find expert advice and many helpful resources on how to implement RTI assistance for students with both behavior problems and academic problems.

Strategies Just for Managing Differentiation Stress

Even though the process of differentiation can be exciting to put into motion, it can be stressful to successfully manage all of it when you are a beginning teacher. Here are some quick tips to help you manage this category of teacher stress:

- Take it easy at first. Start small and keep it simple. You do not have to completely revamp your lesson plans; in fact, it is best to begin with a strategy or two. Practice them until you are comfortable and then add to your repertoire.

- It takes time to find the resources and materials that you need to offer differentiated instruction. Work with colleagues to share ideas and research online to create a bank of activities that you can draw from.

- Work out a simple system to manage the data from formative assessments and to keep track of student assignments. Find a system that is manageable for you and stick with it.

- Take the time to explain to students the purpose of differentiated instruction and how they can help run the class. With their buy-in, classroom management will be much easier.

- Be patient with yourself. It takes time to learn how to manage differentiation. Just as your students are working to improve their skills levels, so are you.

Resources to Help You Learn More about Differentiation

Because of the increasing use of differentiation, there is a great deal of helpful information available for educators who want to learn more. Here are some books and online resources to help you get started:

Books

- McCarthy, J. *So All Can Learn: A Practical Guide to Differentiation.* Lanham, MD: Rowman & Littlefield, 2017.
- Tomlinson, C. A. *How to Differentiate Instruction in Academically Diverse Classrooms.* 3rd ed. Alexandria, VA: Association for Supervision and Curriculum Development, 2017.

Online Resources

- **Differentiation Central (http://differentiationcentral.com).** At the University of Virginia's Institutes for Academic Diversity, you can find many useful resources about differentiated instruction, including Carol Tomlinson's extensive work.
- **Differentiation Daily (http://differentiationdaily.com).** Educator Paula Kluth adds fresh new tips about differentiation to this blog daily. There is an emphasis on material for younger students.
- **Edutopia (www.edutopia.org).** At Edutopia, you can access dozens of well-written, practical articles about differentiated instruction. Use "differentiated instruction" as a search term.
- **Opening Paths (http://openingpaths.org).** At John McCarthy's blog, readers can find a wealth of practical and helpful material about differentiation.

Questions to Discuss with Colleagues

Sharing ideas with colleagues is a helpful way to devise solutions to some of the problems that you must manage successfully at school. Here you will find several topics to open discussions with colleagues about successful instructional practices:

1. You want to provide your students with constructive feedback on formative assessments. What are some of the most effective ways that you can provide encouraging feedback to your students? How can you provide this type of feedback without spending hours writing comments on student papers?

2. You want to assess your students' preferred learning styles but are not sure which assessment instrument you should use. How can you find an assessment that will be effective with your students? Who can help you with this?

3. As you begin a new unit of study, you become aware that your students have various levels of background knowledge about the new unit. What can you do to increase the background knowledge of all students in your class?

4. You have a class with severely mixed ability levels—from very bright to those who struggle to succeed academically. What can you do to meet the needs of the individual learners in your class?

5. Although you want to use formative assessments in your classroom, you are not always sure that the ones you have chosen are producing the most helpful data. What can you do to improve the way you use formative assessments?

Topics to Discuss with a Mentor

Although the topics that new teachers need to discuss with a mentor vary from teacher to teacher and from school to school, there are some that most first-year teachers should be comfortable discussing with a mentor or a trusted colleague. You should ask your mentor about these topics from this section:

- How to obtain any additional materials and supplies you may need for differentiation
- Advice about classroom management strategies specific to differentiation
- How to assess student readiness and use formative assessments
- Suggestions for instructional activity ideas for tiered instruction
- How to create flexible groups

Reflection Questions to Guide Your Thinking

1. What are your biggest concerns about implementing differentiated instruction in your classroom? How can you overcome them? Where can you find help with this?

2. Which formative assessments do you anticipate will work well for your students at this point in the term? What do you need to know and do before administering them?

3. How can you arrange your schedule so that the feedback you provide for students is timely?

4. Which of your students would benefit most from differentiated instruction? How can you determine the best strategies to help them succeed? Where can you find help with this?

5. What are your strengths regarding differentiated instruction? How can you use these strengths to your advantage when planning and implementing differentiated instruction?

SECTION NINE

Design and Deliver Effective Instruction

Lesson planning is one of the most important tasks you have as a first-year teacher, as a second-year teacher, as a third-year teacher . . ., and it will be just as important when you are a seasoned veteran with years of experience. Planning effective lessons is the foundation for success in your classroom and, ultimately, success in your career. There can be no substitute for this process. Successful teachers know that they must carefully plan every lesson.

When you make the commitment to plan lessons carefully, you and your students will benefit in many ways. Here are just some of the benefits you will receive when you make this sound decision:

- You will be more likely to prepare interesting lessons that engage your students' critical thinking skills, leverage their preferred learning styles, and appeal to their interests rather than relying on lackluster routines.

- You will gain confidence from having a clear plan for each lesson. This added confidence will translate into a more successful delivery of material for your students and increased professional credibility for you.

- You will be able to pay attention to the details that will make your lessons successful, such as including technology and real-world activities.

- You will be able to create a logical progression of learning instead of just presenting bits and pieces of information without a clear purpose.

- You will be better able to teach the curriculum that your state and district require of you. With well-planned lessons, you can cover the standards that your students need to master.

How to Develop a Lesson Plan

Because instructional planning is such an important part of any teacher's day, it is not something that educators take lightly. There are dozens of decisions involved in even the most uncomplicated lesson. To ensure that these decisions all work together to facilitate learning, it's necessary to think through each lesson plan carefully. In the next few pages, you will learn how to develop a lesson from the first glimmer of an idea through each step, and finally, to student achievement.

Why Strategic Steps Are the Keys to Success

As you are probably already aware, it is better to begin any project with careful planning, gathering the best possible resources, and making sure you know what to do before you begin. If these steps are important for an ordinary project, just imagine how vital careful planning is when trying to implement various instructional strategies into your classroom. Instead of taking on too much and failing to help your students, be cautious. Take your time. Be deliberate in your approach.

If you learn of a strategy that seems interesting and that you predict would work well with your students, implement it strategically. First, learn all that you can about it. Talk it over with your mentor or with others in your school communities. Next, be thoroughly prepared and have a backup plan in case your untried plan does not work well. Gather data as you implement the strategy so that you can be as accurate as possible when assessing its effectiveness. Finally, take time to reflect. What went well? What do you need to tweak? How can you make sure that this strategy is as effective as possible next time?

Backward Design: Think Big, but Start Small

The iconic term *backward design* was coined by Grant Wiggins and Jay McTighe in their groundbreaking 1998 book, *Understanding by Design*, published by the Association for Supervision and Curriculum Development. Backward design is a productive approach to instructional planning based on the idea that teachers should begin the process by determining the desired end results of instruction. With the final outcomes in mind, teachers can then design and deliver appropriate instruction tailored to help students achieve those predetermined results.

Although thousands of teachers follow the principles of backward design when planning lessons, countless others make the mistake of planning small increments of instruction instead of building a framework of carefully sequenced skills and knowledge. When you begin designing lessons to help your students master the information and skills that your curriculum requires, begin with the big picture. What essential knowledge do your students need to establish a base on which the next unit will build? What skills will they need to move forward in their learning?

Once you have determined the essential knowledge of the content, you will find that it becomes easier to design carefully constructed lessons that combine to form a satisfying sequence of instruction.

Cover the Curriculum or Teach Your Students?

It can be discouraging to assess your students' readiness and background knowledge only to learn that many of them are unable to manage even the most basic work that you ask of them. The discouragement intensifies once you realize that you cannot just ignore the mandated curriculum but are expected to help every student master the material successfully enough to perform well on high-stakes tests.

Although there will never be an easy way to solve the problem of students who are not prepared for grade-level work, teachers do not have to choose between teaching their students and covering the curriculum. Learn to see students with learning deficiencies as students who can succeed and who need to learn the material rather than as problem students. Differentiate instruction, scaffold lessons, offer extra help, and involve other concerned adults in a sustained effort to help every student succeed. If you teach the curriculum with sensitivity to your students' needs, you will not have to make this unfair choice.

How Prepared Should You Be?

One of the easiest mistakes for first-year teachers to make is to not prepare adequately. This is understandable because of the overwhelming newness of each day and the volume of unfamiliar material that you must master, but it is not a sound practice. Put simply, if you are not thoroughly prepared for class, your students will struggle to be successful. Although the amount of necessary preparation varies from teacher to teacher, here are some guidelines on how prepared you should be:

> Think in terms of what you want to get done in class in a week. This tends to make you plan out ahead a little farther, so in case you get through certain activities quicker than you planned, you won't find yourself in that awkward space where you now have to scramble to come up with something.
>
> *Kevin Healy, 11 years' experience*

At the Start of a School Year

- You must be thoroughly familiar with your state's standards.
- You must know the material you will be expected to teach each term.
- You must have a course overview in place as soon as possible.

At the Start of a Grading Period

- You must have plans for each unit you intend to teach.
- You should have enough daily plans for about two weeks. Try to keep at least two weeks of daily plans prepared as often as you can.

Common Planning Problems

Although it is true that all teachers may have occasional problems planning effective lessons, some problems seem to be especially prevalent during the first few years of teaching. The biggest disadvantage you have in creating lesson plans as a novice teacher is that you do not have a storehouse of tried-and-true materials. Every lesson plan you write in your first year is an experiment.

No matter how much effort you put into your plans, a lesson can fail simply because it has unforeseen drawbacks. You can reduce the likelihood of an unsuccessful lesson by paying attention to some of the incorrect ideas you might have about writing your plans. Here are a few of the problems concerning lesson plans that many first-year teachers encounter:

- Neglecting to follow state and district standards and guidelines
- Rushing to cover material instead of teaching students
- Failing to connect current learning to previous learning
- Spending a disproportionate amount of time on one unit
- Failing to include activities that engage critical thinking skills
- Not allowing for differences in learning styles
- Failing to assess students' prior knowledge before starting new instruction
- Testing students on material they have not adequately mastered
- Failing to use data from formative assessments before a summative assessment
- Failing to write a course overview before deciding on unit plans and daily plans

The Practicalities of Planning

As a new teacher, learning to plan instruction efficiently takes time. Be patient as you work out the best ways to manage this important task. With practice, you will soon learn how to find materials and design instruction that can help your students learn. To understand the practical aspects of effective planning, it may help to examine the entirety of the planning process, as shown in Figure 9.1.

Your State's Standards

Each state's department of education has created the standards that indicate the material students must master by the end of each course or grade level. As you begin the process of designing a course of study for your students, the foundation of your lesson plans should be your state's standards. You should plan all lessons with mastery of the state standards as your final objective. To learn more about the standards that apply to you and your students, try these tips on potential resources:

- Access your state's department of education website.
- Access your local school district's website.

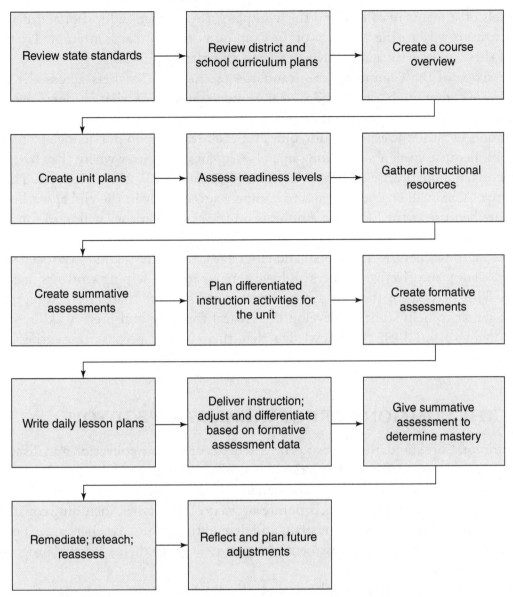

Figure 9.1 The Planning Process

- Begin talking with other teachers at your school to share materials and lesson plans.
- Do your own research involving the textbooks you may be using (if your school uses textbooks) or online sources.

The Common Core State Standards Initiative

The Common Core State Standards Initiative (CCSSI) is a far-reaching reform movement in education coordinated by the National Governor's Association for Best Practices and the Council of Chief State School Officers to provide students with a first-rate, twenty-first-century education regardless of their geographic location.

Concerned about how poorly students performed in recent years in comparison with other students around the globe, as well as with the growing dissatisfaction with the low skill levels of students in college and the workplace, the teachers, educational experts, and administrators who are the designers of the Common Core standards attempted to remedy both of these issues with a carefully researched and planned initiative.

The scope of the Common Core standards reaches far. Teachers across the United States share common objectives and a clearer understanding of what students need to be successful once they leave their classrooms. Transient students should be able to adjust to new schools because the expected outcomes for their learning do not change from school to school. Because students have the same assessments no matter where they live, educators can make more precise comparisons across state and local school districts. The hope is that the CCSSI will enable students to compete successfully in the global workplace of the future because of the increased emphasis on the skills that they will need for the rest of their lives.

K–12 math teachers; K–12 English and language arts teachers; and 6–12 social studies, history, science, and elective teachers all have a major role in helping students master the literacy skills needed for their respective content areas. More than ever before, teachers work together to help students develop the critical thinking and literacy skills that will enable them to build on the knowledge that they already possess to synthesize new learning.

HOW THE COMMON CORE STANDARDS AFFECT YOU

The Common Core standards are results oriented. Accurate data collection and disaggregation are crucial components in instructional planning. The various computer-based benchmark tests, as well as the summative assessment at the end of the year, are not be limited to multiple-choice questions but incorporate a variety of item types, including constructive responses that call for students to explain and defend their work. Teachers are expected to use formative and summative assessments to accurately gauge their students' progress and areas of deficiency.

One very important shift brought about by the Common Core standards is the emphasis on a shared responsibility for literacy across content areas. No longer is the development of good reading skills limited to the work of language arts or reading teachers; every teacher shares the task of helping students become adept at reading and understanding a variety of complex informational texts.

Although the Common Core standards themselves are quite specific, educators have a great deal of flexibility in designing appropriate instruction. There is not a prescribed curriculum that teachers are required to follow. Successful teachers find that a creative approach and careful planning help their students meet the expectations of the CCSSI.

Under the terms of the CCSSI, students must have wide exposure to digital media across content areas. The increased emphasis on employing digital resources in instruction requires teachers to be cognizant of the current best practices in using electronic media and how such media can be used to greatest advantage in their classrooms.

The Common Core standards are rigorous. Students are expected to think critically, to make accurate inferences and judgments about the material they are studying, and to then express those inferences and judgments in a logical manner. Teachers are expected to help their students rise to meet these higher expectations through instruction that is carefully designed and delivered.

HOW TO LEARN MORE ABOUT THE COMMON CORE STATE STANDARDS INITIATIVE

Although your school district will be able to provide you with the local-level information that you need to succeed, here are several other excellent resources that offer useful information on the CCSSI:

- **Common Core State Standards Initiative (www.corestandards.org).** At this informative site, teachers can educate themselves about the scope and history of the CCSSI and can access a wide array of webinars and PowerPoints about the Common Core standards and their implications for educators.
- **Partnership for Assessment of Readiness for College and Careers (http://parcc-assessment.org).** At this site maintained by one of the two consortia involved in the development of the Common Core standards, teachers can learn about the standards themselves as well as about diagnostic assessments, instructional materials, and tools to help make implementation successful.
- **Smarter Balanced Assessment Consortium (www.smarterbalanced.org).** At the website of the Smarter Balanced Assessment Consortium, the second major consortium involved with the development of the Common Core standards, teachers can find valuable teaching resources, information on best practices, and practical strategies for successful implementation of the Common Core standards.

How to Begin Planning Instruction

In the next few pages, you will learn how to begin to plan instruction. Successful lesson planning proceeds in an orderly sequence. After you have thoroughly familiarized yourself with the curriculum that you are expected to teach and gathered the diagnostic data that you need to assess your students' readiness, here's how to begin:

- **Step One:** Create a course overview. This will give you an idea of the scope of the information your students need to master during the entire term.
- **Step Two:** Create unit plans. Divide the material you must teach into smaller units of information and then plan how to teach each one.
- **Step Three:** Create daily plans. This final step in the lesson planning process is the most detailed. At this level, you have the most flexibility in determining the activities your students will complete.

CREATE A COURSE OVERVIEW

Before you can write successful daily plans, you must have a clear idea of what your students are expected to learn by the end of the school term. One of the easiest mistakes to make as a new teacher is to focus on the daily activities that you want your students to complete without fully planning how those activities fit into the bigger picture of the mandated curriculum. To avoid that mistake, first make a general plan of the material you are expected to cover during the term. Here is how to create a course overview that will serve as a useful guide all term long:

- Start with your state's standards. You should begin by thoroughly reviewing the standards for the entire course so that you know what your students are expected to learn by the end of the year.
- Use your district's resources. Review your local curriculum guidelines; they will be aligned with your state's standards.
- Determine the units you need to teach and prioritize their importance. Make a list of the units you must cover to meet state and district objectives. Prioritize your list into three tiers of importance:
  - Units you absolutely must cover
  - Material you would like to cover if you have time
  - Units you plan to offer to students as enrichment or remedial work

As you think through the material that your students need to master as the school term progresses, you can use Teacher Worksheet 9.1 and Teacher Worksheet 9.2 to help prioritize your planning.

Format for a Course Overview

Use this worksheet and your state and district standards to create a brief overview of the material that you are expected to cover before the school year ends.

Essential Units	Optional Units	Enrichment Units	Remedial Units

TEACHER WORKSHEET 9.2

Predictable Dates to Consider When Creating a Course Overview

As you think through the instruction that you must cover for the entire term, it helps to keep in mind some of the important dates that can affect instructional planning. Use this list and your school district's calendar to determine important dates in the school term.

1. _____ The last day of school
2. _____ The first day of school for students
3. _____ The grading periods throughout the year
4. _____ Major holidays when school is not in session
5. _____ Religious holidays celebrated by students
6. _____ Spring break
7. _____ The Hundredth Day
8. _____ District meetings
9. _____ Teacher workdays
10. _____ Evaluation or certification deadlines
11. _____ Open house/back to school/PTA meetings
12. _____ Standardized testing dates
13. _____ Benchmark assessment dates
14. _____ Due dates for district paperwork involving benefits
15. _____ Deadlines for personal and professional goals
16. _____ Professional development meetings

Other dates specific to your school: _____

_____

_____

_____

_____

_____

_____

_____

_____

_____

_____

CREATE UNIT PLANS

Unit plans are the intermediate step between a course overview and daily plans. When you create unit plans, you divide the material into smaller blocks and determine roughly how you will teach it. You should create unit plans after you have an overview of the course for the year and before you attempt daily plans.

In the list that follows, you will find some of the features that will guide you as you plan each unit. You can also use Teacher Worksheet 9.3 to guide your planning process and as a template for your written unit plans.

- Determine essential knowledge. Using state and district guidelines, as well as your textbook and other materials, identify the essential knowledge that students must gain to master the material in the unit.

- Determine your students' prior knowledge. A crucial step in preparing unit plans is to first determine what your students already know about the topic. This will dictate the activities you will include because it will provide you with information about how you should approach the various topics in the unit.

- Determine the length of the unit. To create plans for a unit of study, you must decide how long the unit will take, from the first objective to the final assessment. The length of time you plan to spend on a unit will be an important factor in determining the activities you need to plan.

- Brainstorm and research appropriate activities. Take the time to brainstorm and conduct research to generate activities that will interest your students as you cover the material in the unit. You will need a variety of activities that will interest students, appeal to students with different learning styles, and provide opportunities for students to engage in critical thinking.

- Select appropriate activities. Make a list of the activities that you believe would be most useful to your students in the sequence in which you want to present them.

- Select materials and resources. With a time line and prior knowledge firmly established, you can search for the materials you need. Are there movies or other technology options for you to use? Do your colleagues have materials to share? Finally, turn to other sources, such as the Internet.

- Create assessments. It may seem strange to create the assessments for a unit of study before you write your daily plans, but if you do this, your daily plans will align with the information you plan to assess.

Format for a Unit Plan

Use this worksheet as a template for creating your unit plans, customizing it as necessary to fit your needs.

Unit title: _____

Dates: _____

Objectives: _____

_____

_____

Materials and resources needed: _____

_____

_____

Essential knowledge for mastery: _____

_____

_____

Activities: _____

_____

_____

_____

_____

Formative assessments: _____

_____

_____

_____

Summative assessments: _____

_____

_____

_____

_____

_____

CREATE DAILY PLANS

Although a course overview and unit plans are the basis for your curriculum planning, your daily plans are what will make instruction come to life for your students. Your daily plans should follow a standard format that makes it easy for you to consult them during class. Your school district may have a format that you will be expected to use. If not, then you should create a format that you can use with ease. Many teachers design their own planning templates and either photocopy them, so that they can just pencil in information for each section, or make digital copies. Even if you use a computer-generated template, you may want to print out a copy for quick reference during class.

With your format decision under control, keep these pointers in mind to make sure that the lessons you plan are not only effective but also easy to manage:

- Although you should vary your lessons, routines will keep students on track. Establish some instructional routines so that students can predict what their days will be like. For example, your routines could include a quiz every Thursday, a review game every Monday, or no homework on Tuesday nights.

- No matter what you have planned to do each day, you must include two vital lesson elements. First, you must have an engaging opening that will encourage your students to recall what they did in your class during the last meeting and to look ahead to the current lesson. Second, you must also include a satisfying closure to your lesson. This will help your students reinforce their knowledge of the day's material.

- Your lesson plans should be written for your own use. Even though administrators or other evaluators will probably ask to see your plans from time to time, you should plan for your own benefit. If you are in doubt about how much to write, begin by writing detailed plans to give yourself a needed boost of confidence.

What to Include in Your Plans

The following list will help you as you begin to write your daily lesson plans. There may be other items that you will find useful to include in one class, but the listed items will constitute a good beginning. You will also find that you do not have to cover all the items in this list in one class period. Instead, choose the items from this list that will be most effective in helping your students learn on the day for which you are creating plans.

- Standards: Refer to your district or state guidelines to make sure that the instruction you design is aligned with the standards in the curriculum you are required to cover.

- Specific objectives: Objectives indicate what the result of a lesson will be, not which activities students will complete. The objectives for a lesson should be stated in specific terms and must follow state and district guidelines. For example, an objective for students in a geography course could be: "Learners will be able to identify forty-five of the fifty state capitals."

- Materials and equipment: You should determine what resources you need to teach an innovative and interesting lesson.

- Assessment of prior knowledge: You must assess your students' prior knowledge before you begin teaching a lesson to determine exactly what you need to review or introduce.

- Opening activity: Creating anticipation among your students should be an integral part of the opening activity in your class each day. An engaging opening allows students to shift gears mentally from what they were doing before class began and leads them into the lesson they are about to begin. (For more information on opening and closing strategies, see Section Four.)

- Direct instruction or teacher input: Your input is necessary for a successful lesson. Carefully plan what you are going to do or say to make your points during the day's instruction.

- Student activities: Use a wide range of independent and guided practice activities that will appeal to students with a variety of learning styles. Be careful to include critical thinking activities.

- Alternative activities: Allow for differences in student ability, readiness, and speed of mastery by preparing alternative activities that provide enrichment or remediation. You can also add extension activities for students who finish before their classmates.

- Closure: Close each class with an activity designed to reinforce learning. Allowing students to drift from one class to another without formal closure fails to make use of students' tendency to recall the beginning and end of a lesson with clarity.

- Homework: Homework assignments should arise naturally from the lesson. Because they are part of what you teach, you should record specific assignments in your plans.

- Assessments: You should include a variety of assessments in each unit of study. Be sure to include formative and summative assessments to make it easy to evaluate your students' progress.

- Student reflection: If your students are old enough for this to be appropriate, include time for them to reflect on what they have learned during class, connections with other topics, and what they still need to do.

- Teacher reflection: Leave space in your daily plans to record your successes, failures, or any other information that will allow you to teach this lesson more successfully in the future.

Use Teacher Worksheet 9.4 as a template for creating your daily lesson plans, customizing it as necessary to fit your needs.

TEACHER WORKSHEET 9.4

Format for Daily Lesson Plans

You can use this format to create daily lesson plans that will be easy to follow by filling in the sections you need to cover each day. Although you would not expect to cover all the items in this worksheet every day, you can see at a glance what you have covered and what you may still want to include in your instruction.

Lesson topic: _____ Date: _____

Standards: _____

_____

Specific objectives: _____

_____

Materials and equipment: _____

_____

Assessment of prior knowledge: _____

_____

Opening activity: _____

_____

Direct instruction or teacher input: _____

_____

_____

Student-centered activities: _____

_____

_____

Alternative activities: _____

_____

_____

Closure: _____

_____

Homework: _____

Assessments: _____

_____

_____

Student reflection activity: _____

_____

Teacher reflection: _____

_____

_____

Successful Learning for Nontraditional Schedules

A widespread trend in recent years is nontraditional scheduling. There are countless versions of nontraditional schedules. For example, some classes may meet every day for an extended period for half the school year; some classes may meet every other day for the entire year; still others may meet for varying lengths of time a few days a week for only one grading period. Many districts are also trying year-round school schedules or modified summer schedules.

Although nontraditional schedules have many benefits, they also have drawbacks. It can be difficult to cover all the material the curriculum requires in the allotted time. If students need enrichment or remediation, it can be even more challenging. Student absenteeism while students are on a nontraditional schedule is another serious matter. When students miss a class, they may be missing the equivalent of at least two classes, depending on the type of nontraditional schedule they have.

It is also easy for teachers to waste class time while on a nontraditional schedule because many nontraditional schedules allow for longer class periods. Wasting the end of class by allowing students unstructured time is a poor use of students' time when classes are on a traditional schedule, but it becomes a serious misuse of students' time when a nontraditional schedule is in effect because of the compressed time constraints of most nontraditional schedules.

Despite these problems, many school districts have moved to nontraditional schedules to take advantage of the many benefits such schedules offer.

- With longer class periods, students can finish lengthy assignments, such as experiments or projects, before the end of class.
- With less hall traffic, there are fewer opportunities for discipline problems.

As already indicated, nontraditional schedules have disadvantages and advantages, just as traditional school schedules do; in both cases, you must learn to use the time you have with your students as fully as possible. Here are some strategies that may assist you as you work to master the challenges of a nontraditional schedule:

- Divide the class period you have with students into smaller blocks as you plan. Vary the activities in each of these smaller blocks to keep students alert and interested in working.
- Expect your students to work independently for at least part of the period. Very few teachers can lecture for a sustained length of time and keep the interest of a room full of restless students who are used to a fast-paced world.
- Plan the entire term carefully. You have a limited amount of time to cover the material your students need to know. You must keep your students on track if you are to succeed.
- Plan each day carefully. Always have backup plans to avoid running out of things for students to do.

- Make connections for your students. Spend time at the start of class reviewing the previous day's learning and the last few minutes of each class reinforcing the material that students have just learned.

- Take advantage of innovative activities that require extended periods of time, such as simulations, debates, seminars, or online learning games.

How to Adjust a Lesson

It is not uncommon for students to feel frustrated or to have trouble staying on task. When such behavior seems to last more than a few minutes, you must be prepared to adjust your lesson plan to meet your students' needs. Although the methods of adjusting your plan will vary from class to class, you can quickly correct most situations. The following tips will help you turn a frustrating lesson into a successful one as quickly as possible:

- Resist the temptation to give in to your own frustration by reprimanding your students. Think about why they are off task and solve that problem instead.

- Remember that often just switching to another learning modality will engage students enough that they will work to overcome any small frustrations.

- Either reduce the amount of drill and practice you have assigned or make it more palatable by allowing students to tackle it in pairs or small groups.

- Call a stop to the lesson and assess the situation. Determine what your students already know to avoid needlessly repeating information or leaving them behind by moving to a subject they are not ready to process.

> After a few years, you begin to feel comfortable, but it doesn't start that way. I remember looking at other teachers starting each class with ease and interacting with kids like the Pied Piper. It can be a little daunting at first. Now I walk into classes and actually find myself enjoying the little ways kids try to test you because it's an opportunity to build a relationship. That first year, anything that seems to lead a lesson astray is a travesty in your mind. It's okay to be nervous and to have those moments where you wonder how you're going to get your students to buy in; everybody has them.
>
> *Kevin Healy, 11 years' experience*

- Involve your students in decisions to adjust lessons if they are old enough and mature enough to be helpful. Ask them why the lesson is not working for them and then ask for their suggestions.

Always Have a Backup Plan

Few situations in a classroom are more dismaying than realizing that your students have nothing constructive to do. In a situation like this, you must have a backup plan ready.

When you write your daily plans, you should jot down ideas that would be useful as backup plans. To help you write backup plans, here are two possible ideas that you can adopt for your students.

First, you can brainstorm a list of interesting activities that are related to the general topic under study and will last anywhere from ten to thirty minutes. When you need to use a backup plan, you can quickly scan your list to select an appropriate activity.

Still other teachers keep an eye out for good backup plans all year long. They maintain collections of reading passages, games, and other learning activities. You can begin by compiling a few simple puzzles or other high-interest activities that will provide your students with opportunities to use their time constructively.

In the following list, you will find backup plan options that will help you keep students engaged in learning all class long. Although most of these activities require at least a modicum of planning or preparation in advance, once it is set up, the effort and time you spend on this activity will be rewarding.

- Play an active game, such as Hot Potato, Twenty Questions, or any of the other games you can find later in this section.

- Group students into pairs to share the workload. Have some students do the even problems and others the odd problems, for example. Or have partners take turns tutoring each other.

- If a game is becoming too competitive or rowdy, group students into smaller teams and allow them to consult with one another. They can write their responses as a group instead of shouting the answers.

- Divide the material under study into several parts and have groups of students make presentations that teach the material to their classmates.

- Do a round-robin, whereby students pass around a sheet of paper on which they share their ideas about the material in the lesson.

- Pass out learning cubes and have students work together to answer questions or engage in critical thinking activities. (There is more information on learning cubes later in this section.)

- Have students reorganize the material into their own words by using graphic organizers.

- Have students cover the required material by taking notes as part of a team effort.

- Have students each draw a shape that relates to the lesson on an oversize sheet of paper. After they have done this, have students record their notes inside the shape. They can trade their papers around the room to make sure that they have complete information.

- If a group is not working, move the students to independent work. If independent work is not going well, try collaboration.

- Provide a checklist of the essential tasks that students must complete before they can move on to alternative activities.

- Have students either complete a puzzle or create their own puzzle using the puzzle creation feature at Discovery Education (www.discoveryeducation.com/puzzlemaker).

- Have students list key facts from the lesson and compare their lists with those of other students.

- If students are having trouble understanding the material, ask them to decide on several key points and then explain those points to classmates.

Direct Instruction or Student-Centered Activities?

When you consider all the possible strategies that you can use to present information in such a way that students can master the material, they fall into two categories: direct instruction and student-centered instruction. Direct instruction, on the one hand, involves a teacher standing in front of a classroom delivering information in a lecture-style format. Student-centered instruction, on the other hand, involves a much wider range of activities where students are engaged in such activities as discussion, experiments, and collaborative work.

Both of these categories of instruction have a valid place in a modern classroom when used skillfully and appropriately as part of a well-planned lesson. One mistake that many inexperienced teachers make is to rely too heavily on direct instruction methods. This is only natural because it is frequently what they experienced themselves as students, it is often a good way to present material quickly, and there is an expectation that they should be leading the class when an evaluator drops by.

It's not always easy to determine how much direct instruction is too much or when it is necessary for students to be more actively engaged in learning. As a rule of thumb, student-centered activities should dominate the lesson whenever possible. It is possible to be an effective classroom leader while moving around the room working with groups of students and individuals who are working independently. When you plan instruction, think of yourself as that supportive coach on the side rather than as the sole source of knowledge in the room. With this mindset, it will be easy for you to select activities that engage students more fully than they will be when you lecture.

How to Use Scaffolding to Help Students Learn

Scaffolding instruction is a valuable instructional strategy that can make information more accessible for students. When teachers scaffold instruction, they divide the content into small parts and provide explicit help with each part. Scaffolding differs from differentiation in that the content does not change but rather is presented to students in small, manageable segments.

For example, in a typical lesson, a classroom teacher may want students to learn the material in a certain chapter of a textbook. If the lesson were to be differentiated, that teacher could reduce or expand the amount of text, change the activities that students would use, and offer different summative assessments. In a scaffolded lesson, the teacher would not change the content but would instead break the information into smaller segments with additional instruction for each segment.

Although there are many ways to scaffold instruction, there are some strategies that tend to be more successful than others in helping students access the material once you have broken it into smaller segments. Here are some of those strategies that you can adapt for your students:

- Discuss the specific learning strategies that students can use to unlock the material. When you share ideas about the strategies that help them learn, you empower students to make decisions about effective long-range work habits as well as how to deal with the task at hand.

- Show students videos or movie clips or provide other forms of media to help them understand the material.

- Demonstrate the process you want students to use as they work. While you do the demonstration, carefully explain each step.

- Have students brainstorm all that they know about the content to activate prior knowledge. They can share this information first with partners and then with the whole group.

- Before beginning a segment of the material, teach the terms that students will encounter so that they will be familiar with them as they work.

- As you present information, stop frequently to review the content and check for understanding to ensure that everyone is learning.

- Have students collaborate in groups or pairs to share strategies and information that can help them unlock the content.

- Provide frequent feedback as students work on each segment to prevent student misunderstanding and to encourage mastery.

- Use visual, kinesthetic, and auditory modalities to appeal to student learning preferences.

- Use plenty of models, examples, and samples to make the information as clear as possible for students.

- Ask students to complete graphic organizers so that they can break down the information and express it in their own words.

How to Review Material as Students Learn

To improve the way you deliver instruction, you should treat review time as an integral aspect of instruction. Reviewing the day's instruction is an excellent way not only to reinforce what students have learned but also to gather data as instruction progresses. Although studying for a test is certainly a reasonable purpose of review sessions, it is not the only one—and students do not always have to do the reviewing independently.

Reviewing is not something you should force your students to do immediately before a test. It should be part of the daily fabric of the lessons in your class. When you assume responsibility for creating daily review opportunities and then take care to collect and analyze the data that you gather from reviews, your students will be able to build their knowledge.

If you use the small moments of time that are available each day instead of waiting until right before a test, you will not overwhelm your students with too much information. Here is a list of review activities that can enliven your class and reinforce what your students have recently learned:

- Use a few minutes to teach just one quick and interesting word, fact, or concept about the lesson your students have just learned. Relate it to the earlier lesson in such a way that students will leave your class with something new and interesting to think about.

- Have students predict five possible quiz questions. Ask each student to share one with the class and discuss the answer. To extend this activity, ask students to share how they made the prediction. This technique will not only review facts but also enhance students' test preparation skills.

- Hold a rapid-fire drill session covering some of the facts you have taught recently. You could do this daily, keeping a running tally of the scores for your students or classes and transforming your review routine into a contest or tournament of knowledge.

- Read a brief passage related to the day's topic to your students and then ask for their reactions. An interesting twist on this idea is to read a passage that does not seem to be related to the topic and then ask your students to explain how the two might be connected.

- Divide students into review teams of three or four. Hand each team a large sheet of paper and a marker. Allow three minutes for students to brainstorm as many review facts as they can. The real review occurs when students share their facts with the class.

- Use the last few minutes of class to review the underlying principles of the material in the day's lesson. Reviewing principles in this way on a regular basis will help students focus not only on detailed facts but also on the big concepts in their lessons.

- Reveal a graphic organizer for students to fill out that will help them study the material in a new way. If you have been using an outline format, for example, a Venn diagram might be an effective way to reorganize and reinforce your students' learning.

- Have students link ideas and facts in a knowledge chain. Begin by asking one student to state a fact from the lesson. Next, select another student to repeat the first student's fact and add another fact to it. The next student, in turn, repeats both facts and adds a third. The chain can go on until you run out of facts, students, or class time.

- Teach students to review their notes by underlining, circling, or highlighting the most important terms using colored pencils, highlighters, or pens.

Critical Thinking Skills Are a Crucial Instructional Element

Critical thinking skills are thought processes involving such activities as logical reasoning, problem solving, and reflective thinking. To develop these skills, students need sufficient daily practice. When teachers offer opportunities for critical thinking, watching students become absorbed in their work is only one of the rewards. Critical thinking activities also fall into the student-centered learning category and thus are a necessary element of any lesson.

When you plan instruction that involves critical thinking, students must first have some awareness of the material so that they have information to draw on. If you plan carefully, the activities that involve critical thinking will arise from the lesson itself. Offer your students games, puzzles, real-world problems, or other exercises to stimulate their thinking about a lesson. To incorporate critical thinking into instruction, you can ask students to

- Give reasons for their answers
- Generate problems
- Generate multiple solutions
- Give extended answers
- Make predictions based on evidence
- Relate the lesson to their lives
- Solve brainteasers
- Relate the lesson to other classes
- Trace the origins of their thinking
- Compare and contrast information
- Collaborate on responses
- Determine causes and effects
- Combine ideas from widely differing sources
- Classify items in various ways
- Evaluate one another's work

Here are two excellent and well-respected resources to help you learn more about how to develop your students' critical thinking skills:

- **Critical Thinking (www.criticalthinking.net).** This site provides access to a variety of articles to help guide your thinking about teaching critical thinking skills.
- **Critical Thinking Community (www.criticalthinking.org).** At this extensive site, you can access a wide variety of resources as well as read current articles by scholars and other experts.

Another way to incorporate critical thinking skills into every lesson is to use the essential questions that cover the most important concepts in the lesson. In contrast to questions that ask students to just recall information by rote, essential questions ask students to develop their own answers to complex, open-ended problems. They ask for insight and understanding as well as knowledge. Essential questions

- Can arise from curriculum standards
- Often lead to other questions
- Can be controversial
- Can be revisited repeatedly during the term
- Can draw on personal, community, school, and technology resources
- Are relevant to students' real-life interests and concerns
- Can provide authentic motivation for learning

To begin using essential questions to help your students develop their critical thinking skills, follow these steps:

- **Step One:** Begin with a thematic unit or a strong interest your students may have. For example, your state's standards may dictate that you teach a unit on weather.
- **Step Two:** Work with students to brainstorm questions that appeal to them about this topic. Focus on general, open-ended questions rather than on detail-specific ones—for example, "How do changing weather patterns affect our lives?" Use the classic questions that expand investigations:
  - *Who* is affected by weather?
  - *What* changes are happening now?
  - *When* will the changing weather patterns improve or grow worse?
  - *Where* will citizens be safe from weather disasters?
  - *Why* are weather patterns changing?
  - *How* are we coping with these changes?
- **Step Three:** Work with your students to plan strategies for investigating answers to these questions. Help them make predictions; use planning tools; and select and evaluate materials, resources, and information.
- **Step Four:** As your students gather information and decide how to synthesize it, determine how you want them to present their work.

Maintain a Bank of Activity Ideas

Many experienced teachers maintain a bank of activity ideas to make it easier to save time when planning lessons as well as to ensure that students are engaged in interesting activities geared to help them learn. Some teachers keep digital files of activities and good ideas while others file good ideas in three-ring binders. Still others use a combination of digital and paper files. Whichever method you choose to store activity ideas should be one that is easy to maintain as the term progresses so that you always have fresh ideas handy when you plan instruction. In the list that follows, you will find fifty activity ideas to use as a base for your own activity bank. Use these and some of the activity ideas in the rest of this section to ensure that you have activities that will appeal to your students organized for easy access. Ask students to

1. Create a bumper sticker
2. Take an interactive quiz online
3. Take a virtual museum tour
4. Create a time capsule
5. Make a blog post
6. Maintain a digital portfolio
7. Take and share photographs
8. View a movie clip
9. Play a game online
10. Create a scenario and act it out
11. Write an autobiographical sketch
12. Create a digital portfolio
13. Create a fictional treasure chest
14. Invent and play a board game
15. Write a caption
16. Hold a scavenger hunt
17. Make a collage
18. Create a wall of fame
19. Stage a mock trial
20. Enter a contest
21. Make a video
22. Teach the class
23. Draw a diagram
24. Write an exposé
25. Take a field trip
26. Make a flip-book
27. Make a tabloid newspaper
28. Create a flowchart
29. Set up an art gallery
30. Create a greeting card
31. Make a flag or banner
32. Invent a better way

33. Create a class newsletter
34. Make a map
35. Stage a class skit
36. Observe an unusual holiday
37. Write to a pen pal
38. Design a postcard and send it
39. Plan a journey
40. Hold a press conference
41. Hold a recognition ceremony
42. Make up a questionnaire
43. Decorate a bulletin board
44. Design a T-shirt
45. Reenact an event
46. Text a classmate
47. Take an online survey
48. Photograph class notes and share them
49. Pass a note
50. Make a public service announcement

How to Make Lessons Enjoyable as Well as Effective

When you consider the types of activities that you want to use to help your students master material, take a few minutes to check the enjoyment factor of the activities that you assign. Although every activity does not need to be a fun-packed experience, it is important that your students enjoy their work. Even though the types of activities that students enjoy will vary from class to class, as you get to know your students, you will be able to accurately gauge the types of activities that will engage their interests. In the pages that follow, you will learn about some activities that work well for students of all ages, and you can adapt them to meet the unique needs of your students.

Class Discussions Your Students Will Enjoy

If you have fond memories of classes in which everyone seemed to be involved in discussing a topic of burning importance, you probably want to help your students have that experience, too. Remember how you left the room exhilarated, still debating your points, and in full possession of strong opinions that you did not hold when class began?

Class discussions are an excellent way to deliver instruction that students will remember long after the class is over. Best of all, class discussions create active learners who are perfecting their thinking skills while expanding their knowledge of a topic.

What role should you take in a class discussion? First, envision yourself as the facilitator of the discussion. Your job is to plan the discussion, keep things running smoothly, and wrap up at the end. Think about your role in making this a successful and stimulating method of delivering instruction in three easy components: what to do to prepare for the discussion, what to do during the discussion, and what to do after the discussion is over.

Before the Discussion

- Post procedures in a prominent place in the classroom. You should consider how you want your students to relate to one another and to you. Here are some guidelines you could establish:
  - Wait until the moderator recognizes you before you speak.
  - Do not speak after you have reached your limit of speaking opportunities.
  - Treat other people's opinions with tolerance and respect.
  - Listen more than you speak.
- Convey the purpose of the discussion. What outcomes do you want? Do you want students to analyze an issue? Combine information in a new way? Brainstorm new ideas?
- Create the questions your students will discuss. Successful questions for class discussions require higher-order thinking skills. For the first discussion session, prepare ten thought-provoking questions. Use your students' reactions to gauge how many to prepare for future sessions. When appropriate, give students advance copies of questions so that they can prepare.
- Move the chairs. Set up chairs so that students can see one another's faces. Arranging the seating as you wish the first time will help you to establish how you want it done in the future.

During the Discussion

- Enforce procedures. As the discussion gets under way, remind students of the importance of the conduct procedures for class discussions. Be steadfast in enforcing them. It may be difficult for your students to adjust to them at first, but with persistence, you will succeed in having productive class discussions.
- Introduce the topics of discussion. You can display questions using an interactive whiteboard, write them on the board, or ask students to review their advance copies of the questions.
- Teach your students the importance of supporting their opinions. When someone makes a point, keep probing until enough support has been presented. Students need to realize that it is not enough to express their opinion; they must also be able to defend and support it.

- Encourage deeper thinking. Elicit thoughtful responses by trying these techniques: invite a student to comment on someone else's response, ask for elaboration, ask another student to refute what has been said, or ask for a restatement.

- Allow everyone to participate. Keep outgoing students who want to express themselves at the expense of everyone else in check. One easy way to do this is to give all students the same number of slips of paper. Each time someone speaks, he or she must give up one of the slips. When a student is out of slips, he or she is out of opportunities to speak.

- Recognize speakers. To determine who gets to speak, have an unbreakable object, such as a book or stuffed toy, for students to hand to one another as they take turns speaking.

- Encourage risk taking. Make it easy and nonthreatening for all students to risk answering. Encourage and validate answers when you can.

- Step back. Refrain from dominating the discussion. A class discussion works best when all students are prepared and when all students join in.

After the Discussion

- Have students reflect on the discussion by asking for the following:
  - Written or oral feedback on what went well
  - Suggestions for improvement
  - A retelling of the important points
  - A written or oral summary

The Power of Play: Using Toys to Capture Attention

Rubber ducks in math class? Spinning tops in history class? Not only do toys capture the attention of children of all ages but also the intrinsic contrast between a toy and an academic setting is enormously appealing to almost every audience. Toys of all types can be effective manipulatives that spark students' curiosity and encourage them to use their imaginations as well as their critical thinking skills. Harnessing the power of play in your classroom encourages students of all ages to be engaged with the lesson and invested in collaborating with their classmates.

Depending on your imagination, the lesson, and the ages of your students, toys can be used in many ways before, during, and after a presentation. Try some of these activities to help your students relate the toy to the information in your instruction. Ask students to

- Describe the toy
- Tell how the toy works
- Explain how it relates to the lesson

- Research the history of the toy
- Give other uses for it
- Brainstorm a list of reasons why it is appealing
- Create other names for it
- Share memories about similar toys
- Take it apart
- Find out where the raw materials for it are from
- Estimate information, such as its weight, length, or height
- Use it to illustrate a point

Learning Games Your Students Will Enjoy

Your students love to play games. You can capitalize on this natural interest by playing games often in your classroom. Games are positive learning experiences for the same reasons that activities incorporating toys are: they provide opportunities for interaction, offer immediate feedback, make the work relevant, allow plenty of practice, and motivate students to collaborate on higher-order learning tasks. Consider arranging team games to help students review, teach one another information, or simply work together in a structured fashion. Before your students engage in a classroom game, you must establish ground rules so that the activity will be a successful one for everyone. Here are some suggestions for managing games in your classroom:

- Consider the geography of your room before you begin. Move furniture, put breakable items in a safe place, and plan how you will put the room back in order at the end of the game.
- Teach good sportsmanship in advance of game day. Be very clear with your students about what behaviors you expect from them and what behaviors are not acceptable.
- Make sure there is a sound educational purpose for each game and that you are not simply using it as a pleasant way to pass time.
- Pay attention to safety. If you see that students are so excited that the competition is becoming too intense, stop play at once.
- Select the team members yourself so that no one will be left out. Allow students to make decisions about scoring procedures and rules of sportsmanship. Keep a container of numbers or other markers on hand for students to draw from to determine who goes first or makes other decisions.
- Although you don't really need prizes for class games, consider offering ribbons, stickers, trinkets, or bookmarks.
- Add realistic touches, such as music or other props. These will make it easier for your students to get into the spirit of the game.

- Have students assume the roles of scorekeeper, timekeeper, and master of ceremonies so that you can monitor activities.

- Prepare to move your class to a location where they won't disturb other students if the game gets noisy.

- After a game is over, ask your students to tell you what they learned.

In addition, you can always adapt games you may have enjoyed as a child. To give you some ideas as you begin your adaptations, here are some suggestions:

- Ball Toss: Line up your students in two teams facing each other. As soon as a student correctly answers a question you ask, that student tosses a soft foam ball to a student on the other team. That student must answer the next question.

- Bingo: Many teachers use this game to review vocabulary words. Make and then photocopy a game board with sixteen or twenty-five blocks. Give students a list of words to place in the blanks. They can use bits of paper to cover the words when you call out definitions.

- Board games: Design your own board games to fit your topic. You can make small boards and photocopy them for students to use in a small group, or you can make a large board for the entire class to use. The tasks you assign your students in a board game can range from simply answering questions to solving problems. Many students can be very skilled and creative in designing their own board games. Often they will create games based on such old favorites as Candy Land or Battleship while using the material they have learned in class.

- Chain Making: This is an educational version of the old alphabet game that small children play. One player begins by saying the name of an object related to the unit of study beginning with the letter A. The next student must repeat that clue and add an object beginning with the letter B. The game continues until students are stumped or until they reach the end of the alphabet.

- Flyswatter Badminton: Use masking tape to mark off a small badminton court. Blow up a balloon and hand each student a flyswatter to use as a racket. Divide students into teams and arrange them on either side of an imaginary net (indicated by a taped line on the floor). As you ask questions, students earn points for moving the balloon across the net and for answering questions correctly.

- Hangman: In the traditional version, students guess letters in a word or phrase to keep the figure "alive." In other versions, students can give correct answers to short-answer questions or define vocabulary terms. If you do not want to have your students draw a hanging man on the board, consider using a spider hanging from a web instead. Instead of drawing the head and limbs of a human, your students could add legs to the spider.

- One, Two, and You're Outta Here: Stand at the door at the end of class with a set of flash cards or questions that require quick answers. For a student to leave class, he or she must answer two questions correctly.

- PowerPoint games: The assortment of PowerPoint games available to teachers is almost limitless. You can either create the games yourself or use some of the many templates available for downloading.

- Quiz Bowl: Set up a tournament of quick questions and answers involving as many of your students as possible. To add interest, vary the level of difficulty, rules of play, way of scoring, and incentives.

- Simulations: Although most simulation games are often sophisticated computer ones, you and your students can enjoy low-tech simulations that are simple to construct. Plan the scenario you want your students to enact, then involve them in it by reading them a written description or by role-playing. A very popular version of this game is to have your students imagine that they are shipwrecked on a deserted island and must plan ways to survive. Simulation games can be used to help your students think creatively, learn to work cooperatively, or examine their values—or to satisfy just about any purpose you have in mind when you create the game for them.

- Sporting events: Divide your students into teams and use the board to play games of football, soccer, or whatever sport currently interests them. Students advance by correctly answering questions or completing assigned tasks.

- Tic-tac-toe: Students advance play on a tic-tac-toe board by giving correct answers to questions. Creating a board is easy. Make a grid of three blocks across and down for a total of nine blocks. Photocopy the grid so that students can play in small groups.

Another useful repository of classroom games is the Internet. With just a few clicks, you can find many puzzle and game sites that can engage students in meaningful learning activities. Many teachers, for example, have found that using the search term "free Power-Point games" will yield dozens of free templates to download. At some sites, teachers even share their own games with others who are teaching the same material. The websites listed here are ones that contain a wide variety of puzzles and games that would be appropriate for students of all ages:

- **Boardgames.com (www.boardgames.com).** This commercial site offers a large variety of electronic and traditional board games at reasonable prices.

- **Dave's ESL Cafe (www.eslcafe.com).** Dave Sperling's site lists dozens of classroom games, along with rules and suggestions. Click on the "Stuff for Teachers" tab and then the "Games" tab to access the large list. This site has many other resources for teachers, too.

- **Out of the Box Games (http://ootbgames.com).** This is also a commercial site with a large assortment of games for sale. You can find classic board games, dice games, and word games as well as newer types of games.

Use Graphic Organizers to Engage Students

Can you imagine how hard it would be to make up a seating chart without the chart? You would have to write sentence after sentence explaining who would sit where. Instead of writing it out, you save time by using a graphic organizer. Graphic organizers are useful ways for students to organize information so that they can learn it.

Graphic organizers can help students decode, process, understand, and retain information. Further, graphic organizers can help students solve problems and comprehend material quickly. When students create graphic organizers, they can see the relationships among the important elements in the assignment. Moreover, students of all age and ability levels can use them successfully for a variety of purposes:

- To take notes on lectures and reading
- To describe people, places, events, ideas, or objects
- To compare and contrast
- To determine the validity of assumptions
- To classify and categorize information
- To determine relevant details
- To see how parts make up a whole
- To solve problems
- To predict outcomes
- To plan reading and writing activities
- To understand cause and effect
- To support arguments
- To organize concepts into key components
- To analyze vocabulary words
- To organize textual material

It is easy to find and use comprehensive online resources for help with graphic organizers. To access graphic organizers that are already designed for you and your students, try these websites:

- **Education Oasis (www.educationoasis.com).** At Education Oasis, you will find more than sixty printable graphic organizers.
- **Houghton Mifflin (www.eduplace.com/graphicorganizer/index.html).** Here you will find more than three dozen useful graphic organizers to download.

A special type of graphic organizer is the three-dimensional graphic organizer. To make this type of graphic organizer, students cut, fold, and glue paper in various configurations to create hands-on manipulatives. The best resource for this type of very popular and effective graphic organizer is an educational entrepreneur, Dinah Zike. You can learn more about how to use three-dimensional graphic organizers in your classroom at her informative and helpful website, Dinah (www.dinah.com).

Two Simple Techniques: Learning Cubes and Colored Dot Labels

Two popular and inexpensive ways to deliver instruction sure to engage your students involve learning cubes and colored dot labels. Appropriate for students of all ages and versatile enough to be adapted to any content area, these two simple techniques can enliven lessons.

LEARNING CUBES

Learning cubes can easily be made with just card stock, a marker, and scissors. Either find a cube-shaped box (several brands of tissues have suitable boxes) or make one from the card stock. On each side of a cube, write a direction or question. Students then roll the cube to determine which question to answer or which direction to follow. Although individual students can use them, learning cubes are most effective when pairs or teams of students work with them. To show you how versatile learning cubes can be, here are lists of just some of the directions or questions you can adapt for your classroom:

Idea Set One

1. What is _____?
2. Where is _____?
3. How did _____ happen?
4. Who caused _____?
5. Why did _____ happen?
6. What happened to _____?

Idea Set Two

1. Add _____ and _____.
2. Multiply _____ by _____.
3. Divide _____ into _____.
4. Subtract _____ from _____.
5. Solve _____.
6. Find the square root of _____.

Idea Set Three

1. List _____.
2. Explain _____.
3. Describe _____.
4. Justify _____.
5. Recall _____.
6. Prove _____.

Idea Set Four

1. Summarize _____.
2. Interpret _____.
3. Extend _____.
4. Demonstrate _____.
5. Rephrase _____.
6. Illustrate _____.

Idea Set Five

1. Classify _____.
2. Compare _____.
3. Support _____.
4. State in your own words _____.
5. Contrast _____.
6. Infer the meaning of _____.

Idea Set Six

1. What is the main idea?
2. What are the supporting ideas?
3. What essential concepts can you prove?
4. Which facts provide valid proof?
5. What can you conclude?
6. What is meant by _____?

Idea Set Seven

1. How can you organize _____ to show _____?
2. How can you prove your understanding of _____?

3. What would be the result of _____?

4. What facts would you choose to prove _____?

5. What questions should you ask to _____?

6. What examples can you use to _____?

Idea Set Eight

1. Make use of _____ to _____.

2. Create a model _____.

3. Solve this puzzle: _____.

4. Make a plan to _____.

5. Construct a new _____.

6. Use _____ to _____.

Idea Set Nine

1. Use _____ to simplify _____.

2. Why do you believe _____ is true?

3. What is the chief cause of _____?

4. What conclusions can you draw from _____?

5. What is the evidence to support _____?

6. What is the relationship between _____ and _____?

Idea Set Ten

1. Justify the _____ of _____.

2. Categorize the reasons for _____.

3. Survey classmates about _____.

4. Create a test for _____.

5. Inspect _____ and make inferences about _____.

6. Determine the motives for _____.

COLORED DOT LABELS

Colored dot labels are an inexpensive staple in most office supply stores. Found in a variety of bright colors and sizes, colored dots can be used in engaging ways in a classroom because of their appeal to various learning styles and multiple intelligences and their easy adaptability. To put it simply, students just enjoy sticking the dots on things.

Fortunately, it's easy to take advantage of this inherent appeal. Consider asking students to use colored dots to manipulate items, ideas, concepts, or steps in the following ways:

- To classify ideas
- To identify key concepts
- To group items
- To rearrange ideas
- To categorize concepts
- To place events in chronological order
- To distinguish traits
- To label characteristics
- To match elements
- To reorganize items in a process
- To differentiate items according to various criteria
- To determine cause and effect
- To agree or disagree with statements
- To prioritize items in order of importance
- To recommend as good, better, and best
- To choose items to be combined
- To rank items in order of significance
- To combine multiple ideas
- To evaluate using established criteria

Providing Models, Examples, and Samples

In the rush of planning, it's very easy to overlook this important part of making sure that your instruction is delivered successfully because you are quite naturally focused on the final products that your students will be turning in. However, providing models, examples, and samples of the kinds of work that you expect from your students is key to ensuring that they know what to do and how to do it well. Many veteran teachers find that offering more than one model, example, or sample makes it easier for students to avoid copying and to examine the excellent qualities of each instead.

As a new teacher, you may not have very many exemplars on hand to show your students. To overcome this, create one or two yourself and ask other teachers at your school for help. As soon as good student exemplars are turned in, display them for others to see. These three ways of obtaining good models, examples, and samples are well worth the effort because these items will build your students' confidence and knowledge.

To make sure that you will have plenty of excellent models, examples, and samples for future use and still have sufficient storage space in your classroom, photograph your exemplars and store them in an electronic file for later use. Imagine how convenient it will be next year to show a quick slide show of some of this year's work when you present new instruction.

How to Make Seatwork Appealing

Dull worksheets have no place in today's classroom. Although students do need to complete work at their desks, that work does not have to be tedious. Instead, you can make seatwork engaging and interesting as well as productive.

To give seatwork pizzazz, think of what would delight your students as they sit down to work. Do your students like bright colors? Political cartoons? Clever graphics? Options? You should take advantage of your students' preferences to make their work agreeable. Consider these suggestions to make seatwork a pleasant learning experience in your class:

- Personalize handouts with student names, local places, or student interests. Be sensitive about how you use personal information to avoid inadvertently embarrassing a student.

- Provide access to a key so that students can check their own progress on drill work.

- Provide scrambled facts, words, terms, or other items for students to unscramble.

- If the seatwork has several sections, create a small bar graph for students to fill in as they finish each section. This allows them to see their progress.

- Assign matching exercises, which students of all ages enjoy.

- Offer optional work. When students finish an assignment, they may opt for another activity.

- Allow students to use colored paper, crayons, and colored pencils or pens when appropriate.

- Have students solve puzzles, which hold built-in appeal for learners. Even a brief puzzle or riddle at the bottom of a page will be interesting to your students.

- Allow students to work with a partner or to have access to a study buddy when a question arises.

- Offer choices within the seatwork itself. For example, offer two sections and allow students to choose which one they would like to tackle.

- Ask students to create potential test questions with answers.

- Allow students to be creative. Even such simple activities as making up their own problems or drawing to illustrate a point will please many students.

- Ask students to give their opinions or to respond to questions in a personal way.

- Make all handouts as attractive as possible. Use a readable font, organize each handout clearly, and add clip art when appropriate.

Resources to Help You Plan Lessons

Fortunately for today's teachers, there are countless resources for lesson planning that are just a click or two away. With just a bit of research, you can discover the latest information about the content that you want to teach as well as invaluable lesson planning ideas freely available on the Internet. In addition to the resources available to you online, you also have a great many technology resources that were not readily available to teachers just a few years ago. With this wealth of information and resources at your fingertips, you will find it easy to design and deliver instruction geared to help your students succeed. In the following pages, you will first learn about some of the most common technology resources found in many classrooms and then about some useful websites and apps to enrich your instruction.

Classroom Technology Resources to Aid Your Instructional Practices

Although it can be very tempting to want to incorporate as many technology resources as possible into every lesson, remembering to use small, strategic steps while deciding how to incorporate the latest interactive web page or personal device into next week's lesson plans is a sound idea.

No matter how comfortable you may be with a device or a certain type of software, integrating technology resources into your instructional practices takes careful thought and planning to ensure success. One of the most significant issues that you will have to manage is the inequity that exists in technology use. It is simply neither fair nor reasonable to expect that all students will have the same access to technology resources. As you begin planning how to integrate these resources into your classroom, you will have to determine the best ways to overcome this limitation.

It is best to begin by mastering a base of several resources that you know your students will find useful and then add other technology resources as you have time. To help you get started with this, five of the most common technology resources are listed here, along with tips for how to integrate them successfully into your lesson plans.

CELL PHONES

Once the bane of many a teacher's existence because of their propensity to distract students or because they make cybercheating possible, cell phones are now regarded as valuable classroom tools. Here is a list of just some of the easiest ways in which cell phones can be used to facilitate instruction. Students can use their cell phones to

- Photograph their notes and share them with classmates
- Record homework assignments by using the phone's note features and using the alarm feature to set reminders

- Text questions to one another in advance of a class discussion
- Remind one another of an upcoming project or assignment
- Check a social networking account that they have set up for studying together with classmates
- Stage a scene from a book, photograph it, and share the photo
- Photograph important information on the board that they do not have time to copy, to be downloaded later for use at home
- Record (with permission) a lecture or oral presentation
- Record themselves or classmates studying notes aloud and then play the notes back
- Access school e-mail or a class web page
- Text absent classmates about missing work
- Create brief summaries of important passages or other materials and share them
- Create a photoblog using the phone's camera
- Access maps and other types of related information
- Read e-books or listen to audiobooks
- Watch videos recorded by the teacher in a flipped classroom
- Make videos about the lesson and share them
- Time themselves and classmates during class activities
- Use various apps to access such tools as dictionaries or search engines
- Check or solve problems using the phone's calculator function

INTERACTIVE WHITEBOARDS

There are hundreds of different websites with information, ideas, and lesson plans for using interactive whiteboards. These engaging lesson ideas and activities appeal to all students—from our youngest students to the oldest. In the list that follows, you will find just a few of the ways you can use an interactive whiteboard in your classroom. Teachers can use interactive whiteboards to

- Share student multimedia presentations, PowerPoints, or Prezis
- Have students play review games on interactive websites
- Find and mark errors in written work as well as examples of excellent writing
- Create and share diagrams or other graphic organizers
- Edit assignments and share the results with students
- Have students write exit slips to share
- Provide opportunities for students to take virtual field trips together
- Teach students how to analyze a passage, photograph, film clip, or work of art
- Show students how to compare and contrast different passages or texts

- Have students solve problems while working with classmates
- Share photos of students as they work on projects
- Display interactive maps
- Share exemplary work done by students
- Work out solutions to puzzles with students
- Show review videos in a flipped classroom
- Teach students how their work will be assessed using a rubric
- Work with students to create class poems, stories, or quotations of the day
- Use interesting words from the day's lesson appropriately so that they become part of students' vocabulary
- Show students how to create and use spreadsheets and tables of various types
- Highlight the key features of a text
- Show a brief inspiring video
- Have students correct errors in sentences or problems
- Show a student-made project
- Conduct discussions through a blog or discussion board thread
- Show students how to research databases and archived information
- Have students create graphs and other nonlinguistic representations
- Ask students to create various types of time lines or flowcharts
- Share a daily current event, news article, cartoon, riddle, or unusual fact
- Have students write and share sentences using the word of the day, roots and affixes, or target vocabulary words

iPADS

Although they do function in different ways from laptops and other computers, iPads can serve as helpful and versatile resources in any classroom. If you have even one iPad in your classroom, you can have your students

- Connect with others via global learning project sites; service project sites; and social networks, such as Tumblr or Twitter
- Complete e-projects and share them
- Evaluate the reliability and credibility of websites
- Create interactive time lines
- Create and post book trailers
- Brainstorm collaboratively
- Create and post videos of various types
- Create and share e-books

- Photograph their work and share it with their parents or guardians
- Read and edit one another's work
- Share videos from YouTube, the Teaching Channel, or TeacherTube
- Access the photos at Tag Galaxy (www.taggalaxy.com)
- Donate rice through Freerice (http://freerice.com) by playing learning games
- Collaborate with other students via Skype
- Use Google Docs to interact with one another's work
- Make and share electronic flash cards
- Listen to podcasts on various topics
- Create a photoblog or photocollage
- Take electronic notes on readings or face-to-face presentations

BLOGS

Blogs are among the most versatile technology resources that teachers and students can use and enjoy. Blogs make online sharing an easy and manageable task for even very young students. If you would like to use blogs in your classroom, you can ask your students to

- Maintain a class blog with daily news and updates for absent classmates
- Maintain electronic journals about projects from start to finish and share them online
- Embed videos or artwork that they have made into their postings
- Share ideas about how to study or prepare for assessments
- Compare their work with the work of other students
- Access links and online resources that you have embedded into the class blog
- Review and edit classmates' work
- Complete and share graphic organizers
- Share notes about what they have read or learned
- Respond to writing prompts of various types
- Write entrance or exit slips
- Write responses as they read for pleasure or for a class assignment
- Offer solutions to local problems
- Write reviews of products or books
- Post ideas on a common topic
- Share predictions about what they are reading or upcoming class events
- Practice random acts of kindness and share what they have done with classmates
- Collect and analyze data for a future report posting

- Survey classmates on a topic of interest and share the results
- Create tutorials and post them for classmates
- Share autobiographies or opinions
- Complete daily practice work and share what they have done
- Connect their classroom with another classroom in a faraway location

PODCASTS

Podcasting is simply a way of making digital audio or video files available on the Internet so that others can access them. It is also an intrinsically engaging activity for classroom use because it requires students to apply what they have learned in a new and authentic way. Its rapidly growing popularity is based not only on its usefulness as an instructional tool but also on the ease with which podcasts can be incorporated into lessons.

The process is simple. First, prepare your podcast content and then record it. Next, upload your podcast to a server and publish it. Another good reason to try podcasting is that the equipment you will need to begin podcasting in your classroom can usually be found in any school: a computer with Internet access and a microphone (preferably a USB one) that can record your voice. In addition to the actual equipment you will require, you will need suitable software to broadcast your students' work. Fortunately, there are excellent free software programs available for educators. You'll find a list of sites where you can download these programs later in this section.

Podcasting is a versatile learning activity that can be used with students of all ages. There are limitless possibilities for classroom use. Here are just a few of the many uses suitable for students of all ages for you to consider experimenting with in your classroom:

- Discussion of current events or other topics
- Multimedia presentations of a field trip experience
- Advice on projects or homework assignments
- Demonstrations or explanations
- Tutorials, especially peer tutoring
- Alternative assignments
- Remediation or enrichment work
- Class newsletters or daily logs
- Study guides
- Data gathered for student assignments
- Teacher lectures
- Activities to improve listening comprehension
- Debates
- Riddles, puzzles, and brainteasers to promote critical thinking

Podcasting is an emerging classroom activity, but there are many useful resources to help you get started. Here are a few of the more user-friendly websites that are geared toward classroom teachers:

- **Edudemic (http://edudemic.com).** At Edudemic, use "podcasts" as a search term to access helpful articles about podcasting.
- **Podcasting Tools (www.podcasting-tools.com).** This site hosts a great deal of information, such as tips and directories, for any potential podcaster.
- **Podomatic (www.podomatic.com).** This popular site offers tutorials as well as many podcasts you and your students could access for inspiration.

Useful Websites for Instructional Activities

Here you will find two lists to help you create effective lesson plans for your classes. The first is a list of online resources that are specifically for lesson plans. The second list contains sites that can help you enhance your lesson plans with interesting resources and materials.

ONLINE RESOURCES SPECIFICALLY FOR LESSON PLANNING

Although there are dozens of online sites devoted to lesson plans, the websites in the following list offer a comprehensive assortment of free lesson plans and lesson plan resources for K–12 educators. These sites allow teachers to access lesson plans that cover a wide variety of content areas.

- **A to Z Teacher Stuff (www.atozteacherstuff.com).** A to Z Teacher Stuff is a teacher-created site designed to help teachers find lesson plans, thematic units, teacher tips, discussion forums, printable worksheets, and many more online resources.
- **Discovery Education (www.discoveryeducation.com).** Discovery Education offers an enormous wealth of resources for teachers—digital media, hundreds of easily adaptable lesson plans, worksheets, clip art, and much more.
- **ForLessonPlans (www.forlessonplans.com).** ForLessonPlans is an online directory of free lesson plans for K–12 teachers. Created by teachers, this site offers lesson plans that cover many different subjects as well as links to other resources.
- **Lesson Planet (www.lessonplanet.com).** Founded in 1999, Lesson Planet enables teachers to search more than four hundred thousand teacher-reviewed lesson plans, worksheets, and other resources in an online, professional community. A free trial is available.
- **LessonPlans.com (www.lessonplans.com).** Maintained by the Educators Network, LessonPlans.com offers thousands of teacher-created lesson plans in an easy-to-search format organized by topic as well as by grade level.

- **National Education Association (NEA) (www.nea.org).** The NEA website offers thousands of lesson plans in an easily searchable format. Teachers can also find a variety of lesson planning resources as well as practical tips for classroom use.

- **Scholastic (www.scholastic.com).** Scholastic offers thousands of free lesson plans, unit plans, discussion guides, and extension activities for all grade levels and content areas.

- **Share My Lesson (www.sharemylesson.com).** Share My Lesson is maintained by the American Federation of Teachers and TES Connect. Developed by teachers for teachers, this free platform provides more than 250,000 teaching resources as well as an online collaborative community. Share My Lesson also has a significant resource bank for the Common Core State Standards.

- **Teachers Network (http://teachersnetwork.org).** Teachers Network, a New York City–based nonprofit organization for educators, offers thousands of lesson plans and lesson plan resources covering a wide assortment of topics in a variety of formats for teachers at all grade levels.

- **Teaching Channel (www.teachingchannel.org).** Funded by the Bill and Melinda Gates Foundation and the William and Flora Hewlett Foundation, Teaching Channel is a video showcase of innovative and effective teaching practices schools. Instead of traditional lesson plans, teachers can watch brief videos of effective teaching ideas that they may want to implement in their own classrooms.

Other Useful Resources for Lesson Plan Enhancement

- **Edublogs (http://edublogs.org).** Edublogs is a site that offers a user-friendly way to create and post blogs.

- **Edudemic (http://edudemic.com).** At the resource-rich Edudemic, you can follow the latest trends in educational technology.

- **4Teachers (www.4teachers.org).** This extensive site offers many different tools and helpful resources to make integrating technology easy.

- **Free Technology for Teachers (www.freetech4teachers.com).** Richard Byrne, the creator of this site, offers a wealth of helpful information and links to free educational sites.

- **MasteryConnect (www.masteryconnect.com).** At MasteryConnect, educators can manage information and data relating to the Common Core.

- **Pinterest (https://pinterest.com).** Pinterest is a popular and user-friendly online pin board where you and your students can collect, organize, and share images.

- **Poll Everywhere (www.polleverywhere.com).** Poll Everywhere offers a free plan for educators that will allow students to take and share polls of various types.

- **Skype (www.skype.com).** Skype is a service that can make it easy for students in your classroom to communicate with students in other classrooms.

- **SlideShare (www.slideshare.net).** At Slide Share, teachers can access and download PowerPoint presentations as well as create and share their own.
- **TED (www.ted.com).** At the TED site, you and your students can access videos delivered by great thinkers and experts covering a wide range of topics.
- **Timetoast (www.timetoast.com).** Students can use this site to create and share time lines in just a few minutes.
- **Twitter (https://twitter.com).** Twitter is a very popular microblogging site where students can share their ideas in 140-character increments. You can also join other educators in one of the many PLNs (professional learning network) available on Twitter.

"There's an App for That!"

It is likely that the fastest-growing advance in technology for the average consumer—the apps for our mobile devices—will remain popular and useful for some time. As an educator, you will find that there are apps for just about every aspect of your professional life:

- Tracking grades and data
- Accessing documents when you are not at school
- Reading books with students
- Helping students build vocabulary
- Providing study guides for students
- Having students view a fact or word of the day
- Accessing reference materials of all types
- Finding games for your students to play
- Organizing your classroom
- Ordering supplies
- Editing papers
- Creating lesson plans and sharing them
- Finding video clips to engage students
- Accessing blogs, microblogs, and podcasts
- Searching the web
- Collaborating with colleagues
- Sharing documents with your professional learning community or PLN members
- Creating lesson plan ideas

To learn more about the apps that can increase your knowledge and improve your teaching skills and productivity, one of the best places to begin is with the pages devoted to apps for educators at Kathy Schrock's Guide to Everything (www.schrockguide.net/bloomin-apps.html), where visitors can access information about hundreds of carefully selected educator-recommended apps categorized by device as well as by how they can be used in the classroom.

How to Survive the Homework Debate

One of the most significant issues facing educators today as they plan instruction involves homework. The tension created between students and teachers, teachers and parents, and parents and students over homework has grown in recent years into a contentious national debate. For decades, the issue of homework and its impact on home life has been a concern for families and schools. Although the pendulum of the debate seems to swing with the social climate, homework has remained a staple of education despite the problems associated with it.

Teachers at all levels of experience are judged by their homework assignments. If you assign too much, you are too strict. If you assign too little, you are too lenient. The parents and guardians of your students may also represent two extremes: those who take an active role in homework and those who resent the demands of homework assignments. One thing is clear: teachers cannot please everyone when it comes to homework.

There are many steps you can take to make sure that the homework you assign serves its intended instructional purposes and does not cause conflict between classroom and home. In the paragraphs that follow, you will learn about the strategies that can help homework be a positive learning experience for you and your students alike.

Once, I harshly spoke to a student for not having a homework assignment done. The lack of the assignment precluded her taking part in class that day. She sat outside our work circle. At the end of class, she handed me a folded note. Inside it asked for my forgiveness but told me that, the night before, her mother's boyfriend (one of a long series) had kicked them out of his trailer. She asked her mother what to do, and her mother couldn't give her any suggestions, so she loaded everything she owned into her ragged car and drove to a Walmart one town away. That store had a snack bar and was open all night. She spent the night in the store, then dressed in the store's restroom and came to school. This was a wake-up call for me. Sometimes what we do in class is not the most important part of a student's day. Homework? Maybe not as important as I thought.

Luann West Scott, 42 years' experience

CREATE A HOMEWORK PARTNERSHIP

You can overcome many homework hassles by creating a strong partnership with students and their families. The best way is to communicate your expectations regarding homework in a letter or e-mail home and to be as consistent as possible in adhering to your homework policy.

Many school districts now make it easy to have a transparent classroom by providing homework hotlines, voice mail, e-mail accounts, and class web pages that students and parents can use to access homework information at home. Take advantage of every possible method of communicating with your students and their families about their homework assignments. This is an especially important step if you want to promote the importance of learning as something that continues outside of school. If it is easy for parents and guardians to figure out what you expect in terms of homework assignments, then it will be easier for them to offer support.

If you teach young students, consider a homework folder. Many teachers have found that this is a convenient way to contact parents and guardians. These teachers laminate a folder for every child to take home each night with returned papers and the day's homework assignment tucked safely inside.

If you teach older students, send home frequent progress reports and return other graded work promptly so that everyone involved can see what is required and how to meet those requirements. Don't hesitate to call home to ask for assistance when a student seems to be struggling with homework completion.

Another useful way to communicate freely with the parents of guardians of your students is to send home a letter early in the school term with information about the homework that you intend for your students. You can use Sample 9.1 as a guide for your own letter home.

HOW MUCH HOMEWORK IS APPROPRIATE?

Part of the resistance that fuels the debate over homework concerns the amount of work that students are asked to complete. Parents and guardians complain of assignments that take their children hours and hours of tedious work to complete or that require expensive resources.

As a rule, younger students should be assigned much less homework than older students. Many teachers have found that assigning frequent brief homework assignments to younger students not only reinforces classroom learning but also helps students develop good work habits.

Older students can be expected to handle longer assignments with more comfort and success. Their homework assignments should also involve more independent preparation and practice than the work expected of younger students who may need assistance in completing their assignments.

Although the expected amount of homework time will necessarily vary from class to class, it is generally an acceptable practice to assign about ten minutes of homework per night per grade level. At this rate, young elementary students will have only brief assignments, sixth graders should have no more than an hour, and high school students should have no more than two hours a night in total.

If a student has more than one teacher who will be assigning homework, those teachers should take care to not overload a student if he or she already has a heavy assignment workload in another class. You should talk with those other teachers to make sure that the overall homework load is reasonable.

Sample 9.1

Homework Letter to Parents or Guardians

The following is an example of a letter to parents and guardians outlining a homework policy that you can use to build a homework partnership with students' families.

Dear Parents or Guardians of _____,

Homework is a powerful tool for learning and a necessary part of any student's successful mastery of skills and knowledge. You can expect that your child will have homework on Monday through Thursday nights. These assignments will usually take no longer than thirty minutes to complete. On weekends, I will make no formal assignments, but students can use this time to read, do research, and work on projects.

Homework due dates will be given on the day the work is assigned. I expect students to turn work in on time. If there is a problem, please let me know so that I can help your child. The first time an assignment is not completed, I will speak with your child to see if I can help. After that, I will contact you when assignments are not completed on time.

I will make sure that students write their assignments down each day. I will also record the assignments on my voice mail, which you can reach at _____ and on our class web page at _____.

You can help your child do well on homework assignments by setting aside a study time each night, encouraging good work habits, and contacting me if there is a problem we can solve together.

Please discuss these points with your child. Please sign below and return the bottom portion of this letter to school with your child. Keep the part above the dotted line for your reference.

Sincerely,

. . . .

I have read this homework policy and discussed it with my child.

Parent or guardian signature(s): _____

Student signature: _____

DEVELOPING A HOMEWORK POLICY

Experienced teachers know that making appropriate homework assignments that students will want to complete does not just happen; it requires the same degree of planning and preparation as the assignments that you expect students to complete in class. Remember, you will avoid many of the problems associated with homework if you involve parents and guardians early in the year, communicate with them frequently, alert them promptly if a problem arises, and are organized about homework. One way to begin is by developing a homework policy for your class.

Start by finding out whether there is a formal homework policy for your school district or your school. If there is no formal policy, then you should find out how the other teachers in your school handle homework. When all the teachers in a school have the same expectations for homework assignments, the likelihood of complaints will be reduced.

All homework assignments should be purposefully designed to help students reach mastery of a specific learning objective. Usually homework assignments can be grouped into three basic kinds: assignments that can prepare students for the next day's instruction, such as preparing advance organizers; practice work to review previously taught facts or terms, such as making flash cards; or assignments or independent reading that can extend or enrich the content of a lesson.

In general, your homework policy should provide work that is reasonable in length and in the resources required, designed to reinforce or extend classroom learning, and interesting enough to engage student attention.

SPECIFIC STRATEGIES TO MANAGE HOMEWORK ASSIGNMENTS SUCCESSFULLY

Homework assignments need not be a headache for you or your students and their families. Instead, homework assignments can function as you intend them to: as a logical and helpful extension of the classroom material that you teach. Here are several general homework strategies you can use to help your students find success:

- Allow your students as many choices as you can. For example, you can let students choose to answer the even or the odd problems in their textbook or one of several essay questions. Ask students to research a topic of their own choosing using a database or to review using games from among a selection of online review game sites.

- Consider designating some nights as homework-free nights. This is a good way to dispel some of the complaints about too much homework. If you leave weekends free of new homework assignments, your students can use that time to read for pleasure or to catch up on long-term projects and other work.

- Show plenty of examples, samples, and models. To work with assurance, students need to have a clear idea of what the final product should be.

- Make the work as interesting as possible. Use real-life examples, television shows, popular songs, actual student names, sports, or other eye-catching details to engage students.

- Allow students to consult one another when they all have the same assignment. You should expect that your students will help one another on homework assignments, even ones that you may want them to do independently. Build in collaboration when you can to help your students avoid the temptation to cheat.

In addition to these general strategies, there are several different things to consider when you design and give assignments. Giving effective homework assignments can be broken into three components: before, while presenting, and after the assignment. Use the following suggestions to help make homework a successful experience for you and your students:

Before the Assignment

- Teach the academic work skills that your students need to complete their work with little or no anxiety.

- Allow students to design their own homework assignments when appropriate. If they did not finish an assignment in class, they should have the option of completing it for homework, for example. If students are working in a group, they should have time together to plan the work they need to complete outside of class.

- Have a well-published schedule for homework so that students can anticipate assignments.

- Allow as many options as you can for assignments so that students can do work that is interesting and that encourages them to want to learn more.

While Presenting the Assignment

- Spend enough time going over the assignment and checking for understanding that students know you are serious about it.

- Give plenty of models, samples, and examples, letting students know what their final product should be.

- Don't wait until the last few minutes of class to assign homework. If you want students to take an assignment seriously, it should not be a last-minute item. A sound practice is to go over it at the start of class and at the end of class. Be sure to ask for clarification to make sure all students know what is expected of them.

- Write the homework assignment in the same spot on the board each day. Write it on the board even if you also give your students a syllabus, post it online, and record it on your voice mail.

- Ask students to estimate how long it will take them to do the assignment so that they can set aside the time to do it. With time, students will become adept at planning their work.

After the Assignment

- Send an e-mail, note, or phone call home when a student does not complete an assignment. This will often correct the problem of missing work. If nothing else, it alerts parents or guardians to be more vigilant about checking on their children's homework.

- Offer help to students who may need extra assistance in doing their work. A bit of extra time with you after school will often clear up problems and give students a confidence boost.

- Be reasonable if a student brings in a note from home requesting an extension. Sometimes unforeseen events can cause even the most conscientious child not to complete homework on time.

- Check homework at the start of class on the day it is due. If you do not take homework assignments seriously enough to collect or check them on the day they are due, then your students won't either.

- Because grading homework can be overwhelming, follow these tips to make giving prompt feedback a manageable task:

  - Collect and grade only some of the assignments.

  - Go over the work together as a class. Give a grade for completion.

  - Go over the work with your class and then give a quiz on it.

  - Check the work every day. Have students slip their assignments into a weekly portfolio and then select their best work for you to assess.

  - Have students work in small groups to discuss their answers.

WHAT TO DO WHEN STUDENTS DON'T DO THEIR HOMEWORK

When students don't do their homework, it becomes more than just an assignment; it becomes a headache for parents and guardians, students, and teachers. It can be particularly frustrating if the problem is chronic; has a detrimental effect on the student's mastery of important material; or occurs after you have made sure that the assignment is reasonable, purposeful, and clearly explained. You should make sure that it is posted for students on the board and on a class web page (if you maintain one) and recorded in their assignment planners.

One of the first things you should do is talk to individual students to learn about the problem. There are many reasonable reasons that students might not have done their homework: chronic family dysfunction, a lack of resources, insufficient skills to do the work, and even disorganization, just to name a few. After you know why the problem is happening, you can act to help students overcome the issues that prevent them from doing their assignments.

You should also make sure that you have an explicit homework policy in place so that the positive and negative consequences are clearly spelled out for your students. Once a student has not completed a homework assignment and you have talked with him or her about the problem, you may want to enact your policy if it would be appropriate for that circumstance.

You can also encourage students who have not done their homework to do it and turn it in later. If your school has a policy about accepting late work, you should follow that policy. The most important thing is that students should do the assignment and learn the material it covers.

Finally, if a student appears to have steady problems with getting homework turned in on time, then you should contact the student's parents or guardians to make sure that they are aware of the situation and to ask for their support. One tool that may help you with this conversation is Student Worksheet 9.1. On this form, students explain why they did not do their work. Going over the form with your students or their parents or guardians will make it easier for you to identify any behaviors that may be causing the problem.

Missing Homework Explanation Form

Please complete this form and then return it to your teacher.

Student name: _____ Date: _____

Assignment not completed:

_____

_____

_____

I do not have my homework today because:

_____

_____

_____

_____

_____

_____

_____

Student signature: _____

This information may be shared with a parent or guardian.

From *The First-Year Teacher's Survival Guide, 4th Edition*, by Julia G. Thompson. Copyright © 2018 by John Wiley & Sons, Inc. Reproduced by permission.

WHAT TYPES OF HOMEWORK HELP ARE ACCEPTABLE

One of the most frustrating problems concerning homework is that once students leave the classroom, you have no control over who helps them with their work and how much help they receive. Although you want your students to have the assistance they need to do their work well, some types of help are just not appropriate or helpful in the long run. Inappropriate help tends to fall into two categories: too much help offered by other students and too much help offered by parents or guardians.

When other students are involved, the situation is somewhat easier to manage. Begin by making sure that you have thought out the interactions you would like your students to have with one another when it comes to homework. Be explicit in explaining your expectations to them when you give the assignment. Make these expectations as clear as possible so that students will know when they are cheating on homework assignments.

The second category, too much help offered by parents or guardians, is not as easily managed. Instead of accusing parents or guardians of offering their children too much help, a more effective approach may be to be as encouraging as possible about the types of help that you would appreciate from them. In general, parents or guardians should help their children by setting aside a time and place for homework, being aware of the homework that their children are required to complete, encouraging solid work habits, and communicating with you when there are concerns. As a rule of thumb, if parents or guardians find themselves teaching content at home instead of just supporting good work habits by encouraging successful homework completion, then there may be a problem with the homework assignments.

If you notice that a student appears to be getting what seems to be inappropriate help from home, contact the adults responsible and be as tactful as possible in discussing the problem. Never put the student in the awkward position of having to defend parents or guardians.

HELP STUDENTS MAKE UP MISSING WORK

When a student asks you, "Did we do anything when I was out?," resist the nearly overwhelming urge to respond sarcastically. Your student is only asking for a chance to make up work. Because only very few students have perfect attendance, helping students make up missing work is a responsibility you will have to undertake almost every day.

Assisting students in making up missing work will not be difficult if you establish a policy, make sure that your students understand it, and enforce the policy consistently. Here are some guidelines that will help you:

Establish a Policy

- Learn your school's policy on making up missing work and align your policy with it. If there is no formal policy at your school, ask if there is one for your department or grade level.

- When coming up with a workable policy for making up work, include the revised due date of the assignment, how much and what kind of help a student may receive from others, when you are available to help students make up work, the point at which you will contact parents or guardians, and the penalty for late work.

- If you use a syllabus, encourage absent students to follow it as closely as they can so that they will find it easy to catch up when they return.

Make Sure That Students Understand What to Do

- At the beginning of the term and at subsequent intervals, discuss the issue of making up missing work in class.

- Divide your students into study teams early in the term. Within each team, students can help one another make up missed assignments by calling or texting absent members, sharing notes, collecting handouts, and reviewing the difficult parts of the assignment. Even very young children can help one another by being part of a study team.

- Consider having students rotate the task of recording class events and assignments on a large calendar, on your class web page, or even in a binder each day. When students return from an absence, they can check the class record or logbook to see what they missed and what work they need to do. You will find a sample of a class log page that you can adapt for your own classroom use in Student Worksheet 6.1.

- Keep all papers to be handed back and new handouts in a designated area of the room so that students can pick up missing papers when they return.

- Set aside time each week to meet with students and to help them make up work. Post your hours and be sure to inform parents and guardians about them.

- If a parent or guardian asks you to send work home to an absent student, be prompt and very specific. Give details that will enable the child to complete the work at home. Include a note offering extra help. Such a gesture not only is professional and courteous but also will show your students that you care about their welfare.

Enforce Your Policy Consistently

- Avoid allowing students to make up missing work during class time. Although this practice is certainly convenient, it allows students to miss yet more work. It is better to have students make up their work before or after school rather than miss more class time.

- Make time to speak about missing work with each student who has been absent. Make sure that the child knows what is due and when it is due.

- If a due date is approaching and a student has made no effort to make up the missing work despite reminders from you, call the student's parents or guardians.

This sends a clear message that you are serious about students' making up their work.

- Be flexible. Inevitably, some situations will require you to alter your policy, using your best judgment. For example, if a student is absent because of a serious illness, you should respond with compassion. You will need to adjust the makeup work and the amount of support you offer a student in such a situation.

Questions to Discuss with Colleagues

Sharing ideas with colleagues is a helpful way to devise solutions to some of the problems that you must manage successfully at school. Here you will find several topics to open discussions with colleagues about successful instructional practices:

1. You have a class filled with students who have very short attention spans. They easily become restless and bored. How should you adjust instruction to help them succeed?

2. You notice that your students lose interest in the day's lesson before the end of class. What activities can you use to engage their interest and help them master the content at the same time? Who can help you with this?

3. Your school's curriculum is clearly too advanced for many of your students. You know you should cover all the material in the curriculum guide, but you don't believe it is possible. What should you do? To whom can you turn for help?

4. It's not always easy to balance the amount of talking that you need to do with the amount of independent work that students should do. How can you decide what the right amount of each type of instruction will be for your students?

5. You want to integrate technology resources into an upcoming lesson. How can you plan this so that the implementation goes smoothly and helps students learn?

Topics to Discuss with a Mentor

Although the topics that new teachers need to discuss with a mentor vary from teacher to teacher and from school to school, there are some that most first-year teachers should be comfortable discussing with a mentor or a trusted colleague. You should ask your mentor about these topics from this section:

- How to obtain instructional materials and resources
- Which colleagues can share lesson plan ideas with you
- What restrictions there are (if any) regarding classroom technology
- Suggestions for efficiently planning instruction
- Suggestions for how to adjust lessons that are not going well

Reflection Questions to Guide Your Thinking

1. What kinds of games do your students like to play? How can you incorporate their interests into learning activities? Where can you learn about more games or enjoyable activities that would work well in your classroom?

2. What can you do to make sure class discussions are valuable and enjoyable learning experiences for your students? What do you need to teach your students about their role in class discussions? What do you need to do to prepare for a successful class discussion?

3. What are your strengths as an instructional planner? How can you use these strengths to design and deliver instruction that will help your students succeed?

4. What are your views on homework and how it should be assigned? How can you make homework a positive experience in your classroom?

5. How can you use a variety of learning activities so that students stay engaged? Where can you find these activities? Who can help you with this?

SECTION TEN

Measure Student Progress with Summative Assessments

Summative assessments are those that come at the end of a unit of study, at the end of a grading period, or at the end of a school year to measure how well teachers have aligned instruction with the objectives in the curriculum and how well students have mastered the material they were supposed to learn. No longer do teachers just present information, offer a quick quiz or two, and then give a long test on the material at the end of a unit. Instead, instruction today is data driven.

Teachers who use the data-driven model of teaching first collect and then carefully analyze classroom data to set achievable learning goals for their students. Both formative and summative assessments are part of this process. While formative assessments (see Section Eight for more information about formative assessments) are prescriptive and designed to help teachers adjust instruction to meet student needs, summative assessments measure mastery.

Although most summative assessments are created and administered by a classroom teacher, standardized tests are summative measurements of student progress. The data from summative assessments are often used by schools or even school districts to make broad curriculum decisions.

As you prepare to assess your students throughout the year, it is important to adopt a balanced approach to the process. Formative assessments cannot yield all the information about your students that you require, and neither can summative assessments. You will need to give frequent and varied assessments if your students are to be successful. As you read through the material in this section, you will learn more about the summative assessments that you can use to measure your students' mastery and how to create effective assessment instruments. You will also learn about how to efficiently manage student grades and how to successfully cope with some of the common issues related to summative assessments.

Summative Assessments Must Be Accurate Measures of Mastery

As you create various types of summative assessments to administer to your students, it is important to always keep in mind that those assessments must accurately measure student mastery. It's easy to be so caught up in the process of writing test questions or constructing other assessments that the instruments you create don't accurately measure mastery as they should. To help you with this, try to avoid assessments that

- Are too long to complete in the allotted time
- Don't really assess the information you have taught
- Use a format that is hard for students to follow
- Don't list point values for questions or items
- Ignore higher-level thinking skills
- Contain poorly worded directions
- Don't match your objectives
- Contain trick questions
- Don't match the test-taking skills of your students

The Two Most Common Written Assessments: Tests and Quizzes

Tests and quizzes are the chief written assessment tools that many teachers use to gauge their students' progress. Both tests and quizzes can be classified as either summative or formative assessments depending on the way teachers use the data they collect from them. If you give a quiz or a test and then assign a grade for that assessment, then it is not a formative assessment but a summative one because it is being used to measure mastery and not to gather prescriptive data.

Although tests and quizzes both offer many advantages, using these instruments has a few disadvantages. Too often tests and quizzes focus on lower-level thinking skills, such as asking students to just recall information, or the question formats do not appeal to the learning styles of all students. However, you can successfully handle these problems and design effective assessments to measure your students' progress. The following strategies offer ways to design tests and quizzes that will be fair and valid measures of mastery:

- Aim for validity by making sure that the test or quiz covers the content you want to assess. One way to do this is to create the test or quiz when you plan each unit of study—before you begin instruction.
- Include a variety of question types on each test or quiz. Objective questions do not always give an accurate assessment of your students' thinking. A balanced combination of brief objective questions and questions that require students to write longer answers will provide a better assessment than either type will by itself.

- Write questions that require students to think beyond the remembering level of learning. You can still use an objective format if you model your questions on the format used on many standardized tests. These tests often offer a reading passage or problem followed by questions that require students to apply their knowledge or use another higher-level thinking skill.

- Share questions with your colleagues. If you and other teachers cover the same material, you can save time by using the best questions from one another's assessments. As a new teacher, this will also offer an opportunity for you to learn more about assessment construction from reviewing your colleagues' work.

- Reduce potential confusion by grouping similar question types together.

- Place the point value for each section beside the directions for that section so that your students can judge their own progress.

- Begin any test or quiz with simple questions that your students will find easy. This will help them get over their initial anxiety.

- Make sure to give explicit directions that are easy to follow. When you change question types, you must give new directions, even if the procedure seems obvious.

- Number each page so that students can keep track of where they are in the assessment.

- Build confidence with encouragement, hints, and advice. Suggest how long a section should take to complete, underline key words, or even remind students to double-check their work as well as offer a word or two of encouragement throughout the test or quiz.

- If you type your tests and quizzes, make sure to use a plain font that is large enough for students to read easily. If you write tests and quizzes by hand, make sure that your writing is very easy to read.

- It's not always easy to judge how long it will take students to complete an assessment. To judge the length of your test or quiz, take it yourself and then allow two or three times that amount of time for your students to complete it.

- Save your questions electronically so that you will have ready access to them. Experienced teachers create banks of questions or question ideas that they can use again in a different format or on future tests and quizzes.

SOME SPECIAL CONSIDERATIONS FOR QUIZZES

Quizzes are similar to other assessments in that they require careful attention to fairness and validity. With a few exceptions, you should follow the same guidelines for designing quizzes that you use for tests. Here are some suggestions on how to make sure that the quizzes you design will accurately assess your students' progress:

- Keep quizzes brief. This is easy to do if you think of them as a snapshot of what your students have mastered and not as a comprehensive assessment.

- With fairness in mind, warn your students when you are planning to give a quiz. Students tend to regard pop quizzes as vengeful.

- Bear in mind that verbal quizzes are difficult for students who have trouble processing auditory information. Carefully prepare the quiz document as you would a longer test.

- Use the same care with constructing quiz questions that you do with test questions: give point values, write clear directions, and make sure each question is worded well so that the quiz can accurately reflect what students know.

Create Useful Objective Questions

Objective questions have many advantages for teachers and students. Although it can take a very long time to construct objective questions that can fairly assess what your students know, they can be easy to grade. Also, objective questions are not subject to the grader's bias in the way that more subjective assessments can be. Use the following tips to create different types of objective questions that allow you to assess your students' knowledge and understanding accurately:

True-or-False Statements

- This type of question is less useful than others because students have a good chance of guessing the answer. Use it sparingly if at all.

- Make sure that the answers don't follow a pattern.

- Take care to write statements that are similar in length. Often the true statements tend to be longer than the false ones.

- Avoid giving away the answers with such words or phrases as *not, none, at no time, never, all the time,* or *always.*

- If you would like to increase the thinking skills required on a test with true-or-false statements, ask students to explain their reasoning as part of the assessment.

Matching Questions

- Involve higher-level thinking skills by asking students to do more than just recall information when creating questions that require students to match information. For example, instead of just asking students to match a famous person to an event in history, have students read a brief passage about the event, determine the cause, and then match the cause to the event.

- Take the assessment yourself first to make sure that the answers don't follow a pattern or inadvertently spell out words.

- Encourage students to cross out answer choices as they use them.

- Offer more answer choices than questions.

- Give several short lists of ten to fifteen items rather than a longer list that students will find difficult to follow.

- Arrange matching questions to fit on the same page so that students will not be confused by having to flip the page back and forth.

Short-Answer Questions

- Design short-answer questions to yield responses that can be a word, a phrase, or even a paragraph in length.
- Keep in mind that although it does not take long to create short-answer questions, it does take longer to grade them.
- Short-answer questions are especially good for encouraging higher-level thinking skills because answers are not predetermined, so students must think of their own responses.
- Avoid giving such clues as "a" or "an" to indicate the answer. Instead, use "a/an" to give your students a full range of choices for their answer. For example, your quiz might read, "A wheelwright is a/an _____."
- Make all the blanks in short-answer questions the same length; otherwise, many students will interpret the length of the line as a clue to the answer.
- Short-answer questions take students longer to answer, so you should factor in the extra time when you write the assessment.

Multiple-Choice Questions

- Use multiple-choice questions to measure your students' mastery of both simple and complex concepts.
- Word the stem as a complete question with one of the options containing the answer. This is less confusing for students than a stem that is part of a statement or that asks students to fill in a blank.
- Make each answer choice significantly different from the others to reduce confusion.
- Avoid overusing one letter. You can do this by making up the answer pattern in advance and arranging the questions so that the answers conform to that pattern.
- Provide answer choices that are all roughly the same length to avoid giving away the answer.
- Make every answer choice a possibility by not including options that students can immediately eliminate as likely answers. For example, if your science test includes a question about who discovered DNA, don't give "Superman" as one of the answer choices.

How to Grade Objective Questions Quickly

Among the chief advantages of using objective questions are the ease and speed of grading. Although many schools provide machines that can grade objective assessments quickly with the use of a bubble sheet, not all schools do so, and not all content is appropriate for machine grading. If you are grading objective questions by hand, here are some tips to make grading this type of question easy to manage:

- Group similar items together. For example, place all true-or-false statements together and all short-answer questions together. This will make it less confusing for your students as well.

- Place questions with the same point values together so that you don't have to keep checking the value of each question.

- Keep the number of total points at 100 so that you will be able to quickly add up the missed points and subtract them from 100 to determine the percentage.

- If you ask students to write short answers, provide lines for their answers. They will find it easier to write on the lines, and you will not have to decipher answers that slant off the page.

- If the test or quiz is long, create a blank answer form on a separate sheet that students can use to record their answers. By using an answer sheet, you will only have to manipulate the answer sheet instead of having to flip through multipage tests or quizzes.

- Teach students to use a plus sign for "true" and a minus sign for "false," allowing you to grade true-or-false questions very quickly. It is not always easy to distinguish students' answers when they use *T* and *F*.

- If a student leaves an answer blank, draw a straight line through where the answer would have been in addition to placing an *X* in the blank to prevent students from cheating by adding answers when you go over the graded papers together.

- Ask your students to use dark ink or pencil to take a test or quiz (when appropriate). Dark ink or pencil makes the answers easy for you to read.

- Grade all the same pages at once instead of grading each test or quiz separately. For example, grade all the first pages and then go back and grade all the second pages.

Trading Papers?

Although it may be tempting to have students trade papers and grade one another's work as you call out answers, this is not an acceptable practice for summative assessments. On the one hand, when students are taking formative assessments, it can be appropriate for them to evaluate one another's work and to offer comments and suggestions because there is no grade associated with the assignment. Summative assessments, on the other hand, should be kept a private matter because there is a grade attached to the assignment and because sharing grades has the potential to be embarrassing for some students. It is a teacher's responsibility to grade summative assessments and not the responsibility of classmates.

Conduct Rules for Quizzes and Tests

When your students take quizzes and tests, they should not cheat, and they should not disturb others who may be struggling with an answer. You can prevent both forms of misbehavior from invalidating an assignment by teaching and enforcing rules for your students to follow while taking a quiz or test. These rules will make it easier for you to give quizzes and tests:

- Don't allow students a few minutes to study before a test or quiz. Ill-prepared students may take advantage of this opportunity to write cheat notes.

- Provide students with a cover sheet to allow them to keep their answers hidden from other students seated near them during the test or quiz. You and your students can create colorful ones with inspiring quotations and artwork. Laminate them and use them over and over.

- Limit the materials on students' desks to the minimum of necessary paper and one or two writing utensils. Students with extra paper can use it to hide cheat notes. If students want to pad their paper to make writing easier, teach them to fold their paper in half or give them scrap paper.

- Before giving an assessment, have students neatly stow their belongings under their desks and not beside them. All notes and loose papers should be inside a binder. If your students have cell phones, remind them to turn their phones off and to put them away until all students have completed the assessment and you have given them permission to take them out.

- Require students to sit facing the front of the class, with their knees and feet under the front of their desks. Allowing students to sit sideways during a quiz or test increases the chances that cheating will occur.

- If students need extra paper, pens, or pencils while they have a test or quiz paper, require them to ask permission before searching through their book bags.

- Monitor your students carefully until all papers are in. If students have a question, teach them to raise their hands and to wait for you to come to them. Do not allow them to walk to you.

- Do not allow any talking until all students have turned in their papers. If you allow talking, other students could be disturbed, and you will find it impossible to control cheating.

- Once students turn in their work, don't allow them to retrieve their papers to add answers.

- Set a reasonable but firm time limit. Students who take much longer than others to take a test or quiz have more opportunities to cheat and may cause the rest of the class to become restless while waiting for them to finish.

- If a student's IEP or 504 accommodation allows that student to have extra time on tests and quizzes, you can work with a colleague to provide a quiet place for that student to work for a longer time, offer a shorter version of the assessment, or give the assessment in different stages over a day or two if possible.

- Take the time to check for cheat notes on your students' hands, desks, clothing, and shoes. Students who know you will check will be less likely to attempt cheating.

- Be sure to clean the board to remove any information that will be on the test or quiz.

- Make sure that you do not leave an answer key where students can see it. This is a surprisingly easy mistake to make.

What to Do if Many of Your Students Fail a Test or Quiz

Few things are as discouraging as having several students fail a test or quiz. When this happens, there are three possible causes: the test or quiz itself is flawed, students did not prepare adequately, or you did not sufficiently help students master the material before giving the assessment. Here are some suggestions on how to handle each problem:

- The assessment is flawed: Look at the assessment. Is the format easy for students to follow? Are the point values logical? Do the questions match the way you taught the material? You can correct this situation by designing another test or quiz and using the one that students failed as a pretest and study guide.

- Students did not prepare for the test or quiz: Determine the reasons why your students did not prepare. Ask them to describe how they studied and why they did not study more. Take the time to teach students how you expect them to review and prepare for tests. You can also correct this problem by designing a new test or quiz and by using the one that students failed as a pretest and study guide.

- You did not sufficiently help students master the material: Sometimes teachers overestimate their students' readiness to take a test or quiz. When this happens to you, learn from your mistake and help students master the material before the next assessment. You should also consider the types of formative assessments that you used because the data they provided was not a good predictor of student success. You can correct this problem by using the failed test or quiz as a review guide to help students determine what they don't know. Remedy the situation by providing additional instruction and then retesting.

How to Use Alternative Summative Assessments

Just as the course content and instructional process can be differentiated, so can the way you assess student mastery. One way to do this is to use alternative assessments: methods of determining mastery that often require students to demonstrate understanding in ways other than traditional written tests and quizzes. Students who do not read or write well struggle with tests and quizzes, even though they may know the material as well as students with stronger verbal skills. Recognizing the need for a variety of assessments, educators have developed a wide array of assessment instruments to measure what their students know.

As you plan the types of assessments that you will use to determine your students' mastery of the material, you should use both traditional and alternative assessments. In combination, they provide a more balanced view of what students know, and the combination allows students to comfortably use their preferred learning styles.

Begin slowly, choosing alternative assessments that are easy to manage. As you grow in confidence and as you get to know your students' strengths and weaknesses, you can incorporate assessments that are more extensive. When you make up your next assessments, consider using some of the following types of assessments in addition to traditional measurements:

- Oral reports or performances
- Research projects
- Essays or other writing projects
- Demonstrations
- Creative projects
- Debates or panel discussions
- Multimedia projects
- Work contracts
- Portfolios
- Diagrams or other graphic representations
- Online assessments

How can you determine whether an alternative assessment will be successful with your students? Follow these suggestions:

- Make sure to align the assessment very closely with the material. For example, asking students to demonstrate a process is an appropriate assessment after you have taught them the steps of the process.
- Give scoring information to students when you make the initial assignment. No matter which method of assessment you use, your students need to know the criteria for success before they begin their work. Rubrics, models, samples, and examples are necessary for students to understand what is expected of them.

There are many different alternative assessments you can use throughout the school year. Here, however, is a brief list of some alternative assessments that you may find particularly easy to incorporate into your lessons:

Open-Ended Questions

- When answering open-ended questions, students can reveal what they know about a topic without the constraints of questions requiring fixed-answer responses. Asking open-ended questions based on real-world situations will also yield meaningful responses that require students to use higher-level thinking skills. Here are some examples of well-worded open-ended questions:
  - How did pioneer settlers in 1825 experience hardships similar to the ones you and your classmates experience?
  - Describe several ways that you can learn about another country. If you were planning a trip, which one would you prefer to visit? Why?

Variations on Traditional Tests

- There are many variations on traditional tests that can help you assess your students' knowledge. Use one or more of the following:
  - Group tests: Students work in small groups to answer questions.
  - Pairs tests: Students work in pairs to answer questions.
  - Open-book or open-note tests: Students can refer to their books or their notes when answering questions.

> Talk to the kids. Don't just take the grade on a test or essay. If the kids don't seem to be doing well, talk to them. Find out what they know and what might be holding them back.
>
> *Mary Landis, 22 years' experience*

Performance Assessments

Instead of asking students to write answers, you can give them a task to perform to elicit the information you need to measure. Performance assessments are versatile and easy to adapt to different grade levels and content areas. It is important to be careful to explain the requirements of the assessment, the criteria for success, and such practical expectations as due dates and required materials. Some examples of activities suitable for this type of assessment include these:

- Science experiments
- Oral reports
- Videos
- Skits
- Demonstrations
- Book talks
- Multimedia presentations

Rubrics: Formative and Summative Assessments

A rubric is a sophisticated assessment tool that teachers use to evaluate what their students know. Like other good ideas, rubrics began simply and have grown in usefulness as more teachers have learned how to adapt them for their purposes. Both students and teachers can use rubrics. Students use them as a guide on how to complete assignments, whereas teachers use them to assess student mastery.

The goals for an assignment are very clear when students receive a rubric before they begin. Because students know what to do, their work is usually of higher quality than it is with traditional assessments. Rubrics often help students find and correct mistakes before their teachers subtract points for errors. In this way, they can be used as formative assessments. Rubrics serve as summative assessments when they are used to judge mastery after an assignment is completed.

There are several advantages to using rubrics as summative assessments. One is that because they are explicit about the criteria for the assignment and given to students in advance, they are fair. Students and their parents and guardians know the quality of work that is expected. Another advantage is that rubrics make it easier to give students helpful feedback quickly. There is no need for lengthy marginal comments when the expectations for success are expressed clearly in the rubric.

How can you use rubrics in your class? Although it takes practice and patience to learn how to develop a clearly expressed rubric, you can begin with these steps:

- **Step One:** Determine the criteria by which you will grade an assignment.
- **Step Two:** Decide on the levels of mastery you want in an assignment. Begin by determining the best and the worst levels and then determine the levels in between.
- **Step Three:** Create your own rubric using a chart format similar to the one in Sample 10.1. Using a chart makes it easier for students to see the relationships among the various assessment items.
- **Step Four:** Show students models of acceptable and unacceptable assignments. Demonstrate how you would evaluate each assignment using the rubric.
- **Step Five:** Encourage students to practice using the rubric with several model assignments before you move them to self-assessments of their own work.

Many websites are devoted to the various types of rubrics. To begin refining your knowledge and to access free models, try these sites:

- **ForAllRubrics (www.forallrubrics.com).** This versatile site allows teachers to create rubrics, access student work, and print or share results. It is user-friendly, and the badge feature is particularly appealing to students.
- **4Teachers (www.4teachers.org).** At this helpful site, you will find RubiStar, a tool that allows you to create customized rubrics for all grade levels in English and in Spanish. You can save the rubrics you create online and modify them whenever you need to.

● Kathy Schrock's Guide to Everything (www.schrockguide.net). Along with one hundred rubrics, this extensive site has dozens of informative articles about rubrics, along with examples and instructions for specific types. You can learn how to create or modify rubrics, how to use rubrics in your classroom, or even how to guide students in creating their own rubrics.

Sample 10.1
Simple Rubric

This very simple rubric is one that teachers and students could use with an assignment requiring learners to create a map of the United States.

Quality	Excellent	Above Average	Average	Needs Work
Neatness	Lettering is very neat. States are carefully colored.	Lettering is neat. States are colored.	States are colored. Lettering is sloppy.	States are not colored. Lettering is sloppy.
Accuracy	All capitals, states, cities, and features are correct.	Almost all elements are correct.	More than 75 percent of the elements are correct.	Fewer than 75 percent of the elements are correct.
Details	States, capitals, cities, and all major features are shown.	States, capitals, cities, and some major features are shown.	States, capitals, cities, and few major features are shown.	States, capitals, cities, and no other major features are shown.

How to Manage Student Grades

As summative assessments occur throughout a grading period, it is necessary to manage them competently so that the stress for everyone involved—students, parents or guardians, and teachers—is mitigated. Accurately and promptly recording student grades is a necessary part of any teacher's daily responsibilities. Having a well-organized approach to how you will manage the assignments that you must grade, record, and return promptly will save you time and stress.

As you devise a plan to manage student grades throughout the term, you can talk with your colleagues to learn what works for them. With their advice, and with time and practice, you will soon find the methods that will work for you. As you begin formulating your plan to manage student grades, keep in mind that there are several things that are necessary for a plan to work well. Any grade management plan should

- Be in line with your district's and school's policies and procedures. If you are fortunate, many of the decisions that you will have to make about weighting grades or time lines for recording them will already be in place in those policies and procedures.

- Make transparency easy. Students and their parents or guardians should be aware of grade averages throughout the term. Include ways to keep students and parents or guardians continually informed in your grade organization plans.

- Be easy for you to use. Keeping up with your grading responsibilities takes time. As you figure out how to manage grades, try to keep the process as simple and streamlined as possible so that you can manage the task quickly and efficiently.

GENERAL INFORMATION TO CONSIDER ABOUT GRADES

As you think about the types of grades that you want to use to determine the final average for a grading period or even for the entire term, it is necessary to make some decisions that can have a long-lasting effect on your students. In the list that follows, you will find some general suggestions for how to successfully manage student grades that are fair, in line with your district or school policy, and reflect what your students know:

- You should perform a variety of assessments during a marking period to provide balance in the types of grades your students earn. For example, if you use classwork grades, quiz grades, project grades, portfolio grades, and test grades to determine a student's average, you will have a more accurate assessment of what the student knows than if you rely only on test and quiz grades.

- You should collect several grades each week so that you can have an accurate idea of each student's progress.

- As a rule, formative assessments are not graded since they reflect progress and not mastery.

- You should determine how you will weight your grades before school begins. In general, you should have a greater percentage of objective measurements than subjective ones. The way you weight grades should also align with the way your content area or grade-level colleagues weight grades.

- Many teachers do not assign grades for homework because doing so often skews grades. It is likely that there is already a policy in place for homework grades in your school and district. You should consult a mentor or your colleagues for your district's or school's policies regarding homework grades.

- You must inform your students and their parents or guardians of how you will weight their grades. Many teachers post this information in a conspicuous place and send the information home at the start of the term.

- When you plan your grades, you must also plan how you are going to handle missing work, makeup work, and assignments for students who are homebound. You will need fair and manageable policies and procedures for these.

- Because student grades should reflect mastery of content, reducing grades when a student does not follow directions or turns in an assignment late are practices that are currently under scrutiny. Talk with colleagues and your mentor to determine your district's and school's policies before reducing a student's grade for not following directions or for lateness.

- Don't allow papers to accumulate. Schedule a set amount of time each week to update your grade book. Trying to record hundreds of grades the day before you are supposed to give report cards to students is almost impossible.

- Students' grades are confidential; the Family Educational Rights and Privacy Act (first enacted in 1974) protects them. By law, you should never announce grades, tell a student's grade to a classmate, or allow students to look at your grade book.

> I catch myself always thinking about what I could do in class to make something better, but it's in a good way. When it comes to paperwork, I try to do my best to leave it all at school. That way, when I'm home, I'm home.
>
> *Jared Sronce, 6 years' experience*

Keep Track of Grades

Although you hope it will not happen to you, many teachers have had to produce their grade books as evidence in court. Because a grade book is a legal document, you must maintain it meticulously throughout the year. Your school district will have strict policies about how you are to keep student grade records, and you should follow them precisely.

There are three ways you can record student grades: recording all grades electronically, recording all grades on paper, or using a combination of paper and electronic record keeping.

The combination approach is currently the most common way that teachers maintain grade records. Here's why:

- Electronic grade systems can fail.
- You can lose a paper grade book.
- A paper grade book is usually more portable than an electronic grade book.
- One method can serve as a backup for the other.

To manage both paper or electronic grade books successfully, you will have to be very organized. The following are some tips for success in managing grade books:

Paper Grade Books

- Never leave your grade book where a student can take it. Keep track of your grade book by keeping it in the same place each day. You should either lock it away securely at night or take it home with you.

- Use black ink in your grade book whenever you can. Be very neat.

- Record your students' names in alphabetical order. You should also include student identification numbers if you will be required to use them during the term.

- Be sure to record the name of the assignment, its point value, and the date it was due so that you can quickly identify it later in the term.

- When you record grades, place a line at the bottom of the box where a student's grade will be if the student is absent and needs to make up an assignment. Convert this line to a circle when the student makes up the work. This will be useful when you need to transfer your paper grades to an electronic program or when you average grades by hand because you can add in grades for made-up work quickly.

Electronic Grade Books

- Save your grades in several places. Be very careful to keep all copies secure.

- Be aware that students can read the screen when you record grades while they are present. Place your classroom computer in a spot where you can maintain confidentiality.

- Print or digitally publish grades for students often so that your students will be able to help you correct errors. To maintain your students' privacy, keep the print-outs of their grades in a secure place, just as you would a paper grade book.

How to Personalize a Grade Report

Whether you use a paper grade book or an electronic one, personalizing grade reports is a good idea because it increases the transparency of grades and keeps the vital lines of communication between school and home open. There are two types of information that you can place on a report: general information intended for all parents or guardians and information that is specific to each student.

Many types of general information can be included on a grade report. Parents or guardians will appreciate a notice of upcoming events, such as science fairs, project due dates, or parent conference days. You can also include your contact information, in case parents or guardians want to discuss the grade report with you.

In addition to the general information on a grade report, you should include information that is specific to individual students. Here you can explain such matters as the due dates for any missing work or why the overall grade is what it is; if appropriate, you can write a brief note thanking parents or guardians for their support.

You should also be sure to make a positive comment about the child on each grade report. If you have trouble thinking of fresh ways to write comments about students, you can get ideas from other teachers who have had this problem and have shared their solutions with others. For hundreds of comments that you can use on grade reports, use the online search term "report card comments." You will be able to access hundreds of comments across a variety of websites.

How to Cope When Grades Are Challenged

Although it's not pleasant, it is only natural for students and their parents or guardians to challenge their grades throughout the term. If you do not handle their challenges well, the resulting problems may cause long-term resentment. Here are suggestions for dealing with grade challenges in a way that benefits everyone involved:

- Take a proactive attitude. Anticipating that there will be challenges to both individual grades and grade period averages will allow you to prevent as many problems as you can by being proactive. Here's how:
  - Be careful that your assessments and the weight for each one are in keeping with your district's policies.
  - Make it easy for students and parents or guardians to understand the grading process. Publish the grading scale for your class so that students know just how much weight each assignment will have. Show students how grades are calculated on various assignments as well as how to average their own grades.
  - Be careful to have many assessments for your students and to vary the types of assignments you use so that your students will have several different opportunities to be successful.
  - Make sure that your expectations for success are reasonable and in keeping with your school district's policies.
  - Don't assign a subjective grade for such activities as class participation, paying attention, being on time to class, or even effort because these do not reflect mastery.
  - Make sure that your classroom is transparent: students and their parents and guardians should know what they need to do to succeed in your class.
- Do not take a challenge to grades personally. Focus on the complaint and not on the fact that someone is questioning your judgment.
- Listen to students and their parents or guardians. Their complaints, even if they are not legitimate, are often the result of confusion. Take what they say seriously, and use their complaints to improve your teaching.
- Expect challenges to daily or weekly assignments from students and react positively. When you go over a graded assignment with students, tell them that you could have made mistakes. Ask them to let you know about mistakes you have

made by putting a large question mark beside any item they would like you to reexamine. They should also write a note to let you know why they are challenging the grade. Collect those papers and look at them again. By doing so, you are letting your students know that you will address their concerns in a respectful manner and at a time that is convenient for you. You will also benefit because you won't have a group of students shouting at you because you have made mistakes on their papers.

- Expect challenges to progress reports or report cards. You can preempt many of these challenges by letting students and their parents or guardians know grade averages more frequently than just when progress reports and report cards are distributed. Another advantage of this practice is that students can help you correct errors you may have made in recording grades. Ask students to be sure to double-check their graded assignments against the recorded grades.

- Be respectful of students and their families who are mistaken. When someone challenges a grade and is mistaken, take care to explain the error completely. Thank them for checking with you, and encourage them to continue to be concerned about the work.

How to Handle a Request to Change a Grade

One of those awkward moments that educators dread can occur when a student either is unhappy with a grade on an assignment or wants to raise his or her overall average. Although it is our responsibility to make sure that every assessment is fair and that our students understand how their grades are calculated, teachers can't be expected to abandon their standards when students and their parents or guardians protest grades. Anxiety about grades has many unpleasant causes and regrettable effects. It is our responsibility to make sure that concerns are treated with dignity and respect, even though it is only natural to feel impatient and stressed. To help you manage this problem competently, here are some strategies to use when students ask for special consideration:

- Be sure to set aside enough time to sit down with the student and his or her parents or guardians to work out a solution.

- Stress that you want to work together to make sure that every grade is as fair as possible.

- Be clear that you take their concerns seriously. Treat them with dignity.

- Even though you probably have already shown the entire class how to work out their grades, take the time to go over this again to make sure that students and their parents or guardians know exactly how you arrived at their average or the grade on the assignment.

- Don't offer extra credit to just one student. It is not fair to do this for just one. If you do adjust grades by offering additional work, make sure that the work you offer is not just a quick fix that will skew grades.

Extra Credit Dilemmas and Solutions

Extra credit is often a controversial topic for teachers. Some teachers are adamant about its usefulness, whereas others believe that offering extra credit encourages poor study habits. Either way, extra credit can be a trap for the unwary first-year teacher. When you are trying to establish a workable extra credit policy for your students, follow these guidelines:

- Make sure that your plan for extra credit is in line with your school's policy. If the policy is not in your faculty manual, check with several colleagues to learn how other teachers in your school handle requests for extra credit.

- Before you give in to student pressure for extra credit, decide on your expectations. Don't give in on the spur of the moment just because students want extra points. Extra credit should be carefully planned.

- Be aware of how easy it is to skew grades with extra credit points. If you assign work for extra credit without considering the impact it will have on grades, you may devalue the work you have assigned throughout the grading period.

- If you do offer extra credit, do so at the beginning of a marking period and assign a clear due date and point value for any extra credit assignment. If you don't do this, you will find yourself grading too many papers at the end of the term.

- Offer extra credit to every student in your class if you are going to offer it, not just to students who request it. If you don't offer it to everyone, you can legitimately be accused of favoritism.

- Don't offer extra credit for activities that require your students to spend money. For example, don't give students an extra credit assignment of going to see a local play. Some students will not be able to afford the admission fee, no matter how small it might be.

- If you offer bonus questions on a test, make sure they are not worth as much as the other questions. The purpose of such questions is to encourage students to stretch their minds, not to earn easy points to make up for what they did not know.

The No-Zero Debate

If your school district is like many others, there may already be a policy in place governing how you assign grades for students who have not completed their work or who have done very poorly on it. The ongoing discussions about assigning grades of less than 50 percent even for missing assignments will probably continue for quite some time as educators try to determine a course of action that will be beneficial for all students. On one side are those teachers who believe that students who don't turn in work or who do very badly on assignments should receive the grades that they earn regardless of the impact of those grades on their overall average.

On the other side of the debate are those teachers and researchers who maintain that grades should reflect student mastery of material and that a zero grade is indicative of student behavior and does not measure mastery. Proponents of the no-zero policy also maintain that students may not fully understand the negative impact of even one zero on their grade average and that extremely low grades not only skew the final average but also do not provide an accurate view of what students know.

As a new teacher, you may be firmly in agreement with one side or the other in the debate over grading policy. If your district or school already has a policy in place regarding the types of grades that you may assign, as a professional, you should follow that policy. If you disagree with the policy, you can join forces with other educators at your school to investigate the issue further to determine how it can be adjusted. Until those changes can be made, however, you should not deviate from your school's or district's policy.

Transparency and Other Crucial Grading Considerations

Because grades are a sensitive matter for students and their parents or guardians, there are some special considerations that can make the process of assigning grades more manageable. Here is a brief list of how you can make the grades that you assign as hassle-free as possible for everyone involved:

- Be completely transparent in the way that you assign work and assess it. Your students and their parents or guardians should never be surprised by a low grade. You can prevent this by announcing due dates well in advance, providing plenty of models, giving students rubrics when you first make assignments, and making the criteria for success clear. Publish grades often so that students and their parents or guardians have a clear idea of student progress all term long and not just at the end.

- Be fair in the way that you assess student work. For example, have more objective measurements than subjective ones and take care to appeal to student learning styles as often as you can. Announce all assessments well in advance and allow students who are missing work enough time to make it up.

- Make the workload involved in grading student work and in recording and publishing grades a priority. Do your best to return all graded work as quickly as possible.

- If you make a mistake in grading, admit it freely and correct it quickly. Asking students and their parents or guardians to also check for accuracy is a good way to forestall complaints.

- Carefully follow your school's grading policies. If there is a problem with a grade and a parent or guardian has complained to an administrator, you will have more protection if you have followed the established grading policies.

- Don't be too harsh when you deal with subjective assessments. Use the criteria that you set in advance as a guide instead of being sarcastic or unkind.

- If you notice that a student has not performed well on an assessment or that there seems to be a problem with a student's performance, be proactive in reaching out to parents or guardians to inform them of the situation and to determine the best ways to help the student succeed.

How to Have Difficult Conversations with Students about Their Grades

No matter how young your students are or how disengaged they appear to be from caring about school success, students do not want to fail. As a concerned teacher, it is up to you to encourage students to succeed. The conversations that you have about grades, work habits, and academic success should begin early in the term and continue until students understand that they do have the ability to succeed in your class.

When you talk with students who are not doing well academically, it is important that you take a partnership approach. Tell students that you want to work with them to be successful and that they are not alone in their efforts. Of course, this conversation is one that should be private or with parents and guardians present—and not where other students can overhear.

Be specific about what you have observed as problem areas and about how students can improve. Be as encouraging as you reasonably can about the chances for grade improvement as well. Set goals together so that students have clear ideas about how to proceed.

Finally, start early in the term. Don't wait until it is impossible for students to succeed before arranging a conference. The earlier you can begin to work together, the easier it will be for your students to be successful in improving their grades.

> Teach your students with confidence. Instill the confidence in them that they will be prepared. Don't let your anxiety about tests transfer to students.
>
> *Luann West Scott, 42 years' experience*

Success with Standardized Tests

It is highly likely that your students will have to take at least one standardized test this year. School districts rely on standardized tests to assess not only the performance of individual students but also the performance of schools and how well teachers are achieving the goals of the school district. Because standardized tests have serious implications for everyone involved, the test administrators in your district will probably give teachers a great deal of information about the specific tests that students will take. Standardized tests do not have to be a headache for you and your students if you take care to do three important things: prepare all year long, teach test-taking skills, and assume your professional responsibilities.

YEARLONG PREPARATION

There are several simple steps you can take, beginning at the start of the school year, to make sure that your students are prepared for a standardized test. Spending a bit of time periodically throughout each grading period is a much more sensible plan to help students succeed than just cramming right before the test. Here are some suggestions to follow all year long:

- Provide solid instruction that is aligned with your school district's and state's curriculum guidelines. If your focus is on carefully planning and delivering content instead of just on covering the test, your students will have a greater chance of success.

- Talk about the test. Make students aware of the test, but don't threaten them with it. Threats can intimidate students who are less able or who tend to be anxious.

- Offer a variety of testing formats and instructional activities all year long so that students can naturally develop skills as test takers.

- Use the materials offered by your state's department of education and your local school district as a planning guide. Often there will be course blueprints and ancillary materials that will help you cover the necessary content.

- Offer your students previous tests as practice as often as you can. When they are informed about what to expect, they can take the test with confidence.

- When students practice for the test, gather data and use this information to offer differentiated remediation activities.

TEST-TAKING SKILLS

Prepare your students by making sure they are test wise. They should not feel intimidated by the format or process of a standardized test if you take the time to teach test-taking skills. The tips that follow can help you teach important test-taking skills:

- Teach students to take the time to listen as the test examiner reads the instructions, even if they believe that they are familiar with the directions. They should also reread the instructions for themselves as they work through the test.

- When your students practice taking the test, show them how to pace themselves. Make sure they know where to find a clock at the testing site.

- Practice reading test items together and analyzing what information the answers require. Many mistakes happen because students do not read the questions carefully.

- Be aware that students often become bogged down in a difficult reading passage and just skim the questions. Teach them to read the questions carefully first and then skim the passage, looking for the answers.

- When students have passages to read, teach them to underline or highlight the parts of the passage that are covered in the questions. They can also circle important words or write notes to themselves in the margins.

- Teach the process of elimination regarding answer choices. Students should practice eliminating the answers that are obviously not correct until they arrive at a reasonable answer.

- Because marking a bubble sheet during a test can be stressful for many students, give your students lots of opportunities throughout the year to practice marking their answers on a bubble sheet. If your students will be taking a standardized test on a computer, provide plenty of practice opportunities so that all students are familiar with the format of the test and know how to proceed.

- Encourage students to go back and check their work. If the test is a very long one, or if it is timed, teach students to check the questions they are unsure of first and then check the ones they are sure of as time permits.

YOUR PROFESSIONAL RESPONSIBILITIES REGARDING TESTING

As a classroom teacher, you will have to manage weighty responsibilities when it comes to the administration of standardized tests. It is important that you take care to be as professional as possible when you administer them. It may be helpful to keep in mind that standardized tests are just that—standardized—so that the same testing conditions can be in place for every student. When tests are standardized, they are more likely to be fair assessments of what students know because the testing conditions are the same for every test taker. In the list that follows, you will find some suggestions for making sure that you manage test administration in a professional and competent manner:

- Be aware that you will probably be asked to attend training sessions to prepare for test administration. Take the training seriously and don't hesitate to ask questions.

- Allow yourself enough time in advance of the date of the test to carefully read the procedures and directions for testing. If you are not clear about what you are supposed to do, ask the staff member in charge of testing at your school.

- Familiarize yourself with the directions that you are supposed to read out loud to students during testing. Do not deviate from the script that you will be given.

- Make sure that you have a reliable way to time tests if they are supposed to be timed.

- Do your best to prevent violations of test security. Here are some specific suggestions for this:

  - Monitor students carefully during testing. Don't check e-mail or grade papers during the test, for example. Take care not to look at the tests as you administer them.

- Don't give in to the temptation to quiz your students afterward about what was on the test.

- Be sure to carefully count out the test materials as you distribute them and make sure to account for all copies after the testing period is over.

- Take care that all students turn cell phones or other electronic devices off and place them in a secure place during the testing period.

- Be aware that teachers are often asked to sign an acknowledgment that they have received information about the test that their students will be taking. When you sign such an acknowledgment, you are indicating that you understand the kind of help you can offer your students before and during the test.

- Gently refuse requests for help from anxious students during testing. If you are not sure how to do this in an appropriate manner, ask the testing coordinator at your school for advice before the day of the test.

- If students are supposed to receive testing accommodations, be scrupulous in providing those accommodations.

- If you encounter problems during testing, report them to the testing coordinator as soon as you can. Some of the problems that you may have to report could include a fire drill, loud noises, a ringing cell phone, a student bubbling in patterns instead of taking the test, or a disruptive student.

A final word about success with standardized tests: one of the biggest complaints about standardized tests is that they force teachers to teach to the test. Some opponents of standardized testing claim that the flaws inherent in standardized tests require teachers who want to have successful students to teach only the material that will be covered on the test. Although it is inevitable that there will be flaws in systems of standardized testing, teachers who want their students to be successful certainly do not teach to the test. In fact, teachers whose students are successful test takers make a point of covering the important concepts in the course curriculum instead of dwelling on what may or may not be tested. They may prepare their students by strengthening the test-taking skills specific to their subjects or grade levels, but teachers with integrity do not limit their students by teaching to the test.

Questions to Discuss with Colleagues

Sharing ideas with colleagues is a helpful way to devise solutions to some of the problems that you must manage successfully at school. Here you will find several topics to open discussions with colleagues about successful instructional practices:

1. You have a student who usually does very well on tests. This student failed a recent assessment and has accused you of making an unfair test. What is your goal in this situation? What should you do?

2. Your students do not seem to perform well on traditional tests, even though you spend class time reviewing with them. You feel that they know the material. Which

types of assessments would be effective ways to evaluate your students' progress? How can you use a variety of assessments in your class?

3. One of your students has an accommodation allowing him to have extra time on tests and quizzes. How can you provide this accommodation without compromising the security of the assessment? Who can help you with this?

4. As an alternative assessment, you have assigned a creative project. After students turned it in, however, you realize that the point values that you have assigned for it are not appropriate for the difficulty of the project. How should you handle this?

5. You want to offer alternative assessments but are not sure of the ones that would be most appropriate and manageable. How should you proceed? Who at your school can help you with this dilemma?

Topics to Discuss with a Mentor

Although the topics that new teachers need to discuss with a mentor vary from teacher to teacher and from school to school, there are some that most first-year teachers should be comfortable discussing with a mentor or a trusted colleague. You should ask your mentor about these topics from this section:

- How to learn about your school's policies regarding homework grades and extra credit decisions

- Advice about how to cope when students and their parents or guardians challenge grades

- How to set up shared banks of questions for tests and quizzes

- How to quickly and efficiently grade and return student summative assessments

- How to find advice and information about the standardized tests that your students will be expected to take this term

Reflection Questions to Guide Your Thinking

1. How transparent is the way that you are currently managing student grades? Are you keeping students and parents or guardians as informed as they should be? What can you do to ensure that there are few challenges to the grades students earn?

2. Traditional tests and quizzes can be useful assessments. How can you maximize their effectiveness? How can your colleagues help you with this?

3. What can you do to help students improve their skills at preparing for and taking tests? What strengths do they already have that you can capitalize on? How will you know when you have been successful at helping them with this?

4. What plans have you made to manage your students' grades in an organized way? What does your school district expect of you? What tips can other professionals in your building share with you to help lighten your workload?

5. How have you prepared your students for any standardized tests they will take this year? What test-taking skills are important for them to know? How have you taught those skills? Where can you find more information on how to prepare students for standardized tests?

SECTION ELEVEN

Policies, Procedures, and Rules: The Framework of Classroom Management

A well-managed classroom does not happen by accident. Instead, it is the outcome of a series of intentional choices made by a teacher who has the imagination to predict student behavior and to create a reassuring framework to guide students. A well-managed classroom is one in which the teacher has put a systematic arrangement of complementary policies, procedures, and rules into place so that students can manage their daily tasks with ease and confidence.

In this section, you will be able to learn how to create the policies, procedures, and classroom rules that will make it easier for you to manage your classroom successfully. You will also learn how to set reasonable limits and convince your students to accept your classroom management decisions for the benefit of everyone in the class. In brief, you will be able to establish the vital framework necessary for successful classroom management. Because classrooms are part of the larger school community, it is wise to begin with the policies that you will want to implement.

Develop Policies for Your Classroom

Policies are those general principles that direct the behavior of students and help you make informed decisions about specific actions. Before you can develop a set of policies for your own classroom, you should first consult your school district's policies, your school's policies, and those policies that the other members of a grade-level or content area team to which you may belong already have in place.

For example, your content area team may have a policy that allows students who fail to show mastery on a summative assessment to retake it. Your classroom policy could complement that broader one if your policy were that students who failed an assessment could retake it during a free study period. Some of the areas for which you may need to design policies include these:

- Students who need extra help
- Classroom cell phone use
- Book bags in class
- Food in the classroom
- Missing class work
- Cheating
- Class discussions
- Tardiness
- Appropriate language
- Late or missing homework
- Appropriate homework help
- Conflicts with classmates
- Technology use
- Classroom music
- Grading
- Forgotten materials

To make it easier to take a systematic approach to establishing your classroom policies, consider using Teacher Worksheet 11.1 to work through the process.

TEACHER WORKSHEET 11.1

Planning Classroom Policies

Use this worksheet to jot down your ideas about some areas for which a formal policy is necessary. As you complete this worksheet, consider the policies of your district or school as well as those of your grade or subject area committees or teams when planning for your own classroom policies.

Students who need extra help:

_____
_____
_____

Classroom cell phone use:

_____
_____
_____

Book bags in class:

_____
_____
_____

Food in the classroom:

_____
_____
_____

Missing classwork:

_____
_____
_____

Cheating:

_____
_____
_____

Class discussions:

_____
_____
_____

(continued on next page)

(continued from previous page)

Tardiness:

_____

_____

Appropriate language:

_____

_____

Late or missing homework:

_____

_____

Appropriate homework help:

_____

_____

Conflicts with classmates:

_____

_____

Technology use:

_____

_____

Classroom music:

_____

_____

Grading:

_____

_____

Forgotten materials:

_____

_____

Interactive technology responses:

_____

_____

_____

Establish Procedures for Your Classroom

All students have some common characteristics; one of the most significant is the need for structured time. From energetic kindergartners to sophisticated seniors, students need routines or recurring procedures in their school day to keep them on track. As you begin establishing the procedures for your classroom, it is sensible to think of them as the steps that you want students to follow when performing tasks. The particulars of these procedures will vary from teacher to teacher and from grade level to grade level, but adhering to specific business procedures for the classroom will make the business of the class run smoothly.

Before school begins, you should decide how to handle the classroom procedures you want your students to follow. If you have these in place before the first day of class, you will be rewarded with a positive classroom environment and successful students. Use Teacher Worksheet 11.2 to help you begin to formulate your class procedures.

Just this week I had the occasion to encounter a brand-new teacher in the hallway. She was teary-eyed. I asked her what was wrong, and she said her class had fallen into disarray when she asked a student to put away her phone. I asked if she had a procedure for that, and she didn't yet. She was crying, she said, because she thought they wouldn't like her anymore. I asked if she had friends, and she replied "of course." Then I told her she didn't need students for friends; they needed her for structure. I told her they would like her if they respected her, but they never would if she tried to be their friend. Kind, yes. Fair, yes. Friend, no. Good and fair procedures eliminate tears.

Luann West Scott, 42 years' experience

Planning Classroom Procedures

The following are some of the essential classroom areas that require carefully planned procedures. To determine the best course of action to take for each item, first consult your colleagues or mentor to make sure that the procedures you establish are in line with the procedures that other teachers in your building use.

Beginning class: _____

Ending class: _____

Being tardy to class: _____

Making up work when absent: _____

Handing in work: _____

Using cell phones: _____

Keeping the work area clean: _____

Formatting written work: _____

Using the classroom library: _____

Finishing work early: _____

Pledging allegiance to the flag: _____

Listening to intercom announcements: _____

Being a classroom helper: _____

Lining up: _____

Going to the clinic: _____

Using a computer: _____

Asking questions: _____

Handling emergencies: _____

Managing restroom breaks: _____

Having materials needed for class: _____

Making up missing or late work: _____

Sharpening pencils: _____

Hydration: _____

Assigning homework: _____

Turning in money: _____

Taking attendance: _____

Taking lunch counts: _____

Calling students to attention: _____

Taking tests: _____

Sharing supplies: _____

Conducting emergency drills: _____

Other procedures specific to your class: _____

_____

_____

From *The First-Year Teacher's Survival Guide, 4th Edition*, by Julia G. Thompson. Copyright © 2018 by John Wiley & Sons, Inc. Reproduced by permission.

Teach and Enforce School Rules

The process of creating rules for your classroom begins with the rules that govern everyone in your school. You will prevent many discipline problems and create a positive classroom environment if you take the time to teach and enforce school rules. Consistent enforcement is especially important because some of the conflicts you will have with your students will arise from teachers' having inconsistently enforced rules in the past. Use the following guidelines to create a positive classroom environment:

- Know the school's rules. Often this information is posted in a faculty handbook or in the start-of-school information that goes home with students. Ask colleagues about rules that you are not sure how to enforce.

- Follow the rules yourself. Students are quick to point out hypocrisy. For example, a particularly sensitive area for many students is the dress code. You will find it very difficult to enforce the rules for student dress if you violate them yourself.

- Take the time to teach school rules to your students. One mistake that many teachers make is assuming that someone else will teach school rules. Even though the administrators at your school may have reviewed the rules with students, you should discuss them again during the first few weeks of school to make sure that everyone knows what to do. You will have to repeat the rules from time to time to ensure that students maintain a clear understanding.

- Enforce school rules consistently. If you have a serious reservation about a school rule, you should speak with an administrator about it. No matter what you personally think about a rule, however, you should enforce it. Students are quick to take advantage when teachers are not consistent in enforcement.

> Spending time on routines and procedures will save you time in the long run. Teach them. Model them. Reteach them and return to them often. Use visuals as reminders. Take a picture of what a desk should look like at the beginning of class and then show it before the bell rings. You might not even have to say a word. And if you decide you don't like your procedures, change them. Ask other teachers for ideas, or ask the students themselves what works for them.
>
> *Jennifer Burns, 13 years' experience*

Create Rules for Your Classroom

Class rules provide guidelines for acceptable behavior and protect your right to teach and your students' right to learn. Rules also send the message that good behavior is important and that you expect students to work productively. Although your students may earnestly try to convince you that rules are not necessary, they do not want total freedom. Students of all ages benefit from the guidance that classroom rules provide in establishing a tone of mutual respect, trust, and cooperation. When you create a set of rules, what you are really doing is establishing a common language with your students for your expectation of good behavior.

When creating rules for your classroom, you should follow these guidelines to ensure their success. Class rules should be

- Stated in positive terms
- General enough to cover a broad range of student activity
- Easy for students to remember
- Appropriate for the age and ability levels of your students

To help you get started, begin thinking about your rules by following these four steps:

- **Step One:** Determine what areas your rules need to cover. Begin by asking yourself these questions:
  - What are some behaviors that make it possible for students to succeed?
  - What are some behaviors that make it difficult for students to succeed?
  - What limits can I set to guarantee that all students can exercise their right to learn?
- **Step Two:** Draft a rough set of rules. After you have determined the areas your rules should cover, write a rough draft. At this point, you may want to show your rules to a colleague to make sure they are in line with school rules and appropriate for your students.
- **Step Three:** Word classroom rules positively. Take your rough draft and change the wording as needed to state rules in positive terms, conveying a tone of mutual respect and consideration.
- **Step Four:** State rules in such a way that they are easy to remember. Can you combine any of your rules to cover a general range of student behavior? For example, you could combine "Bring your textbook every day" and "You will need paper and pens in this class" to read: "Bring the materials you will need for class."

Your students will also find it easier to recall your class rules if you have only a few. Many experienced teachers recommend having about five rules for middle school and secondary students. Reduce the number of rules for younger students as appropriate. If you are not sure whether your classroom rules will work, here are some that experienced teachers have used successfully. Adapt them to meet the needs of your students.

- Use class time wisely.
- Do your work well.
- Treat other people with respect.

- Follow school rules.
- Bring your materials to class every day.

If you would like more information about creating class rules that will work well for your students, visit the National Education Association (www.nea.org). On the home page, use "classroom rules" as a search term to yield dozens of articles and strategies for creating useful class rules for students at all grade levels.

Consequences: Positive and Negative

Although it is inevitable that some consequences of broken rules will be negative, astute teachers know that a more effective approach to encouraging students to embrace the rules of their classroom is to promote the positive consequences that arise when everyone works together to follow reasonable rules. From higher achievement to solid feelings of accomplishment, positive consequences are a powerful way to motivate students to behave well.

To help students understand that all actions have consequences and that they choose the kinds of consequences that they will experience, make the connection between behavior and consequences clear to your students. If students are older, a brief class discussion or a few gentle reminders may be sufficient to make the connection clear, whereas younger students may need extra help, patience, and such incentives as stickers or other tangible rewards.

> Let them know *your* rules and expectations. Be *you*. If you aren't true to your expectations and aren't *you*, it will be hard for students to trust you and for you to enforce rules. Start building that connection.
>
> *Jared Sronce, 6 years' experience*

When planning your classroom rules, take the time to consider the types of consequences that would be appropriate when a student breaks a rule. Here are some guidelines to help you make the most effective and suitable decisions about consequences in your classroom:

- The purpose of a consequence is to help students learn how to follow the classroom rules—not punishment. When the focus is on the positive act of following rules instead of being punished for noncompliance, students are more likely to follow rules, not choose to break them.

- Consequences should be timely. Having a student apologize to a classmate for a disrespectful comment several days after the comment happened is not a productive consequence, for example. Instead, a quick, sincere apology in the moment would right the situation without additional drama.

- Consequences should be appropriate in severity. If an infraction is slight, keep the consequence slight. For example, students who make a mess in class should clean it up. Students who speak disrespectfully to you should meet with you privately to discuss the behavior. Students who fall asleep in class should stand quietly beside their desks for a few moments or even get a drink of water to wake up.

- It's easy to be caught up in the moment and to overact when misbehavior happens, but overreacting will cause students to focus on your anger or disappointment instead of learning from the mistake. Calmly enact the predetermined consequence instead.

- Students learn to self-regulate their behavior more quickly if you establish and follow a hierarchy of consequences. Some teachers find it effective to post a notice of the hierarchy in their classrooms. Here's an example that you could adapt for your classroom:
  - First offense: Verbal warning
  - Second offense: Meet with the teacher
  - Third offense: Phone call home

- Consequences should be published well in advance of the possibility of misbehavior so that students know what is expected of them. Discussion at the start of the term, posters displayed in the classroom, and brief verbal reminders early in the term and periodically as needed are all useful methods of making sure students know what is expected. Use Teacher Worksheet 11.3 to plan your classroom rules and consequences.

TEACHER WORKSHEET 11.3

Planning Your Classroom Rules and Consequences

If you want to adjust one of the suggested class rules or create your own set of rules and consequences, begin with these four questions:

What are some behaviors that make it possible for students to succeed?

_____

_____

What are some behaviors that make it difficult for students to succeed?

_____

_____

What limits can I set to guarantee that all students can exercise their right to learn?

_____

_____

Your colleagues can be a helpful resource when creating classroom rules and consequences. Which colleagues would be most helpful?

_____

_____

To be effective, classroom *rules* must meet the following criteria. As you examine each rule, make sure it meets these criteria before you fully adopt it:

_____ Be easy to remember
_____ Create an orderly classroom
_____ Fit within a school district's policies for student behavior
_____ Be stated so that students understand it
_____ Be enforceable
_____ Be as fair to as many students as possible
_____ Satisfy the parents and guardians of your students

To be effective, classroom *consequences* must meet the following criteria. As you examine each consequence, make sure it meets these criteria before you fully adopt it:

_____ Fit within a school district's policies for student behavior
_____ Satisfy the parents and guardians of your students
_____ Be stated so that students understand it
_____ Be geared to helping students follow rules
_____ Be appropriately severe
_____ Be timely
_____ Be published in a variety of ways early in the term

Teaching Classroom Policies, Procedures, and Rules

In the rush to cover the academic material that your students need to learn, it is easy to overlook the importance of teaching the classroom policies, procedures, and rules you have created. All are useless if your students are unsure of what you expect and what they are supposed to do. Teaching appropriate behavior is not something you can complete in one class period; rather, it is a process that will last the entire year.

Time spent explaining the behavior expectations for your class is time well spent. Although you do not want to bore your students, you still need to explain the expectations you have, the positive and negative consequences for each one, and the importance of following them. Several short discussions over a period of several days will serve to make the information memorable for your students.

It is better to spend a few minutes each day or week with brief lessons on classroom policies, procedures, and rules than to spend an hour early in the term and then ignore them afterward. Incorporate the strategies that follow, and the time you spend teaching the rules will save you precious instructional time later:

- Although teaching classroom behavior expectations is a process that will last all term, focus on teaching them during the first three weeks of the term to let your students know that you are serious about creating a positive classroom climate. Revisiting the material periodically will reinforce this early teaching.

- Post a letter about your classroom policies, procedures, and rules on your class web page or send a copy home with your students, thus enlisting the support of parents and guardians.

- Use the walls of your classroom to display appealing reminders of what you expect of your students. If your students maintain a study binder, you can also make copies for students to keep handy.

- When you are ready to teach, don't try to bluff your way through a brief presentation. Instead, present your policies, procedures, and rules in an engaging lesson. Try some of these activities to make the lesson interesting:

  - Model the policy, procedure, and rule yourself. Give students plenty of concrete examples. After you have done this, have students make up their own models and examples to share with classmates.

  - Place students in groups. Have some groups brainstorm reasons why everyone should follow the class expectations. Ask other groups to list what could happen if the expectations were ignored.

  - Ask students to improve the wording of a rule or to make suggestions to streamline a procedure. They can also create examples to explain specific policies or rules.

  - Students can video themselves acting out procedures or following rules and share their video with the class.

  - Ask students to explain the policies, procedures, and rules to you in their own words.

Setting Limits

"But you said!" "That's not fair!" "Are you sure?" "How come we have to do that?" It's clear from reactions like these that many students are used to arguing with the authority figures in their lives. From the howls of protest when we make unpopular decisions to the endless debates about possible answers on a test, many students are clearly accustomed to getting their own way if they nag loudly enough to wear out their exhausted teachers.

One of the most important parts of creating a solid classroom management system involves thinking carefully about what is acceptable behavior in your classroom and what is not acceptable. As you work through the process of creating the policies, procedures, and rules that will govern your classroom, you are providing safe boundaries for students to operate within. Setting limits is a crucial part of classroom management because it relays to students that you care enough to have high standards for their behavior. Although it is sometimes difficult, try to accept the fact that students will test every decision you make, will argue endlessly if given an opportunity, and will continue to push every limit possible, even on the last day of class. When you are aware that your decisions will be tested, it will be easier for you to set limits.

Even though failing to set and abide by firm limits in a classroom can create unproductive behavior, you can avoid this problem. One helpful approach is to remove as much of the emotion from the situation as you can. It's not always easy to resist when students appear ready to stage a tantrum, but those teachers who can take a calm and straightforward approach will find it much easier to deal with student misbehavior.

Another way to manage the issue of setting limits is to take the time when you create a rule, policy, or procedure to put yourself in the place of your students and to anticipate what could go wrong during enforcement. Planning how to handle possible protests will make it easier for you to convince your students to cooperate.

You should also be careful not only to be fair but also to make sure that your students perceive your decisions as fair. Make it a point to preempt student challenges by letting your students know that you intend to be fair to everyone in the class when you make decisions that affect the entire group.

Resist the temptation to be a pushover. Many teachers give in more frequently than they should. In the long run, this will fail as students continually struggle to gain their own way. Adopt the stance that while you are friendly, you are also a teacher who means what you say. Project a matter-of-fact attitude whenever you relay the enforcement of an unpopular decision, and you will find that setting limits and abiding by them is not as difficult as it seems.

How to Say No Courteously

Teachers spend their days bombarded by a steady stream of requests from students who want to go to the restroom, the office, a locker, the clinic, or to call home, open a window, shut a window, sharpen pencils, and hear the directions just one more time. Fielding these entreaties tactfully requires quick decisions not only about whether the request is a sound one but also about how the response will affect the entire class as well as the student making it.

One of the most useful skills that a teacher can develop is the ability to refuse a student's request without causing offense. Although it may seem impossible, this is not as difficult as it sounds. Instead of abruptly refusing, try one of the statements or questions that follow. Each one is designed to deny a student request in a pleasant, nonconfrontational way that preserves the student's dignity. Remember to keep your tone neutral and pleasant.

- Let me think about that for a little while.
- Let's talk about that after class.
- Let's finish this first.
- I don't think that is the best decision because _____.
- Are you sure that's a wise choice?
- What do you think?
- Could you give me a moment?
- Can this wait?
- What are the pros and cons involved in your request?
- How are you planning to do that?
- How will you accomplish that?
- Can you tell me why that would not work?
- Would you ask me again in a moment?
- Have you finished your assignment?
- How will that help you achieve your goal?
- Are you sure that's wise?
- Why don't you give that some more thought?
- Why are you asking?

Empower Your Class with Student Ownership

Many ways of encouraging students to follow class policies, procedures, and rules will be more effective than just imposing your teacher power over students. Spending time at the start of a term enlisting your students' support for class policies, procedures, and rules will result in a more productive classroom environment all year long. Follow these strategies to solicit your students' support:

- Involve students early. The more involved your students are with class expectations early in the year, the more likely those expectations are to be successful. This success will be generated by the sense of ownership your students will gain through their involvement.
- Ask students to tell you the reasons behind a behavior expectation.

- Ask students to suggest policies, procedures, and rules of their own. Assigning students to modify your expectations will enable you to keep them in place while involving students.

- Have students role-play scenarios illustrating various aspects of the class behavior expectations.

- Occasionally quiz your students orally about the rules in rapid-fire bursts of questions at the start or end of class. Make it an enjoyable competition to engage everyone.

- Have students make up songs, chants, gestures, or mottoes for various rules.

- Offer alternative behaviors to students who break class rules, or have them suggest alternatives. Teach them not only to stop a negative action but also to replace it with a positive one. You encourage self-discipline and redirect student energy when you do this.

Moving beyond Crowd Control to Promote Self-Discipline

The ultimate purpose of the thought and effort that we pour into classroom management is not to create mindlessly compliant students but to encourage students to be self-disciplined. When students assume control of their own behavior choices, a positive shift occurs in the classroom. Self-directed students are confident, productive, and on-task far more often than not.

Despite the impossibility of ever knowing for certain just how successful your attempts to help students assume responsibility for their actions will be, you must work toward that goal. You should not only direct your students so that they understand what they should do but also encourage them to be willing to do the right thing at the right time.

Fortunately, you have countless chances to help students in their efforts to become self-disciplined. Here are three that are essential for creating the positive environment that you want for your students:

- Model the behavior you want your students to have. Our actions certainly speak louder than our words when it comes to teaching students the behaviors we want to see from them. This is particularly true of self-directed behaviors. Students need strong, positive role models who will show them the way to succeed.

- Maintain high standards for all students. If you want to see just how capable your students can be, then set limits that are difficult but not impossible for them to achieve. You don't have to expect perfect behavior all the time, but too often our students are much more capable than we give them credit for being. It is especially important to maintain these high standards when students seem to struggle or when less capable students are included in the class. It is a disservice to lower standards instead of helping students rise to meet them.

- Be encouraging and positive with students. Students whose teachers make it abundantly clear that they have confidence in their ability to succeed are students who are more apt to become self-disciplined than those whose teachers doubt their students' abilities. If you want positive actions from your students, then you must show your own positive side. This does not mean you need to be falsely cheerful or to flatter your students; both will surely fail with a spectacular thud.

Resources for Further Exploration

To learn more about the practical aspects of a well-managed classroom, you can explore some of these resources:

- **National Education Association (NEA) (www.nea.org).** Use "classroom management" as a search term to access helpful articles about how to manage a classroom successfully.
- **Smart Classroom Management (www.smartclassroommanagement.com).** Use "class rules" as a search term to access helpful articles about how to establish rules successfully.
- **TeacherVision (www.teachervision.fen.com).** Use "classroom management" as a search term to find dozens of articles and other useful resources.
- **Teaching Channel (www.teachingchannel.org).** Again, use "classroom management" as a search term to find dozens of videos to help you make sound management decisions.

Questions to Discuss with Colleagues

Sharing ideas with colleagues is a helpful way to devise solutions to some of the problems that you must manage successfully at school. Here you will find several topics to open discussions with colleagues about successful instructional practices:

1. You have carefully planned rules and you want to enforce them, yet you are not sure when to be lenient and when to be strict. How can you determine the best course of action to take when enforcing class rules?

2. A couple of teachers at your school seem to abide by their own rules instead of the ones for the entire school. This has created problems for you and your students as you enforce school rules. How can you handle this tactfully and effectively?

3. One of your students repeatedly breaks a classroom rule. The consequences that you have in place are not effective. What should you do?

4. Some of the policies at your school are outdated and not effective any longer. How can you change these policies?

5. What procedures do your colleagues have in place that you think would be effective in your classroom? How can you share ideas about these procedures and how to implement them?

Topics to Discuss with a Mentor

Although the topics that new teachers need to discuss with a mentor vary from teacher to teacher and from school to school, there are some that most first-year teachers should be comfortable discussing with a mentor or a trusted colleague. You should ask your mentor about these topics from this section:

- Suggestions for the rules that would be appropriate for your class
- Advice about how to create different classroom procedures
- How to create appropriate consequences for your students
- Where to learn more about district and school policies that affect you and your students
- How to create student ownership of classroom policies, procedures, and rules

Reflection Questions to Guide Your Thinking

1. What policies do you anticipate needing for your class that are not on the list given earlier in this section? How can you plan for them?

2. What other types of procedures besides the ones in this section would be beneficial to your students? How can you plan for them?

3. What can you do to enforce your classroom rules in such a way that the disruption caused by the rule breakers is minimized? How can you help those students refrain from repeating their errors?

4. What classroom management systems do you currently have in place that are effective? What makes them effective? What can you add to your other classroom management systems to increase their effectiveness?

5. What classroom management techniques have you observed in other classrooms that you would like to try in your own class? How easily could they be adapted to meet the needs of your students?

SECTION TWELVE

Prevent or Minimize Discipline Problems

An out-of-control classroom is every teacher's nightmare. We all dread the thought of having to cope with such disagreeable issues as disrespect, defiance, or work refusal. In fact, discipline problems are often cited as a major source of the stress that many teachers at all levels of experience feel regarding their work. Fortunately, even as an inexperienced teacher, there is a great deal that you can do to avoid the angst of a classroom filled with uncooperative students who seem determined to make your life miserable.

The discipline climate in any classroom is the result of many factors, both positive and negative. As a classroom leader, it is your responsibility to increase the preponderance of positive factors and to reduce the negatives. In addition to such factors as teacher leadership, supportive relationships, and the framework of policies, procedures, and rules discussed earlier in this book, there are specific proactive strategies that you can incorporate into the discipline plan that you have in place for your class.

In this section, you will learn about the strategies and attitudes that can make it easier to prevent or minimize discipline problems. With a proactive approach to discipline problems, you will be able to create the discipline climate that you want for your students. You will feel more confident about how to manage your classroom so that the real business of your class—student achievement—can take place.

Before you begin learning about how to prevent or minimize the discipline problems in your classroom, you can use Teacher Worksheet 12.1 to reflect on how well you are already managing this part of your professional responsibilities and to make informed decisions about the plans you have for creating an optimum discipline climate in your classroom.

TEACHER WORKSHEET 12.1

How Proactive Are You Currently?

As you begin thinking about how you can minimize the negative impacts of behavior problems in your classroom, reflect on your current discipline management approach. Are you doing everything you can to be the proactive teacher you need to be?

Read each of these positive management practices and grade yourself on each one. Use a traditional letter scale: A = excellent, B = very good, C = average, D = needs improvement, and F = failing. If you do not have an A or a B, then that practice is something that you should consider adopting.

1. _____ I consistently enforce school rules.
2. _____ I have a set of positively stated rules posted in my classroom.
3. _____ I use a friendly but firm voice when I ask students to do something.
4. _____ I use nonverbal interventions to keep misbehavior manageable.
5. _____ I have established my authority as a classroom leader through the calm expectation of cooperation.
6. _____ I have established reasonable and appropriate consequences for different types of misbehavior.
7. _____ I have taught my students the routines, procedures, rules, and consequences that will make class run smoothly.
8. _____ I make sure to build relevance and interest into every lesson.
9. _____ I consistently enforce my classroom rules.
10. _____ I make sure that all my students know that I care about them.
11. _____ I make sure that my students perceive that my actions are fair.
12. _____ I involve students in discussions and decisions about discipline matters when appropriate.
13. _____ I contact students' parents or guardians to keep problems manageable.
14. _____ I praise my students more than I criticize them.
15. _____ I monitor my students consistently.
16. _____ I am intentionally proactive in my approach to discipline issues.
17. _____ I respect the dignity of all my students.
18. _____ I cultivate a sense of community to leverage the positive power of peer pressure.
19. _____ When I intervene in a behavior issue, my action is deliberate and carefully planned.
20. _____ I accept responsibility for what happens in my class.

From *The First-Year Teacher's Survival Guide, 4th Edition*, by Julia G. Thompson. Copyright © 2018 by John Wiley & Sons, Inc. Reproduced by permission.

It's Up to You

Neighborhood problems, poor parenting, previous teachers, lack of basic skills—it's easy to blame others when things go wrong in class. After all, you have only a limited amount of time with students each day, and one person probably can't make an impact when there are so many negative influences. If this were true, then how do so many teachers create orderly and productive classrooms? How are so many teachers successful at motivating students to achieve both academic and behavior success? You can do this. You can prevent or minimize the discipline issues that will arise in your classroom.

As a classroom teacher, the responsibility for preventing discipline problems lies with you. Fortunately, preventing or minimizing discipline problems is an easier task than having to cope with serious problems once they have occurred. Teachers with smoothly running classrooms are teachers who assume that they can make a difference in the lives of their students and then thoughtfully set about doing so.

Teachers who take the time to reflect on how they can prevent or minimize discipline problems tend to be more successful than teachers who just react blindly when problems happen. If you find that a discipline problem is beginning to occur in your classroom, a deliberate and systematic approach will make it easier for you to either prevent or minimize it.

> Classroom discipline starts with you. Your manner, your poise, your assurance. Your voice is calm, well moderated, evenly paced, and easily heard. Nothing shakes your calm. You know what is acceptable in your classroom, and you communicate that to your students.
>
> *Anna Aslin Cohen, 40 years' experience*

Your Goal: Instruction without Interruption

Because it's easy be anxious about how you will successfully create the discipline climate that you want for your students, the true goal of those efforts can be obscured. Classroom management for the sake of classroom management alone should not be the result of your effort. Instead, as you work to create an orderly environment by preventing or minimizing discipline problems, keep in mind that your real goal is to be able to teach without interruption. Being able to teach a class without having to stop the flow of instruction to deal with disruptive behavior should be the goal of every discipline strategy that you decide to use. Although cooperative behavior is necessary, try to keep in mind that it is only a means to achieve a much bigger purpose: student learning, student success, and student achievement.

Establish Your Authority with the Calm Assumption of Cooperation

A teacher's anxiety and uncertainty transmit themselves in many subtle ways—none of them conducive to creating a positive discipline climate. Even if you are so anxious that you can feel your knees knocking together, your students still need you to lead them.

Allowing your personal anxiety and lack of confidence to be obvious to your students will only create havoc.

Instead, adopt and then project the proactive stance that you are certain that your students will cooperate. Calmly relay this expectation through body language and tone of voice. Assume a general air of confidence in their willingness to follow your guidance, and your students will respond in a positive way. If you allow your apprehension about how to manage your class to be obvious, then your students will undoubtedly set about testing every boundary for acceptable behavior in your classroom.

A firm voice. A friendly smile. A confident posture. A lot of praise and encouragement. A matter-of-fact tone. These will allow you to deliberately project that calm expectation of cooperation—and ultimately, of success—that can minimize or prevent discipline problems.

Be Aware of the Causes of Most Discipline Problems

If you are to adopt a proactive approach to minimizing behavior problems, then it is important to look at the big picture to understand what's causing them. Even the biggest troublemaker in your class does not always come to school with the sole intention of making your life unhappy and impeding the learning of all his or her classmates. Students are complex beings with complex reasons for acting the way they do.

Your students' misbehavior can become easier to manage once you are aware of the underlying causes and can deal with those causes instead of just reacting to the misbehavior itself. Here are some of the reasons why students may misbehave in class:

- Their work is too difficult, too easy, or just not an appropriate match for their learning style preferences.
- They perceive their teacher as uncaring.
- They perceive their classmates as uncaring and difficult to get along with.
- They are distracted by someone sitting near them.
- They see no connection between school and a successful future.
- They live in a culture with different values from the values of the school.
- They have not learned such social skills as classroom courtesy.
- They don't have the resources they need, such as a computer or school supplies.
- They lack the basic skills to do their work and need special help.
- Their peers mock them for any school success.
- They don't know how to manage their time, materials, or workload.
- No one at home stresses that they need to do well in school.

Easily Avoidable Mistakes Many Teachers Make

To prevent or minimize discipline issues in your class, it's important to avoid some of the mistakes that are all too easy to make. Often new teachers are not always sure about the best course of action to take when confronted with a discipline issue. Although new teachers are not fully expected to know everything about how to manage a class, there are some mistakes that no teacher should make. Even if you don't know which disciplinary techniques will be effective in every situation, you should avoid these harmful mistakes:

- Commanding students to comply with your directives
- Accepting too many excuses or being a pushover
- Making bargains with students to coerce them into obedience
- Making fun of students' culture, neighborhood, home life, or friends
- Allowing students to harass one another
- Blaming the entire class for misbehavior
- Holding grudges
- Allowing small problems to become large ones
- Raising your voice
- Being sarcastic
- Embarrassing students
- Being a poor role model
- Assigning work as punishment
- Nagging students
- Being confrontational
- Ignoring serious misbehavior
- Losing your temper
- Allowing students to sleep in class

> If you lose your cool and have handled a situation badly, make sure to own up to it with the student or students. Explain that you are still upset with their behaviors or actions but that your reaction was not appropriate. This can help them to see you as a human being as well and to respect you even more. Also try as hard as you can to not yell. No one listens or is open to growth when they are being yelled at.
>
> *Shelly Sambiase, 8 years' experience*

Three Crucial Teacher Traits That Make a Difference

Positivity. Consistency. Fairness. These three traits are the hallmarks of successful teachers. Without all three of them working in unison, you will find it difficult to prevent or minimize discipline problems. Once students begin to perceive that you are positive, consistent, and fair, however, you will notice that they will stop testing the limits of what is acceptable (and your patience) to work cooperatively with you.

These crucial traits will make it easier for students to trust you and to be confident that you are the kind of classroom leader they need. If you focus on improving the way you portray these three teacher traits, you will soon see the positive results in your classroom.

BE POSITIVE: NOTHING CREATES SUCCESS LIKE SUCCESS

Although it is very easy to have a positive relationship with those personable students who care about their work and who make it clear that they value their teachers, it is not always easy to have the same positive relationship with those students who struggle with even the most reasonable class requirements. Even though it may not be as effortless as the relationships you build with the more successful students in your class, it is even more important that you work to have a positive relationship with every student—especially those who need you most. Those students who find school difficult need even more positive interactions with their teachers than those students for whom school seems to come easily.

Often, we try to stop misbehavior with a flurry of negative commands and injunctions against behaviors that students find more natural than the more formal or productive ones we try to teach. Most students can recite dozens of things they know they should not do. If those same students are asked to tell what their five greatest strengths are, however, many would be at a loss. Although it would be wrong to unfairly praise or encourage students for behaviors that are not acceptable to their future success, the negative attitudes that many students carry to school are just as wrong.

Although it is natural that we should spend so much time in our profession dealing with the errors our students make or with the things they should not do, we do need to balance this negativity by focusing on our students' successes or strengths as well. The long-term rewards that accrue when we focus on our students' strengths are partly the result of a self-fulfilling prophecy. On the one hand, when our students believe they are capable, they are going to be brave enough to take that extra risk that will generate even more success.

Harshly critical comments, on the other hand, will destroy even the bravest student's confidence. There are many ways to begin to include a more positive focus on your students' strengths in your lessons. Here is a quick list of just some of the ways you can be more positive with your students:

- Pay your students sincere compliments whenever you can.
- Use positive body language to convey your respect and sincerity when you talk with students. Make eye contact. Pat a shoulder or a hand when appropriate. Make sure your expression is pleasant.
- Ask students to share a hidden talent or skill with you.
- Be generous with sincere praise. Students who are aware of what they are doing correctly tend to repeat it.
- Open class by having students tell what they did well on their homework assignments.
- Ask students to tell others what they did right on a difficult assignment so that everyone can benefit.
- When students go over returned papers, have them list the things they did right as well as correct their errors.
- An easy way to make sure all students have the extra help they need is to have student experts share their expertise with others.
- Ask students for their advice or opinions. Students often have important insights and solutions to problems that surprise many adults, even those who know them well.

- Classes seem to take on a personality of their own. Use this to your advantage when you can. For example, if a class is very talkative, turn this into a strong point by giving them lots of opportunity for debate and discussion.

- One of the easiest ways to increase positive behaviors and decrease negative ones is to chart your students' success so that it is a visible reminder to all. When your students see a graphic representation of their positive behaviors, they will understand that good behavior is recognized and appreciated. Use your computer to make and then post a pie chart, a bar graph, or another type of chart to record your class's positive behaviors.

- Be specific and sincere in your praise so that students know what they did correctly.

- Keep the focus of your praise on how positive behaviors will make it easier for everyone to achieve academically. This is a subtle way to remind students that their purpose is to learn and not just to comply with rules.

- Use exit slips to periodically ask your students what they did right during class. How did it make them feel? What did they gain from this good behavior? How did everyone benefit?

BE CONSISTENT: MAKE YOUR STUDENTS COMFORTABLE

As a teacher, you will have to make hundreds of decisions every day. Not only will you have to make many of these decisions quickly but also you will have to make them in front of a crowd of students—all of whom have different needs. You will never have enough time to think through many of the decisions, so you will have to think fast.

The number of quick decisions required of you sometimes makes it difficult to be consistent. However, consistency is one of the most important tools you have in minimizing problems because it gives your students well-defined boundaries for their behavior. Consistent classroom management provides a predictable environment with established rules and consequences. Being consistent will make your students comfortable in class.

Although consistency is crucial to the successful prevention or minimization of discipline problems, it is one of the most difficult skills to develop. You may find it challenging to be consistent if you believe that the consequences of breaking a rule are too harsh, if you believe that overlooking an infraction "just this once" will be acceptable, if the infraction occurs at an inconvenient time or place, or if you have different expectations for students whom you perceive to be less able than others.

If you want to become more consistent in the way you manage your class, there are some easy techniques that can help you get started. Here are several suggestions to create the consistent environment you want for your students:

- Enforce your class rules for all students every day.

- Be a prepared and organized teacher so that you will find it easier to make those tough, quick decisions each day.

- Expect the same high standards for behavior and academic performance from every student.

- Intervene early when students are having problems so that issues remain manageable.

- Teach and reteach the rules and procedures you have established for the smooth operation of your class.

Consistency is really important; you cannot have students wondering what the expectations in class are. Having said that, life isn't just black and white; there's an awful lot of gray out there. Some students may need a little more time, some students are going to have to see that note sheet you had everyone fill out with some answers already filled in. We can bend our rules and expectations in a lot of situations to allow students to get what they need. If a student struggles with writing, the wheels won't come off if we ask him or her for two really strong paragraphs instead of the four we assigned. The hope is to build them to the full assignment down the road. Don't be too rigid.

Kevin Healy, 11 years' experience

- Do not make idle threats. Mean what you say when you talk with your students about their behavior. Expect the same high standards for behavior and academic performance from every student.

BE FAIR: ENGENDER STUDENT COOPERATION

One of the surest ways to create discipline problems is to treat your students unfairly. Even very young students are quick to notice actions that they perceive as unfair and to react accordingly. Conversely, being regarded as a teacher who treats everyone with fairness will minimize many unpleasant discipline issues. Students will be more willing to cooperate with you and with one another if they feel that you regard them as worthy individuals with a right to be treated well. Here are some tips on how to make sure that your students will regard you as a teacher who is fair to everyone in the class:

- Allow students to explain themselves when it seems appropriate. Although you don't want to be a pushover for flimsy excuses, you do want to make it easy for students to talk to you when they experience problems.

- Keep in mind that fair does not mean equal. No students are alike, so they should not all be treated alike.

- Don't play favorites. This is one of the fastest ways to ruin relationships with students.

- Don't give your students unpleasant surprises. Announce tests and quizzes in advance. Publish homework assignments and due dates in various ways so that all students know what is expected of them.

- Make your high expectations clear and make success attainable. Give students examples, models, and samples so that they know what to do to be successful.

- Make sure that the amount of classwork and homework you assign is reasonable. When you divide the work into smaller, manageable chunks, students will not be overwhelmed. You can also work with the other teachers to make sure that your expectations align with the expectations for your grade level or content area.

- Expect your students to observe the same rules as the rest of the students in your school in addition to the classroom rules that you have established.

- Have the same high expectations for academic and behavioral success for all your students.

- When you make a mistake, admit it. Be honest with your students.

- Listen to your students. Teachers who take the time to listen carefully get to know their students well. Once that vital connection is made, students will find it easier to behave in an acceptable manner because they will feel connected to you and to the class.

If You Want to Receive Respect, Show Your Students That You Respect Them

No matter how interesting the subject, how dynamic the instruction, or how well planned the procedures, if we do not have the respect of our students, we are poor teachers. Respect is one of those vital intangibles that is difficult to define. It's the constant delicate balance among the many roles we assume in our workday: disciplinarian, motivator, humorist, listener, adviser, evaluator, entertainer, guide, comforter, and role model.

Having your students' respect is one of the biggest assets any teacher can bring to school each day. When you have earned your students' respect, you will be able to prevent or minimize almost all the discipline problems that come your way.

How do teachers lose the respect of their students? There are lots of ways the unwary teacher can cause students to lose faith. Here are just a few of the more obvious mistakes that are all too easy to make:

- Losing your temper
- Refusing to admit when you make a mistake
- Treating students unfairly
- Assigning an insufficient amount of work
- Assigning work that is inappropriate or not challenging
- Treating students harshly
- Not knowing the material
- Being insensitive to students' needs
- Being emotionally unstable
- Not being a good adult role model

If these are the mistakes that are easy for teachers to make, how then can you earn your students' respect? The best way to ensure that you have earned your students' respect is to fulfill your roles as a teacher. You telegraph respect throughout the school day in the many small professional decisions that you make, such as returning graded papers promptly, being prepared for class, and treating all students with dignity.

There is no better substitute for improving the way you teach than to be self-critical. When teachers examine how they fulfill their classroom roles—assessing their own strengths and weaknesses—then they can work systematically to improve the areas where they are not as strong as they would like to be. This attitude will yield countless rewards for a long time. You treat students with respect when you take these actions:

- Have high expectations for all students' academic and behavioral success.
- Avoid backing students into corners; always allow them a way to avoid embarrassment.
- Help students develop effective work habits.
- Acknowledge complaints and allow students to voice their concerns.
- Make teaching school citizenship and social skills part of the daily fabric of your class.
- Use time-outs and other interventions that can help students compose themselves during a conflict.
- Provide predictable routines and procedures so that students can go about their work confident that they know what to do.
- Avoid power struggles, especially those in front of other students.
- Don't comment on a child's appearance.
- Never threaten a student in front of other students.
- Don't call attention to a child's status or family situation.
- Never insult a student in jest or allow others to do the same.
- Don't allow students to grade one another's work.
- Offer constructive feedback on papers instead of just marking errors.
- Encourage, encourage, encourage.

Withitness: An Attitude, a Skill, and a Necessity

Almost everyone has had at least one teacher who was able to write notes on the board and tell students in the back of the room to stop making faces at each other at the same time. Such teachers' expertise is an inspiration for us all. As amazing and inspiring as it may be, however, no one is born with the trait of *withitness*. Teachers with withitness are said to have eyes in the backs of their heads. But because they never turn their backs on the class, these extra eyes are never necessary.

Educational researcher Jacob Kounin first coined the term *withitness* in his 1977 book published by R. E. Krieger, *Discipline and Group Management in Classrooms*. What is withitness? Simply put, it means that a teacher knows what's going on in class all the time. This continual awareness allows a teacher to manage the competing demands of a classroom and still forestall misbehavior.

As a method of preventing classroom discipline problems, withitness is crucial. Teachers who are alert to what is happening in their classrooms are far more likely to be able to prevent or minimize problems; they are tuned in to all their students rather than checking e-mail or dealing with just one student while ignoring nearby students who may also be misbehaving.

They are also the teachers who have positive relationships with their students. Although positive relationships are valuable for a variety of reasons, these connections often allow a teacher to predict student behavior. Knowledge of students, constant vigilance, and the ability to imagine what could go wrong in classroom situations combine to proactively prevent or minimize misbehavior.

Teachers who have honed their withitness skills know that it's not enough just to actively supervise their students. What is important is that they make their vigilance obvious to their students in many subtle ways—a nod, a friendly smile, a puzzled frown, proximity. Letting students know that you are aware of their behavior often convinces them that misbehavior is just not worth the trouble.

Withitness is easy to master with just a bit of care and effort. Here are some simple tips for cultivating your own classroom withitness:

- Don't *ever* turn your back on a class. Not even once.
- Be alert to stealthy signs and signals among your students.
- Use student arrival time to pay attention to students' emotions. This will allow you to predict and diffuse such situations as a conflict between students, angry outbursts, or more-than-usual distractions.
- Use quiet reminders throughout instruction so that students know what is expected of them and will not misbehave because they are frustrated or bored.
- Be prepared to teach so that you can focus on student behavior as you deliver instruction.
- As quickly as you can, try to learn your students' strengths and weaknesses. This knowledge will make it easier for you to predict their behavior.
- Develop your personal multitasking skills. Teachers with the ability to overlap their attention find it easier to monitor classes. For example, teachers who take attendance with a quick glance around the room at the start of class while students are working on independent warm-up activities will experience fewer problems than those teachers who waste several minutes calling roll.
- Pace lessons so that the workflow can help you manage students. For example, have assignments ready for the early finishers instead of expecting them to just sit quietly with nothing to do while others finish.

- Arrange your classroom furniture so that you can see every student and be seen from every desk in the room.

- It's easy to be too optimistic about the success of an activity when planning instruction. Be aware of this tendency and predict the times in a lesson when more watchfulness could be necessary.

- Be sure to explain the expectations and procedures for each activity that may be new or unfamiliar to your students. This will make it easier to monitor behavior because it encourages more students to stay on task.

- Stay on your feet and monitor your students. Move around the room instead of sitting at your desk or standing in one spot for too long.

Use Teacher Worksheet 12.2 to assess your current level of withitness.

Assess Your Current Level of Withitness

Take a few minutes to reflect on your current level of withitness and to determine where you could improve. Rank yourself on a scale of 1 through 3 regarding how successful you are in practicing the following strategies, with 3 being as successful as possible. Any strategy for which you can't rank yourself as a 3 should be one that you continue to work to improve.

1. _____ I never turn my back on my students for even a few seconds.

2. _____ I take a proactive stance toward preventing or minimizing discipline problems.

3. _____ I trust my intuition. If something seems amiss among my students during class, it probably is.

4. _____ When conducting classroom conferences, I arrange desks so that I face the larger group and the smaller group members face me.

5. _____ I know my students very well. I am familiar with their strengths and weaknesses.

6. _____ I greet students at the door at the start of class to scan for potential problems.

7. _____ I am prepared for class so that I can focus on students.

8. _____ I work on my multitasking skills so that I can overlap my attention in class.

9. _____ I spend more time walking around the class monitoring than I spend sitting at my desk or in one place.

10. _____ I have arranged my classroom so that I can see all my students and be seen by all of them.

11. _____ When I need to talk privately with a student in the hallway, I keep the door open so that I can monitor the rest of the class.

12. _____ I don't allow groups of students to congregate around my desk. I go to them instead.

13. _____ I make a point of spreading out my attention instead of spending too much time with one or two students.

14. _____ I pace lessons so that they flow in a businesslike manner to keep every student engaged.

15. _____ As I work with one group of students, I make a point of trying to remain aware of what the rest of the class is doing.

How to Help the Whole Group Stay on Task While You Work with Small Groups

One of the most difficult classroom withitness skills to develop involves keeping the rest of the class on task while you work with an individual student or small group. This is difficult to manage because often as soon as students see that you are distracted for even a brief period, they will take advantage of the opportunity to misbehave.

What experienced teachers have learned, however, is that with diligence and just a bit of planning, even this difficult skill is one that can be perfected. To begin, try some of these easy suggestions:

- Take care to make your expectations for behavior during small conference time explicit. Spend time at the start of an activity explaining the procedures that you want all students to follow as they complete their assignments. Be sure to include information to help the students who finish their work earlier than the others. Modeling what to do and what not to do can help make expectations clear.

- As you make your lesson plans, the work you assign as you hold conferences should be work that students can complete without the need to interrupt you.

- Arrange for student experts to be available to help those students who need assistance or assurance that they are on the right track as they work. Consciously planning this will make it easier than if you try to include it on the spur of the moment.

- Set aside a place for students to post their questions to be answered later when you are free.

- Furniture arrangement is key. Set up your classroom so that you have a conference area that allows you to face the class: a group of desks in a front corner of the room is ideal. Be sure that your chair faces the class and that the students you are conferring with face you.

- Do not linger with the small group. Have a plan for the conference and stick to it.

- As you work with the small group, scan the room to monitor the other students. Gentle verbal reminders or praise for on-task behavior addressed to the entire group are often enough to keep everyone on task.

Monitoring Student Work Habits

As a teacher, one of the most important skills for you to develop is monitoring—actively overseeing your students from the moment they enter the room until they leave. Although there are many different activities that you could monitor in class, to minimize or prevent misbehavior, it is crucial that you focus on your students' work habits. By paying careful attention to students as they work, you will help them stay on task and be successful. Furthermore, any problems that might arise will stay small if you are actively working to facilitate instruction through continual attention to their progress and needs.

There are several more benefits that you and your students receive when you know exactly what each one is doing at any given moment. When you successfully monitor your students, you

- Create a positive class atmosphere
- Keep problems small
- Reinforce good behavior
- Keep students focused on learning
- Help students develop strong work habits
- Maintain a strong connection with every student

Although monitoring student work habits while they are with you in class is not complicated, it will require effort to become a habit. These suggestions will help you get started:

When You Make an Assignment

- When you assign work, take the time to model how you want students to complete it. Show examples of good work and examples of poorly done work.
- Have students estimate how long it should take to complete the assignment so that they have an idea of how to pace themselves.
- Ask students to share shortcuts or other bits of helpful advice about completing the assignment.

While Students Are Working

- After your students settle down to work, wait about two minutes before you start walking around to see what they are doing. Allow time for students to get started on the assignment and for problems to arise.
- If students are becoming distracted, stand near them for a minute or two. Standing near restless students will often be enough to get them to settle down and to focus on their work. If this does not work, then a quiet word, a glance, or a quick nod will usually suffice.
- Give all students a share of your attention. Many teachers tend to focus on only a few students. To determine how evenly you spread your attention, carry a copy of your class roster. When you speak with a student, place a mark next to the student's name. After doing this for a day or two, you will be aware of the unconscious patterns you follow and will be able to adjust your behavior.
- Try not to allow a large group of students to congregate around you while waiting for help. Instead, try asking students to put their names on the board so that you can see them in order. Or you could have them take a number from a stack of note cards that you have numbered.

> Do your best to get to know your students. Even if you have a tough kid, find *one* thing that you can discuss with the student about his or her life. Find it. It will make a difference in all aspects of your class.
>
> *Jessica Statz, 19 years' experience*

- Have students who have a question that others may also have to write it on the board so that you can address it for everyone.

- Try creating a checklist for your students to follow as they work. If they use the checklist, you will be able to determine their progress as you come by their desks. You can also ask students to show you each item on their checklists as they work through it.

- Ask students to write their names on the board when they have finished. This not only lets you know who is finished but also lets other students know which classmates can help them if you are busy.

- Be supportive by using one of these statements:

  - At this moment, what are you doing that's right?

  - How may I help you?

  - When I come by your desk, please show me _____.

Be Proactive: Three Helpful Activities While Monitoring

There are three specific activities to use while monitoring students that can make a difference in how well they stay on task: how to arrange for students to get help quickly, how to use your "Teacher Look" to its fullest advantage, and how to use brain breaks to keep students energized and on task. All three activities will allow you to use the time with your students productively and to be proactive in preventing or minimizing student misbehavior.

HOW STUDENTS CAN GET HELP QUICKLY

It's important to cut down on the possibility of frustration in any classroom because few students are quiet when they are frustrated. Instead, the problems can run from minor ones, such as heads down on their desks instead of working, to distracting classmates or even to disrespect and work refusal. Savvy teachers make it easy for students to self-monitor the types of help they need.

If you arrange signals to enable your students to indicate when they need help, you can prevent or minimize much of the off-task behavior that can happen when students do not know how to proceed. Signals can be as simple as colored strips of paper on a desk to something as elaborate as a small preprinted flag. To make it easier for your students to communicate with you and to get help quickly, consider some of these ideas:

- Allow students to ask their classmates questions about an assignment before they ask you. This is especially effective if students work in small groups or near study buddies.

- Offer students the opportunity to work on alternative assignments while waiting for your help. They can signal to you that they need assistance by working on the alternative assignments instead of the classwork.

- If the question is one that could be answered with a quick search of the Internet, prearrange a signal with students who can use their phones or other devices to find the answer.

- For each student, tape three note cards together to form a triangle or tent that can stand on a desk. On each side, place a signal that will let you know how a student is doing. A question mark could indicate that the student has a question, a smiling face could mean that the student has no questions, and a frowning face could mean that there is a serious problem.

- Have a supply of red, yellow, and green plastic cups or other similarly colored tokens available for students to use when they need assistance.

HOW TO USE THE TWENTY-FIRST-CENTURY "TEACHER LOOK"

Although you may have vivid memories of a teacher who was able to freeze an entire class into good behavior with just a semi-sinister scowl, there are problems with this technique. Do you really want to glare at students to coerce them into behavior? And does that really work nowadays?

Although a nasty glare may not be the best choice for your students, there are three variations on this nonverbal signal that can be very effective in preventing or minimizing student misbehavior.

- **Teacher Look One:** For slight misbehavior or misbehavior that is just starting, try this variation: Look directly at the offending student and arrange your expression into a look of mild surprise. Your expression should convey your disbelief that such a good student would even consider the behavior.

- **Teacher Look Two:** For more blatant, but still mild, misbehavior: Look directly at the offender and slightly frown. Add a subtle headshake and move close to the misbehaving student at the same time if you need to increase the intensity of this teacher look.

- **Teacher Look Three:** For flagrant misbehavior that can still be quelled nonverbally: Stand next to the student while continuing to speak to the rest of the class. Pause in midsentence and look directly at the offending student. Hold the pause just briefly. At this point, you should have eye contact with the student. If the student's demeanor indicates cooperation, resume teaching. If not, another intervention is required. (You'll find more about this later in this section.)

HOW TO USE BRAIN BREAKS TO KEEP STUDENTS FOCUSED

One of the quickest and most effective ways to prevent or minimize student misbehavior is to provide brain breaks. Brain breaks are brief activities that allow students to move around, engage with classmates, and return to work refreshed, energized, and better able to focus. Students of all ages should be given periodic brain breaks during class.

Because brain breaks allow students to work off excess energy and to focus on their work, they also serve to prevent or minimize the discipline problems that can disrupt a classroom when students are bored and restless. As a bonus, brain breaks can also be a fun time for you and your students where you will find that laughing together and sharing the silliness of a brain break can improve your relationship with students. Here are some things to consider as you plan the brain breaks in your classroom:

- Most experts agree that a brain break every hour is appropriate for students, no matter their grade levels.

- Many teachers keep a list of brain breaks handy so that the novelty of the break can add to the fun. To start your own list of brain break activities, just use "brain break" as a search term. Many educational websites and bloggers have extensive lists of possible activities.

- Another good source of brain break ideas is to ask students to suggest ones that they would enjoy.

- A brain break should be brief—no more than five minutes. Most experienced teachers would recommend breaks that are two to three minutes in duration so that students do not lose the momentum of their work.

- You may also consider having students lead the brain breaks in your class. This could be a rotating classroom job for students.

- You will soon find that your students will have favorite brain breaks. These can also be useful ways to connect with students.

- Older students may want to use the time to check messages or otherwise be on their cell phones. Although this is a pleasant activity, it is often hard to get students settled back on task quickly and so is not a suitable activity to use as a brain break.

Here are some of the more common brain breaks that could appeal to students of all ages:

- Set a timer and have students simply stand and stretch for two minutes.

- Toss out a soft ball or stuffed toy and have students toss it to one another. You can add depth to this by having students call out review facts as they toss.

- Play an up-tempo song. You can ask students to give you the name of a favorite early in the term to help you generate a playlist.

- Watch a funny or inspiring movie clip together.

- Have students walk around the room talking with classmates about three things they like and three things they dislike.

- Have students write their names or draw pictures in the air.

- Start a rhythmic clapping pattern for students to follow along.

- Project the lyrics to a favorite song and ask students to chant them together.
- Have students play the Rock, Paper, Scissors game.
- Students can practice deep-breathing exercises.
- Ask students to turn to a partner and slowly count to ten together.
- For older students, project a video from DoNothingfor2Mintutes (https://donothingfor2minutes.com).
- For younger students, play a brain break video from the free site GoNoodle (www.gonoodle.com).

Intervene Appropriately to Minimize Misbehavior

Like many other teachers, you may sometimes feel unsure about when you should intervene to prevent or cut short a possible problem. When and how you should act depends on the type of problem and its potential for disruption. Classroom discipline problems can usually be divided into two categories: nondisruptive behaviors and disruptive behaviors. Disruptive behaviors require direct interventions and redirection. (Suggestions for dealing with this type of behavior can be found in Section Thirteen.)

Nondisruptive behavior problems affect only the student with the problem and are much easier to manage. Daydreaming, sleeping, and poor work habits are common examples of nondisruptive behavior problems. Often, however, these behaviors can escalate into disruptive behaviors as students become frustrated or assume that they can get away with misbehavior.

Although it's not always possible to catch a misbehavior early enough to keep it in the nondisruptive stage, teachers who monitor their students carefully and who intervene while a problem is still contained to one student will find that it's not hard to keep problems small enough to be easily managed. Try these twenty interventions to prevent or end a nondisruptive behavior problem as soon as you see it starting:

1. Move closer to the student.
2. Remind the entire class to stay on task.
3. Praise the entire class for their good work habits.
4. Maintain eye contact.
5. Praise nearby students for their good work.
6. Ask the student to explain the directions to you.
7. Reassure the student that he or she is on task.
8. Help the student estimate how much longer a task will take.
9. Offer a high five or fist bump with a smile.
10. Point out the correct parts of the work that the student has completed.
11. Send the student to get a drink of water or to take a quick walk.
12. Have the student set a goal to have the work completed by an agreed-upon time.

13. Ask the student to tell you his or her plan for finishing the work.

14. Try the mildest form of the Teacher Look.

15. If appropriate, have the student work with a partner.

16. Praise the work the student has already completed.

17. Offer your help.

18. Gently remind the student of the class rule he or she is breaking.

19. Explain the directions in a different way.

20. Glance or smile at the student.

An Invaluable Tool: The Power of Positive Peer Pressure

One of the greatest tools to prevent or minimize discipline problems is the power inherent in peer pressure. No student, no matter how young or old, wants to look silly in front of classmates. Too often, when students misbehave, they do so because they are not connected to the group; they feel so unattached that they have nothing to lose by misbehaving.

Teachers can harness the human desire to perform well in the presence of peers by making each student feel that he or she is a valuable member of the class. To increase the feeling of belonging that you want for your students and to reduce the incidence of misbehavior, it's important to build a sense of trust among your students through supportive peer relationships. Once you have established the inclusive environment where students feel that they are part of a classroom community, they will be more inclined to behave well so that they can continue to belong.

Questions to Discuss with Colleagues

Sharing ideas with colleagues is a helpful way to devise solutions to some of the problems that you must manage successfully at school. Here you will find several topics to open discussions with colleagues about successful instructional practices:

1. You observe a pattern of misbehavior among your students day after day. How can you discover the reasons for your students' misbehavior? What can you do to prevent or minimize this poor behavior? How can you replace it with more positive behaviors?

2. A student has accused you of being unfair. Although you do not think that you have acted unfairly, the accusation is distressing. How can you handle this situation so that the potential for damaging relationships with students is minimized? Who can help you with this?

3. Which teachers in your school seem to have a highly developed sense of withitness? What can you learn from them to improve your own teaching practice?

4. Sometimes when students are working independently, you notice that too many of them are off task, even though you are monitoring as carefully as you can. What solutions can you generate to solve this problem?

5. What suggestions do your colleagues have for interventions that can prevent or minimize misbehaviors? Which techniques have already been successful for you and your students?

Topics to Discuss with a Mentor

Although the topics that new teachers need to discuss with a mentor vary from teacher to teacher and from school to school, there are some that most first-year teachers should be comfortable discussing with a mentor or a trusted colleague. You should ask your mentor about these topics from this section:

- Advice on how to monitor students as they work
- Suggestions about how to intervene when discipline problems are still small
- How to improve the way you monitor students as they work
- Suggestions for brain break ideas appropriate for your students
- How to increase the positive interactions you have with students

Reflection Questions to Guide Your Thinking

1. When do you find it difficult to be consistent in class? What has made you aware of this? How can you become more consistent in how you manage your classroom?

2. How can you convey the expectation that your students will cooperate with your requests, policies, and rules? What are you already doing to project this attitude? How can you improve?

3. It's tempting sometimes to blame others for the problems that students bring to class. How good are you at avoiding this tendency? How completely do you accept your responsibility for maintaining an orderly classroom? Are you satisfied with your attitude?

4. Do your students respect you? How can you determine this? What are your strengths in this area? How can you improve?

5. What mistakes have you made this term while trying to minimize or prevent discipline problems? What have you learned from these mistakes?

SECTION THIRTEEN

Handle Discipline Problems Effectively

Forgotten pencils, tardiness, excessive talking, defiance—the array of discipline problems that teachers face can be discouraging. Part of the difficulty with classroom management lies in the different types of behavior problems that teachers are expected to handle. Blatantly defiant students can disrupt learning but so can a forgotten pencil. One of the most significant challenges that all teachers face is knowing the right course of action to take when confronted with this wide-ranging assortment of discipline problems.

The behavior issues within your classroom are not the only source of the discipline problems you must manage. Many factors outside your classroom can have a negative effect on how well you handle discipline issues, too. Just a quick glance at the media aimed at young audiences reveals how negative much of what students are exposed to can be. Thousands of messages barrage your students, many of which teach them that opposition to authority is an admirable rite of passage.

Another negative influence on the disciplinary climate in your classroom is that not every parent or guardian will support the decisions you make. When you call a student's home to talk over a problem and find that parents or guardians are unable to help, you may understand why some of your students find it difficult to behave well in your class. Your school's climate may also contribute to classroom behavior problems. If students are permitted to misbehave in other areas of the school, it will be difficult for you to impose order in your classroom. Furthermore, in a chaotic climate, administrators and other teachers may be too overwhelmed to offer the support you need to manage your class effectively.

A final aspect of the disciplinary dilemma that you will have to manage successfully is your inexperience and the ways in which it may contribute to the mix of behavior issues in your classroom. For instance, one mistake that many new teachers make is being too lenient at first to win their students' affection; they soon find out that such permissiveness compounds behavior problems.

As a first-year teacher, however, you have an advantage that your more experienced colleagues may not. You have not had an opportunity to develop poor classroom management habits. Your fresh approach to managing your classroom will make it easier for you to handle discipline problems because the newness of each one will necessitate conscious and careful decisions. Every problem you encounter is an opportunity for you to develop the skills you need to handle discipline issues wisely.

Changing Approaches to Handling Classroom Discipline Problems

As you meet with your colleagues and conduct your own action research, you will have the opportunity to learn more about the exciting shifts regarding classroom management occurring in many schools. Decades of harsh and harmful discipline policies are now being reevaluated and replaced by more supportive philosophies. Thousands of school districts, realizing the ineffectiveness of unforgiving policies, are now adopting more compassionate approaches to classroom discipline problems. As a first-year teacher, you will play a significant part in this new movement in education. In the pages that follow, you will learn about how you can implement a wide variety of thoughtful and effective discipline practices that can help your students succeed.

Restorative Justice and Its Impact on Classrooms

In the last few years, the shift away from punitive and exclusionary school discipline practices, such as suspension and expulsion, has gained momentum as schools discover the effectiveness of creating classroom communities that encourage students who had previously struggled in school. This shift, *restorative justice,* is a philosophy about behavior issues that guides students to participate in positive, supportive, and inclusive interactions with one another.

Because restorative justice (also referred to as restorative practices) is a broad concept, school districts have been able to apply its principles of *inclusion, peer support, open communication, personal responsibility,* and *setting things right* to all grade levels and all classrooms regardless of the age and ability levels of the students involved. Here is a quick look at each of the principles that comprise restorative justice:

- Inclusion: In classrooms where teachers and students practice restorative justice, instead of the teacher being the sole authority figure in the room, students are also included in making decisions that affect the discipline climate. For example, if a student has been caught cheating on a test, the misbehaving student meets with peers and the teacher to discuss what happened and to decide how to correct the problem. Inclusion also refers to the idea that restorative practices do not bar students from school or from the group (except in extreme cases where student safety is at risk). Instead, students work together as a community to solve problems.

- Peer support: A key component of the movement is the idea that students are members of a supportive community composed of their classmates and teacher.

The sense of belonging inherent in this idea is one of the reasons that restorative justice is successful. Students working together to help one another in positive ways is a powerful way to prevent misbehavior.

- Open communication: Students meet in respectful discussion circles to share ideas and to discuss issues that affect all community members, such as how their behavior affects others or how to handle harmful misbehavior.

- Personal responsibility: Students who have misbehaved are supported by the group's open discussion of the situation and work to accept their role in creating the problem. This accountability allows the student who has misbehaved to learn from the mistake and to move forward.

- Setting things right: Once students acknowledge their responsibility for the harm they have caused by their misbehavior, they can then set things right. This can take different forms, such as an apology or other restitution plan decided upon by the restorative justice classroom community.

Here are a few hallmarks of this rapidly growing and highly influential movement that you should be familiar with:

- Teachers who use the restorative justice model in their classrooms find that students are no longer afraid to admit mistakes because of the support of their peers and because of their ability to make things right instead of just being punished.

- In the restorative justice model, mistakes are viewed as normal and to be expected. Misbehavior is also viewed as an opportunity for the offender to learn from the mistake and to grow.

- Although peer mediation has long been at least a small part of school counseling, restorative justice formalizes it and makes the supportive peer community a focus of the program.

- The shift to positive interactions with offending students instead of excluding them from class or from school is one that many educators find immensely powerful.

- The inclusion of students in the process of working out solutions to classroom problems leads to increased student ownership of the class discipline climate and a stronger classroom community.

It is very likely that as the restorative justice movement widens, you could be associated with a school that implements its practices. If that is the case, you will be able to learn more about it from your peers and from local training programs. To educate yourself further, you may want to explore these helpful websites:

- **Fairfax County Public Schools (www.fcps.edu/resources/student-safety-wellness/restorative-justice).** The tenth largest school district in the United States, the Fairfax County Public Schools website offers an extensive information packet.

- San Francisco Unified School District's Student, Family, and Community Support Department (www.healthiersf.org). At this site, use "restorative practices" as a search term to access a wide array of resources, as this school district uses restorative practices in its schools.
- Schott Foundation for Public Education (http://schottfoundation.org). Here you will find implementation strategies as well as many examples of restorative practices in schools. At the home page, again, use "restorative practices" as a search term.

> Be discreet and talk with students privately when there's a problem. When I am frustrated, I give us both time apart before I work through the situation. I need to be clearheaded and to focus on the behavior—the student's action—not the person.
>
> *Laura Moore, 18 years' experience*

An excellent book about restorative justice is *Better Than Carrots or Sticks: Restorative Practices for Positive Classroom Management* by Dominique Smith, Douglas Fisher, and Nancy Frey, published by the Association for Supervision and Curriculum Development in 2015.

The Big Picture: Be Positive and Not Punitive

Although attitudes and practices are changing, punishment is still used far too often in classroom after classroom by frustrated teachers who feel overwhelmed by discipline problems and who are continuing the practices they are accustomed to from their own school experiences. One factor driving this poor decision is the widespread belief that teachers who never punish students are too weak to lead their classrooms effectively.

The problem with punishment as a discipline tool is that although it does work, its effect is temporary compliance and not lasting change. Rising dropout rates and the increase in the number of at-risk students are only two indications that educators need to move away from discipline practices that are mainly punitive to take a more positive approach to classroom discipline.

Students must feel supported by their teachers. They need teachers who value them as individuals and as members of a classroom community. They need teachers who view them as capable of success—who see their possibilities as well as their mistakes.

Instead of punishment, be positive about your students and your ability to handle the discipline problems that will arise. An optimistic attitude about the inherent capacity of your students to achieve success is a much more powerful way to create the smoothly running classroom that you want for yourself and your students than a classroom controlled by out-of-date, negative, and ineffective discipline practices.

What Is Expected of You as a First-Year Teacher?

Although it is not always easy to determine just how permissive or how strict you should be, it's particularly difficult during your first year. Many new teachers make mistakes as they work to become skilled at managing their classes because they have not learned what their school community expects from them. Although expectations for student behavior can vary greatly, there are some common discipline practices that you will be expected to implement when enforcing discipline. As you work to create a safe and productive classroom climate, keep the following expectations in mind. All teachers are expected to

- Maintain an orderly learning climate where students feel a sense of community as they work toward academic achievement.
- Be proactive in preventing or minimizing as many behavior problems as possible to help students stay focused on learning instead of on misbehavior.
- Make thoughtful, informed decisions geared to help students move toward self-discipline.
- Work with students to resolve classroom problems and conflicts instead of merely punishing them.
- Establish, teach, and enforce reasonable class rules, including appropriate consequences for breaking them.
- Make student safety a priority. Never allow any activity that could endanger students.
- Handle most discipline problems on their own, but refer a student to an administrator when school guidelines require it.
- Use the least intrusive and most appropriate interventions and redirections when necessary.
- Respect the dignity of all students.
- Be familiar with the basic laws pertaining to schools, especially regarding their responsibilities, due process, and students' rights.
- Be proactive in seeking the most appropriate help in handling a discipline situation, whether that help is from a mentor, a student's parents or guardians, or another source.
- Maintain accurate discipline records and documentation throughout the year.

Understand Your Legal Responsibilities

As a new teacher, you may feel particularly vulnerable to becoming embroiled in legal problems at school because you are unsure of your responsibilities under the law. Almost all the legal policies involving teachers center on one tenet: teachers are obligated to take care of their students—to protect their safety and welfare at school. Because students don't always recognize danger, even when warned of hazardous situations, teachers have a duty to anticipate and prevent hazardous situations whenever possible.

What are your responsibilities? Use the guidelines in the list that follows to make sound decisions for your students and for yourself:

- Teachers should be familiar with basic school law to understand the laws, policies, and procedures governing their school conduct and duties toward students to reduce the risk of legal problems. An informative source is the sixth edition of *School Law and the Public Schools: A Practical Guide for Educational Leaders* by Nathan L. Essex, which was published in 2015 by Pearson as part of its Educational Leadership Series.

- Once you have learned the basics of school law, you are obligated to act accordingly. Ignorance of the law is not an excuse for allowing a student in your care to come to harm.

- The rules in your classroom must have a clear educational purpose and must be governed by common sense. The consequences of breaking a rule must be appropriate to the rule. You must publish class rules and the consequences for breaking them for your students and their parents or guardians.

- Teachers are obligated to make their students aware of the risks in activities. Whether the hazard is from running with scissors or operating equipment in a vocational class, students need to be taught how to avoid danger.

- In general, younger students need to be more closely supervised than older students.

- Teachers should never embarrass a student in front of his or her peers. Some of the most violent criminal events at schools in recent years have been carried out by students who were not successful academically or socially.

- You should actively monitor your class. If a student in the front of the classroom is seriously injured while you are in the back of the classroom checking your e-mail, you could be considered negligent, for example.

- If you have a student who is aggressive or hostile toward others and you ignore the problem, you have neglected to protect the students who may be assaulted. Be aware of potential problems, and if possible, seek administrative assistance before trouble can occur.

- A student's privacy is protected by law. Do not gossip about a student, post grades, or reveal confidential information. Be especially careful about what you transmit electronically or in writing. Keep confidential material in a secure area.

- A student's freedom of speech and expression is protected by law if that speech or expression does not disrupt the learning environment. For example, if you do not appreciate a student's fashion sense, you have no legal right to enforce your personal taste.

- If your students are required to submit a permission slip signed by a parent or guardian before attending a school activity, such as a field trip, that permission slip does not exonerate you from wrongdoing if a student is harmed. A permission slip is not a legal document that will protect you in court.

- You must supervise your students at all times. Special education students; young students; and those with impulsive, uncooperative, or unpredictable behavior usually require more intense supervision than others. The type of activity that students are engaging in also determines the level of supervision required. Students playing a rough-and-tumble game at recess require more direct supervision than a group of students reading in a quiet classroom. No matter how mature they are, never leave students unsupervised. Never.

- You should design activities with safety in mind. Consider the potential for danger to students when you design active classroom games, lab experiments, group activities, or competitive events that could quickly get out of control.

- It is not a sound practice to allow students to grade one another's final work. Although it may save you time, it is a practice that has been successfully challenged in court.

- If you suspect that a student is becoming involved in gang activity, you must report your suspicions to an administrator who will, in turn, report it to the local police. Do not attempt to confront suspected gang members on your own.

- If you suspect that a student is the victim of abuse, you are legally obligated to report it to the appropriate authorities in your school.

- You must be aware of the requirements and restrictions in a student's IEP or 504 Plan. You are bound by law to follow those requirements.

- The decision to search students' personal property is more complicated than it first appears. Don't take it upon yourself to search student book bags, cell phones, or lockers. Involve an administrator instead.

- Teachers are expected to know about their students' medical needs and behavior problems as well as any other special factors that could put them in harm's way. Take the time to go through students' permanent folders at the start of the term so that you have the knowledge to protect yourself and your students.

- If you have knowledge of student sexting, do not attempt to intervene yourself. Report the problem to an administrator immediately. Because underage sexting is considered child pornography, the administrator is obligated to report the matter to the police.

- Teachers are expected to observe copyright laws when making and distributing materials for their classrooms. A local resource for information about copyright laws in almost every school district is your school library. Librarians generally have up-to-date information about the latest copyright laws and can offer useful resources.

- Keep accurate records of parent or guardian conferences, interventions, student behaviors, and other pertinent information. It is especially important to document misbehavior. Use Teacher Worksheet 13.5 and Teacher Worksheet 6.1 to keep a record that you can refer to if you are asked to give information in court.

- Students have a right to due process, just as other citizens do. If you are not sure about what course of action to take when a problem arises, use your common sense first. If you are still not sure, call in a school official before you act in a way that might be in violation of a student's right to due process.

Due Process Procedures

School disciplinary situations can damage the careers of teachers who are not aware of their own legal rights and the rights of their students. Although by far most of the discipline issues that you will have to handle will be minor, some of the more serious ones, such as possession of illegal substances or fighting, will require you to act decisively. When you do, it is important to keep in mind that one of the most significant rights of students involved in a disciplinary action is the right to due process. Here is a very brief explanation of the conditions for due process:

- School and classroom rules must be reasonable.
- Students must be notified of school and classroom rules and policies.
- When a student misbehaves, he or she must be made aware of the specific charge.
- Students have a right to legal counsel.
- There must be a full investigation.
- There must be documentation of the incident and the investigation.
- The disciplinary action must be fair.
- The student must have an opportunity to file a grievance.
- The student has a right to a hearing.
- The student has the right to appeal the disciplinary action.

How to Handle Discipline Problems if Your School Climate Is Not Positive

Despite the best intentions of providing a positive, productive classroom environment for every student, when the schoolwide climate is negative, teachers struggle to teach and students struggle to succeed. Contrary to what many people may believe, schools with a negative environment are not confined to the inner city or to impoverished rural areas. Any school can have a negative climate.

Although there are many influences that can have a negative bearing on the climate of a school, there are some that are obvious: an unsafe location, a history of low academic success, a strong gang presence, a physical plant that needs cleaning and repair, a lack of effective procedures and policies, and a lack of administrative support for teachers.

Unfortunately, schools with a negative climate are easy to identify. At these schools, students tend to

- Focus on other activities instead of on academics
- Report that they do not feel safe
- Experience little academic success

- Have poor attendance
- Experience problems with their peers as well as with their teachers
- See very little purpose for an education
- Flaunt school rules
- Experience class disruptions due to violence and threats of violence
- Have a high percentage of discipline referrals

If you teach in a school where the environment is not always constructive, there is a great deal that you can do to make a positive difference in the lives of your students. More than other teachers, the effectual educators in a school where the environment is not positive tend to direct their students toward the future. They help students establish goals and develop skills that will lead to a productive and happy life ahead.

To manage this, though, your attitude should be one of realistic optimism. Teachers who are effective in schools with negative climates are not unmindful of the daily challenges that they and their students face. Instead, they acknowledge their problems and then find ways to solve or at least manage them so that students can be successful.

Along with a sense of realistic optimism, successful teachers in a school where the climate is not positive tend to acknowledge the big picture of the school and not just focus on the problem areas. This perspective will allow you to acknowledge the problems you encounter at school and then move forward to help students find success.

Finally, these teachers also tend to believe that change is possible and that they are the agents of that change. With this attitude firmly in place, teachers have been known to inspire entire classes to reach unprecedented success.

With a positive attitude, you will have a much greater chance of successfully managing your daily challenges than if you spend your days bemoaning your school's problems. In addition to these productive attitudes, there are several strategies that you can use to cope with the negative elements of your school's climate:

- Start small. Keep your classroom clean and organized so that students have an orderly place for learning.
- Focus on the positive elements in your school and work to strengthen them. Become a band booster, football team fan, or sponsor of a student club, for example.
- Work with your colleagues to support the development and uniform enforcement of schoolwide rules. A united front on such simple matters as enforcing school rules makes it easier to tackle more complicated issues later because the background work for developing a team is already in place.
- Make sure that all students are aware of school rules, policies, and procedures, along with the positive and negative consequences attached to each.
- No matter what happens in the rest of the school, your classroom should be a place where students are expected to be courteous, respectful, and focused on learning. Don't give in to students who think that bad behavior should be acceptable in your classroom.

- Be realistic about what you can achieve. Although you may not be able to change the total environment of your school quickly, even small changes are worthwhile. Move forward with reasonable, achievable goals.

Focus on These Priorities

Because there are so many aspects of classroom discipline, it's wise to focus your efforts on a few priorities that can make it easier for you to handle the discipline problems that can arise. Here are ten to consider:

- **Priority One:** You have the right to teach and your students have the right to learn. No one has the right to disrupt that process. Make behavior decisions based on the idea that it is student learning that is the goal and not just good behavior for the sake of good behavior.

- **Priority Two:** Use timely and appropriate strategies geared to keep misbehavior as manageable and contained as possible. Keep it small and manageable.

- **Priority Three:** When dealing with a misbehavior, be sure to take the underlying reasons into account. For example, one student's momentary lapse in judgment is very different from another's deliberate flouting of a rule and should be dealt with accordingly.

- **Priority Four:** Accept that behavior problems in even the most meticulously managed classroom are inevitable. What is important is how effectively you handle them, not their presence.

- **Priority Five:** When you react to misbehavior, do so in such a way that you protect the misbehaving student's relationship to the rest of the classroom community. After all, how you treat each student affects how the rest of the students will regard you.

- **Priority Six:** Use the policies, procedures, and rules of your school as a guideline for your classroom. When you do this, the consistency will make it easier for students to comply with your expectations.

- **Priority Seven:** Keep your behavior problems in your classroom. Handle as much as you can without sending a student to the office. Don't hesitate to ask for advice, but assume responsibility for your classroom discipline yourself.

- **Priority Eight:** Be prepared. Have a plan for how you will react when misbehavior happens. Have class policies, procedures, and rules in place.

- **Priority Nine:** Work on your relationship with your students so that there is a sense of mutual purpose and trust. This will prevent many difficulties.

- **Priority Ten:** Manage your stress regarding the discipline issues in your classroom. Once you have done the best you can to manage a problem, mentally leave it at school. Keeping your work-life balance is crucial to your personal and professional satisfaction.

Helpful Attitudes for Your Discipline Anxieties

According to conventional wisdom, it isn't the problems we face that determine our successes or failures; it is our attitude about our problems that ultimately determines whether our teaching is a success or failure. Because discipline problems are inevitable, you will benefit from accepting them as challenges and not as stumbling blocks to success.

Problems move you forward when you choose to work to solve them. When you experience discipline problems, don't be discouraged; they stimulate you to use your creativity and talents to create a well-disciplined classroom.

Small attitude changes can also create substantial patterns of success. For example, many teachers claim that at least one of their classes is terrible. However, when they stop to look at the situation clearly, they do not have a terrible class. What they have is a class with many well-behaved students in it and just a few who are not.

It is necessary to take a positive approach to your students and to your teaching responsibilities if you want to make a difference in your students' lives. There are several significant actions you can take to communicate to your students your positive attitudes about their potential for success.

HAVE CONFIDENCE IN YOURSELF

You must have confidence in your own ability to reach your students. If you are to be successful in overcoming the barriers to a positive discipline climate, you must communicate your belief that your students can grow and change for the better. Few students will try to succeed without a confident teacher who believes in them.

SHOW YOUR STUDENTS THAT YOU CARE ABOUT THEM

Communicate your positive attitudes to your students to show them you care about their success or failure in your class. To do this you must develop a personal relationship with each one. You do this when you show you are interested in their opinions and concerned about their welfare.

PLAN LESSONS THAT ARE CHALLENGING BUT ATTAINABLE

Let your students know you have confidence in their power to succeed by designing lessons where success is attainable. When you plan a unit of study, begin with information that students can relate to previous learning so that they immediately feel confident about what they already know. As the unit progresses, the work should gradually become more difficult so that those students who may have been reluctant to try at first are willing to take a chance and do the challenging work necessary for learning.

CONDUCT YOURSELF PROFESSIONALLY

Present yourself to your students and colleagues as a professional educator. That means doing the things good teachers do—maintain order, be organized, teach innovative lessons, and provide your students with the adult role model they need.

ACCEPT RESPONSIBILITY

Take responsibility for your attitude about the discipline problems in your classroom. Let go of the negative thoughts you have about your students and about the past experiences you have had with them. Concentrate on the positive steps you can take to help your students become self-disciplined.

ADD TO YOUR KNOWLEDGE

Treat every day as an opportunity to add to your knowledge. Even your setbacks will teach you something about how to manage your class. As you get to know your colleagues, you will come to have a supportive network of people who are willing to help you. Each successful day will make it easier for your students to trust you and for you to learn more about them.

Cultivate Grace under Pressure

One of the worst mistakes you can make is to lose your temper in front of your students when you are upset. Giving in to the emotion of the moment will not only cause you stress and sway your good judgment but also may do irreparable harm to your relationship with your students.

Students whose teacher loses control may react in various negative ways. Your outbursts may frighten some students and intimidate others. Still other students will react to your anger by losing control themselves. If you raise your voice at a student, you should not be surprised if the student shouts at you in return.

Learning to control your emotions is not an easy task. If you have had a terrible time with one class, you often may not have enough time to recover from the experience before the next class begins. However, taking out your anger or frustrations on innocent students is wrong. Although your students need to see your human side, they do not need to be subjected to your ill temper. When you are tempted to lose your cool in front of your students, restrain yourself.

Learning the fine art of grace under pressure is not easy, but responding with grace is a powerful tool for any caring teacher. Here are several strategies that other teachers have found useful:

- Remember that losing control will only make the situation worse.
- Count to ten before you speak. While you are counting, make your face appear as calm as possible.

- Instead of shouting, lower your voice to a whisper.

- If there is a great deal of noise and commotion without a threat of violence, stand quietly and wait for it to subside. Shouting at your students to settle them down will only add to the noise.

- Talk to your colleagues to vent your frustration and to plan ways to manage discipline issues differently.

- Remember that you determine what happens in your class. If you lose control, you are not working to solve the problem. Channel your energy toward managing the situation in a positive way.

- Ask your students for help when you are upset. This will redirect their attention toward a productive contribution.

Great Advice: Don't Take It Personally

You are not alone if you tend to take your students' misbehavior personally. After a miserable day, negative student attitudes and behaviors can sometimes cause even veteran teachers to wonder why they bothered to get up, get dressed, and go to school.

If you were to discuss such a day with an experienced teacher, the chances are good that you would hear, "Don't take it personally." This is excellent advice, but it is one of the hardest things for new teachers to learn to do. However, if you are to thrive in your new profession, it is an attitude that you must embrace. Recall these pointers the next time you are tempted to take it personally when your students do not live up to your expectations:

- Students will not always behave well or say the right thing. After all, they are still children—even the seniors.

- Part of being a teacher is setting limits and establishing boundaries for your students. Although this is necessary, it isn't always easy to determine what is acceptable behavior and what is not.

- Teaching is a complicated task. During a typical school week, you will have to make dozens of decisions. Not all of them will be popular with your students.

- As the adult in the classroom, you must consider the needs of all students. When a student disagrees with a teacher, it is often because

Don't allow conflicts to escalate.

I remember a student who I thought was lackadaisical; she deemed me unapproachable (perhaps even a jerk). However, she's the one who had the courage to see me after school. What resulted was an hour-long conversation where we actually *listened* to each other.

What did I take from this? That we don't know what is going on in a student's life outside of school and that we shouldn't expect a student to have the coping skills of an adult who has had multiple life lessons to guide him or her into better decision making.

Michael A. Barrs, 32 years' experience

that student is only considering what he or she wants instead of what would be good for the group.

- Your students do not really know you. They see only one side of you—the teacher part. They react to that part, not to you as a person.

You Could Be Creating Some of the Problems in Your Class

Your inexperience will cause you to inadvertently make many mistakes, and sometimes the mistakes you make will create discipline problems. The good news about the mistakes you make in your classroom is that you have control over them. You can usually prevent them from happening again. In the following list of common teacher-made mistakes, you will find some of the reasons why you may have experienced discipline problems. With each mistake listed here you will also find a way to avoid making it into a discipline problem.

Mistake One: You refuse to answer or give a poor answer when students question you about why they should learn the material you want them to master.

Solution: As you begin a unit of study, be careful to provide students with the reasons they need to learn the material in the unit. Start each class with a review of the purpose for learning the information in the day's lesson. Also, make sure students are aware of the real-life applications for the learning you require of them.

Mistake Two: You present yourself in too tentative a fashion—too easily sidetracked, too unsure, too permissive.

Solution: Approach students with sincere courtesy and confidence. Set limits and take a positive approach to all students, and particularly the challenging ones, by preparing interesting lessons and attending to the classroom management concerns that will make your students more successful in school.

Mistake Three: You are too vague in giving directions to your students.

Solution: Be specific when telling students what they need to do. Instead of saying, "Don't be rude," a better choice is to say, "Please wait until I have finished before talking."

Mistake Four: You are unclear in the limits you set for your students, resulting in a constant testing of the boundaries and of your patience.

Solution: Be as specific as possible in setting limits when you establish your class rules and procedures. Students need to know and understand just what they should do and what will happen if they choose not to follow the directions you have for them.

Mistake Five: You give too many negative directions. This sets an unpleasant tone for your students.

Solution: Replace your negatives with positives. Instead of saying, "Don't play around," you will be more positive if you say, "Get started on your assignment now."

Mistake Six: You try to solve discipline problems without trying to determine the underlying causes.

Solution: Spend time trying to figure out what caused the problem to begin with. If you don't determine the root of the matter, you won't be successful in preventing it from reoccurring. You may also misread the situation and make a serious mistake in trying to solve it.

Mistake Seven: You react to a discipline problem by becoming angry and upset.

Solution: Instead of spending your energy in anger, take the time to examine the problem objectively before acting. Take a problem-solving approach to really deal with it.

Mistake Eight: You neglect to command attention by talking, even though students aren't listening.

Solution: Refuse to give directions or instruction until you have your students' attention. There are many techniques you can follow for commanding attention. Setting a timer, asking a leading question, holding up something unusual, and standing in the front of the room are just some of your choices.

Mistake Nine: You have lessons that are poorly paced. Students either have too much work to do and give up or they don't have enough work.

Solution: Think of your class time in fifteen-minute blocks, and schedule activities that can be completed in that time (or in a longer block with a brief break or change of pace) to keep students at their peak of learning.

Mistake Ten: You make mistakes in assigning punishment by doing so without proof or by blaming the wrong student.

Solution: Determine who did what before you act. Punishing unfairly will create long-lasting bad feelings among your students. This will take longer than rushing to act, but taking your time to assign blame is always a good idea.

Mistake Eleven: You are inconsistent in enforcing consequences. This will lead students to a steady testing of the limits of good and bad behaviors.

Solution: Establish the consequences of rule-breaking at the start of the term and then be as consistent as possible in enforcing the rules. Make sure the consequences are ones with which you will be comfortable in enforcing all term if you want to be consistent.

Mistake Twelve: You punish students for misbehavior while overlooking a more serious situation. For example, you reprimand a student for leaving a book bag in the aisle during a test but neglect to notice that others in the room are cheating.

Solution: Take care to assess a situation as completely as you can before acting. Never punish unless you are sure of what the problem is and who is to blame. Be aware that it is easy to overlook misbehavior if you are distracted.

Could What You Say Create Discipline Problems?

A teacher's words and how they are delivered have enormous power. Be careful to use a tone and language that will calm students and help them choose to behave better. It's not always easy to calmly convey the expectation of cooperation that you want from your students, but to choose otherwise is a mistake.

Your tone, particularly when there is a behavior problem, should remain pleasantly neutral and supportive. Avoid raising your voice. A teacher's soft voice has far more power than a shout.

When you want students to listen to you, move closer to them and lower your voice. Keep your tone neutral, pleasant, and supportive. Your voice should convey that you are confident of compliance. Be direct and clear about what you need for students to do.

It is also very easy to get caught up in the emotion of the moment and to say regrettable things with the power to wound. In the following list, you will find some comments or questions that many teachers tend to use when exasperated with their students. These comments and questions will not make any discipline situation better. Instead, they have the power to frustrate students and to result in an even worse disruption.

- I'll send you to the principal.
- If you don't get to work, you will fail.
- You don't want me to call your mom, do you?
- Who do you think you're talking to?
- How many times do I have to tell you . . . ?
- What am I going to do with you?
- You know better than that!
- Why would you do such a thing?

Are You Too Permissive?

It's not easy to find a balance between being too strict and too permissive when you are just beginning your career. Just how much should students get away with before intervention is needed? When it is okay to bend the rules? When is it necessary to be hard-nosed about a rule or procedure? Finding the balance in the way you interact with your students takes time, but making intentional decisions about that interaction is crucial. One of the most critical issues in earning student respect is the balance you must maintain between being too permissive and being too strict.

The best way to deal with the issue of permissiveness is to make yourself aware of the areas where you may be inclined to be permissive rather than sensible in your approach. If you are still not sure of the best course to take, ask yourself these questions:

- Is this behavior appropriate?
- What will happen if I choose to ignore this behavior?
- What will happen if I choose to deal with this behavior?
- What message about future behavior am I sending to my students in the way I handle this problem?

Teacher Worksheet 13.1 can help you determine how permissive you are.

TEACHER WORKSHEET 13.1

Are You Too Permissive?

Use the items in this checklist to determine the areas where you are too permissive and where you may be too strict. Select the letter of the response that is closest to your own discipline style and put it in the blank. After you have finished all ten choices, check what your responses reveal about how permissive or strict you tend to be.

1. _____ Students jokingly insult one another while waiting for class to begin.
    a. Ignore the horseplay. Class hasn't started yet.
    b. Remind students of the procedure for starting class and the class rule about showing respect for others.
    c. Tell students to stop and to get to work right away.

2. _____ A student is lost in a daydream instead of finishing a reading assignment.
    a. Tell the student that if he or she doesn't get to work, there will be more to do for homework.
    b. Stay at your desk and wait to see how long it takes the dreamer to get back to work.
    c. Move to stand near the student.

3. _____ Students take too long to get their papers arranged for a test.
    a. Remind them to hurry.
    b. Start the test and let the slow ones catch up.
    c. Tell them they have one minute to get ready and then time them by watching the clock.

4. _____ Students ball up papers and toss them at the wastebasket while you are giving directions about an assignment.
    a. Shake your head, frown, and move near them.
    b. Stop what you are saying and reprimand them.
    c. Finish your directions. Go to the students and quietly ask them about the class rule they violated.

5. _____ Students chat while you are explaining the homework assignment.
    a. Ignore it.
    b. Stop, give them your Teacher Look, and wait for them to pay attention.
    c. Tell them to stop talking and start paying attention.

(continued on next page)

(continued from previous page)

6. _____ A student lacks a textbook, pen, or paper.

   a. Share materials from the class storehouse if you have one set up.

   b. Don't allow the student to complete the work in class. He or she can do it at home. This will help all students remember to bring materials next time.

   c. Allow student to borrow from classmates.

7. _____ Students turn in very sloppy or inaccurate work.

   a. Refuse to take it until they redo it.

   b. Take it but give a lecture about work habits.

   c. Talk with students about the reason for the messiness and how to correct it.

8. _____ Students are tardy to class without a good reason.

   a. Enforce your rules regarding tardiness to class.

   b. Refuse to let them in without a pass.

   c. Meet them at the door and ask why they are tardy.

9. _____ Students talk back rudely when you have reprimanded them.

   a. Send them to the office.

   b. Reprimand them privately.

   c. Ignore it after giving them your Teacher Look.

10. _____ Students ignore you when you call for the class to quiet down to work.

   a. Keep asking until they listen to you.

   b. Raise your voice until no one can ignore you.

   c. Give the signal that they recognize as a sign that they need to get quiet.

What Your Responses Reveal about You

You might be *too permissive* if you chose these answers:

1. a
2. b
3. a
4. a
5. a
6. c
7. b
8. c
9. c
10. a

You might be *too strict* if you chose these answers:

1. c
2. a
3. b
4. b
5. c
6. b
7. a
8. b
9. a
10. b

Patience Is Key: There Is No Fast Track to a Good Discipline Climate

Discipline issues do not resolve themselves easily or quickly. Mistakes happen in a classroom. Discipline issues are inevitable. Successful teachers accept this and realize that there is no quick fix—no magic bullet—that can make students grow up any faster than they are capable. Students also do not develop in a steady, linear fashion. Instead, student progress has a mind of its own. Some days will be successful and others will not.

It takes time for students to rise to meet your high expectations. It takes time for them to learn to trust you enough to settle into the rhythm of school. It takes time for them to grow up enough to make the kind of progress that you want for them.

It's especially important to be patient with students at the start of the school year. As a rule of thumb, it takes about six weeks for students to adjust to school and to your expectations. It is also important to understand that the fragile success you have at six weeks tends to vanish as the winter holidays draw near. You will need extra patience then to manage student excitement as the holidays approach. This pattern will repeat itself throughout the year as holidays and special events come and go.

The key to maintaining your equilibrium throughout the school year is to develop patience and then more patience: patience with students, patience with your own skills, and patience with the discipline process.

Think before You Act

Whenever you must deal with a discipline problem, take care to understand the reason for the misbehavior before you act. If you make the effort to determine why your students act the way they do, you will benefit by having a clearer understanding of some of the times when your students are going to have trouble staying on task.

There are many ways to determine why your students act the way they do. Talk to teachers who have taught your students in the past or to parents or guardians. You can also check permanent records to find out more about each student's past, home situation, and abilities. To learn about students' behavior when you are facing a discipline problem, maintain a friendly and supportive relationship with students, listen to what they say, and solicit their input when appropriate. When you do make the effort to learn more about your students' behavior, several beneficial things will happen:

- Your students will feel less frustration because you will be allowing them to talk about their feelings.
- You will gain an understanding of what caused the problem.
- If there are causes other than what you first noticed, you will be able to act on them.
- You will gain insight into how your students think, feel, and react.
- You and your students will have a common ground for discussing other choices they can make in the future.

- You will probably have prevented this problem from recurring.
- Your bond with your students will be stronger because you will have shown them the courtesy of listening to and caring about what they had to say.

How to Investigate When a Problem Happens

In almost every instance, when a negative behavior incident occurs, determining what happened is a pretty straightforward process if you take a commonsense approach. First, be very low key. If you are clearly distressed or excited, students who may be afraid of getting into trouble are not going to volunteer useful information. You will only make a situation worse if you overact.

Don't be surprised if your students are reluctant to tell on one another. Reprisals of various kinds are something that many students fear. If you demand that an entire class tell you what happened, then it is unlikely that you will learn anything useful. A better technique is to ask students to jot down their versions of what happened and turn it in anonymously. Having every student do this and then drop it into a container as they exit the room ensures that their responses will be confidential.

Finally, even though a behavior incident may have disrupted your class, you should never hold students from attending their other classes. If an administrator is involved in the incident, then that person may choose to hold students, but you should not impose on your colleagues by detaining students.

Project a Calm and Confident Demeanor

When handling classroom misbehavior, it's important to convey to your students that you are in control of yourself and the situation, especially in the event of serious misbehavior. To do that, use your body language and your tone of voice, as well as the words you say, to project a calm and confident demeanor.

Stand tall. Hold your head up and shoulders back. Look directly at the class or the offending students and speak calmly and with authority. If necessary, move to the front of the room or closer to the problem to be heard. Give directions in simple sentences without lots of explanation. Be concise. If students sense that you are angry, upset, or uncertain, their misbehavior will undoubtedly worsen.

When students sense that you are calmly in control of the situation, they will stop testing boundaries and listen to you. They will look to you for guidance. They will be calmer. Be the self-assured role model they need in trying times, as well as in the more pleasant times in your class, and you will find it easier to handle misbehavior successfully.

Be Clear about the Behaviors You Should Not Accept

Before you can begin deciding how to manage discipline issues in your classroom, you should have a clear understanding of what the ideal classroom atmosphere should be. Well-disciplined classes share three important characteristics:

- The students and teacher know and understand the rules and procedures that guide the entire class.
- The focus is on learning and cooperative behavior.
- There is a persistent tone of mutual respect among students and between students and the teacher.

When you and your students are working toward establishing and maintaining a well-disciplined class, you should not have to tolerate behaviors that might destroy the fragile positive atmosphere you have established. Here are the most obvious behaviors that teachers and school districts across the nation have deemed unacceptable in any classroom:

- Threats and intimidation: Students are not allowed to threaten or harass one another or you. This prohibition means that no bullying, teasing, hate speech, sexual harassment, or threats of physical harm can be tolerated.
- Substance abuse: Almost every school now has a zero-tolerance policy regarding illegal substances at school. The school nurse or a designee should administer all medications; even such medications as cough drops are regulated under most zero-tolerance policies. It is against the law for students to have alcohol, tobacco, or illegal drugs on school property.
- Interference with others' right to learn: No student has the right to stop other students from learning. This policy is often the rationale behind school dress codes that prohibit students from distracting other students. It also keeps students from making noises loud enough to interfere with the normal routines of a school day and prohibits many other seriously disruptive actions.
- Disrespect for authority: This behavior includes refusal to comply with a reasonable request from a teacher, administrator, or other staff member. It also includes various forms of defiance, both overt and subtle—for example, talking back, sighing, sneering, and other rude behavior directed at an authority figure.
- Failure to complete work: Teachers should monitor student progress closely enough so that all parents or guardians are aware of the situation if a child refuses to complete work or fails to complete it for some other reason.
- Unsafe behavior: Behaviors considered unsafe range from running with scissors, engaging in horseplay, or running in the halls to ignoring safe driving rules in a high school parking lot. Policies to combat unsafe behavior also prohibit students from having matches or other fire starters at school, leaving school grounds without permission, or using school equipment in an unsafe manner.

- Dishonesty: Students should not forge notes from home, cheat on their work, commit plagiarism, or lie to teachers or other school officials. Teachers are required to report almost all incidents of dishonesty to parents or guardians as well as to administrators.

- Tardiness: Students are expected to be at school and in class on time. Tardiness to class is not acceptable and is part of the attendance policy in many states.

> Take the student aside and ask what is going on. You might be surprised that it has nothing to do with you or the class. Ask what you can do to make it better for the student. If you put the onus on the student, the situation usually improves. If it does not, get the parents or guardians involved.
>
> *Deborah McManaway, 23 years' experience*

- Truancy: Almost every state requires local school districts to enforce attendance policies. It is the responsibility of a classroom teacher to maintain accurate attendance records.

- Violence: School districts in all states take violence very seriously. Students are not allowed to fight or to encourage a fight by cheering on the combatants. Regulations against violence include the prohibition of weapons and weapon lookalikes at school.

Respond Instead of Just Reacting

Losing control of your emotions or relying on punishment to effect a change in your students' behavior will not solve discipline problems. What will stop students from misbehaving is a teacher who takes the stance that misbehavior is a problem with a solution.

As the adult in charge of the classroom, you have two choices when confronted with a discipline issue. You can choose to solve the problem with a calm and carefully planned response, or you can choose to vent your frustration and anger. Responding to solve the problem will move you and your students toward a solution; reacting emotionally will not.

Instead of just reacting to a problem, remember this: you have many constructive options when misbehavior happens. If you are to choose the most appropriate action to take, you will need to be aware of which options are likely to be most effective in each situation.

You can select from this list of effectual ways to respond when students misbehave so that you can make wise choices from among the many options you have:

- Consciously choose to ignore the misbehavior. This is an effective option if you plan how to use it, if the misbehavior is fleeting, and if other students are not seriously affected by it—for example, when a student daydreams briefly or gets a slow start on an assignment.

- Delay acting. It is appropriate to delay when the action you plan to take would cause further disruption. As an example, if a student is tardy to class, instead of stopping a presentation, you should delay speaking to that student until you can do so quietly so that other students are not disturbed by your correction.

- Use nonverbal actions. Nonverbal actions, such as physically moving closer to a student, making eye contact, or making inquiring facial expressions, are nonintrusive ways to address student misbehavior. This is often an appropriate choice for dealing with those students who seem to be momentarily off task or gazing out the window instead of working.

- Praise the entire class for its good behavior. Praising the entire group for its positive behavior will encourage those who are doing well to stay on task and will remind those who are not behaving well of what is expected.

- Give a quiet redirection. Giving a quiet verbal reprimand when a student misbehaves will usually end the trouble. Try to be positive instead of negative. "Please open your book and begin working now" will be more effective than a more negative command, such as "Stop playing around this instant."

- Confer briefly with students. In a brief conference, you can remind a student of the rule he or she has broken, redefine acceptable limits of behavior, encourage positive behavior, and discuss the positive and negative consequences of the student's actions.

- Hold a longer conference with students. Schedule a longer and more formal conference with a student when there are several issues to be resolved or when misbehavior is chronic or serious. The emphasis should be on determining the causes of misbehavior and deciding what needs to be done to resolve the problem. You can find more information about this later in this section.

- Contact parents or guardians. If you are having difficulty helping students control their behavior, ask the other adults in their lives to reinforce your efforts. Too often, teachers hesitate to do this or wait until misbehavior is serious. Early intervention in the form of a request for help is a good idea.

- Arrange a conference with parents or guardians. If a student persists in misbehaving and you have tried several interventions, such as phoning a parent or guardian, with no success, then you should schedule a conference with parents or guardians.

- Refer a student to an administrator. You must make this choice when you have exhausted all other possibilities or when the misbehavior is serious. There is more information about how to handle referrals to an administrator later in this section.

For more specific information about how and when to intervene to handle a behavior problem, you can use the chart in Teacher Worksheet 13.2.

TEACHER WORKSHEET 13.2

Behavior and Intervention Guidelines for Prevalent Classroom Misbehaviors

In this chart you will find some misbehaviors that every teacher needs to manage effectively as well as a suggested level of intervention for each one. Although different schools have different interventions for various behaviors, it is best to use the most unobtrusive intervention possible. You should also take care to follow your school's guidelines for handling specific misbehaviors. In this list, the suggested level of intervention applies to the first few incidents of the behavior only. Any small misbehavior can become a serious disruption if it occurs often, and the level of intervention should be increased to meet the seriousness of the disruption.

Behavior	Ignore the Problem	Briefly Delay Acting on the Problem	Intervene to Stop the Problem	Involve an Administrator and Other Adults
Daydreaming	X			
Lack of materials		X		
Chronic lack of materials			X	
Talking while the teacher is talking			X	
Off task and excessive talking			X	
Missing homework assignment		X		
Chronic missing homework assignments			X	
Lying to the teacher			X	
Stealing				X
Cheating on a test				X
Cheating on homework				X
Tardy to class			X	
Chronic tardiness			X	
Cell phone misuse in class			X	
Forged note				X
Lingering in the hallway		X		
Chronic requests to leave class			X	
Name-calling			X	
Intentional profanity directed at the teacher				X
Unintentional profanity			X	
Occasional messy work		X		
Chronically messy work			X	

(continued on next page)

(continued from previous page)

Behavior	Ignore the Problem	Briefly Delay Acting on the Problem	Intervene to Stop the Problem	Involve an Administrator and Other Adults
Getting ready for dismissal early		X		
Sleeping in class			X	
Head down on the desk instead of working or listening		X		
Talking back to the teacher			X	
Rolling eyes		X		
Horseplay			X	
Slow to settle to work			X	
Weapon possession				X
Inappropriate remark			X	
Unkind remark to a classmate			X	
Hate speech			X	
Inappropriate touching				X
Sexting				X
Refusal to work			X	
Refusal to cooperate with a group			X	
Off task while online			X	
Dress code violation		X		
Substance abuse				X
Insignificant vandalism			X	
Serious vandalism				X
Refusing to clean a work area			X	
Brief inattention	X			
Chronic inattention			X	
Ostentatiously acting bored	X			
Eating in class without permission			X	
Out of seat frequently			X	
Unusually loud comment	X			
Challenges and confronts the teacher				X
Challenges and confronts a classmate			X	
Attempting to harm or bully a classmate				X
Rushing though assignments		X		
Negative nonverbal reaction	X			
Talking but shushed by classmates	X			
Insulting or rude to classmates			X	

Take a Problem-Solving Approach

The first step in adopting a problem-solving approach to misbehavior is to develop a proactive attitude to manage your own reactions. Refuse to take student misbehavior personally, even though you may be hurt, frustrated, and angry. Refusing to give in to your first emotional reaction will deescalate the situation to a more manageable level and allow you to handle it in a productive way.

The following steps will help you not only solve problems but also prevent further ones. You will find that Teacher Worksheet 13.3 has space provided for you to write out your responses to each of the steps in the problem-solving process.

- **Step One:** Define the problem. Step back and be clear about what happened. Be specific. Instead of "My class comes back crazy after lunch," define it more clearly as "Fifteen students have trouble settling back to work for the first ten minutes after they return from lunch." Specifically defining the problem will give you the detailed information you need to make rational decisions.

- **Step Two:** Gather information about the cause of the problem from the students who misbehaved. Asking a large group to verbally tell you what happened can lead to chaos, finger-pointing, hurt feelings, and loss of instruction time. Instead, ask students to write out their version of events. At this point, take care to remain nonjudgmental.

- **Step Three:** Check to make sure that your students understand the pertinent rules, procedures, policies, and consequences. Once you have gathered information about the incident itself, take the time to review the rules, procedures, policies, and consequences that apply to the situation with the students involved. This will allow them time to consider the outcome of your response. It's not fair to surprise students with a decision that is not predicated on the expectations you have in place for the class.

- **Step Four:** Tell your students that you will need to take some time to decide. This is especially important if you are upset about the incident. You need time to think through the issue and to arrive at the best possible solution.

- **Step Five:** Generate as many solutions as you can. Take a few minutes to jot down a brainstormed list of the possible solutions to the problem. Try to generate as many as you can while also anticipating the pros and cons of each.

- **Step Six:** Ask an administrator, a team member, or a colleague for advice if you are not sure of the right course of action to take. It never hurts to ask for advice from someone whose judgment you trust. Discuss your brainstormed list. It should not take long to consult one or two people who can help you make the best decision.

- **Step Seven:** Decide on the action that will help keep students from repeating their misbehavior. After thoughtful consideration, choose the action that can provide the best option not only for dealing with current misbehavior but also for making it easier for students to remember what to do in the future.

- **Step Eight:** Decide how you will implement the solution. Remember that your goal is to continue to be able to teach without interruption. Having selected the best option for a solution, implement it in such a way that students can learn from their mistakes and grow from the experience. Take care that the implementation is as fair as the decision itself.

TEACHER WORKSHEET 13.3

Work through Classroom Problems

Use the step-by-step process in this worksheet to help clarify your thinking and guide your decision making as you work through the various problems that you may encounter at school.

Step One: What is the problem?

_____

_____

Step Two: According to the students involved, what appears to be the cause of the problem?

_____

_____

Step Three: Which rules, procedures, or policies apply to the situation?

_____

_____

Step Four: When should you talk with your students about the issue?

_____

_____

Step Five: What possible solutions can you suggest?

_____

_____

Step Six: What advice have you received from an administrator, a team member, or a colleague?

_____

_____

Step Seven: Which course of action will help students not repeat their misbehavior?

_____

_____

Step Eight: How will you implement the solution?

_____

_____

Enforce Your Classroom Rules

Classroom rules empower teachers who want their students to understand that they are serious about good behavior. By consistently enforcing classroom rules, you can prevent many serious discipline problems. When a student breaks a rule and you care enough to spend the time enforcing that rule, you send a powerful message not only to the rule breaker but also to every student in the class, thereby preventing many other infractions.

When a student breaks a class rule, calmly and quietly enforce the rule. Don't threaten, nag, or lose your temper. Instead, enforce the rule with this five-step procedure:

- **Step One:** Ask, "What rule have you broken?"
- **Step Two:** Help the student understand how the rule applies to this occasion.
- **Step Three:** Ask the student to explain the reasons for the rule.
- **Step Four:** Ask the student to tell you the consequences of breaking the rule.
- **Step Five:** Carry out the consequences you have for students who break that rule.

One fact in which you can take comfort is that frequently students will break a rule not from a desire to misbehave but from a momentary lapse in good judgment. By calmly enforcing your rules, you acknowledge that lapse and remind students not to repeat the offense. Here are a few more tips to help you successfully enforce your class rules:

- The first time students break a rule, talk privately with them to make sure they understand the rule and the consequences of breaking it.
- Before you rush to judgment, determine why your students broke the rule. Do they need more attention from you? Did they run out of meaningful work to do? Do you need to explain the rule again?
- Reward good behavior as often as you can. Rewarding students for behaving well will encourage them to continue positive behaviors.
- Accept that enforcing rules is part of your job as a teacher. Be patient. Your students are going to misbehave from time to time.
- Don't be a pushover. Although it may be tempting to make an exception to a rule, think carefully before you do so. You should balance the needs of all your students with the needs of the student who broke the rule.

If you find you are having trouble enforcing a rule, consider asking yourself these questions to see how to get back on track:

- Do all students understand this rule?
- Do students understand and accept the need for this rule? Can they see how it is necessary for the smooth running of the class?
- Has your enforcement of this rule been consistent, or have you sent a confusing message by allowing too many exceptions?

Redirection without Enacting Consequences

Your goal when redirecting students is to quickly and quietly help them get back on task without missing even a moment of instruction. Often all it takes is for you to move closer to the misbehaving student or to make eye contact to let the student know that you are aware of his or her behavior. When delivering simple redirections, to ensure that instruction is not interrupted, strive to be as unobtrusive and as pleasant and supportive as possible. When you notice students off task, try these suggestions:

- Use sticky notes to write reminders and put them on the desks of students who are off task.
- Set a timer and give everyone a two-minute break.
- Change the pace of the assignment.
- Ask students if they would like help from a classmate.
- Use your Teacher Look to remind students to keep working.
- Call home if several attempts to redirect are not successful.
- Remind students of their long- and short-term goals.
- Ask students to restate the directions.
- Ask students to estimate how long it will take to finish the assignment.
- Count "One, two, three," and wait for everyone to pay attention to your directions.
- Ask students who are struggling with an assignment if they need help.
- Move to stand near the students who are off task.
- Have students stand, stretch, and then return to work.
- Discreetly remove distractions.
- Ask students who are off task to sit near you.
- Pleasantly remind students of the behavior you would like to see.
- Sometimes the problem is not off-task behavior but noise. You can also establish signals such as these with your students to let them know that they need to moderate their noise level:
  - Flick the lights.
  - Fan them so that they "chill out."
  - Tell them to use a six-inch voice.
  - Ring a bell.
  - Wave your hands over your head.
  - Snap your fingers until students snap back.
  - Blow a whistle.
  - Play calming classical music.
  - Raise your hand until they raise theirs.

- Clap your hands until they clap with you.
- Clap twice until they clap three times.
- Stand near a noisy group.
- Give them a thumbs-up when they are quiet.
- Give them a thumbs-down when they are noisy.
- Shush the nearest group and have them pass it on.
- Place your finger over your lips and have them do the same.
- Hold up your hand in a *V* for volume sign.

Redirection Involving Consequences

Even though you may have done everything possible to prevent a discipline problem from occurring and then exhausted an array of subtle redirections without consequences, students will still make mistakes—many of which are age appropriate and to be expected. When this happens, it is necessary to enforce consequences as you redirect students to attend to their work and to the business of the class.

The purpose of consequences is not to punish but to help students remember the classroom rule, policy, or procedure that they should observe. Consequences should also help students understand that their misbehavior is detrimental to their classmates' ability to learn as well as to their own success. When delivering redirections with consequences, there are a few things to keep in mind:

- Because the purpose of a consequence is not punitive, the specific consequence should match the offense in a logical way so that students see the connection between it and their actions. For example, it would not make sense to have a student clean a work area if the offense was that the student said unkind things to a classmate. Instead, a more appropriate consequence would be for that student to apologize.

- The consequence should fit the severity of the misdeed. For example, being moved away permanently from a work group where the student is usually happy and productive is not necessary for minor off-task behavior. Being removed for the rest of class is more appropriate.

- Students should not be surprised that their behavior is not acceptable because of the previous work you have done to make sure that class expectations are clearly evident to all students.

- A redirection with consequences should be delivered in a quiet, calm voice. Ideally, you should be close enough to the student so that only you and the student are involved in the conversation.

- Even when a student has misbehaved, that student should be treated with respect.

- Never threaten a student, especially when enforcing a consequence. Simply enact the consequence.

- Deliver the consequence in a neutral tone. If you are angry or upset, students will focus more on your reaction rather than on the consequence.

- Briefly explain the reason for the consequence and how it will be enforced. For example, if a student has repeatedly refused to work despite your interventions, you could say, "This work needs to be completed for you to learn this material. Instead of going out to recess today, you need to stay in the room with me to finish it. If you need help, I will be here. If you finish it before recess is over, you may join your classmates."

- Avoid arguing or chatting with the misbehaving student when explaining the consequence. Be concise. Be serious. Stick to explaining the consequence and nothing else.

- Usually consequences fall into three broad categories. Here are those categories with some brief examples:
  - Students must make amends for behavior.
    - Apologize to an offended classmate
    - Repair or replace something broken
    - Redo messy work
    - Turn in missing assignments
  - Students must have a temporary time-out to gain self-control.
    - Move to another part of the classroom
    - Move to a nearby classroom where you have made prior arrangements with that teacher
    - Go to a counselor or other adviser
    - Step into the hall for a few moments and then return
  - Students must lose a privilege.
    - Not allowed to have free time to read or to use a computer
    - Must sit near the teacher
    - Must walk near the teacher if in the hall
    - Cell phones sent to the office

You Must Preserve Student Dignity When Redirecting

No matter how upset and frustrated you may feel when a student misbehaves, it is crucial that you preserve that student's dignity when you offer redirection. There are many valid reasons for this that will help you remain in control of your emotions when you work with misbehaving students.

If the purpose of a redirection is not only to contain a misbehavior but also to prevent it from happening again, embarrassing a student will not achieve that goal. Students who feel humiliated will not be able to think clearly because they will be overwhelmed by their emotions. They will not be able to listen or to focus on anything other than their own misery.

Teachers who embarrass a student in front of classmates will make those other classmates uneasy as they wonder who among them will be next. This will harm your relationship with the entire group because they will lose trust in you when they perceive your unpredictable behavior.

Embarrassing a student will also seriously harm your relationship with that student. Students who are prone to misbehavior are so used to being called out by adults that they tend to tune them out as just another annoying authority figure. Instead of a productive relationship, teachers who humiliate students find that they have created students who are more likely to misbehave because of the poor relationship.

Ignoring the need to preserve a student's dignity when redirecting will also harm that student's relationship with the rest of the class. The fragile threads of a classroom community are easily broken; embarrassing a student is a sure way to damage the relationship that student needs to feel connected with the group. Here are a few suggestions for what to do and what not to do when trying to preserve a student's dignity. To preserve a student's dignity, be careful *to*

- Take the student's concerns seriously
- Use a kind voice when talking with the student
- Be as patient and understanding as possible
- Try to be as fair as possible when delivering a reprimand
- Ask sufficient questions to be sure that you understand the incident
- Work to resolve problems and not just punish the student
- Assure the student that you believe that the misbehavior will not happen again
- Make every effort to see the entire child and to not be affected by a moment of bad judgment

To preserve a student's dignity, be careful *not* to

- Call a student a name, even in jest
- Compare one student to another
- Reprimand a student in front of the class if at all avoidable
- Allow a confrontation to build in front of others
- Ignore a student who needs your attention
- Raise your voice
- Be sarcastic or insulting in an attempt to have the student learn from a mistake

Finally, is embarrassing students the way you want to conduct your professional life? You did not become a teacher to harm children emotionally. Neglecting to preserve a student's dignity at the crucial moment of redirecting will certainly cause more harm than good.

How to Obtain Discipline Assistance When You Need It

Just as teachers are expected to work in collaboration with colleagues to solve curriculum issues, they are also expected to work together to solve discipline problems. Although you may feel overwhelmed at times, you are not alone.

It's not always easy to ask for help, especially with such an anxiety-producing topic as classroom management. Because you will certainly not be the first teacher at your school to need help with discipline issues, you will find that there are many supportive colleagues who will be willing to offer assistance if you just take the time to ask.

In fact, it is much better to ask for help and advice early when your classroom issues are easier to solve than if you wait until later in the term. Being proactive in the way you ask for help will indicate that you are aware of the problem and are willing to listen to advice. By seeking help, you portray yourself as a serious professional.

The first person you should talk to about discipline issues is your mentor, if you have been assigned one. If you do not have a mentor, then consult a colleague who appears to be competent at classroom management and who seems open to extending a helping hand. Be respectful of that person's time, but be honest about the problems you are experiencing and your willingness to solve them.

One of the most valuable ways to ask for help with the way you manage your classroom is to ask several teachers to make snapshot observations while you are teaching. (See Section One for more information about classroom observations.) If you are open-minded as you receive their suggestions, you will make it easier for your advisers to offer honest and helpful counsel.

How to Talk with Parents or Guardians about Behavior Problems

In a perfect world, your greatest allies in dealing with classroom management problems would be the parents or guardians of your students. However, this is not a perfect world, and not all parents or guardians are as helpful as you need them to be.

Even though some parents or guardians are not helpful, most will be if they perceive that you conduct yourself in a professional manner, maintain an orderly classroom where students feel valued and successful, and want the best for their children. The important positive relationship that you have carefully developed with the parents or guardians of your students will be put the test when there is a discipline issue serious enough to warrant a phone call home or a face-to-face meeting.

The positive and productive relationship that you want with the parents or guardians of your students can be maintained if you take the time to treat them with respect when a problem arises. Here are some suggestions for how you can demonstrate your respectful regard and still successfully handle the discipline problems that may arise in your classroom as you talk with parents or guardians about a discipline issue:

- Communicate early and often. Keep discipline issues small by asking for help early in the year.

- Make it clear that you like their child and that you want him or her to achieve both academic and behavioral success.

- Ask for their help. Make it clear that you want to work with them to help their child do well in school.

- Although you should say positive things about their child as a prelude to a conversation about a problem, it is wise to focus on the behavior at hand. Convey that the behavior is the problem and not their child.

- Be an active listener. Allow parents or guardians to explain their viewpoints, offer suggestions, and give you background information that can help you understand their child better.

- When you make a phone call, be sure to ask first if they have time to talk with you. If not, arrange a time that would be good for you both. Avoid trying to cram in a phone call home when you have only a few minutes.

- If you leave a message, be circumspect about what you say so that their privacy can be protected. Be especially guarded if you call parents or guardians at work so that they will not be embarrassed in front of their peers or, even worse, supervisors.

- It is always better to call instead of e-mail about a discipline problem.

- When you describe the details of an incident, be concise and factual. Stick to exactly what happened instead of generalizing about it. Be specific and precise about what you say.

- If other students were involved, try not to mention them by name if possible. Absolutely do not make negative comments about those students and their parents or guardians, even if the person you are speaking with does.

- If you are upset, wait until you have yourself under control before speaking with parents or guardians so that your purpose—solving the problem—will be evident instead of your emotions.

- If a parent or guardian becomes abusive, resist the urge to reply in kind. Instead, speak with an administrator as soon as possible to report the phone call. It is likely that the parent or guardian will also contact that administrator, so don't delay on this.

> If there is a tricky situation and a parent is not treating you with respect, do not hesitate to call in a supervisor. We have all been there. You need help navigating some of those tough situations. Don't be too proud to ask for that help. It will make it much easier in the long run.
>
> *Mary Landis, 22 years' experience*

How to Hold Successful Conferences with Students Who Have Misbehaved

Student conferences can be a powerful tool for teachers who want to establish a positive relationship with a student who has misbehaved. When the two of you sit down together to work out solutions to a problem, you will both benefit.

Holding a successful conference with a student who has misbehaved is not difficult. Use the strategies that follow to guarantee success by making it clear that you have thought about the student's concerns and how the two of you can work together to resolve problems:

Before the Conference

- At least twenty-four hours in advance, notify the parents or guardians of any students you intend to keep after school.

- Make sure that the conference time is workable. Younger students should consult their parents to coordinate their ride home. Be as cooperative about the time as you can.

- Arrange a place to meet that is as free from distractions as possible. Do not confer with students while other students are in the room.

During the Conference

- Be courteous in your greeting. This will set the tone for the rest of the meeting.

- Make the area as comfortable as possible. Offer a pen and paper for taking notes, and sit at student desks or at a table. Do not sit behind your desk.

- To protect yourself from charges of misconduct, when you are meeting one-on-one with a student, sit near the door to the room, and make sure the door is open. If you believe that a conference will be uncomfortable, arrange for a colleague to be in the same room with you and your student.

- Be very careful not to touch a student for any reason during a conference. Even an innocent pat on the back can be misinterpreted.

- Begin the meeting by stating that the purpose of the conference is to work together to resolve a problem between the two of you. Avoid rehashing unpleasant details, blaming the student, or showing your anger.

- Take the initiative by asking the student to tell you why you are meeting. Make sure that you each have a chance to state the problem as you see it.

- Listen to the student without interrupting.

- When you discuss the student's behavior, focus on the misdeed itself, not on your student's negative personality traits.

- After the student has spoken, restate the problem in your own words. Make sure you understand the problem and express your sincere interest in solving it.

- Be positive but firm in conveying that it is the student's responsibility to change his or her behavior.

- Brainstorm solutions with the student. Ask questions about how the student could handle the situation differently in the future.

- Agree on a plan that satisfies both of you. Make sure that you are comfortable with implementing it.

- Calmly explain the negative consequences you will impose if the student fails to carry out his or her part of the plan.

- Once again, state that you are willing to help the student be successful.

At the End of the Conference

- Ask the student if there is anything else that needs to be said. State your willingness to listen.

- Be very clear that you consider the student's misbehavior to be in the past and that you will not hold a grudge now that a resolution has been reached.

- Thank your student for taking the time for a conference and for deciding to work with you.

Document the conference as soon as possible so that the details are still fresh. Maintain this documentation until the end of the school year. You can use Teacher Worksheet 13.4 to help with this task.

TEACHER WORKSHEET 13.4

Student Conference Documentation

Teacher present: _____   Student present: _____

Date: _____   Time: _____   Place: _____

Reason(s) for the conference:

_____

_____

_____

Topics discussed:

_____

_____

_____

The teacher's future responsibility:

_____

_____

_____

The student's future responsibility:

_____

_____

_____

Positive consequences:

_____

_____

_____

Negative consequences:

_____

_____

_____

Teacher signature: _____

Student signature: _____

How to Refer a Student to an Administrator

For the discipline process to be meaningful, teachers who need assistance with students who make learning difficult for others must have some recourse. Usually, this recourse takes the form of an administrative referral. Referring students to an administrator during your first year as a teacher is, at best, a nerve-racking experience. It is often hard to determine when a referral is necessary. There is no question that you should refer a student to an administrator for any of these behaviors:

- Persistent defiance
- Bullying
- Stealing
- Sexual harassment
- Vandalism
- Deliberate profanity
- Bringing weapons to school
- Substance abuse
- Making threats
- Violent behavior
- Truancy
- Cheating
- Persistent disruptions
- Habitual tardiness

Before the Infraction Occurs

- There are usually preliminary measures you should take before you refer a student to an administrator. Talking with the student and contacting parents or guardians are two of the most important early interventions you should try.
- Make sure you are familiar with the school rules and procedures that apply to your students. Be aware of the ways the school board and your other supervisors expect you to handle student misconduct.
- Prevent misbehaviors through sound educational practices and consistent enforcement of rules.
- Handle routine misbehaviors yourself. If a phone call to parents or guardians would be effective, there is no need in most cases to involve an administrator. Establish your rules, policies, and consequences early in the term and follow through when necessary. Document the methods you use to handle these routine misbehaviors.
- Make sure you have the necessary referral forms on hand so that you don't appear disorganized if a time comes when you must refer a student to an administrator.

- If a problem with a student or situation has been brewing for a while, you probably have already been in touch with the administrator to ask for advice and support. This is a sound idea because it will enable the administrator to see that you have been diligent and professional at working on a solution.

After the Infraction Has Occurred

- Once a student has misbehaved to the point that you will refer him or her to an administrator, make sure you prevent a bad situation from becoming worse by maintaining the student's dignity and privacy in front of classmates.

- When you talk with a student about an infraction, don't threaten or bully the student, even if you are angry. Calmly state your policy and the consequences for misbehavior.

- Calm down before you write the referral. Your language should be as professional and objective as possible. Many different people will see the referral. Use language that is behavior oriented and factual. Do not state your opinion of the student's behavior or sink to name-calling or sarcasm.

- Call the student's parents or guardians before the end of the day to inform them of the incident and of your action in referring their child to an administrator.

- Make sure you also tell the student when you refer him or her to an administrator. The best way to do this is privately at the end of class.

- Once you have referred a student to the office, let go of it emotionally. By completing and turning in a referral form, you have put the matter into someone else's hands.

What to Do When Students Are Violent

In the last few years, there has been a dramatic increase in the number of fights at school; sadly, some of these conflicts have involved the use of weapons. As an educator, you can do a great deal to reduce violence by taking a proactive stance.

Expectations for Teachers

- Follow your school district's procedures for handling student fights.

- If you are assigned to hall duty, cafeteria duty, or any other duty, don't miss it. Be on time and be alert. A strong adult presence deters many fights.

- Act quickly to prevent fights by reporting student rumors about fights to administrators or security personnel. This is what your school district will expect you to do.

- Don't leave the fight area. Send students for help instead.

- Keep your students as safe as you can when a fight erupts.

- Take reasonable measures to stop fights without putting yourself or others in danger.

- Be prepared to provide an accurate witness report and appear in court.

- Don't allow a fight to hinder the rest of the day's instruction. Settle students down as quickly as possible. A written assignment usually will focus their attention on their work.

- Do not try to restrain violent students without help from other adults. Teachers who inadvertently hurt students while stopping them from fighting have been sued successfully. Other teachers have been injured themselves.

Do What You Can to Prevent Violence at School

- Familiarize your students with your school's policy concerning students who fight at school.

- Make sure that your students are aware of their options besides fighting in a peer conflict situation. Remind them of the severe penalties for fighting.

- Be alert to the signs that a fight is building: rumors, a high level of excitement, and remarks about what will happen later.

- If you see that two students are beginning to square off, remind them of the serious penalties for students who fight. Often students will take this as an opportunity to back down without losing face because they can claim that they do not want to be expelled.

- Immediately contact an administrator about a possible fight. Also, contact the parents or guardians of the students who are threatening to fight.

- Make sure that all your students are aware of the school policy on weapons and how to report weapons to an adult.

- Teach your students about bullying and sexual harassment. Make sure that they understand the limits they should observe when interacting with one another and what they should do if they are bullied or harassed.

- Encourage good behavior by refusing to allow students to insult one another, even in jest. Good-natured insults can quickly generate anger and violence.

- Teach your students that they can be punished for inciting others to fight and for blocking the area so that adults cannot get through to stop a fight.

If Violence Occurs Near You

- Immediately get help from other adults by sending students to fetch them. Do not try to restrain or step between students without another adult present.

- Make the safety of all students at the scene your first concern. Do not leave the area.

- Be very clear with students who are watching the fight that you want them to leave the area or, if the fight is in your classroom, to sit down.

- Be very careful about how you approach violent students so that no one, including yourself, is injured.

If There Are Weapons Involved

- If you hear a rumor that there is a weapon in the building, contact an administrator at once. You should not attempt to handle this situation by yourself.

- When a weapon is used during a fight, do not allow other students to take it. The weapon may be used as evidence. If you can, confiscate it and turn it over to an administrator.

If There Are Injuries

- Send a student for the school nurse. Deal first with any injured students and then with the other students at the scene. Do not leave the area.

- Assist the more seriously wounded students first. Be careful that the aid you offer does not injure students further.

- Protect yourself and others from contact with blood or other body fluids.

- If you are even slightly injured, seek medical attention promptly.

What to Do After You Have Witnessed School Violence

- As soon as you can, jot down the details of what happened. As a witness to the fight, you may be called on to remember these details in court, sometimes months after the incident, so be as specific as you can when you write your notes.

- If a fight took place while students were under your supervision, contact their parents or guardians so that you can work together to prevent a recurrence.

- Model the calm response you want from your students. Resume teaching immediately, without rehashing the fight or allowing students to do so.

Warning Signs of Trouble You Should Not Ignore

One of the saddest aftermaths of school violence is the realization that some teachers have had that they may have been able to prevent a dangerous situation had they only recognized earlier that a student was severely troubled. Although it may not always be easy to identify seriously troubled students, it is important to get to know your students well so that you can be alert for signs of potential problems. One significant way to make this task easier is to forge a bond with the parents or guardians of your students so that you can be aware of any problems as quickly as possible. Although the warning signs of potentially violent students can include the following list, if you observe two or more of these in combination, you should be alert to the potential for serious problems:

- A lack of adult supervision
- Cruelty to animals
- A fascination with gangs and gang activity
- Increased conflicts with peers
- Evidence of being bullied
- Membership in a gang
- An increase in the frequency of discipline issues
- Evidence of bullying others
- Incidents of abusive language and threats
- Lack of school-related motivation
- Incidents of misplaced or inappropriate anger
- Increased truancy
- A fascination with violence
- Repeated blaming of others
- Poor academic progress in general
- Evidence of substance abuse
- A sudden drop in academic performance
- Persistent isolation from others

For more information about the signs that all teachers should be alert to in their students, try these resources:

- **Keep Schools Safe (www.keepschoolssafe.org).** Helpful information about school violence issues can be found at Keep Schools Safe, an organization devoted to school safety, security, and the prevention of violence.
- **National Crime Prevention Council (www.ncpc.org/topics/school-safety).** At this site, educators can access tips and resources geared to keeping schools safe.
- **National School Safety Center (www.schoolsafety.us).** This website offers many free resources to help educators learn how to prevent school violence.

Help Students Move Forward after a Discipline Problem

Once a discipline problem has occurred in a classroom, it is up to you not only to resolve it but also to help students who have misbehaved move past the incident. This is a vital step in the process of handling all types of discipline problems successfully because without it, both your relationship with the offending student and that student's sense of self-worth will be damaged.

Because some discipline problems are easier to handle than others, you may not need to spend a long time on this part of the process with every issue. A quick nod of the head, a smile, or a comment such as "I know you've got this" will all be sufficient to reassure the student that you still find him or her likeable and capable of future success.

When a behavior problem is serious or time consuming, it is even more important to make sure that the student feels included, valued, and trusted again. Without that feeling, the student has little reason to try to perform well in your class. Spend a few minutes with misbehaving students, reassuring them that you have every confidence in their ability to be successful in the future. It's a step well worth the trouble.

Maintaining Behavior Documentation All Year

Keeping accurate records about the discipline issues in your classroom is a necessary professional responsibility, no matter what grade you teach. Because discipline issues can affect all aspects of a student's life and can also be a point of contention between home and school, the documents you keep about how discipline problems occur and are resolved should be accurate and up-to-date.

Behavior records serve several purposes. They will allow you to see the maturity of your students as the year progresses. When you review them, you will be able to see what worked and what did not; this will enable you to make informed decisions when future problems occur.

The notes you keep about a behavior incident that happened at the start of the school term could be invaluable at the end of the year if a parent or guardian challenges their child's grade in your class. Being able to refer to your notes about the various times you offered support and attempted redirection could be helpful in defending your discipline decisions.

Well-maintained records will also make it easier for you to recall the details of a behavior incident long after the incident has passed. Behavior documentation is also especially important if a behavior incident is serious enough to warrant the attention of a court official or police officer. You may be asked to testify in court and so will want accurate notes.

If you make it a habit to complete the records you need to maintain as soon as an incident is resolved, you will find that it is easier to recall the details of the incident when needed. To make the record-keeping task as simple as possible, you may want to adopt some of the forms in Teacher Worksheets 13.5, 13.6, 13.7, 13.8, and 13.9 to fit the needs of your teaching practice.

Behavior Incident Report

Use this form to record your notes about the details of a behavior incident so that you will have a clear record of the event.

Teacher: _____ Student: _____

Date and time of incident: _____

Place of incident: _____

Description of incident:

_____

_____

_____

_____

Actions taken by teacher:

_____

_____

_____

_____

Results of teacher actions:

_____

_____

_____

_____

Parent or guardian contact:

_____

_____

_____

_____

Notes:

_____

_____

_____

_____

From *The First-Year Teacher's Survival Guide, 4th Edition*, by Julia G. Thompson. Copyright © 2018 by John Wiley & Sons, Inc. Reproduced by permission.

TEACHER WORKSHEET 13.6

Behavior Observation Form for a Class

This worksheet is a useful tool for helping you gather the data that you need to make discipline decisions because it will allow you to record specific behaviors quickly. After you have made your observations, you should then be able to use the recommendations column to jot down the ideas you have for remediating problems. As an alternative, you could ask a colleague to make the observations while you teach.

Date: _____   Class: _____

Number of students in the class: _____

Observed Misbehaviors	Number of Students	Recommendations
Tardy to class		
Lack of materials		
Talking while the teacher is talking		
Off task and excessive talking		
Missing assignment		
Cheating		
Cell phone use in class		
Unintentional profanity		

(continued on next page)

(continued from previous page)

Observed Misbehaviors	Number of Students	Recommendations
Intentional profanity		
Sleeping in class		
Disrespectful to the teacher		
Disrespectful to classmates		
Horseplay		
Refusing to work		
Misuse of materials or equipment		
Negative verbal reaction		
Negative nonverbal reaction		
Disorganized work space or materials		
Asking to leave room		
Distracting other students		
Distracted		

TEACHER WORKSHEET 13.7

Behavior Observation Form for an Individual Student

Use this form after you have already determined a student's specific behaviors that you want to observe. You can either do the observations yourself or have a colleague observe your students as you teach.

Observer: _____   Student: _____

Date and time: _____

Targeted Behavior 1 _____

Frequency:

_____

Level of disruption: Self   Nearby students   All students

Possible triggers:

_____

_____

Teacher response:

_____

_____

Result of teacher response:

_____

_____

Insights or reflection:

_____

_____

Next steps:

_____

_____

(continued on next page)

(continued from previous page)

Targeted Behavior 2 _____

Frequency: _____

Level of disruption:　　　　Self　　　　Nearby students　　　　All students

Possible triggers:

_____

_____

Teacher response:

_____

_____

Result of teacher response:

_____

_____

Insights or reflection:

_____

_____

Next steps:

_____

_____

TEACHER WORKSHEET 13.8

Behavior Intervention Documentation for an Individual Student

This form is suitable for documenting the responses you have made to a student's misbehavior so that you can be sure that you have a complete record of the steps you have taken to help the student succeed.

Student:_____   Class period:_____

Major concern(s): _____
_____
_____

Level of Success

Record the success of each intervention you have tried in the last column by using these numbers:

1: Not successful
2: Somewhat successful but needs modification
3: Successful

Date	Behavior or Concern	Intervention	Level of Success

Behavior Intervention Documentation
for a Difficult Class

This worksheet allows you to quickly record and analyze the behavior interventions that you have tried with a class that you find difficult.

Class period: _____ Major concerns: _____

_____

_____

_____

_____

Record the success of each intervention you have tried in the last column by using these numbers:

1: Not successful
2: Somewhat successful but needs modification
3: Successful

Date of Intervention	Intervention	Level of Success
	Recorded or videoed self to determine how I could be contributing to the problem	
	Asked a colleague to observe the class and provide feedback	
	Analyzed the time used by students at the start of class, during various activities, and at the end of class	
	Made sure that expectations are clearly expressed in several modalities and taught to students	
	Made sure that procedures for all activities are in place and known to students	
	Made sure that students are aware of the class rules and the positive consequences for following rules as well as the negative consequences for disregarding rules	
	Held individual conferences with key students	
	Held a brief conference with the entire class to solicit their suggestions	

(continued on next page)

(continued from previous page)

Date of Intervention	Intervention	Level of Success
	Used exit slips or other written formats to elicit student suggestions	
	Adjusted the pace and types of instruction	
	Increased student choices for instructional activities	
	Praised the positive behavior of the entire class	
	Made student successes as concrete and visible as possible	
	Involved other staff members in creating solutions	
	Involved students' parents or guardians in creating solutions	
	Shared a pleasant activity together to build a sense of community	
	Made sure all students have access to materials and supplies	
	Worked with individual students to set and achieve goals	
	Worked with the entire class to set and achieve group goals	
	Made sure that the level of work is neither too easy nor too difficult	
	Used all available class time in a productive way	
	Offered a variety of relevant learning activities, including games and technology-based instruction	
	Taught courteous behaviors to replace negative ones	
	Included motivational activities in the lesson to increase engagement	
	Provided positive opportunities for students to be in the spotlight	
	Established signals for students to indicate that they need help	
	Involved students in as many helpful roles in the classroom as possible	
	Established ways for students to productively help one another	
	Offered a combination of tangible and intangible rewards	

(continued on next page)

(continued from previous page)

Date of Intervention	Intervention	Level of Success
	Taught students how to modulate their noise levels	
	Made it obvious that the purpose of class is to learn, not to misbehave	
	Posted encouraging mottoes to remind students to stay focused	
	Allowed students to redo a failed assignment to encourage effort	
	Communicated a strong belief in students' ability to succeed	
	Established predictable routines so that students know what to do	
	Provided various role models and mentors for students	
	Appealed to a variety of learning styles in each lesson	
	Established a time-out area so that students can gain self-control	
	Gave students a second chance when appropriate	
	Made sure the lesson was as exciting as possible	
	Gave written and verbal directions that are easy for students to follow	
	Made sure the class traffic flow is conducive to on-task behavior	
	Offered frequent checks for understanding to reduce frustration	
	Involved students' interests in the lesson	
	Acknowledged student effort	
	Ignored as much bad behavior as was possible and prudent	
	Involved students in teaching a lesson	
	Varied instructional activities to include interaction and independent work	
	Kept expectations for academic and behavioral success high	

From *The First-Year Teacher's Survival Guide, 4th Edition*, by Julia G. Thompson. Copyright © 2018 by John Wiley & Sons, Inc. Reproduced by permission.

Questions to Discuss with Colleagues

Sharing ideas with colleagues is a helpful way to devise solutions to some of the problems that you must manage successfully at school. Here you will find several topics to open discussions with colleagues about successful instructional practices:

1. Several of your students are often off task and have made it clear that they are not interested in the subject matter you are teaching. How can you intervene and redirect while treating each one with respect and dignity? What is your goal in this situation? How can you prevent this behavior from occurring in the future?

2. What are the most common misbehaviors that you observe among your students? How do the other teachers at your school handle them? What advice do they have for you as you work to establish an orderly classroom environment?

3. You would like to learn more about restorative justice and how it could be used in your school. How can you and your colleagues learn more about this movement and how to integrate it into your school? Who can help you with this?

4. When students misbehave, it is often hard to manage the stress that a discipline problem brings with it. How can you manage your stress related to discipline problems? What suggestions do your colleagues offer to help you with this?

5. Although you accept that the discipline issues in your classroom are your responsibility, it is apparent that some of them are caused by the poor discipline climate at your school. What can you and your colleagues do to improve the overall discipline climate?

Topics to Discuss with a Mentor

Although the topics that new teachers need to discuss with a mentor vary from teacher to teacher and from school to school, there are some that most first-year teachers should be comfortable discussing with a mentor or a trusted colleague. You should ask your mentor about these topics from this section:

- Advice about referring students to an administrator
- Suggestions for redirecting students who are off task
- How to learn more about your legal responsibilities as an educator
- Information about which behaviors you should overlook and which require intervention
- Advice about how to respond to and document behavior problems

Reflection Questions to Guide Your Thinking

1. What are your skills regarding handling students who have misbehaved? How can you capitalize on your strengths? What can you improve about how you deal with misbehaving students?

2. Why do students misbehave in your class? Can you notice a pattern or a time when misbehavior is most likely to occur? What can you do to prevent problems from happening?

3. What plans do you have in place for handling serious student misbehavior, such as fighting? What is your school's policy about teacher intervention in a student fight? What can you do to keep your students and yourself safe when serious misbehavior erupts?

4. What do your supervisors expect from you in terms of discipline? What do the parents or guardians of your students expect of you? How strict do they expect you to be?

5. What attitudes can you adopt to increase your confidence in your ability to cope with discipline issues? How can you improve your ability to manage the discipline concerns in your classroom?

SECTION FOURTEEN

How-to Quick Reference Guide to Common Classroom Discipline Problems

This section is designed to help you cope with some of the pervasive classroom behavior problems that both novice and experienced teachers encounter in their teaching practice. This quick reference guide is organized to help you find the behavior management advice you need to cope successfully with these problems.

Even though there may be some overlapping information, you'll find the problems here are divided into four categories:

Category One: Problems Associated with Individual Students

In this category, the negative influence of the behavior is generally limited to individual students and not to an entire group of students.

- How to react when students want to sleep instead of work
- How to react when you suspect substance abuse
- How to help students who are chronically disorganized
- How to deal with students who are tardy to class
- How to help students who are truant
- How to help students who are abused or neglected
- How to help students with chronic misbehavior
- How to help students who lack materials
- How to cope with students who tell lies
- How to manage cell phones in class

Category Two: Problems Associated with the Enforcement of School Rules or Policies

This category covers the discipline issues that can arise when a teacher attempts to enforce school rules or policies, including his or her legal responsibilities.

- How to cope when there's a classroom theft
- How to cope when students use profanity
- How to help students who cheat
- How to react when students engage in sexting
- How to react when dress code violations occur
- How to handle hallway problems
- How to deal with students who engage in horseplay
- How to deal with students who are bullies
- How to manage name-calling

Category Three: Problems Associated with Misbehavior during Instruction

This category involves misbehavior either by an individual student or by a group of students during instructional time.

- How to handle work refusal
- How to handle a class that is slow to settle to work
- How to cope when students misbehave for a substitute teacher
- How to handle classes that are too noisy

Category Four: Problems Associated with Students' Relationship with Their Teacher

In this category, the misbehaviors are the result of a damaged relationship between teacher and student.

- How to deal with defiant students
- How to cope with a difficult class

One day in the cafeteria, I noticed a young man who was not his usual fun self. I walked by, stopped, and asked him quietly if everything was all right. He said yes, but I knew it wasn't. I told him he knew where I was if he needed me and then moved on. The next morning, I found a note on my desk, all folded, teen style. In the note, this young man thanked me for asking him if he was okay. He said he had been struggling with some very hard news and was really thinking of doing something stupid, but I had made him rethink his decision. I was awed at the power teachers have. As teachers, we never, ever know the full extent of our effect on those lives entrusted to us. We must truly exercise caution in how we interact with young people. I carry that note, now more than thirty years old, in my wallet every day of my life, to remind me of this moment. The good news: this young man is now a productive member of our community with a lovely wife (who was also my student) and three great children. What greater reward could any teacher desire?

Luann West Scott, 42 years' experience

- How to help students who are disrespectful
- How to manage classroom power struggles

Each entry begins with a general description of the problem so that you can easily recognize it should you experience the discipline issue in your teaching practice. This description is then followed by a list of some of the mistakes that teachers often make when attempting to cope with each problem so that you can avoid these errors. Finally, you will find classroom-tested strategies that can guide you to make informed decisions about how to handle these discipline problems when they appear in your classroom.

Category One: Problems Associated with Individual Students

HOW TO REACT WHEN STUDENTS WANT TO SLEEP INSTEAD OF WORK

Sometimes students are sleepy. When that happens only now and then, sleepy students are not a problem. The behavior becomes a problem when a student repeatedly falls asleep in class or chooses to sleep instead of work. Then the behavior is symptomatic of a larger issue that requires adult intervention and support.

Mistakes to Avoid

- Don't let your students miss valuable instructional time. Because sleeping students are not involved in class, they can't learn. For this reason, you must not overlook this passive misbehavior.
- If the sleeping students in your class are the ones who tend to misbehave when they are awake, it is tempting to allow them to sleep. Don't give in to this teacher temptation. Instead, work with them to be more productive and better focused on working in class.
- Don't take this behavior personally. Instead, work with the student to solve it.
- Never ask other students to wake up a sleeping classmate. This not only interrupts their work but also puts them in an awkward position.
- Don't make fun of students who are sleeping. Gently awaken them instead.

Strategies That Work

- When you speak with a student about sleeping in class, don't be unpleasant. Instead, decide how to work with the student on the problem.
- Before you act, determine the cause. Speak to sleepy students in private to find out why they want to sleep. Do they stay up too late at home? Is there a medical

problem? Do they have an after-school job that requires long hours? Are they bored with school?

- If talking to a student does not solve the problem, contact his or her parents or guardians to elicit their support.

- Try not to disrupt the entire class by calling too much public attention to a sleeper.

- When you see that a student is becoming sleepy, allow that student to stand up, move around, or perhaps go to the water fountain.

- Give students a reason to stay awake. When students decide that they cannot succeed in a class, they sometimes choose to sleep rather than be frustrated. Involve these students in activities in which they can be successful and that they will enjoy more than napping through class.

- If you notice that several of your students are tempted to sleep, reconsider the way you are presenting information. Few students can sleep through a lively, active class.

HOW TO REACT WHEN YOU SUSPECT SUBSTANCE ABUSE

Many teachers are not sure what to do when students brag about a weekend party or smell of cigarette smoke and may want to believe that educating students about substance abuse is someone else's job. The problem with this assumption is that many families are unable to cope with the problem or are themselves the root of the problem.

As a classroom teacher, it is important that you know and follow your district's guidelines about how teachers are required to deal with substance abuse by students. It is also important that you know which staff members to turn to for help as soon as you determine that a problem exists.

Mistakes to Avoid

- Don't assume that young students are exempt from the problem because of their age. Even young elementary students can be affected by substance abuse problems.

- Don't ignore substance abuse problems among your students; such problems do not go away by themselves.

- Don't overreact. For example, if a student makes a passing mention of a weekend party, don't lecture or notify a counselor. Instead, speak privately with the student about making sound decisions.

- Don't attempt to handle a serious substance abuse problem without involving other adults. If you have a student with a substance abuse problem, keep in mind the serious nature of the problem and recognize that it needs to be handled with support from all the adults in the student's life.

- Don't forget that you are a role model. Teachers who talk about the fun they had at college parties do not help students make wise choices for themselves.

Strategies That Work

- There are many different things that a caring teacher can do to help students who have problems with substance abuse. Here you will find advice on helping prevent substance abuse as well as on how to intervene if you notice that a student has violated school policies.

Prevention

- Do not spend hours of instructional time teaching students about illegal substances. Instead, when the subject arises, be clear about your position on the issue.
- Give your students the facts about substance abuse, thus enabling them to make wiser choices based on real information rather than on the opinions of their friends, who may be just as confused as they are.
- Remember that many students, especially younger ones, are simply not aware of the health risks and social consequences of substance abuse. Make sure that students are aware of these risks as well as the legal penalties for substance abuse.
- Make sure that your students understand school policies concerning student use of tobacco, alcohol, and drugs, including the consequences of violating those policies.

Intervention

- Quietly question the student to determine whether there is a problem.
- Immediately and calmly put your school's policies into effect.
- Contact the staff member at your school who is designated to handle substance abuse problems and explain the issue as you see it. That person will conduct a search, if one is necessary, and will involve the student's parents or guardians and other appropriate personnel.
- Help the student see you as a supportive and caring person. Students with substance abuse problems need support and assistance, not blame.

HOW TO HELP STUDENTS WHO ARE CHRONICALLY DISORGANIZED

Although the problems caused by a chronically disorganized student would appear to affect only that student, this is not the always the case. Disorganized students waste everyone's time. When a student spends time frantically searching for homework assignments and trying to borrow paper and pencils instead of listening to directions, you will be distracted and so will your students.

Mistakes to Avoid

- Do not rush to judgment. Many students struggle with managing their papers and supplies. Teach strategies to help them instead of being irritated.
- Don't embarrass a student in front of his or her peers.
- Instead of impatiently halting class to deal with the offending student, ask him or her to wait quietly until you can help. Get everyone else settled and then help the disorganized student.
- Don't neglect to teach organization strategies throughout the term. Learning to work efficiently is an important school skill that all students need to develop.

Strategies That Work

- Make a point of checking in with disorganized students frequently to see that items are stowed away in a logical place from which they can be easily retrieved. With periodic checks, the problems with disorganization can stay small.
- Keep the requirements for paper management as simple as possible. For example, ask students to use just one folder or binder for class instead of requiring them to keep up with several items, such as a binder, a spiral notebook, and folders with pockets.
- Help students develop routines for keeping belongings in good order. These routines should be as simple as possible so that they are easy to follow.
- Be aware that many students benefit from working with a study buddy so that they can check each other's folders, binders, and book bags before leaving class.
- Although creating methods of organization may seem obvious to you, be explicit in directing your students. For example, say, "Clip this handout into the assessment section of your binder" instead of "Put your papers away."
- Allow enough time at the end of class for students to pack away their belongings neatly.
- Because turning in work completed at home is often a continuing problem for disorganized students, there are several different options that you can offer to make sure that students turn in the work they complete at home. Consider which of the suggestions in the following list would be most appropriate for your students:
  - Accept an electronic version of the work if the parents or guardians are willing to scan and send it for younger students or if older students will e-mail it to you. You could always accept a hard copy of the work later.
  - Consider asking parents or guardians to contact you via e-mail at night to confirm that the homework has been completed and packed into the proper binder and book bag to be turned in.
  - Be willing to think outside the box. For example, you can create a daily routine whereby the disorganized student turns in homework as soon as he or she arrives at school instead of waiting until class begins.

HOW TO DEAL WITH STUDENTS WHO ARE TARDY TO CLASS

Very few students can attend school for an entire term without being tardy at least once. Students have many reasons to delay their arrival in class, and by the end of the first few weeks of school, you will have heard many creative excuses. Tardy students cause a disruption, no matter how quietly they try to slip into the class. Furthermore, if students see that their classmates can be tardy with no teacher reaction, then they will believe that it is okay for them to be tardy, too.

Tardy students set a negative tone in a class by tacitly sending a message that the activities you have planned for them are not important enough for them to make the effort to be on time. As a result, class focus may shift from learning to a power struggle between you and the students who are testing the boundaries of your patience.

Mistakes to Avoid

- Never embarrass tardy students with sarcastic remarks, such as "Glad you decided to join us." Sarcasm will not solve the problem, nor will it earn you respect; instead, it will make tardy students even more reluctant to enter the room.

- Do not be a pushover who accepts unreasonable excuses; instead, enforce the consequences of tardiness.

- Never stop what you are doing to interrogate a tardy student in front of the rest of the class; instead, allow the student to slip into class while you continue giving instruction.

- Don't allow students to stand in the doorway before class starts. Students who block the entrance interrupt the smooth start of class because they delay their classmates from getting to their seats on time.

Strategies That Work

- Define tardiness for your students and be reasonable in your definition. Most teachers will agree that a student who is inside the classroom but not in a seat is not tardy; others are more particular and insist that a student who is not actually sitting down is tardy. Note, however, that the second definition is difficult to justify to your students and their parents or guardians.

- Make it important for your students to be on time to your class. Begin class quickly, with assignments that students will find enjoyable. Make the first few minutes of class as meaningful as the rest.

- Enforce your tardiness policy consistently. Be sure that your classroom policy is in line with your school's policy. Chronically tardy students respond particularly well to a policy with escalating consequences because it forces them to take their actions seriously.

- Involve parents or guardians if a student is tardy more than twice in a marking period. This is an especially important step if the tardy student is late to school and not just late from another teacher's class.

- Be aware of your school's policy for handling habitual tardiness. At some point in the process, you may be expected to refer the student to an administrator for action. Be sure to follow your school's procedures regarding tardiness.

- Model the behavior you expect. Your students will be very quick to point out your hypocrisy if you are tardy and then reprimand them for the same offense.

- Keep your attendance records accurate. It is sometimes confusing to stop class and change an absence mark to a tardy mark, but you must do so nevertheless. When you refer a student to an administrator or when you talk to parents or guardians, you will need to provide the dates when the student was tardy.

- Move a chronically tardy student to a seat near the door to minimize disruptions. When you pass out materials and the student is not present, place materials on the desk to prevent disruption when that student arrives.

- Find out about the backgrounds of chronically tardy students. Their tardiness can often be the result of a disorganized family life in which the student has not been taught to be punctual.

- Whenever you talk with your students about their tardiness, put the responsibility for their behavior where it belongs—on them. Ask tardy students what steps they plan to take to eliminate the problem. Offer support, but remain firm in your expectations.

HOW TO HELP STUDENTS WHO ARE TRUANT

Many factors may contribute to a student's poor attendance. A consistent pattern of poor attendance usually develops from his or her earliest days onward. For instance, when a family is in turmoil, a student finds it difficult to attend school. Frequent illness may also be a factor, especially with the rise in respiratory illness among young students.

Another factor that causes some students to miss school is having a family that does not value education and does not encourage regular attendance. Students who are parents themselves find it almost impossible to overcome the difficulties associated with having a child and attending school. Sometimes older children must stay home to take care of younger siblings or other family members for various reasons.

Take an active role in encouraging students to attend school regardless of the reason for their absenteeism. Encouraging your students to attend school on a regular basis is one of the most important tasks you will face in your career.

Mistakes to Avoid

- Don't assume that absent students want to miss school.
- Don't ignore attendance problems—doing so could encourage students to miss more school.

- Don't make it difficult for students to make up missing work. Give students the assignments that were missed and a reasonable length of time in which to complete them.

- Because attendance records are crucial documents that can be called for if students are involved in legal difficulties, it is important to keep accurate and up-to-date documentation. If you are going to help students improve their attendance, you will need to be able to access accurate data quickly.

Strategies That Work

- When you realize that a student has an attendance problem, do not ignore it. It is up to you to help that student in the most appropriate way.

- Be aware of your students' attendance patterns. Find out the reasons for a student's absenteeism so that you can offer assistance.

- Remember that students who feel connected to their school, their classmates, and their teachers rarely miss school without good reason. Encourage regular attendance by building a strong relationship with each of your students. Student should feel that they are missed when they are absent.

- Contact the parents or guardians of students who have excessive absences to ask them to work with you on the problem. Some parents or guardians may request that you contact them any time their child is absent. Try to honor this request whenever you can.

- Maintain accurate attendance records and follow your school district's procedures for reporting and handling attendance, especially if you want to seek assistance for truant students. It is not always easy to keep up with attendance records, but students and administrators need to have an accurate accounting of attendance throughout the term.

- Consider sending a letter home with any student who misses a third day of your class. Keep a copy of the letter as documentation that you have contacted the student's parents or guardians.

- Encourage students and their parents or guardians to record the days that students miss school on a home calendar. Some parents or guardians do not realize just how often their child is out without such a reminder.

- Ask a counselor to speak to students who are having trouble with their attendance so that the students will have a clear picture of their options. Many believe that they can drop out and then pick up a GED certificate later, not realizing how difficult the test for this certificate can be.

- Talk to students about their absences. If your students are having family problems or social problems, seek help for them. Have them talk to a guidance counselor to enlist further support for maintaining regular attendance.

HOW TO HELP STUDENTS WHO ARE ABUSED OR NEGLECTED

One of the most serious responsibilities that an education professional has is to keep students safe from harm. Although most of that responsibility involves classroom issues, such as adequate supervision or sensible rules and procedures, keeping students safe also involves intervening when you suspect or when a child reports abuse and neglect. As a teacher, you are morally and legally obligated to act when you suspect or when a student discloses abuse or neglect. Failure to act appropriately and promptly may put the student in even more danger.

There are many different online resources available for teachers who want to learn more about this problem; here are two particularly helpful ones:

- **U.S. Department of Health and Human Services (www.childwelfare.gov/ pubPDFs/educator.pdf).** Here educators can learn more about the symptoms of abuse and neglect as well as how to help abused or neglected students.
- **U.S. Department of Justice (www.justice.gov/sites/default/files/ defendingchildhood/legacy/2011/09/19/tips-teachers.pdf).** This tip sheet for teachers provides concise information about abuse and a teacher's responsibilities.

Mistakes to Avoid

- Don't neglect to familiarize yourself with your district's policies and expectations regarding how teachers are required to handle suspected or reported abuse and neglect.
- Because it is your role to report and not investigate, do not contact a student's parents or guardians if you suspect abuse or neglect. Report it to the designated staff member at your school or to police instead.
- Don't promise the student that you will keep the situation a secret.
- Don't talk about the situation with colleagues or community members. Respect the student's right to confidentiality.
- Don't hesitate to act quickly. Because teachers are regarded as mandated reporters, you must act to protect students.

Strategies That Work

- When you suspect abuse or neglect or when a student confides in you, keep in mind that it is your role to report this information immediately to staff members who are trained to deal with it or to police. Act quickly.
- Familiarize yourself with the most common signs of abuse and neglect so that you can protect your students.

- Listen carefully and nonjudgmentally to the student who may be confiding in you. Do not allow your personal reactions to show, as they might interfere with the student's willingness to talk to an adult.

- Be compassionate. Acknowledge to the student that you are aware that talking to an adult is difficult and that he is she is not alone. Reassure the student that what happened is not his or her fault.

HOW TO HELP STUDENTS WITH CHRONIC MISBEHAVIOR

Chronic misbehavior comes in infinite varieties of disruption, stress, and teacher misery. From tattling in kindergarten to senioritis, chronic misbehavior is something that all teachers must deal with. Sometimes the misbehavior is contained to one or two students and sometimes it is a problem involving an entire class. In either case, chronic misbehavior, like other types of misbehavior in a classroom, requires a thoughtful and deliberate problem-solving approach.

Mistakes to Avoid

- Don't expect a quick fix. Chronic patterns of misbehavior usually take a long time to develop and a long time to change.

- Don't focus too much of your energy on troublemakers. They are used to being singled out for their poor decisions. Instead, treat them with the same calm expectation of success that you do the rest of the class.

- Being angry with students will not help the situation.

- Don't neglect to manage your own stress. Be proactive about how difficult it can be to figure out how to help students stop misbehaving.

Strategies That Work

- Attend to safety issues first. It is your responsibility to act decisively and quickly to keep all your students safe. Never allow behavior that jeopardizes student health, safety, or welfare.

- Stay positive in your approach. Work to resolve it instead of just reacting negatively.

- Help your students who struggle with chronic misbehavior by setting a clearly established goal for improvement and measuring the steps in their journey toward it.

- Show students how they are supposed to behave. Use plenty of models, examples, and explicit details so that your misbehaving students can have a clear idea of just how they are supposed to act.

- Let your policies, procedures, and rules do the hard work. Enforce them consistently and fairly and students will eventually stop testing boundaries.

- Be supportive and encouraging rather than negative. With this combination of positive and supportive attitudes, you will be far more likely to change your students' misbehavior than if you just react negatively.

- Keep disturbances as unobtrusive as possible. Respect students' dignity so that they do not need to act out to have a voice. You'll send a strong message that the focus in your class is not on misbehavior but on learning instead.

HOW TO HELP STUDENTS WHO LACK MATERIALS

When students occasionally forget their textbooks or other materials, this is a problem that can be solved by the loan of a book from the extras in the classroom or sharing with a friend. The problem with forgetting materials comes when students repeatedly forget or when they distract others trying to borrow materials.

Mistakes to Avoid

- Allowing the same students to repeatedly borrow materials from their classmates is not a sound practice because it does not promote self-discipline, and it places a burden on the students who feel obligated to lend their materials to a classmate.

- If you don't plan how to handle the problems caused by missing materials, you will have to deal constantly with the situation. Spend some time and effort in preventing the problem instead.

- Never allow the lack of materials for any reason to cause a student to refuse to work.

Strategies That Work

- Prevent problems with materials by reminding students what they will need to have with them when class meets again. You can do this by telling students what they will need at the beginning of class and then at the end by asking them to tell you what they should bring. Make it part of their homework assignment, send home digital or paper reminders, and display reminder signs.

- Ask students for advice about what would make it easier for them to remember to bring their materials to class. You should not be the only person in the room who is concerned about this issue.

- Try to have extra books in the classroom so that you will be able to lend one to almost any student who slips and forgets. Three are not too many to keep track of if you are busy, especially if you have the students who borrow books from you write their names on the board to remind you that they have one.

- When you notice that students seem to have a problem keeping up with their materials, it's time to talk with them privately about how to solve the issue. Sometimes all it takes is for a supportive teacher to show students how to stay organized or help them figure out how to remember what they need for class.

- If forgotten materials continue to be a problem, even after all that you do to prevent it, then you should call home to speak to parents or guardians about your concern.

- If missing pencils are a problem in your classroom, set up a system where students can borrow from a shared bank of supplies. This system promotes self-discipline because students run it themselves and are responsible for contributing to it. Here's how:

  - Create a bank of shared materials by asking students to volunteer to donate a pencil or two at the start of the term when many students have new supplies.

  - Ask for volunteers, assign it as a classroom job, or select several students to oversee the shared materials bank.

  - When students borrow pencils from the bank, the students who oversee distributing them should record the name of the borrower on the board. This will remind students to return it at the end of class. The students in charge of the supplies bank should check the board at the end of class to remind classmates to return the pencils.

- If you have students who are unable to afford school supplies, discreetly lend them the materials that they need with collateral until they can purchase their own.

How to Cope with Students Who Tell Lies

On the day that an important assigned project is due, several students tell you that they can't turn in their work because their printer was out of ink, there was no printer paper at home, the power went out, the dog ate it, and other obvious lies. Sadly, students of all ages seem to find it convenient to lie to their teachers about a wide variety of topics. One of the most difficult issues that many teachers must manage is what to do when they realize that a student has been lying to them. Unfortunately, no teacher escapes this responsibility.

Mistakes to Avoid

- When you find that a student has lied to you, privately deal with that student. Don't compound the problem by humiliating the student in front of classmates with an angry confrontation.

- Be sure of your facts before accusing a student of being untruthful to you. A false accusation can destroy a student's fragile trust in you.

Strategies That Work

- Strive to see student falsehoods as a problem that you can cope with instead of just reacting to the issue in an emotional way. Try to remove the negative emotion you may feel at being tricked and redirect your energy in a positive way.

- Instead of accusing the student directly, ask questions that will lead him or her to admit the truth. This is especially important and effective with students who have had a momentary lapse of judgment and integrity and who will self-correct when given an opportunity.

- Contact the student's home when necessary. Sometimes it takes a united front to tackle the underlying issues that have encouraged a student to lie. Be compassionate and understanding when speaking with a parent or guardian. Spare them embarrassment with a quiet problem-solving attitude rather than accusing their child or backing them into a corner.

- Once you and the student have worked out the problem, assure the student that the matter is resolved and that you intend for both of you to move forward. Be calm and friendly in your dealings so that this can happen.

- Be a role model of integrity yourself. This is crucial if you are to be able to tackle the issue successfully.

HOW TO MANAGE CELL PHONES IN CLASS

Cell phones can create distractions that disrupt the learning environment in significant ways. Students can misuse their phones by texting one another in class, bullying other students, taking unflattering photographs or recordings of teachers, or using phones to instigate fights that they then post online. Phones also are attractive targets for thieves. Perhaps the most significant negative impact that cell phones can have in a twenty-first-century classroom, however, occurs when students use them to cheat on tests and other assignments.

Although there are disadvantages to cell phones in school, there are also many positive uses for this ubiquitous tool. (See Section Nine for more information about this.) It's clear that the cell phones themselves are no more of a problem than pencil and paper; it is student misuse of these devices that creates problems.

Mistakes to Avoid

- It is a mistake to allow students to have their phones on and handy when they do not need to use them because phones are such a tempting distraction.

- Don't be inconsistent in your enforcement of a cell phone policy. If you want students to learn to self-govern the way they use phones in your class, firmly enforcing your expectations for cell phone use is key.

- Don't allow students to take mental breaks during class to play on their phones. It is often too difficult to capture their attention again, which results in a loss of instruction time.

- Don't take a student's phone. If you lose it or if it is stolen from your desk, you will be held responsible.

Strategies That Work

- Follow the guidelines set forth by your school district concerning student cell phones.

- Make sure all students are aware of your policies so that they understand the times when they can use their phones and the consequences for not following school policies.

- Be consistent in your enforcement to help students learn to be self-disciplined about their cell phone use.

- Many teachers have had success with cell phones by asking students to leave them turned off and zipped into book bags. This can work well if students get into the habit of managing their phones at the start of class and if teachers are vigilant and consistent in enforcing the procedure.

- Still others have had success with a designated cell phone area of the room where students can stow their phones upon entering the classroom.

- Ask several other teachers in your school how they handle cell phones in class. This will enable you to make sound decisions that are similar to what other teachers do. When there is a consistent approach like this in a school, students will find it easier to comply.

Category Two: Problems Associated with the Enforcement of School Rules or Policies

HOW TO COPE WHEN THERE'S A CLASSROOM THEFT

Just as other forms of dishonest behavior cause classroom problems, so does stealing. Once a theft has happened in your classroom, it will be up to you to make sure that the problem is solved in such a way that the thief can remain a valued member of the class, the disruption is minimal, and the victim's belongings are returned.

Mistakes to Avoid

- Don't accuse students or continue to talk about the situation. Try to maintain as normal a class atmosphere as you can to minimize the disruption.

- Always lock your classroom on leaving, and never give your keys to students. Discourage students from taking items from your personal space at school.

- Don't use the words *steal* or *theft* because they make it difficult for students to come forward with information. Instead, make it easy for the thief to have a change of heart and "find" the missing object. This will allow the thief to save face in front of peers, minimize disruption, and encourage the positive class community you want for your class to continue.

Strategies That Work

- The suggestions for dealing with students who commit theft in your class fall into two categories: how to prevent theft and how to manage the situation once a theft has occurred.

Prevention

- Be aggressive in preventing theft. Don't leave your personal belongings in the open or on your desk. Many teachers do not carry much cash at school and leave their credit cards at home.
- Be very careful about how you handle money you collect from your students. To avoid problems, deposit it as quickly as you can.
- Don't expect students to tell on one another, and don't expect a student to confess in front of the class.
- Remind your students that they can prevent theft by taking good care of items that are attractive to thieves: calculators, headphones, pens, money, jewelry, electronic devices, hats, books, notes, and yearbooks.

Dealing with a Theft

- If the stolen item belongs to you, don't threaten your students. Instead, offer a small reward for its safe return. Promise to ask no questions, and honor that promise. If the item is not returned, you may want to alert other teachers about what has happened so that they also can be on the lookout for the missing item.
- If the stolen item belongs to a student, remain calm and ask that anyone who may have picked up the item by mistake return it. If no one returns the item, notify an administrator. Your students may need to be detained, and an administrator's help is necessary for this.
- When you catch a student stealing, keep that information as private as possible. You must involve an administrator and the student's parents or guardians, but try to preserve the student's dignity.

HOW TO COPE WHEN STUDENTS USE PROFANITY

Our society's standards about what is appropriate language to use at school have relaxed considerably in the last few years. Not too long ago, the expression "School sucks!" was considered indecent language. Now most people regard it as rude but not necessarily indecent.

Although there are various ways to effectively deal with the problem of profanity in your classroom, most of the incidents of inappropriate language fall into one of two categories: unintentional profanity and intentional profanity.

Unintentional Profanity

In this category, students simply make a slip of the tongue while they are chatting with one another. In this category, students do not mean for you to overhear them. Sometimes this type of profanity happens in the hallways where students don't think adults can overhear them.

Mistakes to Avoid

- Be careful when you overhear cursing not to turn to a student and say, "What did you just say?" unless you want to hear the curse word again. You can usually tell by the shocked looks on the faces of the students near the guilty one that the word was inappropriate.

- Often students who have cursed accidentally will try to convince you that they really said something else. Don't accept this.

- Even though cursing is more common now than it used to be, you should not allow even mild words to just slip by without acting unless you want your students to believe that you think swearing in class is acceptable.

- No matter how tempted or angry you may be, never swear in class yourself. Your students need you to be a role model.

Strategies That Work

- Discuss the problem of swearing at the start of the term. Have students brainstorm reasons why this type of language is not acceptable everywhere. Explain that everyone has various levels of language and that students need to practice a more formal one at school so that they will be able to speak correctly in situations where it is expected.

- Establish a hierarchy of consequences to help students remember not to swear. Here is a possible sequence:
  - First offense: Warning
  - Second offense: Teacher conference
  - Third offense: Phone call to parent or guardian

- Pay attention if a student is genuinely remorseful and immediately apologizes. At that point, the negative consequences should not have to be enacted because the student has enough self-discipline to realize that the mistake should not have happened and has tried to undo the error. If the student continues to forget, then you should enact the consequences.

Intentional Profanity

These are the hateful words that students throw at you or other students when they are out of control with anger. As soon as students say them, they know they have gone over the line of acceptable behavior. This is a very different situation from the first category, where a student does not mean to curse in front of you. In this type of incident, students deliberately use language to try to hurt the object of their anger. Most of the time, these incidents also involve other problems: racial slurs or insults.

Mistakes to Avoid

- You should not deal with this situation by yourself. This is an important matter and should be taken seriously.

Strategies That Work

- You have two choices to make, depending on the severity of the offense:
  - If you are convinced the student is out of control with anger, send for help and have the student removed from the classroom. You should then follow through with a written referral to an administrator and by contacting the student's parents or guardians.
  - If you think the student will not further disturb class, you may allow him or her to remain, but you should refer the student to the attention of an administrator before the school day is over. The situation should be dealt with before the student returns to your class.
- You should also phone the student's parents or guardians to let them know what happened and that you have referred their child to an administrator.

HOW TO HELP STUDENTS WHO CHEAT

Cheating is an unfortunate and ubiquitous part of school life that requires a multifaceted solution. Sometimes students cheat because they have copied other students' work for so long that they really don't understand that doing so is not just cooperating with a classmate but cheating. Others cheat because they have a very real fear of failure and are not prepared for class. Still others cheat because they do not see the relevance of the tasks they are asked to perform.

When you deal successfully and consistently with cheating incidents as they arise, you make your students aware that cheating is not going to be tolerated in your classroom. Dealing with cheating should be something you do consistently every day in your class, not just when you nab an offending student.

Mistakes to Avoid

- Don't assume that students know what constitutes cheating on an assignment. Go over the expectations for acceptable collaboration and use of resources when you make the assignment.

- The worst action you can take is to ignore an incident of cheating. At the very least, you should speak privately with a student who has cheated in your class.

- Never publicly accuse a student of cheating. Don't chat about a cheating incident with others. Cheating should be treated confidentially.

- Don't ask a student to confide in you about another student's cheating. This is awkward and unfair to both students.

- Never accuse a student unless you are sure that cheating has occurred. You must have proof before you act.

Strategies That Work

Step One: Preventing Cheating from Occurring

- Know your school's policy on student cheating and follow it. If all teachers in a school consistently enforce a schoolwide policy on cheating, then the battle is almost won because students will know they are not supposed to cheat and what the consequences will be if they do.

- During class discussions encourage students to talk about cheating. They will surprise you with the insights and experiences they are willing to share with a concerned adult.

- Model honest behavior by annotating photocopied material and by respecting copyright laws for films, software, books, and other material.

- Help your students see cheating as part of the big picture of life choices. Listen and advise. Don't lecture.

- Keep desktops and work areas clean so that you will notice if answers are written on them or if a stray cheat note is visible. Keep cleaner on hand to wipe away any notes or answers.

- Before a test, ask students to neatly stow away their books, papers, phones, and other materials as part of preparing for the test. Make it obvious that you are checking.

- Talk to your students about taking a commonsense approach to avoiding the appearance of wrongdoing. Students should not turn sideways in their seats during a test. Students should also not talk to one another during a test or quiz.

- Don't leave tests or quizzes on your desk where anxious students might be tempted to peek at them.

- If your students need a cover sheet for tests, provide it for them. Recycled paper is a good option if you do not have permanent cover sheets.

- Don't allow students to have extra paper on their desks as a writing pad. Allow them to fold the test paper or issue an extra sheet of recycled paper to create a softer writing surface instead. Extra paper is an obvious hiding place for disguising cheat notes.

- Any questions your students may have during a test should be directed only to you. Walk over to the student who has a question. Students should remain seated during tests to avoid inadvertently seeing another's paper.

- Monitor your students very closely during a quiz or test. You can't do this by sitting at your desk. Move around the room frequently.

- Give several different versions of a test or quiz—even during the same class period.

- For a test where you expect lots of detailed memorization, consider allowing your students to bring in a small legal cheat sheet. Determine the limits of the size and the information on it in advance; an index card works well. This will lessen their anxiety and reduce the temptation to cheat.

- When students finish a test early, either have them keep their papers until you collect them all at once or have them turn them in and begin another independent assignment immediately.

Step Two: Dealing with Cheating Once It Has Occurred

- If you have caught a student cheating, the first thing you should do is arrange a private conference with the student to determine the reasons why he or she cheated. Whatever the reason, talk with the student in a calm manner to determine what went wrong and to help the student see other options that could prevent future cheating.

- When you catch one of your students cheating, contact his or her parents or guardians at once. Cheating is, without question, an issue that involves parents or guardians, the teacher, and the student.

- Put the school's policy on cheating incidents into action. Sometimes this means involving counselors and administrators. Make sure when you speak to parents or guardians that they understand what actions you will take.

- Unless your school's policy prohibits it, you should allow the student to make up or redo the assignment.

- If you suspect that a student is cheating on another teacher's assignment while under your supervision, don't accuse the student outright. Collect the work if you can and discuss it with the other teacher.

- If you do catch a student cheating, protect the student's dignity.

- If a student confides in you that another is cheating, counsel that student about the best way to cope with this additional pressure. Make sure you take such confidences seriously and act with discretion to take the necessary steps to solve the problem.

- Once you have settled an incident with a student, forgive and forget. Convey this attitude to all guilty students, and you will provide them with an incentive to start fresh and to put their mistakes behind them.

Cybercheating

Although technology has greatly enhanced education for millions, it can also be used for a less positive purpose: cheating. Students who cybercheat do so in a variety of ways, including the following:

- Purchasing essays
- Photographing tests and quizzes and sending the digital image to classmates
- Texting answers to classmates
- Plagiarizing parts of essays or reports
- Accessing notes stored on phones

Although the problem of cybercheating is widespread and growing rapidly with new developments in technology, there are several things that savvy teachers can do to manage the issue.

- Educate your students about what constitutes cheating. Many students are so accustomed to cutting and pasting information into essays and reports or sharing information with classmates that they may not always understand what constitutes cheating.
- Make sure your students know that you are aware of the issue and that you will be checking their work for evidence of cheating.
- Browse some of the many online cheating advice sites maintained by less-than-ethical people. To access dozens of the most current sites, use a search term such as "how to cheat in school." When you browse these sites, you will learn some of the many ways that students cheat while in class as well as tips for how to recognize that students are cheating electronically.
- Ask students to show their work on projects and essays. They should submit notes and drafts as well as final copies.

HOW TO REACT WHEN STUDENTS ENGAGE IN SEXTING

Sexting is the act of digitally transmitting or receiving sexually explicit messages, photographs, or videos. Although the most common device used for sexting is a cell phone, other electronic devices can also be used. One of the most significant problems that sexting poses for teachers occurs when the students who are involved in sexting are underage; the material they send is then considered child pornography.

Mistakes to Avoid

- When a student confides in you, resist the urge to ask the student to show you the material or to take a student's phone or device. Doing either could have serious legal implications for you.

- If a student confides in you, don't hesitate to act quickly.
- Don't violate the victim's right to confidentiality. Sexting is not something that should be discussed casually with colleagues.

Strategies That Work

- Begin by educating yourself about the problem. Sexting is a widespread and extremely harmful trend among students who have access to electronic devices. Sexting is not only the transmission of sexually explicit photos but also can include text messages, social network messages, and e-mails.
- Make sure that you are familiar with your school district's policies on sexting and aware of the steps that are required of you. Most school districts have very clear policies about how sexting should be handled.
- When you learn of a sexting incident, remain calm and follow your district's policies about how to handle the matter.
- Contact an administrator immediately to report the incident—this is your responsibility as an educator. The school administrator will report the offense to the local police and notify parents or guardians.
- Do not confiscate the cell phone or device. That should be done only by an administrator or the police. Make every effort to protect yourself from criminal charges by refusing to read the message or look at any images, as they could constitute child pornography. Take care. School officials have lost their jobs by mishandling incidents of student sexting.
- For more information about sexting and how to prevent it among your students, use "sexting" as a search term on the "Safety" page of Wired Safety (www.wiredsafety.org). This national organization provides excellent information on a variety of tech safety topics.

HOW TO REACT WHEN DRESS CODE VIOLATIONS OCCUR

In court case after court case, the right of a school district to enforce a student dress code that is reasonable and that promotes a safe school environment without violating a student's right to free speech has been upheld. School districts do have the right to ban clothing that is vulgar or provocative or that would disrupt normal school activities.

As a classroom teacher, you will almost certainly be required to deal with student dress code violations from time to time. Although different schools have different dress codes and even enforce their own dress code inconsistently, it is still up to the teacher to determine if the student's attire is in violation of the prevailing standard and to decide the best manner to manage it with tact and sensitivity.

Mistakes to Avoid

- Be careful not to violate the dress code yourself. It will be impossible for you to enforce it if you are also in violation.

- Be careful that your decision to enforce the school's code is based on the code and not on your personal taste. For example, you may think that oversize pants on students are not appropriate for school. If your school's code does not address the issue, however, it would be wise for you to follow the school policy instead of your own preference.

- Some students who live in poverty will not have the same access to clean, appropriate, well-fitting clothing as other students. Be careful to take this into account when dealing with the issue.

- Because students are extremely sensitive about their appearance, take extra care to be clear with students in violation of the code that it is the dress itself that is the issue and not the students.

- Because of the potential to embarrass a student, never handle a dress code issue in front of other students. Be discreet as you ask the student quietly to speak with you in the hallway or some other spot where the rest of the class cannot be an audience.

Strategies That Work

- Make sure that you are familiar with the dress code rules before you try to explain them to your students.

- Make sure that your students understand the rules. If violations seem to be a problem with your students, post the dress code so that they can check it for themselves.

- If you are dealing with a student of the opposite gender, you may be more comfortable asking a colleague or administrator to discuss the problem with the student rather than to take it on yourself.

- Call home when a dress code violation happens. Enlisting support from a student's parents or guardians for this issue is not always easy, but it is respectful to involve them in the process.

- Be alert to gang activity expressed through student clothing. Speak with other staff members to learn about specific gang colors and types of clothing in your area.

- Be careful to preserve your students' dignity when enforcing the dress code. Sometimes students may not have anything else clean to wear. If students are wearing inappropriate clothes to be defiant, you do not want to give them an audience by attempting to discuss the issue where others can overhear.

HOW TO HANDLE HALLWAY PROBLEMS

Hallway problems vary widely depending on the age of the student. In high school, teachers generally are required to supervise their students less than those teachers who work with younger students. Usually, all that is required of secondary teachers is that they stand in their doorways, monitor, and urge students to hurry to class.

Hallway problems involving younger students, however, are more complicated and can occur when teachers need to supervise students closely as they walk their students to the school cafeteria, the library, or similar destinations. The problems associated with these students can range from excessive noise, horseplay, and not following the procedures for hallway behavior.

Mistakes to Avoid

- Don't assume that students know how to move quickly from one destination to another. They do not. The procedures for forming a line and moving through the hallways of your school must be taught.

- Don't overlook the potential for having fun with hallway behavior as you work to strengthen your classroom community. When working together to line up quickly and move quietly is a shared problem, students learn to the importance of collaboration and problem solving.

Strategies That Work

- Be proactive in your approach to this problem. To begin, make sure you know the expectations for hallway behavior at your school.

- Consider adopting the ideas that work for other teachers at your school, thereby presenting a united front to any students who may be confused about what is expected of them.

- Talk with your students about why they need to follow the procedures for hallway behaviors to build student ownership of the problem.

- Have silly awards for students who manage their line duties well.

- Make it enjoyable for students to comply with procedures. Play games such as calling out "One, two, three, freeze!" at some point in the trip to have students form themselves into human statues, or have them line up according to their age, eye color, birthday month, or favorite food. You can also find enjoyable ideas for hallway behavior just by searching online. Try a search term such as "lining up strategies" to find dozens of ideas to make this an enjoyable part of your school day.

- Set a timer to try to set a class record for the shortest lining up time. Chart the results so that students can see how they are meeting their goal.

- Keep in mind that good hallway behavior, just like any other student behavior, requires explicit instructions from you, time for students to practice, and lots of praise for those students who behave well.

- If your students lapse in their good behavior after a while, take the time to calmly reteach the behaviors you expect from them while they are in the hallway.

HOW TO DEAL WITH STUDENTS WHO ENGAGE IN HORSEPLAY

A friendly push, a quick grab from behind, running in the hall, or throwing book bags are behaviors that are all too common when students gather. Horseplay has been a part of school life for as long as schools have been in existence. So, too, have the serious consequences associated with horseplay. In addition to the disruption and loss of instructional time that horseplay causes in a learning environment, there are other, far more serious problems.

It is all too easy for students who are "playing around" to injure themselves as they knock one another about. Bystanders can also be injured when the students who are roughhousing bump into them or into furniture. Finally, the most significant detrimental effect of horseplay is that often what starts as friendly fun escalates into an unfriendly or even violent event when one of the students is injured or decides to retaliate.

Mistakes to Avoid

- Don't overlook the problem. Be proactive in making sure that students know the expectations you have regarding horseplay.

- Allowing some horseplay will only confuse students who will test the limits of your tolerance for this type of misbehavior. Horseplay is a behavior with no gray areas. Stop it at the first sign.

Strategies That Work

- Teach students the importance of respecting others' personal space. Be explicit about explaining what is acceptable behavior and why it is important.

- Most horseplay occurs when students are in transition times, such as moving through the hallway, entering class, at lunch, or in the restroom. Be extra careful to monitor students during these less-structured times of the school day.

- Stand at your classroom door when class starts, but position yourself so that you can monitor students in your class as well.

- To reduce or eliminate the problems caused by horseplay, strictly enforce the class procedure that requires students to go directly to their seats upon entering the classroom.

- Have clearly spelled out and well-timed dismissal procedures so that students do not have enough time to roughhouse as they pack to leave class.

- Carefully consider the traffic flow of your classroom to eliminate unnecessary wandering. Are the paths to the trash can, the area where students pick up or turn in papers, and the pencil sharpener efficiently laid out so that students will find it easy to stay on task?

- If you have students who continue to engage in horseplay even after you have warned them and enacted consequences, you should call their homes for additional support.

- It is highly likely that a student who is engaging in horseplay in your class is doing the same in other classes. Contacting other teachers to work on the problem together is a sound idea.

HOW TO DEAL WITH STUDENTS WHO ARE BULLIES

Schools are not always safe places for teachers. Each year, thousands of teachers report that they have been insulted and threatened by their students. School can be an even tougher place for students. Every year, thousands of students report that a classmate has physically attacked them. Others report that they have been too afraid to attend school on at least one occasion. These statistics reveal only what is reported to authorities; far more harassment occurs than is ever reported.

One of the worst aspects of the problem of harassment is that teachers have been slow to react to complaints from victims in the past. Some teachers seem to feel that victims of harassment bring it on themselves or are overreacting. Many teachers, despite recent incidents of school violence, are still inclined to overlook harassment. The situation is exacerbated by the fact that many teachers are not sure about when they should intervene.

The first step you can take to stop this serious threat is to understand exactly what harassment is. It can take three forms: physical abuse, verbal abuse, and cyberbullying. Cyberbullying is a growing threat as more and more students use social networking sites, cell phones, and other forms of electronic communication to connect with their classmates. When students are abused physically, teachers are usually quick to respond. However, verbal abuse in the form of rumors, racial slurs, and teasing is the most widespread form of harassment; unfortunately, it is far more likely to be tolerated by teachers. Cyberbullying is even more difficult to manage because it rarely takes place in a classroom, although its effects can be devastating. As an educator, you have certain responsibilities that you must fulfill regarding bullying:

- You must know your school's policy about harassment as well as your responsibilities for handling it.

- You are expected to take necessary steps to prevent harassment by teaching your students about it and by supervising them adequately.

- Because harassment is such a serious offense, you must involve administrators, parents or guardians, and other support personnel according to the guidelines specified by your district if one of your students is involved in harassment.

Mistakes to Avoid

- Never ignore the situation. If you observe an incident, no matter how mild it may appear to you, take action.

- Don't make things worse for the victim by causing him or her unnecessary public humiliation. Be sensitive to the embarrassment such a student feels at being a target and having to ask for help.

- Never assume that victims bring it on themselves.

- Don't neglect to teach your students about harassment, the forms it can take, the consequences of perpetrating it, how to report it, and why they must report incidents to adults.

Strategies That Work

Before an Incident Occurs

- Make teaching social skills part of your classroom procedures, no matter how old your students are. Some of your students simply do not know which behaviors are appropriate and which are not.

- Be alert for the early or subtle signs of bullying. Listen carefully to what students say both to and about one another. For example, if you notice that several students have targeted one of their classmates or that a student is having trouble adjusting, be alert that more may be going on that you don't see.

- Promote acceptance by praising students when they are helpful to one another. It is particularly effective when you can label an entire class as helpful, initiating a positive self-fulfilling prophecy.

- Boost the self-esteem of all students, particularly those who may be tempted to harass others because of their own poor sense of self-worth and those who may be targets of harassment.

After an Incident Occurs

- Because of the serious nature of bullying, you should not attempt to manage this without administrative help. As soon as you are aware of an incident of bullying, quickly put the school's procedures into action by formally reporting the incident to an administrator. Be as accurate and factual as possible in your report.

- Respect the confidentiality of the students involved and do not discuss the incident with others.

- Support the victim. Often, just talking with an adult will help the bullied student relieve some of the anxiety that he or she is feeling.

Cyberbullying

Cyberbullying is often more insidious than other types because victims are never free of the threat if they carry a cell phone or belong to a social networking site. Cyberbullies, too, are often more aggressive because they are not face-to-face with their victims.

Although it is not your responsibility to police how your students use their personal electronic media to communicate with one another when they are not in class, teachers do have a privileged position in the lives of their students. Here are some tips on how to handle a cyberbullying incident should you have to:

- If a student confides that he or she is the victim of a cyberbully, the first step that you should take is to talk with the student to learn the details of the harassment.

- You should involve other professionals who can help your student at once. Just as you would report face-to-face bullying, so should you report cyberbullying to an administrator.

- At this point, the administrator should assume the primary role in helping your student with the issue. You should, however, continue to offer your support and encouragement to help the victim.

- To learn more about what you can do to prevent and deal with digital harassment, there are several organizations that can offer you and your students advice and support. One of the foremost of these organizations is the Cyberbullying Research Center. This group maintains an informative and helpful website at www.cyberbullying .org. Another helpful site for educators is maintained by the U.S. Department of Health and Human Services: StopBullying.gov (www.stopbullying.gov).

HOW TO MANAGE NAME-CALLING

Almost every person has experienced name-calling at one time or another, either as the person using the name or as the victim. When name-calling is affectionate or friendly, it is an accepted part of relationships. When it is intended as a weapon, name-calling can cause a great deal of anguish and embarrassment.

To be clear, even though name-calling is a fairly common school experience, when it persists, even though the victim has indicated that it should stop, name-calling becomes bullying and must be handled as such. When name-calling is occasional, or when it is misguided, it can be dealt with as a mistake in judgment instead of as harassment.

In either case, as concerned adults, teachers cannot allow name-calling to be a part of the school environment. Fortunately, there is a great deal that teachers can do to manage name calling successfully.

Mistakes to Avoid

- Do not engage in even friendly name-calling yourself. Model the adult behavior you expect from your students instead.

- Students can be quick to pick up on a teacher's problem with pronouncing a classmate's name or frustration at a student's misbehavior. Do not give students reasons to call one another names.

- Don't accept excuses. Some students will try to convince you that they meant no harm. Continue to be firm in your efforts to stop the name-calling.

Strategies That Work

- Be alert. Even pleasant and cooperative students can call one another hateful names. Often the offense happens when the teacher's back is turned; when students are moving from one place to another; or in a less supervised place, such as the cafeteria, playground, or hallway.

- Be aware of the students in your class who may be at risk for name-calling. Students whose appearance and behavior differ from those of their classmates are particularly vulnerable.

- Act quickly and decisively as soon as you hear name-calling. Stop the misbehavior at once. Be matter of fact and calm, but make it obvious that name-calling will not happen in your class.

- Sometimes students lack the social skills or the maturity to realize that name-calling is hurtful and not acceptable. Take a few minutes to educate students who may not be aware of the effect of their actions on others.

- As unobtrusively as possible, offer appropriate support to students who are the victims of name-calling. If you are not sure of the types of support you should provide, consult a school counselor, a colleague, or your mentor for advice.

- If you notice that students persist in name-calling after your efforts to stop it, you must treat the situation as bullying and not just as name calling.

Category Three: Problems Associated with Misbehavior during Instruction

HOW TO HANDLE WORK REFUSAL

Students who refuse to do even the most engaging assignments are the embodiment of a teacher's frustration. Work refusal can be a passive behavior, such as when a student sleeps, forgets to do homework, or is absent on the day of an assessment. It can also appear in a more obvious form, such as a disrespectful response to an assignment or an outright confrontation. In either case, the problem of work refusal can affect the rapport you want to have with your entire class as well as with individual students.

Mistakes to Avoid

- Don't delay acting quickly when a student refuses to work. The problem will only compound itself when the student falls further behind because of not working.

- Avoid overreacting or being negative with students. Take a problem-solving approach instead.

- Don't neglect to enact the consequences that you have in your classroom management plan for students who are not cooperative.

- Don't overlook the importance of setting small, achievable goals with students so that they can see the purpose of their effort and their progress toward reaching a goal.

Strategies That Work

- Be encouraging and supportive but also firm in your expectations.

- Prevent as much work refusal as you can by designing instruction that is meaningful and relevant and by ensuring that students understand the purpose of their assignments.

- Working on your relationships with students who refuse to work is important. Make sure that they perceive you as someone who has their best interests at heart and who is willing to help them succeed.

- Consider assigning study buddies to all students. When students can turn to friendly peers for support, it will be easier for them to stay on task and to complete their work.

- Although you should be subtle so as not to embarrass students who refuse to work, remove as many distractions as you can so that it's easier for them to stay on task.

- If the problem persists after you have offered help and made your expectations clear, then you must enforce your class rules for completing work.

- Call home to enlist the support of parents or guardians when you see a pattern beginning to develop. Working as a team with other supportive adults is often an effective way to manage the issue of work refusal.

HOW TO HANDLE A CLASS THAT IS SLOW TO SETTLE TO WORK

Classes that are slow to settle to work often enter the classroom energized from a previous class or an active event in their day. Returning to the room after lunch, recess, or physical education class can be particularly difficult for some classes who have trouble making the transition from a lively environment to a quieter one.

Mistakes to Avoid

- Don't take a harsh or negative approach to this problem. Instead, make it a shared responsibility involving everyone in the class.

- Don't miss the opportunity to have fun at the beginning of class and to get students off to a great start by providing them with a series of opening exercises that will help them focus on the work ahead instead of the class or event they just left.

- Don't give in to the temptation to bribe students into good behavior.

Strategies That Work

- Be patient when trying to solve this problem. Classes that are slow to settle to work will not learn to focus in just a day or two. Be persistent.

- Make sure that the expectations you have for the time it takes your class to settle are realistic. It takes a large class longer to settle down than a smaller one. It is reasonable for students to chat as they get ready for class.

- Does the traffic flow of your class allow students to settle to work quickly, or do they need to move around the room to pick up materials and supplies from different places? Make it easy for students to find their seats and to settle to work right away.

- Discuss the issue with students and ask for their suggestions to solve the problem. Because it is a problem that affects the entire class, it should be a problem that the entire class can solve by working together.

- Have the materials that students need for class ready as soon as they enter the room so that they can start working right away.

- Have consistent routines and procedures in place so that students can confidently anticipate what is expected of them at the start of class.

- Set a class goal for the time that it should take all students to be settled and working. Post this goal in a conspicuous place and remind students of it as they enter the room. Chart their progress on the board so that they can have a visual representation of their own progress.

HOW TO COPE WHEN STUDENTS MISBEHAVE FOR A SUBSTITUTE TEACHER

Even usually dependable students can regard the presence of a substitute teacher as an excuse for a free day—no boring routines, no demanding work, and no hovering teacher. The result is frustrating misbehavior and lost instruction time. As if writing the detailed plans required for a substitute teacher weren't enough trouble, having to deal with the aftermath of students who misbehave for a substitute teacher just adds to the burden caused by a teacher's absence.

Mistakes to Avoid

- Don't overlook student misbehavior when you have a substitute teacher taking your place. You must address it. Overlooking misbehavior sends the message that students should behave well only when you are present instead of learning to be self-disciplined.

- Don't react without first taking the time to think and gather information. Reacting hastily instead of carefully taking a problem-solving approach could injure your relationship with your students.

- Leave work that students can complete without a great deal of extra help from a substitute. When students have difficulty doing their work or are unsure about what to do, their frustration will invariably result in misbehavior.

Strategies That Work

- If a substitute teacher left a note about student misbehavior, be sure to seek clarification about what happened before acting. One way to do this is to ask students to give you their version of events. Having the entire class jot down their thoughts to be turned in anonymously instead of expecting them to express themselves in front of their peers will result in more accurate information for you to use. Then you can enforce the consequences that would be appropriate based on your class rules.

- Keep in mind that much of the misbehavior that happens when a teacher is absent can be prevented by preparing students for your absence and by being as explicit as possible about the expectations for student behavior. You can find more information about how to prepare for your absence from school in Section Three.

- Be sure that the work that you leave for students is work that is important and not just busywork. Have the substitute collect the work at the end of class. This not only will allow you to see how much work your students accomplished but also will give students an incentive to complete the work, since turning it in will hold them accountable.

HOW TO HANDLE CLASSES THAT ARE TOO NOISY

Each teacher has unique teaching methods, classroom management styles, and learning philosophies. Despite these individual differences, however, there is one problem that we all have in common. None of us—from the most skilled veteran to the recent graduate struggling with that difficult first semester—escapes this discipline problem. We all must find ways to successfully manage the problem of unacceptable noise levels and excessive talking.

Although the days of silent students have passed, the noise level in a class must still be appropriate for the activity that is under way. When students are off task, they seldom amuse themselves quietly. The noise level in an unproductive class can be deafening. Students and their teacher alike suffer when this happens.

Mistakes to Avoid

- Never talk over noise or shout to be heard in your classroom.

- Don't allow noise to get out of control. Once students are very loud, you must take extreme measures to get them to stop being noisy. You'll find it easier if you begin to control noise levels as soon as class begins.

- Don't try to assume control of a noisy class without enlisting the cooperation of your students. Ask for suggestions from your students about how to manage noise.

- Sometimes you are the problem. When your students are working quietly and productively on an assignment, don't keep talking to the class in general. When you repeatedly interrupt their work by distracting them with your own conversation, you make it harder for your students to work quietly.

Strategies That Work

- Make it clear that some noisy activities are just not acceptable. Teach your students that it is never acceptable to talk across the room to classmates, to shout at any time, or to talk during a media presentation, when you are giving instructions, or during a test and other quiet activities,

- When you plan activities that have the potential to be noisy, consider moving to a part of the building where you can't disturb other classes.

- Don't plan group activities without teaching students how to control the noise level of their groups. One way to do this is by using distances as noise measurements. For example, students should find a one-foot voice useful for working in pairs and a three-foot voice useful for working in groups. When you give directions for an assignment, tell students the acceptable noise level for the activity.

- Model the noise level that you want from your students. If you speak softly, your students will follow your lead. If you shout, you will dramatically increase the noise level in your class because students will see this as permission for them to shout, too.

- Be emphatic with your students when you speak with them about this problem. You should make it very clear when it is okay for them to talk and when you want them to work silently. If you are clear in communicating your expectations to your students, they will not repeatedly test the limits of your tolerance for noise.

- Avoid the sound-wave effect of a loud class time followed by a quiet one followed by a loud one again by consistently enforcing the rules in your class about excessive talking.

- Help your students feel they can succeed in your class. Students who feel they are part of a worthwhile experience have a reason to stay on task and to cooperate with you. They show respect for themselves and for their classmates when they have a reason to work. Students who do not care about their work, your expectations, and their classmates have no reason to respect the class rules about talking.

- Begin every class with an activity that will focus your students' attention on the work they will be doing. This focusing activity will help them make a transition from the casual chatting they may have done in the hall on the way to your class to the purposeful work that you want them to begin.

- If you have a group that likes to talk, capitalize on this by getting them talking productively about the lesson. If you are successful at doing this, their need to interact with one another and your need to have them master the material can both be satisfied.

- If your students tend to talk when they have finished an assignment and are waiting for others to finish, sequence your instruction so that there is always an overlapping activity for your students to begin right away. This could be another in a series of assignments, a homework exercise, or even an optional assignment for enrichment.

- Sometimes when students are very excited, allow them to spend a minute or two talking to clear the air so that they can focus on their work. Be clear in setting brief time limits when you do this.

- Stay on your feet when your class has a problem with talking and excessive noise. Eye contact, proximity, and other nonverbal cues will help. Persistent and careful monitoring will encourage students to stay focused on their work rather than on conversation.

- During a movie or oral presentation, prevent students from talking instead of listening by giving them an activity to do. Students who are taking notes or filling out a worksheet will not have time for chatter.

- If the noise level is too loud, give students quiet activities that require them to write or read independently. These assignments should be designed to engage and instruct, not just to keep the class busy.

- Shifting gears from one activity to another is difficult for many students. Make transition times as efficient as possible in your class to avoid this problem.

- If the entire class persists in having a problem with excessive talking, chart their behavior so that they can see tangible evidence of it. Create a bar graph each day where you rank their success at managing their problem with talking on a scale of one to ten. Sometimes students are not aware of the severity of a problem until they can see it in a format such as this.

- Use good-natured but firm signals to indicate that students should stop talking. Some signals that are appropriate include the following:
  - Writing a reminder on the board
  - Holding up a silly sign on a poster

- Saying a code word that your students recognize
- Counting backward from ten
- Flicking the lights
- Ringing a bell
- Turning music on or off
- Putting your finger to your lips
- Holding your hands over your ears
- Writing a time-limit countdown on the board
- Holding your hand up and counting by folding your fingers
- Standing in the front of the room obviously waiting
- Having them put their pens down when you call for attention
- Timing an activity and obviously watching the clock

Category Four: Problems Associated with Students' Relationship with Their Teacher

HOW TO DEAL WITH DEFIANT STUDENTS

Defiant students can be angry, loud, abusive, and confrontational, or they may mutter, show disrespect, and refuse to work. Oddly enough, the more aggressive and confrontational student is easier to deal with because the intensity of the outburst demands immediate action. The less-violent confrontational student is much harder to manage because it's not easy to correct students who may only be mumbling under their breath or rolling their eyes. Attempts to correct this behavior can result in vehement denials and accusations of unfairness. Defiant students of either type have a serious impact on a discipline climate. They not only cause trouble for themselves but also can perplex even the most caring teacher.

Mistakes to Avoid

- Although you should take an angry outburst or other sign of defiance seriously, you should not lose control of the classroom situation. Wait a moment or two to gather your thoughts. Often this brief delay will allow the student to calm down.
- As tempting as it may be to simply tell a student to leave the room, keep in mind that many school districts have policies that discourage teachers from simply removing a student from the class without a prearranged destination, such as a counselor's office or a time-out area.
- Absolutely refuse to reply to a defiant student in a rude way. Silence is better than a sarcastic retort or insisting on compliance. Do not argue or raise your voice. Stay calm and remain in control of your own emotions.

Strategies That Work

- Many problems with confrontational students can be prevented or minimized with early action. Monitor students as they enter the room and continue to do so throughout class. If you see that a student is frustrated or upset, offer help and support as quickly as you can. Some of the signs of impending trouble are
  - Refusing to work
  - Inattention
  - Muttering under their breath
  - Angry or exaggerated movements of their hands
  - Loud voices
  - Facial expressions that signal distress
  - Imminent tears
  - Work done poorly or not at all
  - Slamming books or materials

- Prepare yourself by planning what steps you will take to keep the disruption minimal. The following are some questions you should consider before a disruption occurs:
  - How can I tell when I should act?
  - Where can I send an angry student to ensure the safety of others?
  - What signs should I pay attention to that will let me know a problem is brewing?
  - Which of my students is already heading in this direction?
  - What can I do in class tomorrow that will ease some of the stress that my defiant students may be feeling?

- You must act calmly and quickly because the student has forced a showdown with you in front of the rest of the class. You should show you are serious, concerned, and in control.

- As quietly and calmly as possible, remove the defiant student from the room. This not only will keep the disruption under control but also will save more embarrassment for the student who has misbehaved. You cannot begin to help a defiant student in front of an audience. Be sure to have a specific destination for any student you send out of class. Arrange for students to have a time-out with another teacher, send them to a counselor, or refer them to an administrator.

- Acknowledge their feelings of anger and frustration as quickly as you can. Although these are not excuses for bad behavior, the student needs for you to pay attention to the reasons that the outburst happened. After this important first step, deal with the outburst and its causes.

- Having appropriate and meaningful work with a clear purpose will eliminate many problems.

- If the situation persists, involve the student's parents or guardians and an administrator. Meet with them and the student to work out a plan to solve the problem.

- Continue to work on your relationship with a defiant student. A positive relationship with this student will go far in preventing potential conflicts.
- It is up to you as the adult in the classroom to make sure that you have a positive relationship with all the students in your class, even those who are confrontational or defiant. Because all students need to be treated fairly, the same standards should apply to every student in your class—regardless of whether a student is frustrated or not.

HOW TO COPE WITH A DIFFICULT CLASS

Teaching a difficult class can be an unnerving and exhausting experience. A rude or disrespectful class can turn your enthusiasm into a desire to just make it through one more day. What causes a class to be difficult? Here are just a few of the many and varied reasons a class can give you trouble:

- An unequal distribution in the ability levels of students is causing frustration.
- A negative label has become a self-fulfilling prophecy.
- There is an unpleasant chemistry between you and your students.
- There is an unpleasant chemistry among students.

Perhaps the most serious reason why classes can be difficult lies in the way students regard themselves and their ability to succeed academically. Students who do not believe they can succeed have no reason to try. Teachers who achieve success with difficult classes turn the negative energy in a class into a positive force by persistently communicating their faith in their students' ability to achieve.

Mistakes to Avoid

- Don't be a pushover in hopes of winning your students' affection. They will soon learn that it is easy to manipulate you with insincere shows of affection.
- Not all students in your class are difficult. Not every class is difficult every day. Learn to see the good in individual students and in the entire group to gain a balanced view of the situation.
- Never allow students to sit with nothing to do but disturb others. Keep them engaged in productive learning for the entire class period.
- Don't give up on a difficult class. You can turn a difficult class around with patience, planning, and persistence.

Strategies That Work

- Smile at your class. If you were videotaped while teaching, would your body language reveal positive or negative feelings about your students?

- Keep the expectations for your class high. Children live up to the expectations of the adults in their lives, so let them know that you expect a lot from them.

- From the first class meeting onward, establish that you control the class. Demonstrate that you will oversee the behavior in your classroom for the good of all students.

- Call parents or guardians as soon as you can when a problem arises.

- Plan activities to fit your students' short attention spans.

- Make sure that activities offer plenty of time for practice and review.

- Make sure that the work you assign is appropriate for your students' various ability levels and that you differentiate it appropriately.

- Offer incentives other than grades. Students who have never received a good grade may not be motivated by grades. Offer small, frequent rewards instead, such as stickers, computer time, or bookmarks until the positive behaviors you expect become routine.

- Praise good behavior as often as you can. Difficult students do not always know when they are behaving well. When you praise your class for good behavior, you are encouraging all your students to repeat the behavior.

- Take the time to teach and reteach the rules and procedures that you want your students to follow.

- Although you do want students to share their feelings with you, don't allow them to engage you in an argument.

- Give students opportunities to help one another. Students who are sharing their knowledge with a classmate will be so busy being productive that they will not have time to disrupt class.

- Acknowledge the rights of individuals in your class. Showing students that you are fair will ease many sensitive situations.

HOW TO HELP STUDENTS WHO ARE DISRESPECTFUL

One of the most difficult aspects of working with students who are disrespectful is that their words and behaviors are often meant to hurt—and they do. It's not always easy to control the feelings of frustration and dismay that follow an incident of disrespect. Often, too, when a student is disrespectful in front of other students, it's easy to be embarrassed, even as you worry if the disrespect is going to spread.

When students are disrespectful to their teachers, there are usually issues with classroom leadership and with teacher-to-student relationships that need to be addressed. When teachers present themselves to their students as knowledgeable professionals who are firmly in control of the class and who like and respect their students, the prospect of disrespect will decrease. When students are disrespectful, it is wise to reflect carefully on what led up to the incident and what you could have done to prevent it, in addition to deciding on the best way to handle it so that it does not occur again.

Although your role in sparking the disrespect may have been a very minor one, as the classroom leader, it is incumbent upon you to at least consider how you could have prevented it. Here are some questions that may help you reflect on your role in creating a classroom climate where disrespect occurs:

- Are your classroom policies, procedures, and rules serving their purpose? What needs to be adjusted?

- Are the instructional activities appropriate for all students so that their frustration levels are low?

- Are you monitoring your students adequately so that they can be engaged and on task?

- Do you take the time to relate well with your students as a group and as individuals?

- Are you sensitive to students' cultural backgrounds and how these affect their attitudes about class and about you?

Mistakes to Avoid

- Work to educate students about the right way to work out their frustrations without being disrespectful.

- Don't be surprised to learn that students who are disrespectful to you are also disrespectful to the other significant adults in their lives. Because their disrespectful responses are ingrained, it's more difficult to deal with the problem.

- Don't embarrass a student who has been disrespectful to you. This will only force him or her to save face by being even more disrespectful to you. It will not solve the problem.

Strategies That Work

- Take a problem-solving approach to the situation instead of escalating the confrontation and ill will with unkind words of your own.

- Fewer behavior incidents are more stress-inducing than student disrespect. Make time to deal with your stress levels. (See Section One for more information about dealing with school stress.)

- Even though it can be very difficult, try to keep your reaction as neutral as possible so that the disrespectful student will not have the pleasure of irritating you, the disruption will be minimal, and you can help the student learn from the mistake and move forward.

- Don't interrupt class to deal with an incident of disrespect if you can help it.

- Take the intent of the comment or action into account. Often students misjudge a situation and say things or use a tone of voice that is innocently wrong. A helpful way to manage this is to quietly say, "I don't think you meant to be disrespectful just now, right? It came across that way."

- Show students a better way to express their frustrations by rephrasing their comments to be respectful to the entire class community. You could quietly say, "Instead of telling someone to shut up, in this class we are polite to one another. Try 'Could you not talk for a minute?' instead." Modeling the right way to speak to others is a necessary step in successfully managing the situation.

- Don't forget that some problems will take longer than others to solve. Be patient and persistent.

- Although it is natural that you would have something to say in your own defense, resist the temptation to argue with or reprimand the student in front of the class.

- Ask the student to step into the hall for a private conference when you are calm enough to manage the situation well. Talk with the student about the effects of disrespect on you and on the rest of the class. Enact your classroom rules and consequences.

- Make an agreement with students who feel the need to talk back. Tell them that you want to hear what they have to say and are willing to listen but that they need to speak to you privately and respectfully. When you take this friendly attitude, you offer students a chance to approach you in a positive manner, a way to deal with frustrations, and an opportunity to learn how to resolve conflicts respectfully.

HOW TO MANAGE CLASSROOM POWER STRUGGLES

Although students who want to engage in power struggles with the adults in their lives can appear in different guises, teachers can unfortunately find some power struggles easier to recognize than others.

- The student who complies with your directions—but at a deliberately and maddeningly slow pace
- The class clown who disrupts the flow of instruction with attention-grabbing comments
- The defiant student who is openly confrontational, oppositional, and rude
- The disrespectful student who somehow manages to be just rude enough not to be referred to the office
- The passive-aggressive student who consistently does not have materials or completed work
- The student who can do well in school but who chooses not to
- The student who has perfected the fine art of eye rolling when you give directions

Sometimes the frustration, stress, and misery caused by a student who wants to engage you in a power struggle may make intervention appear not worth the trouble. After all, unlike some discipline problems, power struggles often build slowly and require long-term solutions. Many teachers find it easy to adopt defensive attitudes.

- I can't change her anyway. Why even try?
- Only five more minutes of class left . . .
- It's May. Soon this will be another teacher's problem.

The long-term, heavy toll of a power struggle on students and their teachers makes action imperative. If teachers don't choose to act to resolve a power struggle, the results can be disastrous: a loss of instructional time, distracted students, the escalation of misbehavior, and unhappy and unproductive students.

Mistakes to Avoid

- Don't lose sight of the student behind the behavior. Focus on helping the student learn more appropriate ways to engage your attention.
- Don't just react or hope that it will resolve itself. A power struggle requires a problem-solving approach.
- A power struggle is frustrating and difficult. Don't ignore the stress you feel when you must deal with a power struggle in your class.
- Ignoring the problem will only allow it to grow until it becomes harder to manage. Intervene as quickly as you can.
- Don't delay getting help with students who want to engage in power struggles. Involve parents or guardians and other concerned adults early. A united front of supportive adults sends the power-hungry student a strong and decisive message.
- Don't reward the students you are engaged in a power struggle with by allowing them to see your frustration or anger.
- Don't use an office referral as a solution instead of as short-term relief. Work on your relationship with the power-seeking student instead.

Strategies That Work

- Turn negative student leaders into positive ones with a delicate touch. What they want to do and are already pretty good at doing is simple: leaders want to lead. A wise teacher will give them plenty of constructive opportunities to do so. Here are just some of the small actions you can take that will allow leaders to be productive instead of destructive influences in your classroom. Class leaders can
  - Be the person who makes sure everyone knows the homework assignment
  - Serve as the moderator in role-play situations

- Lead a class discussion
- Be the reporter for small-group discussions
- Speak for their peers at class meetings
- Monitor groups working on class assignments
- Take class votes, collect money, and assume responsibility for issuing texts and passing out papers
- Run errands and pick up supplies
- Consult with other students about choices in due dates, projects, and materials and report to you
- Greet guests and be the helper when there is a substitute

- Be as overwhelmingly positive with your class leaders as you can. Never belittle them. You will only appear foolish as the rest of the class immediately takes sides sympathetically with their classmates. Praise class leaders as often as you sincerely can.

- Reinforcing positive behaviors is the best strategy you can take with students who want to engage you in a power struggle. You will gain their cooperation as well as the approval of the entire class when you make it clear that you want everyone in the class to succeed.

- It's important to maintain a level-headed approach to the problem. You won't be able to win over every student despite your obvious sincerity and very best efforts. It is unrealistic to expect otherwise of yourself and of your students.

> My first year teaching, I was complaining to a veteran teacher that my students were not learning as much as I wanted them to. My mentor shook her head, looked at me, and said, "Vivian, you know where your grade book is, and you are not weeping openly in front of your students. You're doing fine." I realized then that, even if I was not living up to my own expectations, I was exceeding other people's. I could cut myself some slack.
>
> *Vivian Jewell, 25 years' experience*

Questions to Discuss with Colleagues

Sharing ideas with colleagues is a helpful way to devise solutions to some of the problems that you must manage successfully at school. Here you will find several topics to open discussions with colleagues about successful instructional practices:

1. One of your students is chronically late to school because a parent drops him off late many mornings. You have tried talking over the situation with the parent, but the child is still late. What should you do?

2. Two of your students turn in homework papers that are very similar. You believe that one of the students copied the other's work. However, you do not have any proof. What are your school's policies about how you are to handle this? What mistakes should you avoid? To whom can you turn for help?

3. You have a class right after lunch that is very hard to settle down. How can you help them focus and get to work quickly without raising your voice or feeling frustrated? To whom can you turn for help?

4. You notice that one of your brightest and most cooperative students has something hidden in a book bag. You suspect that it could be an illegal drug. To whom can you turn for help? What should you do?

5. You suspect that some of your students appear to be harassing another student, but you have not actually caught them, and the harassed student denies any trouble. What should you do? Who can help you with this?

Topics to Discuss with a Mentor

Although the topics that new teachers need to discuss with a mentor vary from teacher to teacher and from school to school, there are some that most first-year teachers should be comfortable discussing with a mentor or a trusted colleague. You should ask your mentor about these topics from this section:

- Advice about the classroom discipline problems you can expect to encounter
- How to learn your school's policies regarding tardiness and truancy
- How to prevent the problems that you may be experiencing from becoming worse
- Advice about defiant or disrespectful students
- How to manage student cell phones and other electronic devices

Reflection Questions to Guide Your Thinking

1. What is the most serious discipline problem that you have had to cope with to date? How well did you handle the situation at the time that it occurred? How well did you prevent it from occurring again? What did you learn from the experience that you can use in the future?

2. How orderly is your classroom? Are you satisfied with the way you are handling discipline problems? What areas would you like to work on? Who can help you with this?

3. A student who is normally pleasant and well prepared is suddenly rude to you. What should you do? How prepared are you to manage student rudeness? Do you have a workable plan in place to cope with students who are rude or disrespectful?

4. Your students seem to be obsessed with their cell phones. How can you manage the way your students use their phones and other devices so that they can focus on learning? What do other teachers in your school do to manage cell phones in class? Where can you learn more about what is expected of you regarding student cell phones?

5. What is your biggest worry regarding classroom discipline issues? What can you do to manage not only the issue itself but also your stress levels regarding it? How can you use your personal strengths as a classroom teacher to manage discipline problems? What weaknesses are you aware of, and how can you overcome them?

A Final Word

As a first-year teacher, you are on the threshold of an exhilarating time in your life—a career path that stretches far into the future. You will have many good days at school, but, like every other educator, you will also have some tough days.

Maintaining a healthy balance between your personal life and your professional life is one of the most important responsibilities that you have as an educator—and as a human. Be proactive about managing your stress. You are worth it.

To help you with this, I have one more strategy to share with you. It's one that I learned during my own first year and that I continued every year since. I am so glad I did. You will be, too. Here's my final advice to you.

Find an old shoebox and label it "Bad Day Box." In that box, store all the expressions of gratitude and other encouraging reminders that come your way: thank-you notes, student-crafted cards, encouraging notes from colleagues, endearing smiley faces drawn on scrap paper, and precious homemade gifts that students give you. Store the parts of your day that touch your heart and remind you why you wanted to become a teacher.

When you come home after a tough day, get out your Bad Day Box and let the contents renew your faith in yourself. Soon you will not only be surprised by how many good things come your way but also by how much you have learned and how much you have grown as an educator. You'll be able to put those tough times in perspective because they are just one small part of your school life.

Your Bad Day Box will remind you that being a teacher is about so much more than the daily grind of paperwork, plans, and routines. It's about changing lives and helping students achieve their dreams. It's about taking good care of yourself and learning to balance the tremendous responsibilities of being a teacher with the sure knowledge that what you do *matters*.

Julia Thompson

Index

Page references followed by *fig* indicate an illustrated figure.

How to Access Additional Content Accompanying *The First-Year Teacher's Survival Guide, Fourth Edition*

Video Clips, Templates, Checklists, and More!

The *Survival Guide's* web page features downloadable versions of the book's checklists, forms, worksheets, and self-assessments. Visit www.wiley.com/go/fyt4e; the password is the last five digits of this book's ISBN, which are 70366.

The companion contents include the following:

- Teacher worksheets on lesson study observation, checklists for the first day of school, and even how to gauge your own level of "withitness"!
- Student worksheets such as how to set and achieve goals, a class log, and even a worksheet for missing homework explanations!
- Parent worksheets on your students' assets and needs
- Video learning, including working with parents and administrators and increasing positive behavior in the classroom

---

For more information on how you can have a successful first year,
visit www.juliagthompson.com, juliagthompson.blogspot.com,
or on Twitter @TeacherAdvice.
